Pro ASP.NET Web API Security

Securing ASP.NET Web API

Badrinarayanan Lakshmiraghavan

Apress®

Pro ASP.NET Web API Security

ISBN 978-1-4302-5782-0

ISBN 978-1-4302-5783-7 (eBook)

President and Publisher: Paul Manning
Lead Editor: Ewan Buckingham
Developmental Editor: Barbara McGuire
Technical Reviewer: Fabio Claudio Ferracchiati

Coordinating Editor: Mark Powers
Copy Editor: Teresa Horton
Compositor: SPi Global
Indexer: SPi Global
Artist: SPi Global
Cover Designer: Anna Ishchenko

Distributed to the book trade worldwide by Springer Science+Business Media New York, 233 Spring Street, 6th Floor, New York, NY 10013. Phone 1-800-SPRINGER, fax (201) 348-4505, e-mail orders-ny@springer-sbm.com, or visit www.springeronline.com. Apress Media, LLC is a California LLC and the sole member (owner) is Springer Science + Business Media Finance Inc (SSBM Finance Inc). SSBM Finance Inc is a Delaware corporation.

For information on translations, please e-mail rights@apress.com, or visit www.apress.com.

Apress and friends of ED books may be purchased in bulk for academic, corporate, or promotional use. eBook versions and licenses are also available for most titles. For more information, reference our Special Bulk Sales–eBook Licensing web page at www.apress.com/bulk-sales.

Any source code or other supplementary materials referenced by the author in this text is available to readers at www.apress.com/9781430257820. For detailed information about how to locate your book's source code, go to www.apress.com/source-code/.

To Him, who is able to be both larger than the largest and smaller than the smallest.

To my mother and father.

Contents at a Glance

Contents

Foreword

Everybody who knows me also knows that identity and access control in distributed applications are very near and dear to my heart. Having spent many years in the WS* security space (or WS-Deathstar as many called it), I was happy to see that Microsoft finally built a web service framework that really embraces HTTP instead of abstracting it away.

It is also fair to say that the "web API idea" has taken the world (and its developers) by storm. Even if the technology is not really new, having such capabilities in a mainstream framework like .NET makes adoption really easy. In the short period of time since its first release, it has gained a lot of traction.

As with many other Microsoft technologies, for the first version they mainly concentrated on the core framework, extensibility points, and a limited set of common use cases. The same is true for ASP.NET Web API: Although all the foundational work has been done, the main focus in the security space was Windows authentication and (simpler) AJAX scenarios. There was no built-in support for cross-domain scenarios like basic authentication, client certificates, and token-based authentication (SAML/JWT), let alone two-factor authentication or emerging standards like OAuth2, although it was technically totally possible.

Luckily Badri took that challenge and spent a lot of time exploring all these technologies and their integration into ASP.NET Web API for you. I was totally impressed with how complete and strong this book is on both the "broad" axis and the "deep" axis. In many ways this is the book that I wanted to write for years but never found the time for it. Excellent job!

You, the reader, have quite a journey ahead of you. The world is moving to the web API approach to model services, and the security scenarios are becoming even more complex. OAuth2 is the protocol that enables many of these new architectures, but it will make your head hurt at first. It is also really hard to write a good security system that does not get in the way of legitimate users. If you do your job really well no one will notice it, and for everything else they will blame you! But a working system is very rewarding, and I still very much enjoy doing security every single day.

With that said (and because I am not a big fan of overly long forewords), I wish you a lot of fun and many "a-ha" moments while reading this really comprehensive and interesting book! Mind those tokens!

Dominick Baier
`http://leastprivilege.com`
`http://thinktecture.com`
`https://twitter.com/leastprivilege`

About the Author

Badrinarayanan Lakshmiraghavan has more than fourteen years of information technology experience in all phases of the software development life cycle, including technology consulting and advisory roles in multiple technologies. He has been programming on the Microsoft technology stack from the days of Visual Basic 3.0.

Badri currently is a senior technology architect with Global Technology Consulting - Microsoft Center of Excellence of Cognizant (NASDAQ: CTSH), a Fortune 500 company. He speaks three languages: Tamil, English, and C#.

Badri's coordinates are 12.9758° N, 80.2205° E on the third rock from the yellow-dwarf star that lies close to the inner rim of the Orion arm of the Milky Way Galaxy.

About the Technical Reviewer

Fabio Claudio Ferracchiati, a prolific writer on cutting-edge technologies, has contributed to more than a dozen books on .NET, C#, Visual Basic, and ASP.NET. He is a .NET Microsoft Certified Solution Developer and lives in Milan, Italy. You can read his blog at `Ferracchiati.com`.

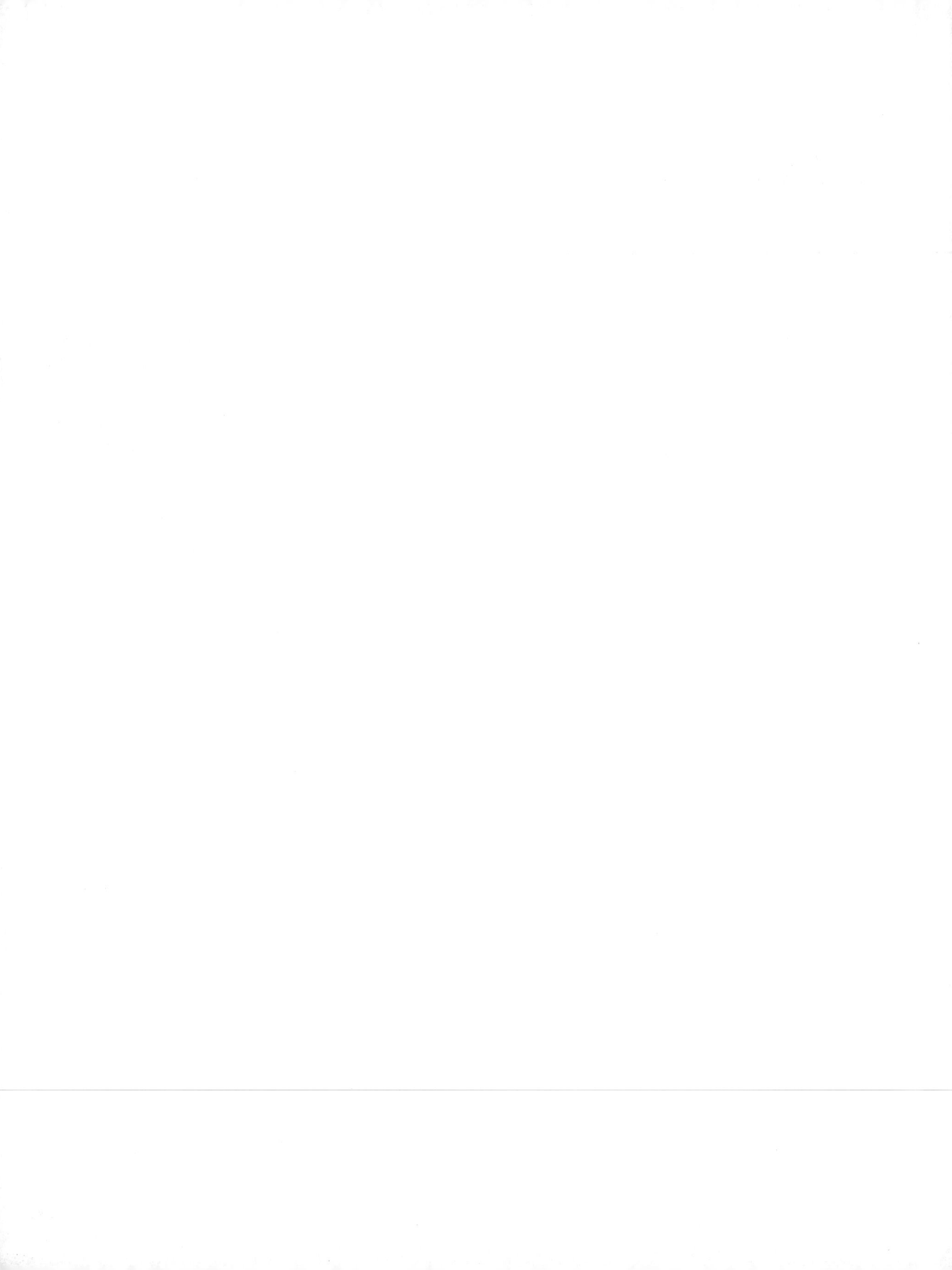

Acknowledgments

Whether you seek general information on .NET security or specific information on claims-based identity and ASP.NET Web API, you likely will find the answers you need on his blog at `http://leastprivilege.com` or in one of his posts in a technical forum such as MSDN. No points for guessing who it is: Dominick Baier, the ultimate voice of wisdom when it comes to ASP.NET Web API security! I deeply appreciate Dominick for all his help and guidance, including taking time from his busy schedule to write the foreword for this book.

Just about every book author acknowledges the team assembled by the publisher, and I won't be any different. Cliché or not, I must gratefully thank the following individuals who are part of the Apress team (in the same order as they got involved).

- Ewan Buckingham, lead editor, for his patience answering all my relevant and irrelevant questions and helping me all the way from the proposal stage to manuscript completion.
- Mark Powers, coordinating editor, for his helping nature and promptness (I have yet to see an instance where Mark has not replied to my mail two hours from the time I clicked the Send button despite being on the other side of the globe).
- Fabio Claudio Ferracchiati, technical reviewer, for catching the subtle things that I overlooked.
- Teresa Horton, copy editor, for putting up with my writing, notably my problem with the usage of articles.
- The SPi Global production team for diligently incorporating all the changes I asked for.
- Barbara McGuire, developmental editor, for her patience in reading through my jumbles, giving structure and order to the content. Thanks very much, Barbara; you might be last on this list, but definitely not the least!

My thanks also to Arvind TN of Cognizant GTC Microsoft CoE for asking THE question that resulted in this book.

Finally, a huge thank you to my family—my wife Poornima and my sons Anirudh and Aparajith—for their understanding and enormous patience. My special thanks to Anirudh for understanding, without any complaints, that his dad has to sit in front of the computer typing away, unable to watch with him such exciting things as an asteroid hitting the earth and obliterating Triceratops, T-Rex, Stegosaurus, and Alamosaurus.

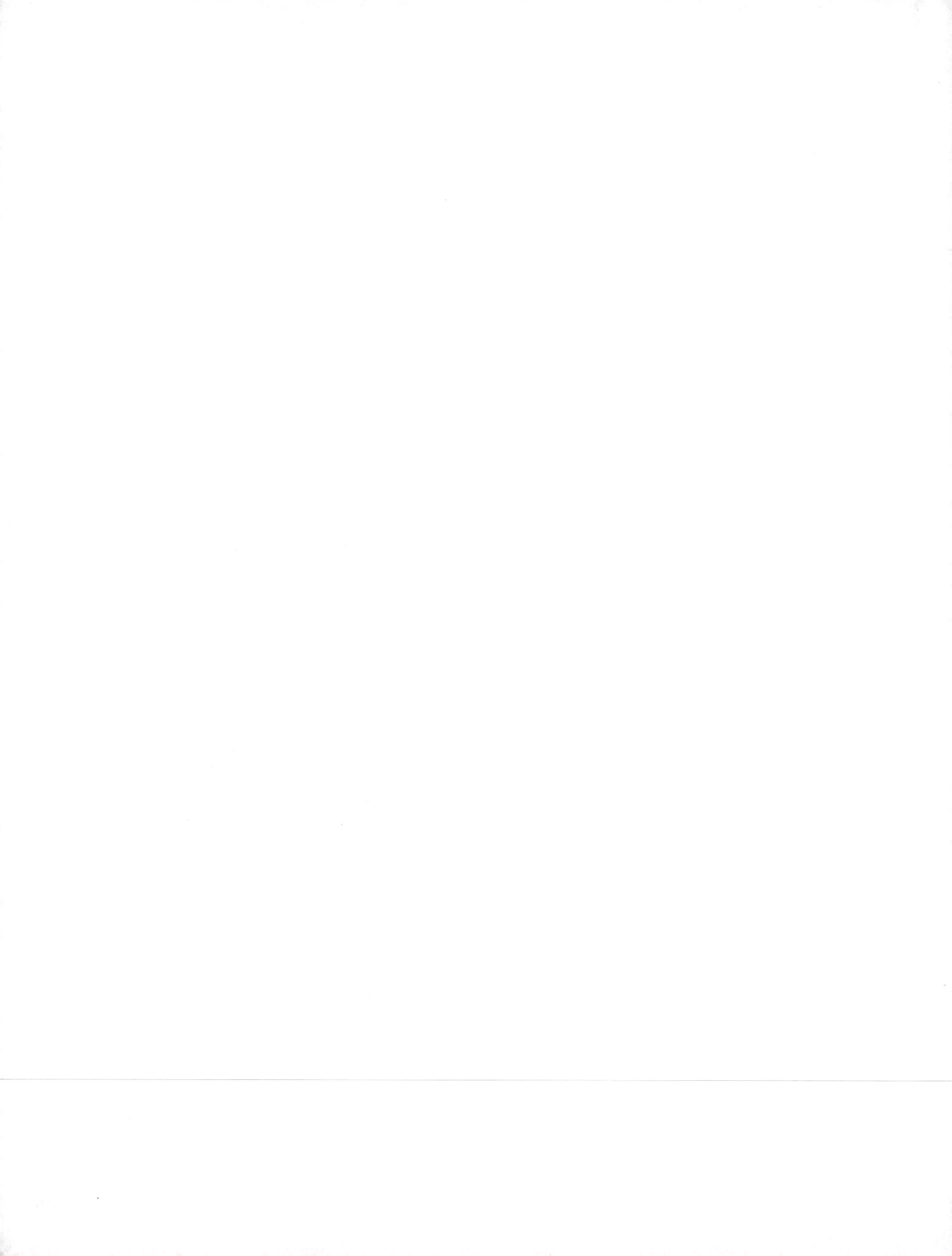

Introduction

Risk comes from not knowing what you're doing.

—Warren Buffett

Few organizations can afford to have dedicated people working on application security. More often than not, a developer or a lead developer from the team is entrusted with the responsibility for retrofitting security into the application or a service. In this quest, the developer looks around, maybe Googles some information, asks a question or two in forums, and rolls his own security implementation without knowing fully the underlying concepts and the implications of the choices he made. This path of least resistance is usually taken because of the project schedule pressures and the lack of emphasis or the focus that the nonfunctional aspect of security generally deserves.

Not reinventing the wheel is a great policy for application development teams because reusable components like libraries and frameworks help get things done efficiently and the right way, incorporating best practices. The flip side of reusable components, open source or not, is that they result in a "black box" syndrome: Things just work and continue to work until the time they stop working. Also, if a reusable component provides options, a developer must know the different choices available as well as the advantages and disadvantages of those choices to make a knowledgeable decision on the methods to be employed for the security requirements at hand.

Compared to the SOAP-based Windows Communication Foundation (WCF) services that enjoy the support of mature security specifications such as WS-Trust, WS-Security, and so on, REST-based ASP.NET Web API currently has very little support. OAuth 2.0, which is the equivalent for WS-Trust and WS-Security in the REST world, is nascent: The OAuth 2.0 framework and the bearer token specifications were published in October 2012.

Even if you have simple security needs that can be met by the direct authentication pattern of a client presenting a password to your ASP.NET Web API for authentication, will you implement Windows Authentication, which is a popular choice for intranet ASP.NET applications, or Forms Authentication, which is a great choice for Internet ASP. NET applications, or widely supported HTTP-based basic or digest authentication? There are pros and cons with every option, and there is no one-size-fits-all solution available for securing a web API.

This is where this book comes in and presents to you the various options available for securing ASP.NET Web API, along with the merits and demerits of those options. Whether you roll your own security mechanism or use a reusable component in the form of a library or a framework, you will be able to make informed decisions by learning the underpinnings of the mechanisms and the implications of the choices you make.

However, this book does not give you any ready-made, penetration-tested code to copy and paste straight into your production implementation. It does not give you fish, but instead teaches you to catch fish. Using this book, you can gain a solid understanding of the security techniques relevant to ASP.NET Web API. All the underlying concepts are introduced from basic principles and developed to the point where you can use them confidently, knowing what you are doing. If you want to get your hands on proven, production-strength code, there are a couple of excellent open-source resources:

- **Thinktecture.IdentityModel.45** features an extensible authentication framework for ASP.NET Web API supporting SAML 1.1/2.0, JSON Web Token (JWT), Simple Web Token (SWT), access keys, and HTTP basic authentication. It also has support for protected cookies and Cross Origin Resource Sharing (CORS). See `https://github.com/thinktecture/Thinktecture.IdentityModel.45`.

- Thinktecture's **IdentityServer 2**, a lightweight STS built using the .NET Framework 4.5, ASP.NET MVC4, WCF, and web API that supports both WS-Trust and OAuth 2.0. See `https://github.com/thinktecture/Thinktecture.IdentityServer.v2`.

What You'll Learn

- Identity management and cryptography
- HTTP basic and digest authentication and Windows authentication
- HTTP advanced concepts such as web caching, ETag, and CORS
- Ownership factors of API keys, client X.509 certificates, and SAML tokens
- Simple Web Token (SWT) and signed and encrypted JSON Web Token (JWT)
- OAuth 2.0 from the ground up using JWT as the bearer token
- OAuth 2.0 authorization codes and implicit grants using DotNetOpenAuth
- Two-factor authentication using Google Authenticator
- OWASP Top Ten risks for 2013

How This Book Is Organized

Pro ASP.NET Web API Security is divided into fifteen chapters. Although it is not divided into parts, the chapters do tend to fall together into several related groups. The first three chapters constitute one such group that pertains to the core ASP.NET Web API framework. Chapter 4 is a stand-alone chapter on HTTP. Chapters 5, 6, and 7 form a group on .NET security topics of identity management and cryptography. Chapter 8 is a stand-alone chapter on knowledge-factor security, and Chapters 9 and 10 are related to ownership factors. Chapters 11, 12, and 13 form the OAuth 2.0 group. Chapter 14 is a stand-alone chapter on two-factor authentication. Finally, Chapter 15, another stand-alone chapter, focuses on OWASP security risks.

The way the chapters are organized in this book takes into account the dependencies one chapter might have on another. If you are confident, you can feel free to skip chapters, but trying to read the chapter on SWT without understanding the basics of digital signing will likely not be very productive. Similarly, trying to implement implicit grant flow without understanding the implications of same-origin policy and the related CORS will be a challenging experience. For this reason, the best way to derive the maximum benefit from this book is to read the chapters sequentially, starting with Chapter 1 and skimming any text that you are already familiar with.

Chapter 1: Welcome to ASP.NET Web API

We start off with understanding what a web API is in general before moving on to a primer on RESTful web API, followed by a review of how Microsoft's ASP.NET Web API framework can help you build web APIs. We complete the chapter with a primer on security that looks at all aspects of security, above and beyond a login screen accepting a username and password, which for many people is the meaning of the word *security*.

Chapter 2: Building RESTful Services

An HTTP service that handles XML and/or JSON requests and responds to HTTP methods such as GET, POST, PUT, and DELETE is not necessarily a RESTful service. This chapter introduces you to Roy T. Fielding's constraints that must be satisfied for an HTTP service to be called RESTful and builds our first web API, a simple Hello-World kind of API.

Chapter 3: Extensibility Points

The ASP.NET Web API framework has various points of extensibility built into the web API pipeline for us to extend the processing pipeline. This chapter focuses on understanding the web API extensibility points such as filters and message handlers from the point of view of leveraging the same for securing ASP.NET Web API to deal with threats at the earliest available opportunity. It also highlights the trade-offs associated with selecting the web API extensibility point of a message handler over the ASP.NET extensibility point of the HTTP module for authentication and authorization.

Chapter 4: HTTP Anatomy and Security

This chapter introduces you to Hypertext Transfer Protocol (HTTP), the protocol behind the World Wide Web. Understanding HTTP is a prerequisite to understanding the security aspects of ASP.NET Web API. Instead of fighting against it or abstracting it away, web API embraces HTTP. For this reason, understanding HTTP is all the more important: A house is only as strong as its foundation! This chapter also covers some of the advanced concepts of HTTP, things that are a must to create production-grade, performant, secure web APIs such as Web Caching, ETags, Cross-Origin Resource Sharing (CORS), cookies, proxy servers, HTTPS, and the ultimate tool of HTTP debugging, Fiddler.

Chapter 5: Identity Management

Identity management is an important aspect of application security. In this chapter, we focus on how a subject or an entity gets authenticated and how the actions an entity attempts to perform are authorized by an application in the context of the .NET Framework. This chapter introduces you to the interfaces `IIdentity` and `IPrincipal` that form the basis of role-based access control (RBAC) and compares it with the more flexible and granular claims-based access control (CBAC), which is built based on the claims. Readers get to the take a first peek at the security tokens and the three major formats: SAML, SWT, and JWT.

Chapter 6: Encryption and Signing

Windows Identity Foundation (WIF) hides away the nuts and bolts of tokens and lets the developers work with a set of claims without bothering about the aspects of cryptography. As we step out of the realm of WCF/WIF, securing RESTful ASP.NET Web APIs without depending on WIF classes for the cryptographic heavy lifting means understanding the nuts and bolts of encryption and signing. This chapter covers encryption and decryption and signing and validation using symmetric keys and asymmetric keys: public–private keys generated using RSACryptoServiceProvider as well as a self-signed certificate generated using the Makecert tool.

Chapter 7: Custom STS through WIF

One of the key components in the WS-Trust scheme of things is Security Token Service (STS). WIF allows you to build your own custom STS, although it is highly recommended that you buy one instead of building one. This short chapter introduces you to WS-* protocols, specifically WS-Trust, and goes through the steps for creating a custom STS to enhance your understanding of STS and how STS creates and issues tokens.

Chapter 8: Knowledge Factors

A knowledge factor is something a user knows, such as a password or a PIN. This chapter explores the knowledge-factor authentication mechanisms that can be used to secure ASP.NET Web API. Login credentials of a user ID and password combination is probably the most widely used knowledge factor, and this chapter focuses on the mechanisms leveraging this factor: the two authentication schemes defined in HTTP specification, namely basic and digest authentication, and the Windows-OS-powered Integrated Windows Authentication (IWA), more commonly known as Windows Authentication.

Chapter 9: Ownership Factors

An ownership factor is something a user owns or possesses, such as a key, a certificate, or a token. This chapter examines ownership-factor authentication mechanisms for securing ASP.NET Web API, such as preshared keys (PSKs), more commonly called API keys, X.509 client certificates, and SAML tokens.

Chapter 10: Web Tokens

This chapter is an extension of the previous chapter on ownership-factor security, for web tokens are ownership factors just like SAML tokens. However, web tokens deserve a chapter of their own because they are a better fit for RESTful services. Hence, this chapter is dedicated to web tokens and takes an in-depth look at the two most popular web token formats by studying the anatomy of the Simple Web Token (SWT) and the JSON Web Token (JWT), including both signed (JWS) and encrypted (JWE) forms.

Chapter 11: OAuth 2.0 Using Live Connect API

OAuth 2.0 is an open standard for authorization. Roughly speaking, it can be considered the WS-* of the REST world. We start our exploration of OAuth 2.0, mainly from the point of view of a client consuming a web API that implements OAuth 2.0. We review the four types of grants and take a detailed look at implicit and authorization code-based grants using Microsoft Live Connect API.

Chapter 12: OAuth 2.0 from the Ground Up

In this chapter, we move to the other side of the table. Instead of focusing on a client that consumes an API, we now develop a web API implementing OAuth 2.0, specifically the authorization code-based grant. Implementation is performed from scratch using two ASP.NET MVC web applications so you can understand the nuts and bolts.

Chapter 13: OAuth 2.0 Using DotNetOpenAuth

Although it is possible to build on the OAuth 2.0 implementation from the previous chapter and develop your production-strength OAuth 2.0 implementation, this chapter implements the same authorization code-based grant using DotNetOpenAuth (DNOA), which is a well-established open source .NET library that helps you write production-grade OAuth 2.0–based authorization for your web API, in conformance to the principle of not reinventing the wheel.

Chapter 14: Two-Factor Authentication

When you have an authentication mechanism that leverages a combination of two of the knowledge, ownership, and inherence factors, it is called two-factor authentication (TFA or 2FA). This chapter covers TFA by leveraging the knowledge factor of a password, the ownership factor of an X.509 client certificate, and TFA on a need basis realized through the use of TOTP codes provided by Google Authenticator.

Chapter 15: Security Vulnerabilities

This chapter looks at important and potential security risks or vulnerabilities, points of interest pertaining to ASP.NET Web API, and things to look out for while building a secure, production-strength ASP.NET Web API. The coverage includes the top risks, per OWASP 2013, as well as best practices such as logging and validation.

Appendix: ASP.NET Web API Security Distilled

This appendix is a grand summary of the book, a recap of the various security mechanisms covered in the book. Because there is no good or bad mechanism in an absolute sense, the idea of this book is to present you with all the mechanisms and let you decide based on your needs. This appendix provides an overview of the options.

What You Need to Use This Book

At a bare minimum, you need Microsoft Visual Studio 2010, although all the code listings and samples in this book were developed using Visual Studio 2012 targeting the .NET Framework 4.5. If you use Visual Studio 2010, you will need the WIF runtime as well as the WIF SDK, which are available as stand-alone installations.

One important point to note is that WIF has been fully integrated into the .NET Framework starting with the .NET Framework 4.5, both the tooling as well as the classes. As part of this process, there are changes to the classes and the namespaces the classes were part of in the .NET Framework 4.0 compared to the .NET Framework 4.5. If you use Visual Studio 2010 and the .NET Framework 4.0, you will need to look at sources outside of this book to figure out the .NET Framework 4.0 equivalents of the code and configuration settings used in this book.

The language of choice for all the code written in this book is C#. Although there are Visual Basic.NET folks out there, it is not feasible to show the Visual Basic.NET equivalent, as that would bloat the size of the book. Understanding C# syntax is not that hard, after all!

ASP.NET Web API is part of ASP.NET MVC 4.0. It ships with Visual Studio 2012. Again, if you have the constraint of having to work with Visual Studio 2010, you must install ASP.NET MVC 4.0 by visiting `http://www.asp.net/mvc/mvc4`.

The bottom line is that Visual Studio 2012 and the .NET Framework 4.5 are strongly recommended. If you are really determined, you can get away with using Visual Studio 2010 targeting the .NET Framework 4.0. However, you will not be able to run the code samples provided with this book as is, and you will need to massage the C# code and configuration settings to make them work with the .NET Framework 4.0. All the samples in this book are coded and tested in Windows 7 using Visual Studio 2012 targeting the .NET Framework 4.5. Also, you need IIS 7.0.

The browser we use is mostly Internet Explorer 9.0; for some specific cases, we use Mozilla Firefox or Google Chrome. We also use the HTTP debugging tool called Fiddler. One of the chapters optionally uses Google Authenticator software that runs in iOS, BlackBerry, and Android-based mobile phones.

Who This Book Is For

No prior experience with .NET security is needed to read this book. All security-related concepts are introduced from basic principles and developed to the point where you can use them confidently in a professional environment. A good working knowledge and experience of C# and the .NET Framework are the only prerequisites to benefit from this book.

CHAPTER 1

Welcome to ASP.NET Web API

"Begin at the beginning," the King said gravely, "and go on till you come to the end: then stop."

—Lewis Carroll, *Alice in Wonderland*

If you have chosen to read this book, which is on ASP.NET Web API security, it is highly likely that you are familiar with ASP.NET Web API. In case you are not or simply would like me to begin at the beginning, this introductory chapter along with the next chapter will help you gain a quick understanding of the basics of ASP.NET Web API and help you appreciate the need for the emphasis on security for ASP.NET Web API applications.

ASP.NET Web API Security: If we break this down, we get multiple terms—Web API, ASP.NET Web API, and Security. We start by understanding what a web API is in general before moving on to a primer on RESTful Web API, followed by a review of how the Microsoft ASP.NET Web API framework can help you build web APIs. We complete the chapter with a primer on security that looks at all aspects of security, above and beyond the login screen accepting a username and password, which for many is synonymous with the word security.

What Is a Web API, Anyway?

It all started with the launch of *Sputnik* in 1957, by the Union of Soviet Socialist Republics (USSR). The United States, under the leadership of then President Eisenhower, started the Advanced Research Projects Agency (ARPA) to advance the United States in the technology race, in the light of the *Sputnik* launch. One of the ARPA-funded projects was ARPANET, the world's first operational packet switching network. ARPANET led to the development of protocols that allowed networks to be joined together into a network of networks that evolved into the ubiquitous **Internet** of today.

The terms *Internet* and *World Wide Web* or simply *Web,* are generally used interchangeably, but they are separate although related things. The Internet is the infrastructure on which the World Wide Web has been built. The Internet connects islands of smaller and bigger networks into one huge network.

The **World Wide Web** builds on this network by providing a model to share data or information with the computer users who are all part of the Internet. Servers or web servers serve data in the form of documents or web pages to the clients, called web browsers, which display the documents in a format readable by human beings. Typically, a web page is created in a language called Hyper Text Markup Language (HTML) and is served to a browser by the web server as a result of both parties following a protocol, Hyper Text Transfer Protocol (HTTP). The Web is just one of the ways information can be shared over the Internet. Just like HTTP, there is Simple Mail Transfer Protocol (SMTP) for e-mail, File Transfer Protocol (FTP) for transfer of information in the form of files, and so on.

Initially, web pages were just static pages existing in the file system of some computer with data that hardly changed. As the World Wide Web started to grow and the user base started to expand, there was a need for web pages to be generated on the fly. Web servers started delegating this responsibility to engines such as the Common Gateway Interface (CGI) to generate web pages on the fly. The dynamic web pages and the introduction of the client-side JavaScript scripting language led to a new generation of software applications called **web applications**. The end user of a web application is a human being with an objective of performing a task.

Because the end user of a web application is a human being, there is a user interface associated with a web application. The browser is what provides this interactive interface for a user. In addition, there is a need for nonhuman entities such as a machine running some software to communicate and exchange data over the World Wide Web. Enter the **web service**. Although not mandated, a web service uses HTTP to exchange data. Unlike a web application, which is mainly about HTML over HTTP, for a web service it is mainly Extensible Markup Language (XML) over HTTP. A client sends a request in XML, and the server responds with an XML response. This XML can be **Plain Old XML** (POX), which is typically a nonstandard XML only the client and server will be able to make sense out of, or it can be standard **Simple Object Access Protocol** (SOAP).

To appreciate the value SOAP brings to the table, let us pretend we got some XML response representing an employer in an organization, as shown in Listing 1-1.

Listing 1-1. Response XML

```
<employee>
        <firstname>John</firstname>
        <lasttname>Human</lastname>
        <salary>2000</salary>
        <doj>06/01/1998<doj>
        <lastlogin>10/20/2012 09:30:00</lastlogin>
</employee>
```

To do anything useful with this in our application, this XML might need to be loaded into some data structure, say an object as defined by a class in the case of an object-oriented programming (OOP) language. If I'm programming, how will I define the data type of the field to store salary? Will it be an integer or a fractional number? What if my request to get the employee fails because there is no such employee or there is some other problem? How will I know where to look in the XML if the request has failed? SOAP helps us with questions like these by providing a basic messaging framework on which web services can be built. SOAP has Microsoft roots, although it is currently maintained by the World Wide Web Consortium (W3C).

Microsoft technologies such as the ASMX-based web service, which is currently a legacy technology, and its successor Windows Communication Foundation (WCF) all have great affinity toward SOAP. An ASMX-based web service allows the exchange of SOAP messages over HTTP and that's pretty much it. WCF builds on this and tries to abstract away the infrastructure from the programming. If I have an Employee service that returns the details of an employee, I can host the service to be consumed over HTTP, over Transmission Control Protocol (TCP), through Microsoft Message Queuing (MSMQ), or any combinations thereof. By having the same contract with the client, I can have multiple binding for multiple ways my service can be reached. In both cases, though, the payload will be SOAP, by default. An important aspect of SOAP-based web services is the availability of a Web Service Definition Language (WSDL) file, which allows tooling to be built that helps in consumption of services. For example, Microsoft Visual Studio can generate proxy classes reading WSDL definitions, and the client trying to consume the services (i.e., the programmer writing the client code) can directly work with the generated classes, with the whole existence of the web service hidden from the programmer.

A **web API** is a service. Technically, there is no difference. What is different is the manner in which a web API is intended to be used. Let's say I have a web application where a user can post his thoughts in the form of a short message. A user can log in to my application from a browser, add new posts or update the ones she posted in the recent past, or even delete the old ones. In other words, users can perform create, read, update, and delete (CRUD) operations on their posts using my web application. My application became so popular that there are folks who want to integrate this CRUD functionality into their mobile apps so that users can perform CRUD operations from their mobile devices without logging on to my web application while they are away from their normal computers.

I can now create a web service to support the CRUD operations. Technically it is a web service, but it is an application programming interface (API) to interact with my web application, except that it is over the Web. Traditionally, APIs are a bunch of classes with properties and methods that are part of a reusable component to interact with another application. This scenario is exactly that, except that my API is not available in the form of a software component, but over the Web instead. It is a web API!

Although it is fundamentally a web service, the intention is to use it to manipulate application data, and that is what makes it an API. One important characteristic of most of the typical web APIs in use, although not a defining characteristic, is that web APIs tend to be RESTful web services as compared with SOAP-based web services. A web service can very well be REST based, so this is not the defining characteristic. By using REST, a web API tends to be lightweight and embraces HTTP. For example, a web API leverages HTTP methods to present the actions a user would like to perform and the application entities would become resources these HTTP methods can act on. Although SOAP is not used, messages—requests and responses—are either in XML or JavaScript Object Notation (JSON).

A Primer on RESTful Web API

RESTful Web API, as the name indicates, is a web API or web service implemented using HTTP and is based on the REST architectural style. To be exact, a RESTful service must satisfy the constraints, as defined in the doctoral dissertation of Roy T. Fielding.[1] We will look at RESTful services and all the constraints in Chapter 2, but here is a primer on RESTful Web API.

A central concept to REST is the existence of resources that can be identified through a uniform resource identifier (URI). If you equate resources to nouns, then actions on a resource are verbs and are represented by HTTP methods such as GET, POST, PUT, and DELETE. One of the key characteristics of RESTful Web API is that the URI or the request message does not include a verb. Let us look at a few examples to see what is not RESTful.

1. To retrieve the details of an employee, the URI is `http://server/hrapp/getemployee?id=12345`

2. To retrieve the details of an employee, the URI is `http://server/hrapp/employee?id=12345&action=GET`

3. To retrieve the details of an employee, the URI is `http://server/hrapp/employee` and the request message determines the action to be carried out. For example, the XML fragment <GetEmployeeDetails><Id>12345</Id></GetEmployeeDetails> in the request indicates to the service to fetch the details of the employee with an identifier of 12345.

Now, let us see how the employee details can be retrieved with a RESTful service. The URI will be `http://server/hrapp/employees/12345`. The URI itself will include the employee ID and serves as an identifier to the resource, which is an employee in this case. Actions on this resource are accomplished through HTTP verbs. The action that we are trying to perform against the resource is retrieving the details. Therefore, the request will be an HTTP GET on the URI `http://server/hrapp/employees/12345`.

To update this employee, the request will be an HTTP PUT on the same URI. Similarly, to delete this employee, the request will be an HTTP DELETE request, again on the same URI. To create a new employee, the request will be an HTTP POST to `http://server/hrapp/employees` (without the identifier).

In the case of POST and PUT, the service must be passed the employee data or the resource representation. It is typically XML or JSON that is sent as the HTTP request message body.

The RESTful service responds with the HTTP status code indicating success or failure. For example, if the employee with identifier 12345 does not exist, the HTTP status code of 404 - Not found will be returned. If the request is successful, the HTTP status code of 200 - OK will be returned.

The RESTful service sends responses in XML or JSON, similar to the request. For example, a GET to `http://server/hrapp/employees/12345` results in a response containing JSON representing the employee with an ID of 12345.

---

[1]Fielding, Roy Thomas. "Architectural Styles and the Design of Network-based Software Architectures." Doctoral dissertation, University of California, Irvine, 2000.

Hello, ASP.NET Web API!

Now that you have a 10,000-foot overview of RESTful Web API, let us look at how ASP.NET Web API can help you build RESTful Web API or web services.

ASP.NET Web API is a framework for building RESTful services on the .NET Framework. So, we have this URI `http://server/hrapp/employees/12345` and a client issues a GET. To respond to this request, we need to write code somewhere that retrieves the employee details for 12345. Obviously, that code has to be in some method in some C# class (C# is the language of choice for this book). This is where the concept of routing comes into play.

The class in this case will be a class that derives from the `ApiController` class, part of the ASP.NET Web API framework. All you need to do is to create a subclass of the `ApiController`, say `EmployeesController`, with a method `Get(int id)`. The ASP.NET Web API framework will then route all the GET requests to this method and pass the employee ID in the URI as the parameter.

Inside the method, you can write your code to retrieve the employee details and just return an object of type `Employee`. On the way out, ASP.NET Web API will handle serialization of the employee object to JSON or XML. The web API has the capability of content negotiation: A request can come in along with the choices of the response representation, as preferred by the client. The web API will do its best to send the response in the format requested.

In case of requests with a message payload such as POST, the method you will need to define will be `Post(Employee emp)` with a parameter of type `Employee`. ASP.NET Web API will deserialize the request (XML or JSON) into the `Employee` parameter object for you to use inside the method. If you have experience working on the ASP.NET MVC framework, the web application framework from Microsoft that implements the Model-View-Controller (MVC) pattern, you can relate the preceding paragraphs to routing and model binding in ASP.NET MVC.

ASP.NET Web API enables you to create HTTP-based services through the powerful ASP.NET MVC programming model familiar to many developers. Some of the great features from ASP.NET MVC like routing, model binding, and validation are all part of ASP.NET Web API as well.

Like MVC, there are extensibility points available to tap into and extend the processing pipeline, such as action filters. There are additional extensibility points available, the most notable one being message handlers. Like MVC, a web API lends itself very well to automated unit testing.

In the case of ASP.NET MVC, all controller classes inherit from the `Controller` class of the MVC framework. Similar to that, all controller classes in a web API inherit from the `ApiController` of the web API framework. MVC dispatches a request to an action method inside a controller by mapping the uniform resource locator (URL) to an action method. The web API dispatches a request to an action method based on HTTP verbs rather than the action name from the URL.

ASP.NET MVC 4 ships as part of Visual Studio 2012 and as an add-on for Visual Studio 2010 SP1. ASP.NET Web API is a part of MVC 4.0. There is a new project template called WebAPI available to create web API projects. You can have both API controllers and MVC controllers in the same project.

■ **Note** The MVC controller base class is `System.Web.Mvc.Controller`, whereas the API controller base class is `System.Web.Http.ApiController`. The classes in the two frameworks are in different namespaces. Even if the class name is the same, as in the case of `AuthorizeAttribute`, they will be part of different namespaces.

WCF vs. ASP.NET Web API

Is ASP.NET Web API the only means to create RESTful services in .NET? The answer is no. You can use WCF as well. If you have been associated with the .NET Framework for a nontrivial amount of time, you have for sure encountered the term Dub-See-Eff (WCF), the one-stop framework for all service development needs in the .NET Framework, including RESTful services. Why a new framework then?

The short answer is that ASP.NET Web API is designed and built from the ground up with only one thing in mind—HTTP—whereas WCF was designed primarily with SOAP and WS-* in mind, and REST was retrofitted through the WCF REST Starter Kit. Well, if you are interested in doing one kind of task, such as opening a beer bottle, which would you prefer: a simple bottle opener or a Victorinox SwissChamp?

The programming model of ASP.NET Web API is similar to ASP.NET MVC in that it is simple and convention based, as compared to defining interfaces, creating implementation classes, and decorating them with several attributes. However, ASP.NET Web API is not supposed to supersede WCF. If you want to open a wine bottle, you can't use a simple bottle opener, can you?

It is important to understand the coexistence of WCF and ASP.NET Web API. WCF has been around for a while and ASP.NET Web API is a new kid on the block, but that does not mean WCF is meant to be replaced by ASP.NET Web API. Both WCF and ASP.NET Web API have their own place in the big picture.

ASP.NET Web API is lightweight but cannot match the power and flexibility of WCF in certain cases. If you have your service using HTTP as the transport and if you want to move over to some other transport, say TCP, or even support multiple transport mechanisms, WCF will be a better choice. WCF also has great support for WS-*.

However, when it comes to the client base, not all platforms support SOAP and WS-*. ASP.NET Web API–powered RESTful services can reach a broad range of clients including mobile devices. The bottom line is it is all about trade-offs, as is the case with any architecture.

Programming Model Differences

Let's try to understand the differences in programming models by looking at a simple example: an employee service to get an employee of an organization, based on the employee ID. WCF code (see Listing 1-2) is voluminous, whereas ASP.NET Web API code (see Listing 1-3) is terse and gets the job done.

Listing 1-2. WCF Way

```
[ServiceContract]
public interface IEmployeeService
{
        [OperationContract]
        [WebGet(UriTemplate = "/Employees/{id}")]
        Employee GetEmployee(string id);
}

public class EmployeeService : IEmployeeService
{
        public Employee GetEmployee(string id)
        {
                return new Employee() { Id = id, Name = "John Q Human" };
        }
}

[DataContract]
public class Employee
{
        [DataMember]
        public int Id { get; set; }

        [DataMember]
        public string Name { get; set; }

        // other members
}
```

Listing 1-3. ASP.NET Web API Way

```
public class EmployeeController : ApiController
{
        public Employee Get(string id)
        {
                return new Employee() { Id = id, Name = "John Q Human" };
        }
}
```

A couple of things are worth mentioning here: First, the web API is exactly the same as a normal MVC controller except that the base class is `ApiController`.

Features of MVC that users like, such as binding and testability typically achieved through injecting a repository, are all applicable to a web API as well. Routing in ASP.NET Web API is very similar to ASP.NET MVC. The only difference is that the HTTP method is used to choose the action method to execute, as compared with the URI path in MVC. The naming convention followed in naming the method is sufficient enough for the framework to map this method to HTTP GET. Of course, the name of the method has to just begin with Get. It therefore can be `Get` and it can very well be `GetEmployeeByIdentifier` and ASP.NET Web API would still map the action method to HTTP GET.

If you are experienced with ASP.NET MVC, you could be wondering how different a web API is while the MVC controller's action method can return `JsonResult`. With `JsonResult` action methods, a verb gets added to the URI (e.g., `http://server/employees/get/1234`), thereby making it look more RPC-ish than REST-ish. Actions such as GET, POST, PUT, and DELETE are to be accomplished through HTTP methods rather than through anything in the URI or query string.

ASP.NET Web API also has far superior features, such as content negotiation. ASP.NET MVC's support for `JsonResult` is only from the perspective of supporting AJAX calls from the JavaScript clients and is not comparable to ASP.NET Web API, a framework dedicated to building RESTful services.

Scenarios in Which ASP.NET Web API Shines

Let us now review the scenarios where ASP.NET Web API can add value to an application or system architecture. The following are the scenarios where ASP.NET Web API, as the back end, brings the most value to the table.

- **Rich client web applications:** ASP.NET Web API will be a good fit for rich client web applications that heavily use AJAX to get to a business or data tier. Client applications can be anything capable of understanding HTTP. It can be a Silverlight application or an Adobe Flash-based application or a single-page application (SPA) built using JavaScript libraries such as JQuery, Knockout, and so on, to leverage the power of JavaScript and HTML5 features.

- **Native mobile and nonmobile applications:** ASP.NET Web API can be a back end for native applications running on mobile devices where SOAP is not supported. Because HTTP is a common denominator in all the platforms, even the native applications can use a .NET back-end application through the service façade of a web API. This is especially useful when a mobile application is a secondary user interface (UI) channel with an ASP.NET MVC application being the primary UI channel. Also, native applications running on platforms other than Windows such as a Cocoa app running on Mac can use ASP.NET Web API as the back end.

- **Platform for Internet of Things (IOT):** IOT devices with Ethernet controllers or a Global System for Mobile Communications (GSM) modem, for example, can speak to ASP.NET Web API services through HTTP. A platform built on .NET can receive the data and do business. Not just IOT devices, but other HTTP-capable devices such as radio frequency ID (RFID) readers can communicate with ASP.NET Web API.

■ **Caution** ASP.NET Web API is meant for developing web APIs. In other words, although it can technically work, it is not the right candidate for supplementing your web application's AJAX needs, especially when the AJAX use cases are very few.

ASP.NET Web API as a service layer or tier need not always be the optimum solution from a performance standpoint, because there is an HTTP overhead with every call. For a service tier that is used by the presentation tier, with both tiers in the same network within the safety of firewalls, TCP or Named Pipes could be better choices and WCF can outshine a web API in this area.

A typical service tier or layer in a .NET technology stack gets realized through WCF. Such WCF services are consumed by a front-end application such as a web application (ASP.NET WebForms or MVC) or thick client application (WPF or WinForms). With the exception of Silverlight apps that consume WCF services, a majority of the typical architecture scenarios see WCF services sitting comfortably behind the firewall outside of the DMZ, whereas web servers running the front end or the web application sit within the DMZ and are more prone to attacks. The web API tends to be similar to web applications, as they get typically consumed over the Internet just like an Internet web application and hence get hosted in the servers in the DMZ.

Figure 1-1 illustrates a typical deployment associated with ASP.NET Web API. It is worth noting that ASP.NET Web API is well suited for communication across the firewall, especially given the friendly relationship port 80 enjoys with corporate firewall policies. Native mobile apps, browsers, and other devices are typically outside the firewall and this basically boils down to the fact that ASP.NET Web API has to live outside the protection corporate firewalls offer and be exposed to the Internet. Security will be a major factor in architecting and designing ASP.NET Web API.

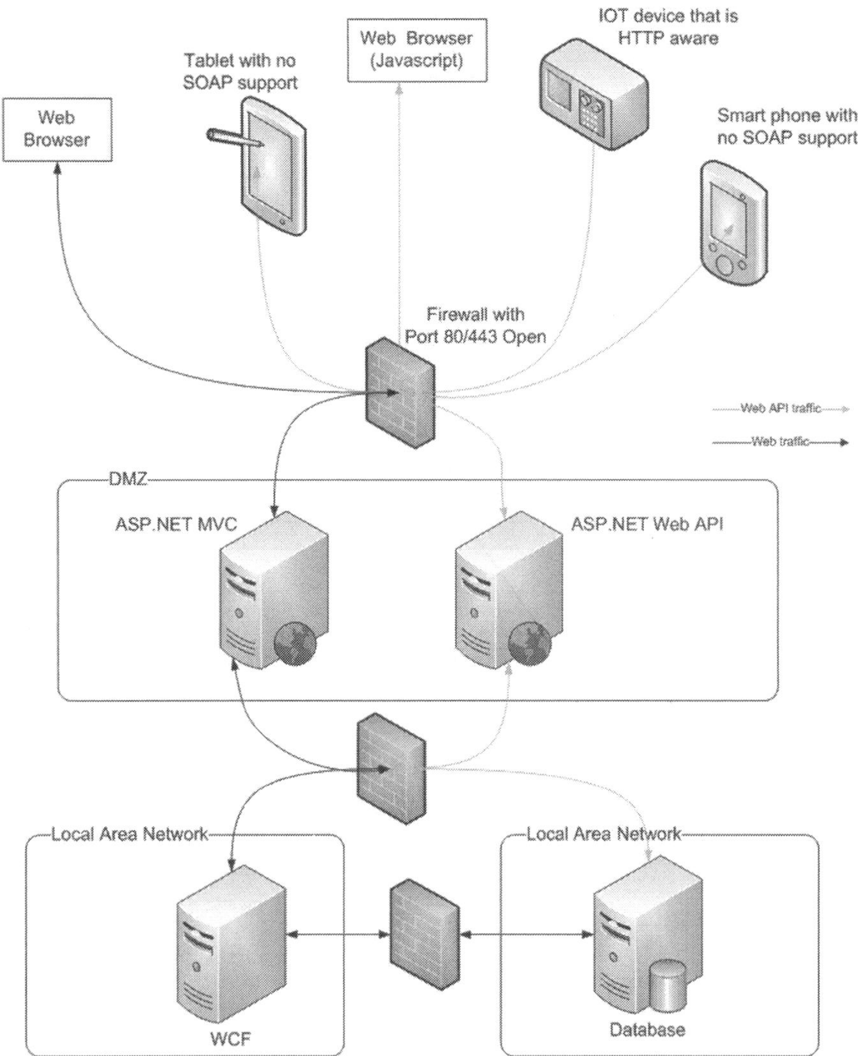

Figure 1-1. *Deployment diagram illustrating the typical deployment associated with ASP.NET Web API*

A Primer on Security

We have seen quite a bit on RESTful Web API and the ASP.NET Web API framework. Finally, we move to the main topic, security. This is a very broad term, but in general it signifies the state of being secure, or freedom from danger. This book is about ASP.NET Web API security, so obviously our focus here is information security. As per U.S. law, the term *information security* means protecting information and information systems from unauthorized access, use, disclosure, disruption, modification, or destruction to provide the elements of the CIA hierarchy.

- Confidentiality, which means preserving authorized restrictions on access and disclosure, including the means for protecting personal privacy and proprietary information.
- Integrity, which means guarding against improper information modification or destruction, and includes ensuring information nonrepudiation and authenticity.
- Availability, which means ensuring timely and reliable access to and use of information.

Confidentiality is about preventing the disclosure of information to unauthorized entities. Encrypting sensitive data and storing hashed passwords are examples of ensuring confidentiality. We look at encryption in Chapter 6 and hashing in Chapter 15.

Integrity is about preventing modifications to the data by unauthorized entities (an entity is a user or an external system that uses the application). This means, first and the foremost, that an entity must be identified. **Identification** is the process of simply identifying the entity. It is different from **authentication**, which is about ensuring that the user really has the identity that she claims to have.

As an example, consider an application where a user, John Q. Human, with a user ID of jqhuman and some password is trying to log in to the application. As soon as the application gets the user-entered identifier of jqhuman, it can identify the user. At that point, the user is an identified user, but not yet authenticated. Once John enters the password, the application compares the user-entered password with the one in its records; if they match, the identified user is considered an authentic user. It is important to note that identification must precede authentication, because only after the user is identified can the application retrieve the password from the data store for comparison against the user-entered password to complete the authentication process.

Authentication can be based on three factors: **knowledge, ownership,** and **inherence**. In the preceding example, the user John uses his user ID and password. The password is something the user knows or remembers and hence the password is a knowledge factor. Authentication can be based on things a user owns or possesses, such as a security token or a client certificate, which are ownership factors. The third factor, the inherence factor, is something a user is, such as a fingerprint or DNA sequence. It is also possible to combine one or more of these factors for authentication. If two factors are involved, it is a **two-factor authentication** (TFA or 2FA). An example of TFA would be authentication based on an X.509 client certificate and a user ID–password combination. We cover knowledge-factor-based security in Chapter 8 and ownership-factor-based security in Chapters 9 and 10. Two-factor security is covered in Chapter 14.

Once an entity is authenticated, actions that the entity wishes to perform on the application can be access controlled. **Authorization** is the process that ensures only those entities with permission to perform a task do perform the task. We look at **identity management** in depth, mainly from the point of view of the .NET Framework and the concepts of authentication and authorization, in Chapter 5.

Authorization ensures entities get to see and operate on what they are allowed to access, but there are cases where an entity would like to open up its own data or information in one application to another application, mostly on a temporary basis. There are standards available in this area, such as **OAuth**, which we look at in depth in Chapters 11, 12, and 13.

Authentication and authorization are important for ensuring integrity, but those two factors alone do not constitute the exhaustive list of things needed to ensure integrity. There are other requirements, too. For example, let's say our application is a web application and a user posts an HTML form with data based on which application data store will be updated. Of course, the application enforces authentication and authorization, but what if someone in the middle tampers with the data in transit? Then, integrity is said to be compromised.

It is common to handle situations like this by securing the layer that transports the data; in the case of web applications, this means using transport security through HTTPS/TLS. We look at **HTTPS** in depth in Chapter 4. An alternative to transport security is message security, where the message is protected without protecting the transport layer. Message security typically involves encryption and signing of messages or the data transmitted, which are covered in depth in Chapter 6.

Similar to man-in-the-middle attacks, where an adversary in the middle attempts to tamper with data, there are multiple other forms of attacks and associated security risks. The Open Web Application Security Project (**OWASP**) is a worldwide, not-for-profit organization that publishes a list of the top ten current security risks. Risks from this list that are relevant to ASP.NET Web API are covered in Chapter 15.

So far, we have focused on the confidentiality and integrity aspects of the CIA triad. The third aspect, availability, is about an application being available for legitimate users. There are forms of attacks such as denial-of-service attacks, which are all about making an application unavailable for users. DoS and brute-force attacks are covered in Chapter 15, but availability from a security standpoint is mostly attributed to IT administration and operation activities involving specialized hardware and software, and is not typically related to application programming.

Related to that point, security is a team effort among the IT administration, operations, and development teams. All the areas need to be covered to call a system or an application secure. You might painstakingly architect, design, and implement a secure application, but if the platform running the software is not hardened or patched diligently, you are opening your system to attacks. Similarly, if you have a sound and secure platform and infrastructure, yet you don't design or code the right way, you are equally vulnerable. One coding bug related to SQL injection is all it takes to open up your application to attacks, even if your design, architecture, and infrastructure are top notch. However, this book is for software developers, designers, and architects, and throughout its chapters, you will see that the focus is on integrity and confidentiality aspects of the CIA triad from a programming perspective.

From an IT operations perspective auditing is an important aspect. We have authentication, authorization, and other protection mechanisms in place, but there could be legal or business requirements to keep track of activities in the application, in terms of who does what. This is called **security auditing,** covered in Chapter 15.

Finally, a short note on **nonrepudiation**, a term that is typically seen in a legal context. To repudiate is to deny, so nonrepudiation is basically ensuring that someone cannot deny something. A digital signature based on an X.509 certificate is very common to ensure nonrepudiation. Signing and encryption using certificates are covered in Chapter 6, but there is no coverage specific to nonrepudiation, as the legal requirements can vary. Figure 1-2 provides an overview of the security topics discussed throughout the book, along with the chapters in which they are covered.

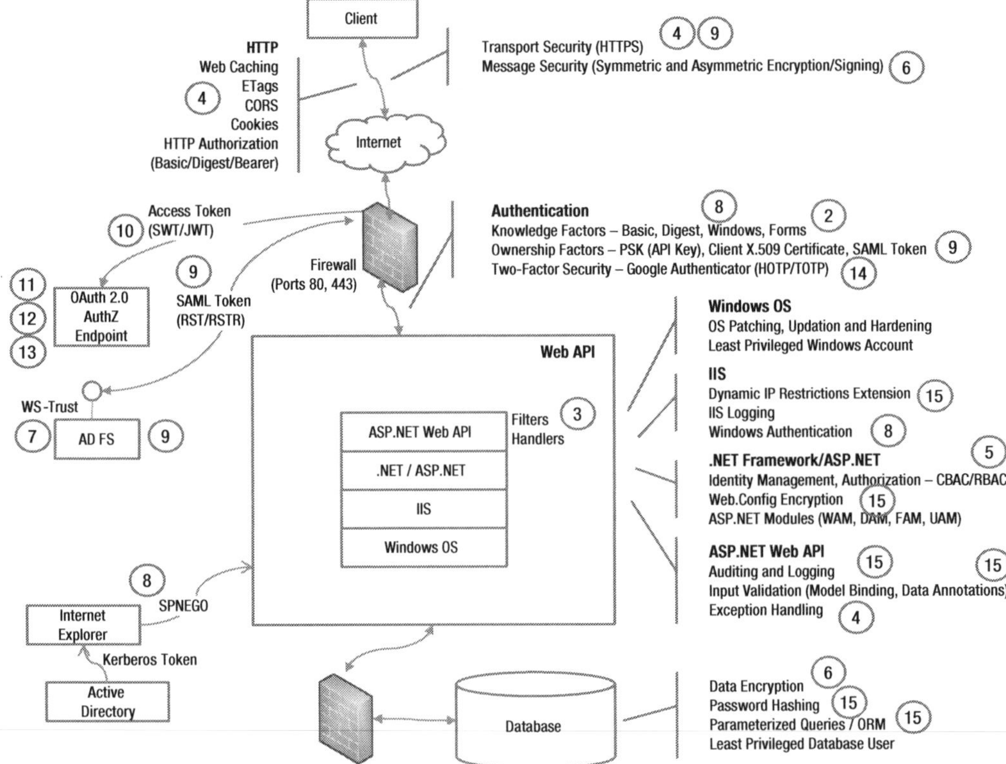

Figure 1-2. *Security overview with chapter references*

Summary

We looked at what a web API is, what ASP.NET Web API is, and why we need this new ASP.NET Web API when there is WCF. We looked at a quick example to get a taste of how easy it is to create a web API with very few lines of code, preferring convention over configuration. We then reviewed the typical scenarios, where ASP.NET Web API brings value to an application or system architecture. Finally, we reviewed a primer on security, specifically information security with a focus on the confidentiality and integrity aspects of the CIA triad.

CHAPTER 2

Building RESTful Services

One of the important characteristics of the popular web APIs in use today is that they are RESTful services, or at least they are not SOAP based.

Just because I have built an HTTP service that handles XML or JSON payloads and respond to HTTP methods such as GET, POST, PUT, and DELETE, I cannot claim that I have built a RESTful service. In this chapter, we see what it takes for an HTTP service to be called RESTful. We then build our first web API, a simple Hello-World API.

What Is a RESTful Service?

Representational State Transfer (REST) is an architectural style. The term REST was introduced and defined by Roy T. Fielding in his doctoral dissertation in the year 2000. A service that conforms to the REST constraints is referred to as being RESTful. To be RESTful, a service has to conform to the following mandatory constraints.

1. **Client-server constraint**, which is based on the separation of concerns, is about separating user interface concerns from data storage concerns. Clients are not concerned with data storage, which is a concern of servers, and servers are not concerned with the user interface or user state, which are concerns of clients.
2. **Stateless constraint** is about each request being an independent self-contained unit with all the necessary information for the server to service the request without looking at anything else for the context.
3. **Cache constraint** is about the server being able to label a response as cacheable or not, so that the client handles the response appropriately from the point of view of later use.
4. **Layered constraint** is about composing the system into layers, with each layer being able to see and interact with only its immediate neighbor. A layer cannot see through its neighbor. Between the client and server, there could be any number of intermediaries—caches, tunnels, proxies, and so on.
5. **Uniform interface constraint** is about providing a uniform interface for identification of resources, manipulation of resources through representations, self-descriptive messages, and hypermedia as the engine of application state.

How can we build a service that satisfies the given constraints using the ASP.NET Web API framework? Client-server constraint is an easy one to satisfy out of the box. ASP.NET Web API is all about responding to the client request with the data, without bothering about client state or how data will be presented to the end user.

Stateless constraint can also be easily satisfied out of the box, unless something horrible is done such as using the ASP.NET session state from the web API.

ASP.NET MVC supports the `OutputCache` attribute that can be used to control output caching. ASP.NET Web API has no support out of the box, but it is easy to roll out our own action filter attribute. The bottom line is that the

Cache-Control response header is the lever ASP.NET Web API can use to label a response as cacheable or not. By default, Cache-Control is set to no-cache and the response is not cached. Chapter 4 covers the topic of web caching, including ETags.

Layered constraint is more along the infrastructure line—proxies, firewalls, and so on. There is nothing special that needs to be done from ASP.NET Web API to satisfy this constraint.

Uniform interface constraint includes the following four constraints and is a key factor in deciding if an HTTP service is RESTful or not.

1. Identification of resources
2. Manipulation of resources through representations
3. Self-descriptive messages
4. Hypermedia as the engine of application state (HATEOAS)

We now look at uniform interface constraint in detail through each of the four constraints.

Identification of Resources

A resource is any data that a web API sends to its clients. Examples could be a product that your company sells, a purchase order received from a buyer, a list of employees in your company, or an individual employee in a department. In the real world, a product or an employee could be uniquely identified through an identifier, such as a product ID or an employee ID.

In the case of RESTful web services, a resource is identified by a URI. An employee with an identifier of 12345 will be represented by `http://server/employees/12345`. In the case of ASP.NET Web API, the URI can be slightly different and it includes api by default in the URI, so it will be more like `http://server/api/employees/12345`. If you fire up an instance of Internet Explorer, type that URI in the address bar, and press Enter, Internet Explorer does an HTTP GET and you will get the JSON representation of the resource, which is an employee with the ID of 12345 in this case.

From the .NET code point of view (see Listing 2-1), the corresponding class will be `EmployeesController`, which is a subclass of `ApiController` and the method that executes to create the resource representation to be sent back to the client in its `Get(int)` method.

Listing 2-1. Identification of Resources

```
public class EmployeesController : ApiController
{
        public Employee Get(int id)
        {
                // return employee
        }

        public IEnumerable<Employee> GetAllEmployees()
        {
                // return all employees
        }
}
```

In Listing 2-1, the resource that is a noun has the URI representation of `http://server/api/employees/12345`. This resource was accessed through GET HTTP method, which is the verb. Like one single employee, a list of employees is also a resource and its identifier will be `http://server/api/employees`. The corresponding method is `GetAllEmployees()`, which returns `IEnumerable<Employee>`.

Manipulation of Resources Through Representations

The example of a user typing `http://server/api/employees/12345` in Internet Explorer can be described as a user requesting a resource using the GET verb and getting back the employee JSON, which is the representation of the resource. GET is guaranteed not to cause any side effect and is said to be nullipotent; nothing happens to the system's state, even when called multiple times or not called at all. In other words, the system state will be the same for all the following scenarios: (1) method was not called at all, (2) method was called once, and (3) method was called multiple times.

Other important verbs are POST, PUT, and DELETE. POST is for creating a new resource, PUT is for updating an existing resource, and DELETE is for deleting an existing resource. PUT and DELETE are idempotent; the effect to the system state will be the same as that of the first call, even when called multiple times subsequent to the first call.

To create a new employee, the client sends a POST request, with the new employee (JSON or XML representation) in the body of the request. This request gets mapped to a method with a name starting with Post, which is `Post(Employee)` in this case.

Updating an employee is the same as creating a new employee except that the PUT verb is used and mapping is based on the name starting with Put. One important difference compared to POST is that PUT is idempotent. If a user sends multiple requests to update an employee to the same state, no error must be sent back.

Deleting an employee is similar except that a resource representation is not needed. A DELETE request against the URI will be sufficient to delete the resource. Similar to PUT, the DELETE method is also idempotent. Even if the underlying data source sends an error back when the employee to be deleted no longer exists, because it is already deleted in response to the previous request, no error must be sent back.

See Listing 2-2 for an example of how ASP.NET Web API supports manipulation of resources through different action methods.

Listing 2-2. Manipulation of Resources

```
public class EmployeesController : ApiController
{
        public Employee Post(Employee human)
        {
                // Add employee to the system
        }

        public void Delete(int id)
        {
                // Delete employee from the system
        }

        public void Put (Employee employee)
        {
                // Update employee in the system
        }
}
```

Table 2-1. Manipulation of Resources

Action	Resource Identifier	Verb	Request Body	Response Body
List of all employees	`http://server/api/employees`	GET	None	JSON/XML representation of the resource requested, which is the list of employees.
Get a specific employee	`http://server/api/employees/12345`	GET	None	JSON/XML representation of the resource requested, which is the specific employee.
Create a new employee	`http://server/api/employees`	POST	JSON/XML representation of the resource getting added, which is the new employee	JSON/XML representation of the resource, which is the new employee that just got added into the system. The difference between this representation and the one in the request body could be that the employee ID that got generated by the system could be present in the response representation.
Update an existing employee	`http://server/api/employees/12345`	PUT	JSON/XML representation of the resource getting updated	None
Delete an existing employee	`http://server/api/employees/12345`	DELETE	None	None

For all the preceding actions, a status code is the means through which the status of the action is communicated back. By default it is 200 – OK, indicating success. As a special case, 201 – Created gets sent for POST, when a resource was created. 401 – Not authorized gets sent when a user requests an action on a resource that requires the user to be authenticated and that user has either not provided the credentials or provided invalid credentials. 404 – Not Found gets sent when the user has requested an action on a resource that does not exist. There are multiple other status codes.

We will see in detail how ASP.NET Web API supports some of these status codes in Chapter 4.

Self-Descriptive Messages

A resource can have multiple representations, JSON and XML being just two examples. A request body having a specific representation of a resource must have a self-description of the representation so that it is parsed and handled correctly. The same holds for responses.

In ASP.NET Web API, the Multipurpose Internet Mail Extensions (MIME) type determines how the web API serializes or deserializes the message body. There is built-in support for XML, JSON, and form-url encoded data.

Let's take the case of a request to create a new employee, the corresponding action method shown in Listing 2-3, to review a few scenarios.

Listing 2-3. Self-Descriptive Messages

```
public Employee Post(Employee value)
{
      // Create the new employee and return the same
}
```

Scenario 1: JSON Representation

Here is an example of a request-response message pair with JSON being the content type for both messages. The web API determines the media-type formatter to be used based on the content type. Because it is JSON, it uses JsonMediaTypeFormatter to deserialize JSON in the CLR object of type Employee named value. Again on the way out, the CLR object to be returned, in this case an object of Employee type, is serialized into JSON.

If the request content type comes in as XML, XmlMediaTypeFormatter would have been used to deserialize and this whole process is seamless to the action method code, as it always receives the Employee object. This is one of the powerful features of ASP.NET Web API.

Request Sent

```
POST /api/employees HTTP/1.1
Content-Type: application/json; charset=utf-8
Content-Length: 49

{"Name":"John Q Law", "Department":"Enforcement"}
```

Response Received

```
HTTP/1.1 200 OK
Content-Type: application/json; charset=utf-8

{"Department":"Enforcement","Id":"123","Name":"John Q Law"}
```

Scenario 2: No Content Type

What if there is no content type specified in the request header? ASP.NET Web API will not know what to do with the message. The web API returns 500 – Internal Server Error with a message that no MediaTypeFormatter is available to read the object of type Employee with media type undefined.

Request Sent

```
POST /api/employees HTTP/1.1
Content-Length: 49

{"Name":"John Q Law", "Department":"Enforcement"}
```

Response Received

```
HTTP/1.1 500 Internal Server Error
Content-Type: application/json; charset=utf-8

{"ExceptionType":"System.InvalidOperationException","Message":"No 'MediaTypeFormatter' is available
to read an object of type 'Employee' with the media type ''undefined''.","StackTrace":"   at
System.Net.Http.ObjectContent.SelectAndValidateReadFormatter(..."}
```

Scenario 3: XML Representation

If the content type is specified for XML and the XML representation of the resource is sent in the request message body, it starts to work again. The web API uses XmlMediaTypeFormatter, although this time around the resource sent back in the response also becomes XML.

Request Sent
```
POST /api/employees HTTP/1.1
Content-Type: application/xml; charset=utf-8
Content-Length: 80

<Employee><Name>John Q Law</Name><Department>Enforcement</Department></Employee>
```

Response Received
```
HTTP/1.1 200 OK
Content-Type: application/xml; charset=utf-8

<?xml version="1.0" encoding="utf-8"?><Employee xmlns:xsi="http://www.w3.org/2001/XMLSchema-
instance" xmlns:xsd="http://www.w3.org/2001/XMLSchema"><Id>123</Id><Name>John Q Law</
Name><Department>Enforcement</Department></Employee>
```

Scenario 4: Mix and Match

It is possible to mix and match, that is, send the XML representation of the resource in the request body and ask for JSON to be returned or vice versa. If a web API is capable of handling the content type specified in the Accept header, it will send the resource in that representation. In the following example request, the client sends the request body as XML and indicates the same by specifying application/xml in Content-Type. However, the client prefers the response to be returned as JSON and indicates that preference by specifying application/json in the Accept header.

Request
```
POST /api/employees HTTP/1.1
Content-Type: application/xml; charset=utf-8
Accept: application/json
Content-Length: 80

<Employee><Name>John Q Law</Name><Department>Enforcement</Department></Employee>
```

Response
```
HTTP/1.1 200 OK
Content-Type: application/json; charset=utf-8

{"Department":"Enforcement","Id":"123","Name":"John Q Law"}
```

The key point to note in this transaction is that the client **asks** and not **tells** the server. If the Accept header of application/pdf, application/json is sent in the request, ASP.NET Web API will not be able to send the response back as PDF, by default, and hence switches to the second choice, JSON. This process is therefore called Content Negotiation.

It is interesting to note that a web API switches to XML if the Accept header has just application/pdf. It can't send a PDF for sure but there is nothing else specified as the second choice, so it switches over to the MIME type of the request, which is XML in this case.

Hypermedia as the Engine of Application State

The HATEOAS constraint requires a client to enter a RESTful service through a fixed URL. From that point onward, any future action a client takes will be based on what the client gets to discover within the resource representation returned by the service.

Let's take an example. A client makes a GET request to the resource with identifier `http://server/api/employees`. In other words, the client is asking for a list of employees. As the next step, if the client needs to GET an employee, how will it go about doing it? One option is that the client "knows" it! Then, the client has to know quite a bit about the service. Another option is hypermedia, or hypertext. A service that satisfies the HATEOAS constraint returns not just data, but data and links.

In the previous example of the employee listing, each employee can have multiple links: one to look at employee details, or one perhaps to fire him, for example. Of course, the links available will be based on what the client is authorized to do. For a user who is not authorized to fire employees, there is no point in sending the firing link. Here is an example JSON representation of an employee resource with links.

```
{
   "Department":"Enforcement",
   "Id":"123",
   "Links":[
      {
         "Rel":"GetDetails",
         "Url":"/api/employees/56789"
      },
      {
         "Rel":"Fire",
         "Url":"/api/employees/56789"
      }
   ],
   "Name":"John Q Law"
}
```

One obvious problem is what the client will do with the links. To get details, GET has to be executed and for the next one, DELETE, probably, but how will the client know? The answer to the question is forms, which will contain all the needed information for the client to make the next move.

HATEOAS is not supported by ASP.NET Web API out of the box, if you expect a web API to provide links or forms intelligently without ever writing a line of code. However, it is possible to include them in the resource representation returned by writing your own custom code.

Implementing and Consuming an ASP.NET Web API

Let us now go through the steps of creating an ASP.NET Web API that returns a list of employees. Our web API, in this case, will be consumed by an ASP.NET MVC Razor view through JQuery AJAX. Fire up Visual Studio and create a new web project as shown in Figure 2-1. I'm naming it TalentManager.

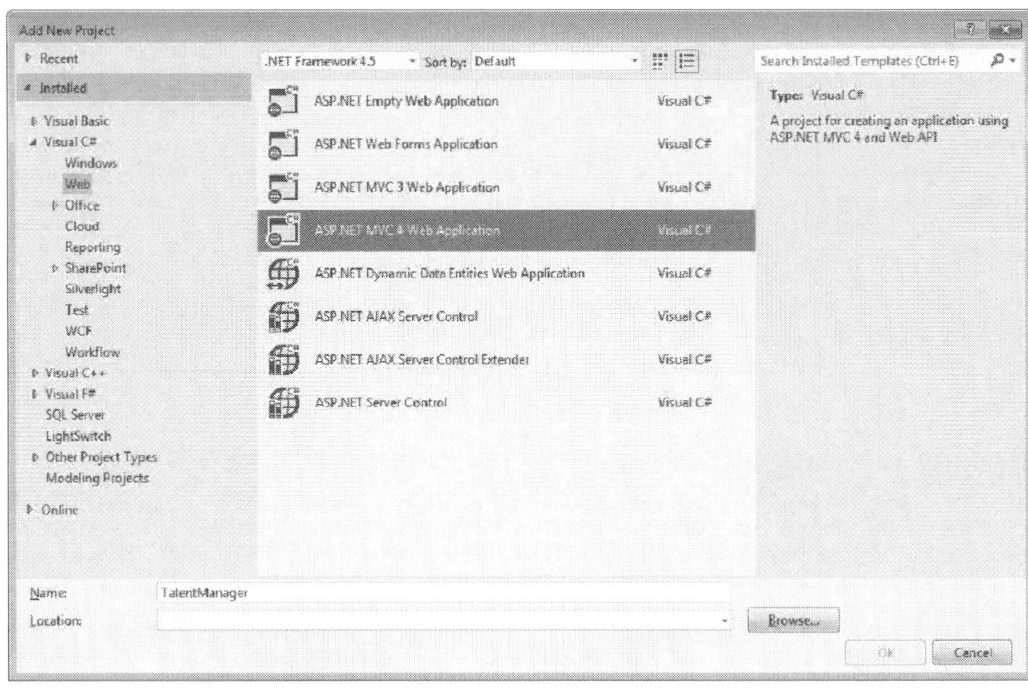

Figure 2-1. *New ASP.NET MVC 4 project*

Select the web API template in the next screen, as shown in Figure 2-2.

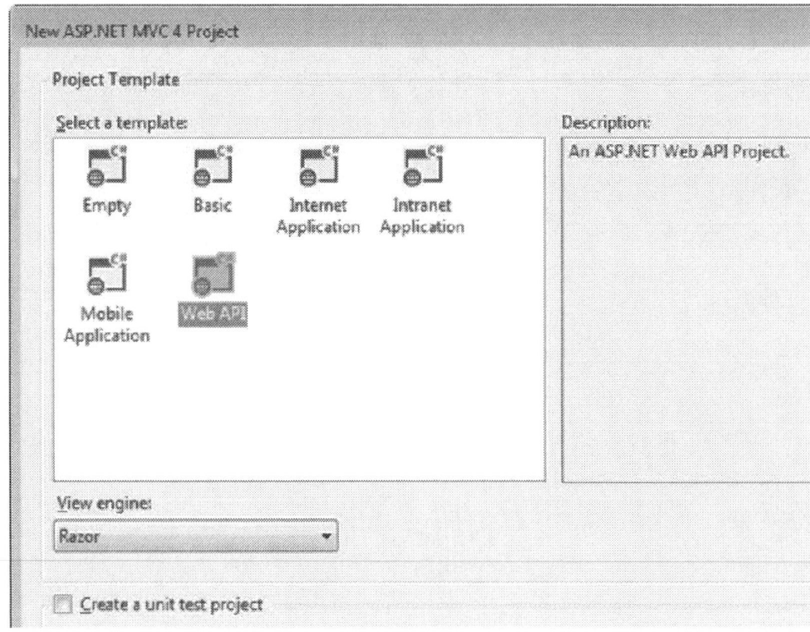

Figure 2-2. *Web API template*

■ **Note** I'm using Visual Studio 2012, which comes with ASP.NET MVC 4.0 out of the box. Also, I'm using the .NET Framework 4.5. All the samples in this book will target the .NET Framework 4.5.

If you are using Visual Studio 2010 and targeting the .NET Framework 4.0, you will need to download ASP.NET MVC 4.0 from `www.asp.net/web-api` and install it. If you have done so, you will get an option to create an ASP.NET MVC 4 Web application. If you have not downloaded MVC 4.0, now is the time to do so!

Delete the `ValuesController` added by Visual Studio and create a new WebAPI controller by right-clicking the controller folder in Solution Explorer and selecting Add ➤ Controller in the pop-up menu. Select Empty API Controller as Template in Scaffolding Options and assign a name such as `EmployeesController`. Copy and paste the code from Listing 2-4. Create the `Employee` class under the Models folder.

Listing 2-4. Get Employee – ASP.NET Web API

```
public class EmployeesController : ApiController
{
        public Employee Get(int id)
        {
                return new Employee()
                {
                        Id = id,
                        Name = "John Q Law",
                        Department = "Enforcement"
                };
        }

        public IEnumerable<Employee> GetAllEmployees()
        {
                return new Employee[]
                {
                        new Employee()
                        {
                                Id = 12345,
                                Name = "John Q Law",
                                Department = "Enforcement"
                        },
                        new Employee()
                        {
                                Id = 45678,
                                Name = "Jane Q Taxpayer",
                                Department = "Revenue"
                        }
                };
        }
}
```

```
public class Employee
{
        public int Id { get; set; }
        public string Name { get; set; }
        public string Department { get; set; }
}
```

■ **Note** Unlike the general naming convention followed in .NET, the controller name is plural. This is done so that the resulting URI of the resource follows the REST conventions. We have two action methods here: one to handle GET on a specific employee resource using an identifier and the other one to handle GET requests on all employees with corresponding return types, *Employee* in the former case and *IEnumerable<Employee>* in the latter.

When Visual Studio created the web project, it created a HomeController with an action method named Index. Let's go to the corresponding view View/Home/Index.cshtml and replace the content with code from Listing 2-5.

Listing 2-5. Get Employee - JQuery

```
@section scripts{
    <script type="text/javascript">
        $(document).ready(function () {
            $('#search').click(function () {
                $('#employees').empty();

                $.getJSON("/api/employees", function (data) {
                $.each(data, function (i, employee) {
                      var content = employee.Id + ' ' + employee.Name;
                      content = content + ' ' + employee.Department;

                      $('#employees').append($('<li/>', { text: content }));
               });
          });
            });
        });
    </script>
}
<div>
    <div>
        <h1>
            Employees Listing
        </h1>
        <input id="search" type="button" value="Get" />
    </div>
    <div>
        <ul id="employees" />
    </div>
</div>
```

If you now go to /Home/Index of the MVC application and click the Get button, it will get the JSON from Web API /api/employees and render the data in the form of an unordered list (see Figure 2-3).

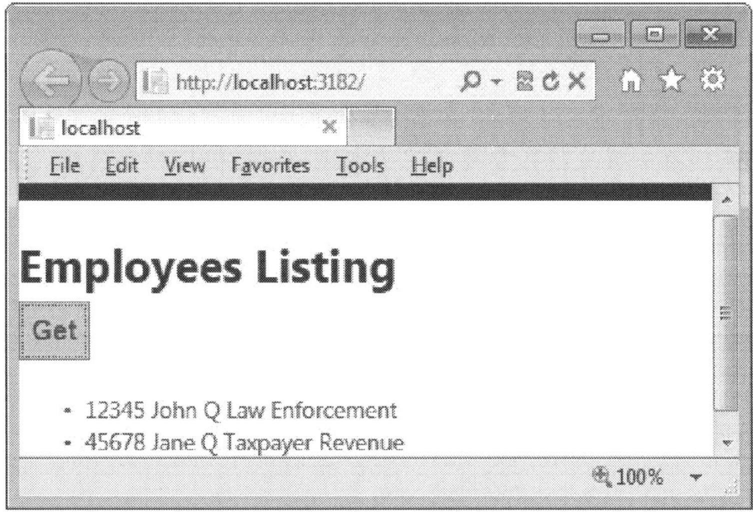

Figure 2-3. *Employees listing user interface*

Our First Attempt in Securing a Web API

The web API and the web application we have developed so far, when deployed in an Internet Information Services (IIS) server opened up to the Internet, can be accessed by anyone who knows the URL. This is undesirable for most, if not all, web applications. For public-facing web sites, this is acceptable, but web applications typically have restricted access. A mechanism for authenticating the users will be required at a bare minimum.

There are multiple ways of authenticating users. If an ASP.NET web application is targeted exclusively for an enterprise user base, Windows Active Directory–based authentication is a great option. If the user base can extend beyond the reach of Active Directory, Forms Authentication is a popular choice for both ASP.NET MVC and ASP.NET WebForms, with user credentials typically stored in a database against which authentication is performed.

Forms Authentication

Forms authentication is a ticket-based mechanism. An authentication ticket gets created at the time of user login, stuffed into a cookie (typically), and sent back to the browser for the browser to keep sending the cookie with the ticket in all subsequent requests until the time cookie expires. As long as the cookie is sent by the browser and the cookie contains the valid ticket, the user is considered an authenticated user.

Forms authentication is applicable to any kind of ASP.NET application: WebForms, MVC, or even web APIs. In the TalentManager application, we have the MVC controller and the web API controller in the same project or application, so we try to secure them both with forms authentication.

When IIS receives a request, it will try to authenticate the user. If anonymous authentication is selected, as is the case by default, IIS creates a token to represent the anonymous user and passes that on to ASP.NET. Next, ASP.NET will try to authenticate based on the `mode` attribute of the `authentication` element defined in Web.config. The default configuration is `<authentication mode="None" />`, which means ASP.NET will also not authenticate the user.

To enable forms authentication, we need to make sure a specific IIS module, FormsAuthenticationModule, is hooked into the life cycle of our ASP.NET application. This can be accomplished by removing the default authentication element and adding a new entry as shown in Listing 2-6.

One more step is required to deny access to anonymous users and make authentication mandatory: the addition of one more element, authorization (see Listing 2-6).

Listing 2-6. Web.config Entries

```
<authentication mode="Forms">
      <forms loginUrl="Login"/>
 </authentication>

<authorization>
         <deny users="?"/>
</authorization>
```

With these two config elements in place, forms authentication begins to take effect. UrlAuthorizationModule, another module in the pipeline, determines whether or not the current user is authorized to access the requested URL. This is where the second configuration setting in Listing 2-6 comes into play.

By specifying that all paths are denied to nonauthenticated users, UrlAuthorizationModule sends a 401 – Unauthorized response when a nonauthenticated user accesses any path. However, a response with a 401 status code never gets sent back to the client, because FormsAuthenticationModule reads this and redirects to LoginController's default action, as specified in the loginUrl attribute, in the preceding example configuration.

The user at this point provides the credentials (user ID and password) and submits the form. LoginController validates the credentials, creates the ticket, and writes the cookie into response.

The browser, on receiving this cookie, starts to send the cookie in all subsequent requests. FormsAuthenticationModule reads the cookie and establishes the identity based on the authentication ticket in the cookie.

Figure 2-4 shows the sequence diagram of the interactions associated with forms authentication. FormsAuthenticationModule and AuthorizationModule are from the ASP.NET framework.

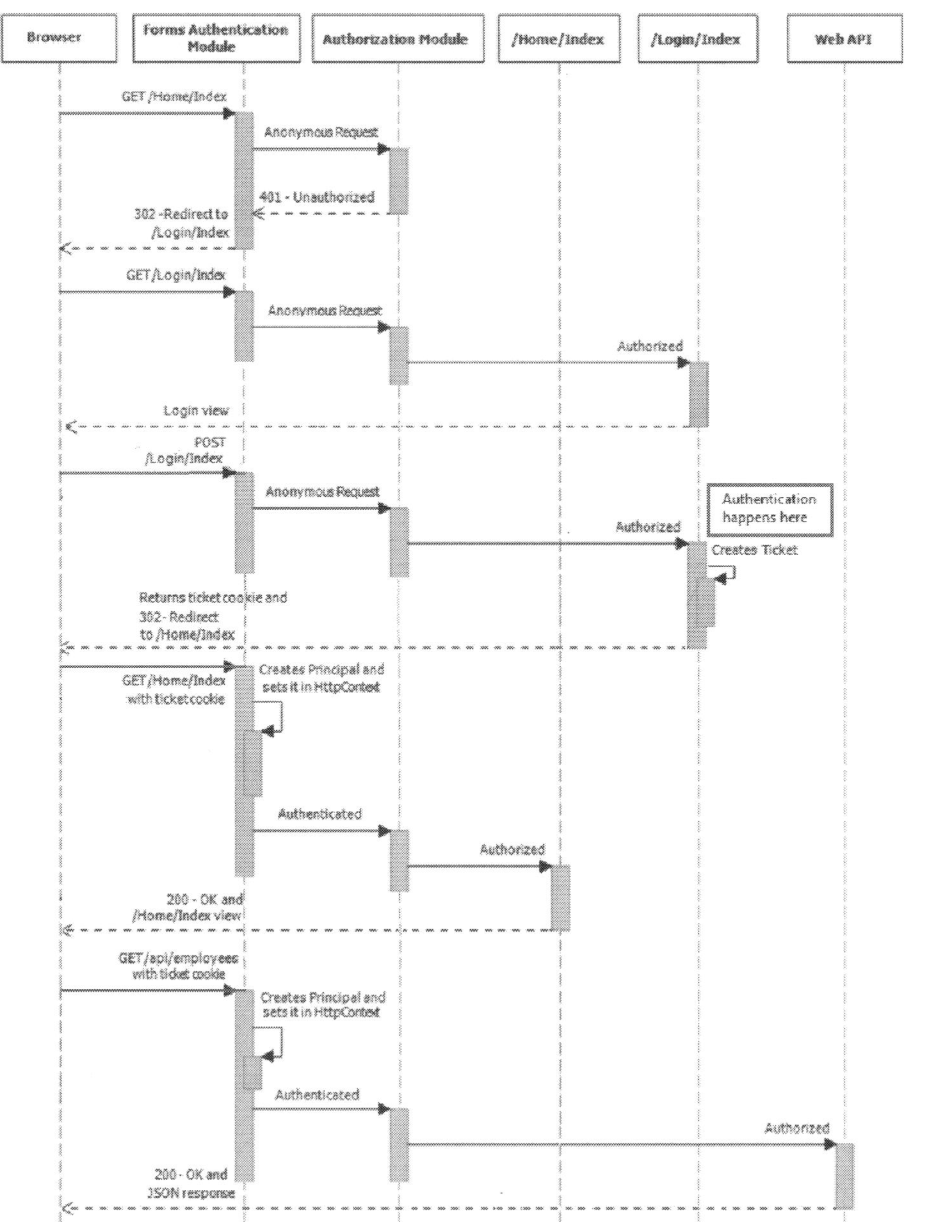

Figure 2-4. *Forms authentication sequence*

To enable forms authentication for the Talent Manager application, first modify the Web.config file, as shown in Listing 2-6. Then, add an empty MVC controller with the name `LoginController`, as shown in Listing 2-7.

Listing 2-7. Login Controller

```
public class LoginController : Controller
{
    public ActionResult Index(string returnurl)
    {
        return View(); // present the login page to the user
    }

    // Login page gets posted to this action method
    [HttpPost]
    public ActionResult Index(string userId, string password)
    {
        if (userId.Equals(password)) // dumb check for illustration
        {
            // Create the ticket and stuff it in a cookie
            FormsAuthentication.SetAuthCookie("Badri", false);
            return RedirectToAction("Index", "Home");
        }

        return View();
    }
}
```

The action method that handles HTTP POST is where the actual authentication (i.e., comparing the user-entered credentials against the stored credentials) happens. If credentials are valid, an authentication ticket gets created and stuffed into a cookie through the call to `FormsAuthentication.SetAuthCookie()`. For the sake of brevity, the authentication I'm doing is just making sure the user ID and password are the same.

Right-click Index action method and select Add View in the shortcut menu, then click Add in the subsequent dialog box. Copy and paste the code in Listing 2-8 into Index.cshtml under the Login folder. The view corresponding to the Index action of the Login controller will be the login page; it gets the user ID and password from the user and posts it back to itself.

Listing 2-8. Index View of LoginController

```
<h1>Sign In</h1>
@using (Html.BeginForm())
{
    <div class="editor-label">
        @Html.Label("userId")
    </div>
    <div class="editor-field">
        @Html.TextBox("userId")
    </div>

    <div class="editor-label">
        @Html.Label("password")
    </div>
```

```
    <div class="editor-field">
        @Html.Password("password")
    </div>

    <input type="submit" value="Login" />
}
```

Now, with the changes to Web.config and the addition of `LoginController`, the application is no longer a free-for-all application. When you go to Home/Index, which is the home page, you get redirected to the login page. On entering the right credentials (in our case any string as user ID and the same as password), you come back to the home page. If you then click Get, the view makes a call to ASP.NET Web API and displays the list of employees correctly. Very nice!

■ **Note** A cookie is not mandatory for forms authentication and it is possible to send the ticket in a query string, but it gets really ugly to see those in every request. It is not good from a security standpoint, either.

One important point to note in the sequence associated with forms authentication is the `FormsAuthenticationModule` creating the `GenericPrincipal` object and attaching it to `HttpContext` and `Thread.CurrentPrincipal`. Identity associated with the principal will be `System.Web.Security.FormsIdentity` with the same name that is passed in while creating the ticket.

It all seems to be working very well, only because ASP.NET Web API is accessed only after the home page was accessed. Nothing prevents a direct HTTP GET to /api/employees. There are multiple ways to do this. The simplest way is to type the URI of `http://localhost:<port>/talentmanager/api/employees` directly in the browser. If you do that, you get directed to the login page, which is not nice at all! You are accessing an API—a service—and you get redirected to a web page. If you do not use a browser but, say, a C# program that uses `HttpClient`, you will be getting a 302 redirect. It is nice for a web application but not so nice for a web API.

Although forms authentication has served us well in the preceding example of accessing an API through the web app, it is not always an ideal solution to securing ASP.NET Web API. For nonbrowser clients, forms authentication feels like fitting a square peg into a round hole!

The problem with using forms authentication with ASP.NET Web API is not just about getting a 302. The problem of 302 redirects can be worked around by not specifying the `authorization` element in Web.config and instead adding an instance of `System.Web.Http.AuthorizeAttribute` to the `HttpFilterCollection` and an instance of `System.Web.Mvc.AuthorizeAttribute` to `GlobalFilterCollection`, as shown in Listing 2-9.

Listing 2-9. Enabling Authorize Filter at Global Level

```
public static class WebApiConfig
{
    public static void Register(HttpConfiguration config)
    {
        config.Routes.MapHttpRoute(
            name: "DefaultApi",
            routeTemplate: "api/{controller}/{id}",
            defaults: new { id = RouteParameter.Optional }
        );

        config.Filters.Add(new AuthorizeAttribute());
    }
}
```

```
public class FilterConfig
{
    public static void RegisterGlobalFilters(GlobalFilterCollection filters)
    {
        filters.Add(new HandleErrorAttribute());
        filters.Add(new AuthorizeAttribute());
    }
}
```

This will have the same effect of redirecting all unauthorized requests to the login page in the case of MVC and sending back a 401 response code in the case of a web API.

However, the real problem is the forms authentication itself. It is a mechanism designed for web applications that have the cookie and redirect support and is not a natural fit for RESTful, stateless ASP.NET Web APIs. Cookies do bring Cross-Site Request Forgery (CSRF) attacks into the equation as well (see Chapter 15 for more information on CSRF). We are in need of security mechanisms better than what forms authentication can provide, to be a better fit for ASP.NET Web API!

Summary

Not all HTTP services are RESTful services. Just because an HTTP service that handles XML or JSON payloads responds to HTTP methods such as GET, POST, PUT, and DELETE, it is not always true that this service is RESTful. We looked at Roy Fielding's constraints that an HTTP service must meet to be called RESTful.

We built our first web API and consumed the API from an ASP.NET MVC application using JQuery AJAX. We tried to secure our web API using the popular forms authentication. The takeaway from that attempt is that techniques popular with other ASP.NET applications—Web Forms and MVC—most notably forms authentication, might not be appropriate for ASP.NET Web API.

CHAPTER 3

Extensibility Points

ASP.NET Web API is a framework. The key defining attribute of a framework is that it is in control of the execution flow and calls the application-specific code written by developers like us at the appropriate time. We don't call the framework code but it calls us, in line with the Hollywood principle. The most fundamental lever that we use to harness the power of the ASP.NET Web API framework in building a service is the `ApiController` subclass that we write. It is the business end where all the application-specific action happens.

The ASP.NET Web API framework receives an HTTP request and goes about processing it. At some point in time during the processing, it calls the method we have implemented in the `ApiController` subclass passing in the parameters, if any, and takes the output returned by our application-specific code and continues the processing to ultimately send an HTTP response back to the client. The sequence of steps that happens from the time a request is received to the time the response is sent back defines the processing architecture of ASP.NET Web API.

ASP.NET Web API, being a framework, has various points of extensibility built in, for us to hook our code in and extend the processing. In this chapter, we look at the processing architecture of ASP.NET Web API framework with focus on the extensibility points.

The What and Why of Extensibility Points

Why do you need to bother about the processing architecture? The more you know about something, the easier it is to secure the same. Securing a black box is a very difficult task, for we do not know what it does. A good understanding of the processing architecture, the extensibility points available, and the sequence of steps puts us in a position where we can deal with malicious intentions at the earliest available opportunity.

You also might wonder why you need to understand the extensibility points. The core concerns of an ASP.NET Web API powered service stay in the action methods of `ApiController` subclasses. Security, being a cross-cutting concern, does not fit directly into `ApiController` subclasses.

The most simplistic approach to implementing security (which is far too simple to be deemed production strength) is to have the code in separate classes and call them from the action method. By doing so, we are mixing concerns. This mixing results in a code base that is hard to manage, with code duplicated all over the place. Most important, a failure to call the method of the appropriate class due to lack of knowledge or just plain sloppiness results in security loopholes.

Another possible approach is to create a base `ApiController` class with security-related code from which all the controllers inherit, instead of inheriting directly from `ApiController`. Inheritance has its own disadvantages in terms of flexibility and there will always be a developer who inherits his controller class directly from `ApiController`.

What other options do we have? Enter extensibility points. They offer a standard set of extension points to hook our security code in. All the developers on the team need not bother about the security-specific code. A designated one or few can extend the web API processing through these points. The ASP.NET Web API framework calls this code at the appropriate point in time just as it calls the action method in `ApiController`. By leveraging the extensibility points, we are making sure security code is not repeated and the overall application code stays clean and modular.

Moving the responsibility of calling the security-related code to ASP.NET Web API from the developers means we are idiot-proofing our application to a greater extent. After all, ASP.NET Web API is a framework and calling our code is what it is good at!

Finally, what are all the extensibility points available for us to use? There are several, but we focus mainly on two of them—filters and message handlers—because these are the most relevant ones from the security point of view. Both have merits and drawbacks. The requirements at hand typically determine which one to choose over the other.

ASP.NET Web API Life Cycle

First, let us take a look at the ASP.NET Web API life cycle for web hosting (ASP.NET) before we dive into the depths of filters and message handlers. The application domain gets created first. Then, ASP.NET creates core objects such as `HttpContext`, `HttpRequest`, and `HttpResponse`. The ASP.NET Web API application is started by creating an instance of the `WebApiApplication` class, which is derived from the `HttpApplication` class. The `Application_Start` event gets fired and the corresponding handler in Global.asax.cs is called. So far, the flow is just like any other ASP.NET application.

The application startup maps the route template, as shown in Listing 3-1, by calling `WebApiConfig.Register(GlobalConfiguration.Configuration)`. `MapHttpRoute`, an extension method to `RouteCollection`, adds a new `HttpWebRoute` object, with the `Handler` property set to `HttpControllerRouteHandler` singleton, to `RouteTable.Routes`.

Listing 3-1. Map Route

```
config.Routes.MapHttpRoute(
                name: "DefaultApi",
                routeTemplate: "api/{controller}/{id}",
                defaults: new { id = RouteParameter.Optional }
           );
```

The application object goes about handling the request in the usual ASP.NET style and gets to the point where a route handler has to be chosen. `RouteTable` is used to get the matching route handler (`HttpControllerRouteHandler`) corresponding to the request and the `GetHttpHandler()` method is called off the handler, which returns a new instance of `HttpControllerHandler`.

`HttpControllerHandler` converts the ASP.NET-specific `HttpRequest` into a web API abstraction of `HttpRequestMessage` and dispatches it to an instance of `HttpServer`, which is a `DelegatingHandler`. Figure 3-1 illustrates the Web API life cycle and handler pipeline.

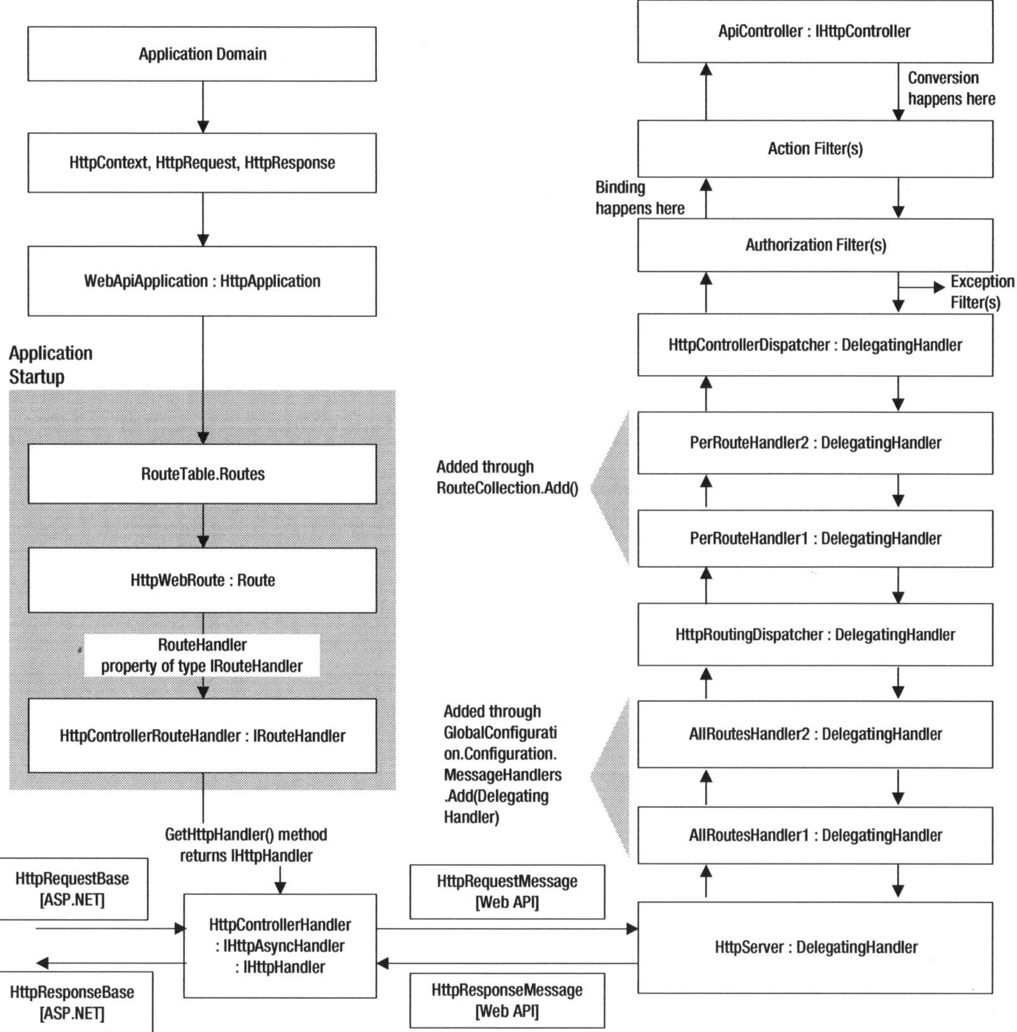

Figure 3-1. *ASP.NET Web API life cycle and handler pipeline*

`HttpServer` is one of the key classes of the web API pipeline, as this is where host agnostic processing starts, with `HttpServer` dealing only with the web API abstractions of the request and response, `HttpRequestMessage` and `HttpResponseMessage`, respectively. `HttpServer` gets the list of delegating message handlers (common to all routes) configured in Global.asax startup and creates Chinese boxes of handlers (or Russian matryoshka dolls, if you prefer them to boxes) by setting the `InnerHandler` property of each handler in such a way that handlers are invoked in a top-down fashion: The first handler to receive the request is the last one to be passed the response and vice versa. `HttpServer` makes sure the last message handler in the all-route message handlers pipeline is `HttpRoutingDispatcher`.

First up is the per-route message handler pipeline. `HttpRoutingDispatcher` dispatches to the message handler specified in the route. If multiple handlers (Chinese boxed through InnerHandler) are specified for the route, all message handlers are invoked in the same fashion as all-route handlers. `HttpRoutingDispatcher` makes sure the last message handler in the pipeline is `HttpControllerDispatcher`.

HttpControllerDispatcher dispatches to IHttpController (ApiController). The ExecuteAsync() method of ApiController runs authorization filters, performs model binding, runs action filters, invokes the action method in the controller, and runs exception filters. As you can see from Figure 3-1, there are two pipelines available: filters and message handlers (DelegatingHandler). Message handlers run right after HttpServer and hence they have early visibility in the requests. Filters run right before the action method and hence by the time a request gets to them, that request could have been through multiple other classes. Both the pipelines are extensible and we now look at filters and message handlers in depth.

Filters

A filter is a great way to encapsulate a cross-cutting concern like security and apply it to action methods. Filters can be applied to individual action methods, all methods in an ApiController, or all methods across all controllers by configuring the filter as a global filter. As shown in Figure 3-1, filters run just before the action method in the pipeline. This behavior can be considered disadvantageous if you would like to stop malicious requests earlier in the pipeline. An advantage with filters is the granularity or the level at which they can be applied, which is at the action method level.

Authorize Filter

The Authorize filter is a special out-of-the-box filter because it runs ahead of the normal action filters. There can be more than one Authorize filter defined per action. An Authorize filter can be specified at the action level or at the controller level. It can also be added to global filters like GlobalFilters.Filters.Add (new AuthorizeAttribute()). See Listing 3-2 for an example of an Authorize filter in action.

Listing 3-2. Authorize Filter

```
[Authorize(Roles = "HumanResourceTeamMember")]
public class EmployeesController : ApiController
{
    public IEnumerable<Employee> Get()
    {
            return new List<Employee>()
            {
                    new Employee() { Id = 12345, Name = "John Q Human" },
                    new Employee() { Id = 23456, Name = "Jane Q Public" }
            };
    }

    public Employee Post(Employee human)
    {
        // Add employee to the system
        human.Id = 12345; // Id produced as a result of adding the employee to data store
        return human;
    }

    [Authorize(Roles = "ManagementTeamMember")]
    public void Delete(int id)
    {
        // Delete employee from the system
    }
```

```
    public void Put(Employee employee)
    {
        // Update employee in the system
    }
}
```

The Authorize filter attribute accepts a CSV of users or roles authorized to perform the action. When no users or roles are specified, it just makes sure the identity associated with the principal object is an authenticated identity. When users or roles are specified, it performs the additional steps of ensuring that the name of the identity associated with the principal is in the allowed users list or at least one role associated with the principal is present in the roles list. If any of the authorization checks fail, 401 - Unauthorized is set as the response status code.

Subclassed Authorize Filter

Out of the box, the Authorize filter accepts users and roles as CSV. Unless an application has one or two of these, it will be very difficult and even impractical to manage.

Also, you don't want to compile and deploy in production for making authorization adjustments, do you? Inheriting from the out-of-the-box filter and implementing the application-specific logic is an option. See Listing 3-3 for an example of a subclassed filter.

Since the subclass filter derives from the Authorize filter, the subclass filter inherits the drawback of the parent. As I mentioned earlier, the security checks happen just before the actual action method executes in the ASP.NET Web API pipeline.

Listing 3-3. Subclassed Authorize Filter

```
public class TimeShareAttribute : AuthorizeAttribute
{
        protected override bool IsAuthorized(HttpActionContext context)
        {
                IPrincipal principal = Thread.CurrentPrincipal;
                // If principal.IsInRole("TimeSharer")
                // Check if current time is between allocated slot start and end times
                // If not, return false
                return true;
        }

        // If 401 - Unauthorized is okay for you, no need to override
        protected override void HandleUnauthorizedRequest(HttpActionContext actionContext)
        {
               base.HandleUnauthorizedRequest(actionContext);
        }
}
```

ALLOWING ANONYMOUS ACCESS SELECTIVELY

`Authorize` filters authorize access to individual action methods if applied at the action method level or all methods in a controller if applied at the controller level. By specifying the `Authorize` filter globally, it is possible to enforce authorization checks on all action method invocations across all controllers. Imagine a scenario where you would want to enforce authorization on all methods on a blanket basis except, say, two methods. Will it not be a nightmare from a maintenance and security standpoint to apply the `Authorize` filter individually on all the action methods with the exception of two? Fortunately, there is a special marker filter called `AllowAnonymous` that can work with the `Authorize` filter and help you out of this unpleasant situation. The `AllowAnonymous` filter allows us to apply the `Authorize` filter globally and specify those two methods on an individual basis to be exempted from the blanket authorization. An important point to note is that the `AllowAnonymous` filter works only with the `Authorize` filter.

ActionFilter

Action filters are the generic filters, as opposed to the `Authorize` filter which is an out-of-the-box filter meant specifically for authorization. Action filters are generic enough to be used to encapsulate any cross-cutting concern. Action filters are classes that inherit from `FilterAttribute`.

Security is not just about authorization. There are scenarios for which you will need to write an action filter. A use case for such an action filter is enabling CORS selectively for a few action methods. CORS is covered in Chapter 4. For a sample implementation of an action filter, refer to Listing 4-7 in Chapter 4, where I use an action filter to enable ETags.

It is quite possible to authenticate and authorize in a custom action filter. If the `Authorize` filter run is too close to your comfort level, please be informed that this runs just one step before the action. `ApiController` runs all the `Authorize` filters, performs binding, and starts running action filters. It is possible that so much of the code written in the application could have been already executed, before execution ever gets here, and all those lines of code are exposed to servicing an unauthorized user's request.

Message Handlers

Authorize filters are run by the `ApiController`'s `ExecuteAsync()` method. In other words, if you are banking on these filters to stop unauthorized access, you need to understand that the unauthorized request has come in all the way through the delegating handlers and is getting stopped just a few steps before the execution of the action.

Better late than never, of course, but if you do not want to let some intruder into your house, will you allow him all the way to the bedroom door just because you happen to be in the bedroom at that time? You probably want him stopped even before he sets his foot on your property. If this is the case, you will need to handle the authentication and authorization somewhere else, preferably in a message handler, which has the opportunity to take care of unauthorized requests earlier in the pipeline.

Although a message handler running earlier in the pipeline can be advantageous in dealing with malicious requests at the earliest available opportunity, the message handler runs for all action methods, or at least all the action methods of a route. This is something to consider when selecting the message handler to solve a problem.

In the ASP.NET Web API pipeline, the first message handler to run is `HttpServer`. All the other custom message handlers run after `that`. A custom message handler is a class that inherits from the class `DelegatingHandler`. Ideally, your custom message handler that handles important security aspects like authentication or authorization should run immediately after `HttpServer`, as the second message handler in the pipeline. Let us now take an in-depth look at message handlers. Every second you spend in this section is worth it.

In the ASP.NET Web API message handler pipeline, the incoming request goes through the handlers in order, starting with `HttpServer`. In other words, `HttpServer` gets to look at the request before anybody else. For the outgoing response, the last handler in the chain gets to see the output first and `HttpServer` gets to see the response last.

This is a great model because your important handlers get to see the request first and they are the last ones to do anything to the response. If a bad request (whatever the criteria is for the request to be classified bad) comes in, your important handlers see it first and they can decide if the inner handlers should be allowed to see the request or if the request should be stopped at that point in the pipeline.

Similarly, on the way out, the important handlers get to decide as late as possible in the pipeline to send the response out, stop it, or make a last-minute alteration to the response. Figure 3-2 is an illustration of the call sequence.

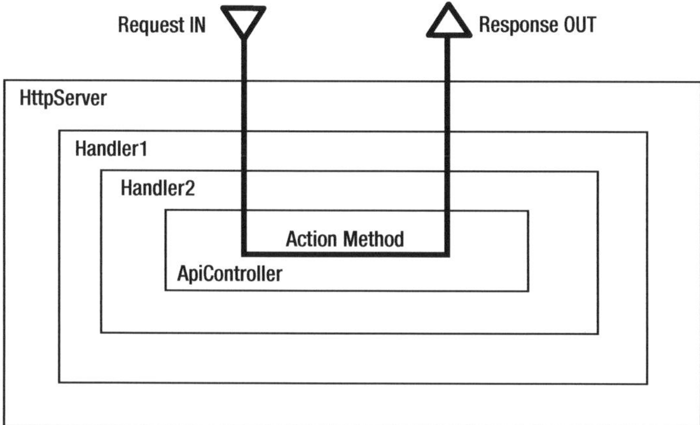

Figure 3-2. *Chinese boxes of message handlers*

To create a message handler, we must inherit from the `DelegatingHandler` class and override the SendAsync method. If we must write some code to execute while receiving the request and some other code to execute while sending the response, it is natural that there will be two methods to override: one for request processing and one for response processing. However, the power of `Task` helps us write code for both the cases in one method, as shown in Listing 3-4.

Listing 3-4. DelegatingHandler

```
public class MyHandler40 : DelegatingHandler // Handler for .NET 4.0
{
        protected override Task<HttpResponseMessage> SendAsync(HttpRequestMessage request,
                                                                CancellationToken cancellationToken)
        {
                // Inspect and do your stuff with request here

                // If you are not happy for any reason,
                // you can reject the request right here like this

                bool isBadRequest = false;
                if (isBadRequest)
                {
                        return Task<HttpResponseMessage>.Factory.StartNew(() =>
                        {
                                return request.CreateResponse(HttpStatusCode.BadRequest);
                        });
                }
```

```
                return base.SendAsync (request, cancellationToken)
                        .ContinueWith((task) =>
                        {
                                var response = task.Result;

                                // Inspect and do your stuff with response here
                                return response;
                        });
        }
}
```

In the .NET Framework 4.5, the handler shown in Listing 3-4 can be written with even fewer lines of code, thanks to the async and await keywords, as shown in Listing 3-5. From this point onward, for coding message handlers we will stick to the .NET Framework 4.5 style using the async and await keywords because the .NET Framework 4.5 code is concise and easier to read. Also, at the time of this publication the .NET Framework 4.5 is the latest version.

Listing 3-5. DelegatingHandler in the .NET Framework 4.5

```
public class MyHandler : DelegatingHandler
{
    protected override async Task<HttpResponseMessage> SendAsync(HttpRequestMessage request,
                                                                  CancellationToken cancellationToken)
    {
        // Inspect and do your stuff with request here

        // If you are not happy for any reason,
        // you can reject the request right here like this

        bool isBadRequest = false;
        if (isBadRequest)
            return request.CreateResponse(HttpStatusCode.BadRequest);

        var response = await base.SendAsync(request, cancellationToken);

        // Inspect and do your stuff with response here

        return response;
    }
}
```

To hook the handler up in the configuration so that it becomes a part of the Chinese box of delegating handlers, the handler needs to be added to the MessageHandlers collection as shown in Listing 3-6, in WebApiConfig.cs under App_Start folder. When set up this way, the handler becomes an all-route handler, which executes for all requests and responses regardless of the route. It is possible to specify multiple handlers by adding more handlers, as shown in Listing 3-7.

Listing 3-6. Single All-Route Handler

```
public static class WebApiConfig
{
    public static void Register(HttpConfiguration config)
    {
            config.Routes.MapHttpRoute(
                    name: "DefaultApi",
                    routeTemplate: "api/{controller}/{id}",
                    defaults: new { id = RouteParameter.Optional }
            );

            config.MessageHandlers.Add(new MyHandler());
    }
}
```

Listing 3-7. Multiple All-Route Handlers

```
config.MessageHandlers.Add(new MySecurityHandler());
config.MessageHandlers.Add(new MyHandler());
```

The order in which handlers are added **does** matter. In this case, `MySecurityHandler`, which is a more important message handler that deals with security, is added first, followed by `MyHandler`. This order ensures `MySecurityHandler` gets to inspect the request before `MyHandler` and vice versa for the response. This way, `MySecurityHandler` can perform the necessary security checks such as authentication and authorization before allowing the request to pass to `MyHandler`. If need be, `MySecurityHandler` can short-circuit the processing of a malicious or bad request and prevent `MyHandler` or any other code in the pipeline downstream from seeing the request. On the way out, `MySecurityHandler`, by virtue of being the first handler in the chain, gets to see the response as the last handler. This way, it has the final say to pass the response along or make a last-minute decision to not send a response with a 200 - OK status code and instead send an error.

To hook up a handler specific to a route, the handler can be passed into `MapHttpRoute`, in WebApiConfig (under App_Start), as shown in Listing 3-8.

Listing 3-8. Route-Specific Handlers

```
public static class WebApiConfig
{
        public static void Register(HttpConfiguration config)
        {
            var handler = new MyPremiumSecurityHandler()
            {
                InnerHandler = new MyOtherPremiumSecurityHandler()
                {
                    InnerHandler = new HttpControllerDispatcher(config)
                }
            };

            config.Routes.MapHttpRoute(
                name: "premiumApi",
                routeTemplate: "premium/{controller}/{id}",
                defaults: new { id = RouteParameter.Optional },
                constraints: null,
                handler: handler
            );
```

```
            config.Routes.MapHttpRoute(
                name: "DefaultApi",
                routeTemplate: "api/{controller}/{id}",
                defaults: new { id = RouteParameter.Optional }
            );
        }
}
```

Listing 3-8 specifies `MyPremiumSecurityHandler` with `MyOtherPremiumHandler` as the inner handler, so the order of execution will be the same as the all-route example. Here the handlers are specific only to the premium route. For example, GET `http://server/premium/employees` will result in the handlers participating in the pipeline, whereas GET `http://server/api/products` will not engage the handlers.

HTTP Modules

There are extensibility points available to extend the ASP.NET pipeline itself, an HTTP module being one such point. By implementing an HTTP module, you can have your authentication code execute even before your first all-route message handler runs. If you have a web API and other resources such as HTTP handlers, pages, or MVC controllers in the same application and you want to establish identity in one place and share the same, an HTTP module is a great option.

The following list shows the key points you must consider before designing your authentication mechanism. This list is from Microsoft's ASP.NET Web API web site (`http://www.asp.net/web-api/overview/security/authentication-and-authorization-in-aspnet-web-api`).

- An HTTP module sees all requests that go through the ASP.NET pipeline. A message handler only sees requests that are routed to Web API.
- You can set per-route message handlers, which lets you apply an authentication scheme to a specific route.
- HTTP modules are specific to IIS. Message handlers are host-agnostic, so they can be used with both web hosting and self-hosting.
- HTTP modules participate in IIS logging, auditing, and so on.
- HTTP modules run earlier in the pipeline. If you handle authentication in a message handler, the principal does not get set until the handler runs. Moreover, the principal reverts back to the previous principal when the response leaves the message handler.

The last two points are very important considerations for using the components in the ASP.NET pipeline that expect authentication to happen earlier in the ASP.NET pipeline, when the `AuthenticateRequest` event was fired and the same identity to remain through the entire processing of the ASP.NET pipeline.

Message handlers do run earlier in the ASP.NET Web API pipeline, but it could already be late from the perspective of the components running in the ASP.NET pipeline. If you use a custom HTTP module that you have written or the out-of-the-box module from ASP.NET that needs an authenticated identity to work, authenticating in the message handler could be too late. For example, the `ResolveRequestCache` event is fired right after the `AuthenticateRequestand` `AuthorizeRequest` events. ASP.NET `OutputCacheModule` or your own custom HTTP module listening for the `ResolveRequestCache` event can service the request from the output cache even before the ASP.NET Web API pipeline starts running. It is worth noting that there is no `OutputCacheAttribute` available for ASP.NET Web API at the time of writing of this book.

Also, IIS will not log the principal you could be setting in `Thread.CurrentPrincipal` from your message handler. So, if web hosting is a given and you want to leverage ASP.NET fully through its extensibility points, implementing your authentication and authorization logic in HTTP modules makes a lot of sense. On the other hand, if you prefer not extending or leveraging the ASP.NET pipeline and letting the requests come to the ASP.NET Web API pipeline before any processing starts, using a message handler to perform authentication is a great option.

The flip side of using an HTTP module is that your design is no longer host-agnostic and you are taking a dependency on web hosting (IIS). I use message handlers throughout this book because it is host-agnostic but you must be aware of the trade-offs involved in choosing a message handler over HTTP module or vice versa. Listing 3-9 shows an HTTP handler that hooks into `AuthenticateRequest` and `EndRequest` events.

Listing 3-9. HTTP Handler

```
public class MyHttpModule : IHttpModule
{
    public void Init(HttpApplication context)
    {
        context.AuthenticateRequest += OnApplicationAuthenticateRequest;
        context.EndRequest += OnApplicationEndRequest;
    }

    private static void OnApplicationAuthenticateRequest(object sender, EventArgs e)
    {
        var request = HttpContext.Current.Request;
        var authHeader = request.Headers["Authorization"];
        if (authHeader != null)
        {
            // Authenticate here using the credentials from authorization header

            // On successful authentication, set principal
            var identity = new ClaimsIdentity(new[] {
                                            new Claim("type", "value") }, "AuthnType");
            var principal = new ClaimsPrincipal(identity);

            Thread.CurrentPrincipal = principal;

            if (HttpContext.Current != null)
                HttpContext.Current.User = principal;
        }
    }

    private static void OnApplicationEndRequest(object sender, EventArgs e)
    {
        var response = HttpContext.Current.Response;

        // Do anything with response such as checking status code and
        // adding response headers
    }

    public void Dispose() { }
}
```

To let this module run in ASP.NET pipeline (integrated), make an entry in Web.config, as shown in Listing 3-10.

Listing 3-10. Web.config Change

```
<system.webServer>
        ...
        <modules>
          <add name="MyHttpModule"
                         type="namespace.MyHttpModule, assembly"/>
        </modules>
        ...
<system.webServer>
```

Summary

In this chapter, we looked at the processing architecture of web-hosted ASP.NET Web API and explored the two important extensibility points available within the ASP.NET Web API pipeline, namely filters and message handlers.

Filters run later in the pipeline but can be applied at the more granular level of the action method. Out of the box, the `Authorize` filter can be applied to action methods or at the controller level to enforce authorization. If need be, the `Authorize` filter can be extended by subclassing to add more functionality. While the `Authorize` filter is specific to authorization, a generic action filter can also be used to add other security-related functions.

Message handlers run earlier in the pipeline and can be chained together to form Chinese boxes of message handlers, with the first handler in the chain getting to inspect the request first before passing it on to the second in the chain. On the way out, the first handler will be the last one to inspect the response and hence has the final say on the response.

We looked at all-route message handlers that get to inspect the request and response for all action methods across all routes. We also examined route-specific handlers that get to inspect the request and response for action methods in a specific route.

We leverage the understanding gained from this chapter to implement the security-related code in all the upcoming chapters, as these extensibility points are fundamental to plug in the security aspect, which is a cross-cutting concern.

CHAPTER 4

HTTP Anatomy and Security

The primary benefit of creating an HTTP service is reachability. A broad range of clients in disparate platforms can consume your HTTP services. A client application on an Apple iPhone running iOS can talk to ASP.NET Web API hosted in an HP ProLiant server running the Microsoft Windows 2012 OS. Similarly, an application on a Microsoft Surface tablet running Windows 8 Pro can talk to an HTTP service hosted on the IBM System z. HTTP is the secret sauce behind these disparate device-platform interactions.

ASP.NET Web API is a framework that makes it easy to build HTTP services. The ASP.NET Web API framework embraces HTTP instead of fighting against it or abstracting it away. Because the underpinning of an HTTP service is the HTTP protocol, understanding the protocol is a prerequisite to securing ASP.NET Web API powered HTTP services. After all, a house is only as strong as its foundation!

A good understanding of HTTP is a must in implementing an HTTP-compliant service. For example, developers don't want an HTTP service to send a response with a 200 - OK status code and a message in the body stating authentication failed because of invalid credentials. Instead, developers who have a good understanding of HTTP want an HTTP service to send a 401 - Unauthorized status code, which is a standard way of communicating the authentication failure and hence is understood by all clients.

In this chapter, you learn how to apply the fundamentals of HTTP to create a secure HTTP-compliant service. You also learn advanced concepts such as caching, ETags, CORS, and HTTPS that are essential to create a production grade, performant, and secure web API.

HTTP Transaction

HTTP is an application layer protocol based on a reliable transport layer protocol (read TCP). The two endpoints of the communication based on HTTP are a server and a client. The client sends a request to the server; the server processes the request and sends a response back to the client that includes a status code denoting if the processing is successful or not. These steps constitute an HTTP transaction. The client typically is a web browser such as Internet Explorer, and the server is a web server such as IIS. A web server services multiple clients simultaneously. The HTTP client initiates an HTTP request by connecting to a port (typically 80) on the web server.

Web servers host resources that are uniquely identified through an identifier called the Uniform Resource Identifier (URI). The Uniform Resource Locator (URL) is a URI—it identifies a resource but it also specifies how a representation of a resource can be obtained. For example, `http://www.server.com/home.html` is a URL that includes three parts.

1. Scheme, which is `http://`. The scheme denotes the protocol used (HTTP).
2. Server, which is `www.server.com`. The server is the server that hosts the resource.
3. Resource path, which is `/home.html`. The resource path is the path of the resource on the server.

Figure 4-1 illustrates a typical HTTP transaction.

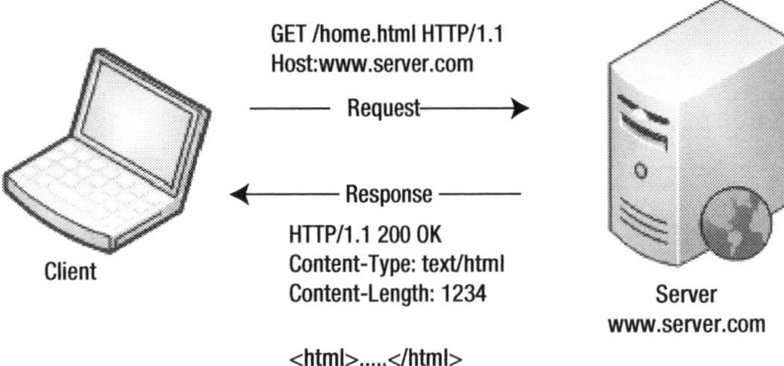

Figure 4-1. *HTTP transaction*

A client requests the server to take an action on a resource. There is a noun and a verb associated with the request. The noun is the resource identified by the URI. The verb is the action or the HTTP method. In Figure 4-1, the client requests GET on /home.html. The server responds with a 200 OK status code and sends the text/html representation of the resource. The server specifies the representation (text/html) in the Content-Type response header. The content type is also called the media type.

HTTP Request

An HTTP request has the request line as the first line of the request. The request line starts with the HTTP method followed by a space, followed by the URI of the resource requested, a space, and then the HTTP version. The request line is terminated by a Carriage Return (CR) and a Line Feed (LF) character, as shown in Figure 4-2.

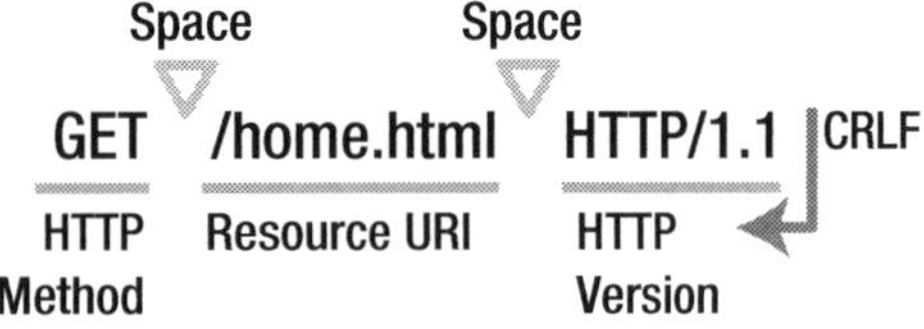

Figure 4-2. *Request line*

Following the request line are the request headers. The header fields are colon-separated key-value pairs, terminated by a CRLF, just like the request line. The end of the header fields is indicated by an empty field—two consecutive CRLF pairs—as shown in Figure 4-3.

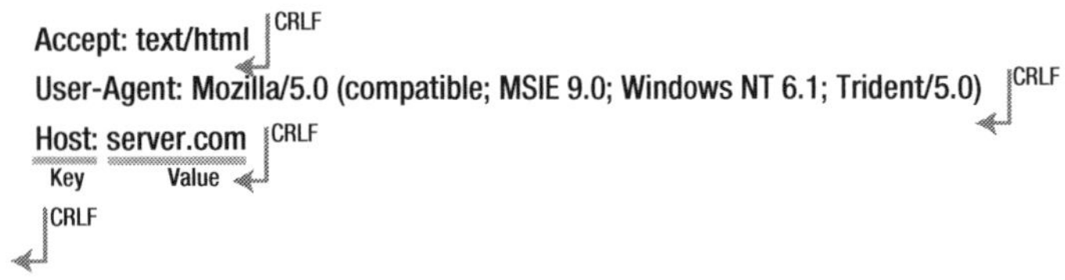

Accept: text/html CRLF
User-Agent: Mozilla/5.0 (compatible; MSIE 9.0; Windows NT 6.1; Trident/5.0) CRLF
Host: server.com CRLF
Key Value
CRLF

Figure 4-3. *Request headers*

Finally, following the request headers is the optional request body. Depending on the HTTP method used, the request body can be present or absent.

Request Headers

The request headers allow a client to send additional information about the request or the information about the client itself to the server. Although there is no limit specified for the number of headers or the length of the headers, for practical reasons there is a limit imposed by the client and the server participating in a transaction. The host is the only mandatory request header for HTTP 1.1. The User-Agent header has the user agent string and identifies the user agent that is making the request. Although this is not mandatory, this header is almost always present.

In Chapter 2, we examined a few request headers. We saw how the Accept and the Content-Type headers are used in the content negotiation by ASP.NET Web API. The most important header from the point of view of security is the Authorization header, which is used for sending the credentials for authentication. We see in later chapters how this header is used for securing ASP.NET Web API. There are many headers related to web caching and ETags. We look at them at work later in this chapter. The Accept-Language and Accept-Encoding headers are not supported by ASP.NET Web API out of the box at the time of writing this book.

In addition to the standard headers, there are nonstandard headers named with an X- prefix as a convention. The most common one, X-Requested-With: XMLHttpRequest, is used by most of the JavaScript frameworks such as JQuery to identify the AJAX requests.

HTTP Methods

The HTTP methods denote the action that a client requests on a resource. Table 4-1 shows the eight methods defined in the HTTP 1.1 specification.

Table 4-1. *HTTP Methods Comparison*

Method	Description	Side Effect
GET	Gets a representation of the resource	Nullipotent; no side effect
PUT	Updates a resource	Yes, but idempotent
POST	Creates a new resource or updates the resource	Yes
DELETE	Deletes a resource	Yes, but idempotent
HEAD	Same as GET but without response body	Nullipotent; no side effect
OPTIONS	Methods supported for the URI	Nullipotent; no side effect
CONNECT	Converts the request connection to a TCP tunnel, usually to facilitate HTTPS through an HTTP proxy; there are security implications with supporting this method	Nullipotent; no side effect
TRACE	Gets the request back, as received by the server with all changes introduced by intermediate servers; generally not recommended from a security point of view	Nullipotent; no side effect

Currently, ASP.NET Web API supports all the methods except CONNECT and TRACE through convention. By implementing a method with a name starting with the HTTP method in the `ApiController` subclass, you can let the ASP.NET Web API framework route the HTTP requests to the corresponding method in the controller class. For example, by implementing a method `GetEmployee()` or just `Get()` in `EmployeesController`, you can handle an HTTP GET request.

For the CONNECT and TRACE methods, you must apply the `AcceptVerbs` attribute on the action method to get the requests routed appropriately. Listing 4-1 shows how you can support TRACE by adding a specific action method to the `ApiController` and applying the `AcceptVerbs` attribute on the action method.

Listing 4-1. TRACE Method

```
[AcceptVerbs("TRACE")]
public void Echo(){}
```

■ **Note** If a request for an unsupported method comes in, ASP.NET Web API responds with a response status code of 405 – Method Not Allowed.

Figure 4-4 shows what a typical request message looks like when we put all the pieces of the HTTP request together. Because it is a GET, there is no message body.

```
Request Line      GET /home.html HTTP/1.1

Request Headers   Accept: text/html
                  User-Agent: Mozilla/5.0 (compatible; MSIE 9.0; Windows NT 6.1; Trident/5.0)
                  Host: server.com
                  [Blank line indicating the end of request headers]
```

Figure 4-4. *Request message*

Method Overriding

RESTful services allow the clients to act on the resources through methods such as GET, POST, PUT, DELETE, and so on. GET and POST are the most frequently used methods.

Most of the corporate firewalls allow port 80, the typical port of HTTP. However, some do have restrictions in terms of the HTTP methods allowed. GET and POST methods are very common, but others such as DELETE can be disallowed.

The X-HTTP-Method-Override header can help you work around this problem. A typical solution involving this header is to send X-HTTP-Method-Override in the request with the actual verb intended (DELETE or PUT) and submit the request using POST; that is, the request line with the dummy POST verb tricks the firewall into allowing the request.

In ASP.NET Web API, a message handler, such as the one shown in Listing 4-2, can replace POST with the method specified in X-HTTP-Method-Override. The message handler runs early in the pipeline and is the best extensibility point suitable for this purpose.

Listing 4-2. Method Override

```
public class MethodOverrideHandler : DelegatingHandler
{
    protected override async Task<HttpResponseMessage> SendAsync(HttpRequestMessage request,
                                                        CancellationToken cancellationToken)
    {
        if (request.Method == HttpMethod.Post && request.Headers.Contains("X-HTTP-Method-Override"))
        {
            var method = request.Headers.GetValues("X-HTTP-Method-Override").FirstOrDefault();

            bool isPut = String.Equals(method, "PUT", StringComparison.OrdinalIgnoreCase);
            bool isDelete = String.Equals(method, "DELETE", StringComparison.OrdinalIgnoreCase);

            if (isPut || isDelete)
            {
                request.Method = new HttpMethod(method);
            }
        }

        return await base.SendAsync(request, cancellationToken);
    }
}
```

To test the preceding `MethodOverrideHandler`, you will need a tool like Fiddler, covered in depth later in this chapter. Fiddler is useful in capturing and analyzing HTTP traffic. Also, it lets you hand-code a request complete with request headers and send it to an endpoint with an HTTP method of your choice. Figure 4-5 illustrates how you can make a POST request with an X-HTTP-Method-Override header set to PUT. If `MethodOverrideHandler` is plugged into the pipeline by making an entry in WebApiConfig.cs file under App_Start, this request will invoke the PUT action method in the controller instead of POST.

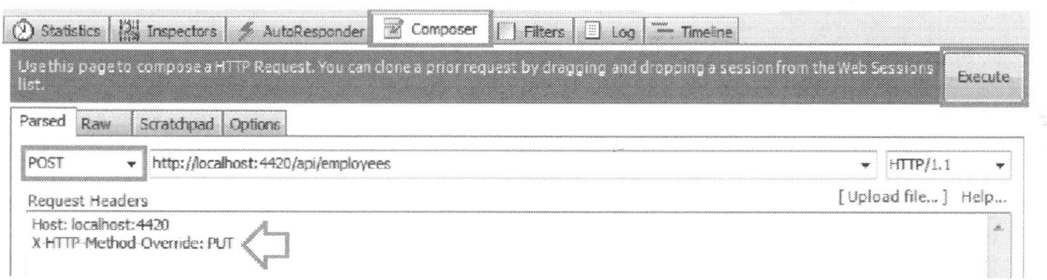

Figure 4-5. *Fiddler Composer*

HTTP Response

The HTTP response has the status line as the first line of the response. As shown in Figure 4-6, the status line starts with the HTTP version, followed by a space, followed by the status code and a space, and then the reason phrase. The request line is terminated by a CR and an LF character.

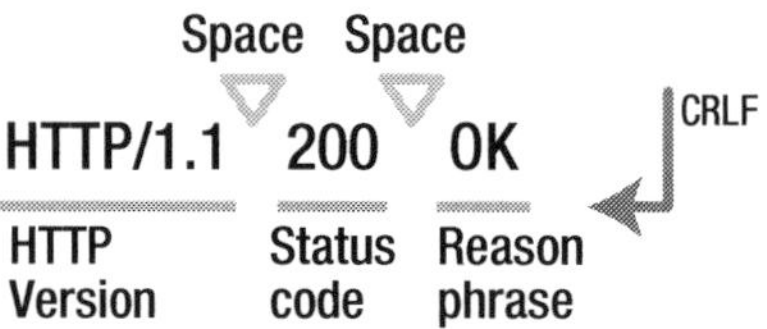

Figure 4-6. Status line

Status Codes

The HTTP response status code is a three-digit number. The first digit defines the class of the response: 1—Informational, 2—Success, 3—Redirects, 4—Client-side error, and 5—Server-side error. Table 4-2 shows some of the most common status codes. Sending the appropriate status code for the situation is an important aspect of embracing HTTP. By doing so, you can leverage the broad acceptance of HTTP.

Table 4-2. *HTTP Status Codes*

Status Code	Description
200 OK	The request has been successfully processed.
201 Created	The request has been fulfilled and resulted in a new resource being created. The URI for the new resource is returned in the Location response header. In ASP.NET Web API, such a response can be created like this: `Request.CreateResponse<Employee>(HttpStatusCode.Created, employee);`
204 No Content	The request has been successfully processed, but no content is being returned. A void action method in ASP.NET Web API returns this status code. Also, a delete action method can send this code to denote the resource has been deleted.
400 Bad Request	The request could not be understood by the server due to malformed syntax.
401 Unauthorized	The request requires user authentication. If the credentials are already provided, a status code of 401 indicates the provided credentials are invalid.
403 Forbidden	The server understood the request, but is refusing to fulfill it. This status code can be used even when valid credentials are provided; for example, if the user corresponding to the submitted credential is not allowed to access the resource. Typically, the server sends back the reason why it is refusing to fulfill the request along with this status code.
404 Not found	The server has not found anything matching the request URI. The 404 status code can also be used in 403 scenarios, when the server does not want to send back the reason why it is refusing to serve the request. A good example is when the server senses some kind of an attack, which might be a brute force attack. In this case, the server responds with a 404 Not found instead of a 403 Forbidden and an explanation.

The Curious Case of an Unhandled Exception

When an exception is thrown and it is not handled, ASP.NET Web API returns a 500 Internal Server Error. Listing 4-3 shows an action method that throws an `ArgumentException`, but there is no handler to catch this exception.

Listing 4-3. Unhandled Exception

```
public class EmployeesController : ApiController
{
        public IEnumerable<Employee> Get(string department)
        {
                if(!String.Equals(department, "HR", StringComparison.OrdinalIgnoreCase))
                        throw new ArgumentException("Bad Department");

                return new List<Employee>()
                {
                        new Employee() { Id = 12345, Name = "John Q Human" }
                };
        }
}
```

When a GET request is made for the department of "HR," a response status code of 500 is returned. In this case, the response body has the stack trace details.

```
{"Message":"An error has occurred.","ExceptionMessage":"Bad Department","ExceptionType":
"System.ArgumentException","StackTrace":"   at ...
```

Sending a stack trace is a security risk. By specifying the `Never` option for the error details inclusion policy in WebApiConfig.cs under the App_Start folder, the stack trace can be stopped from getting to the client.

```
config.IncludeErrorDetailPolicy = IncludeErrorDetailPolicy.Never;
```

However, this is not useful from the client perspective. The client has the status code of 500, which basically indicates something is wrong with the service. This is obvious and not useful in determining what is wrong. By throwing an `HttpResponseException`, we can have better control of what is being sent to the client and can control the status code and other things to be more meaningful, as shown in Listing 4-4.

Listing 4-4. HttpResponseException

```
public Employee Get(int id)
{
        if (id > 999999)
        {
                throw new HttpResponseException
                        (
                                new HttpResponseMessage()
                                {
                                        Content = new StringContent("Invalid employee id"),
                                        StatusCode = HttpStatusCode.BadRequest
                                }
                        );
        }
}
```

Instead of a generic status 500, 400 – Bad Request gets sent back along with the message stating the employee is invalid.

```
HTTP/1.1 400 Bad Request
Headers go here

Invalid employee id
```

This gets the job done, but there is an extensibility point in the form of `ExceptionFilterAttribute` available to map standard .NET exceptions to standard HTTP status code (see Listing 4-5). Such a filter added to the global filter collection will keep the code dry from the point of view of having to build an HTTP response with different status codes at different places.

Listing 4-5. Exception Filter

```
public class ExceptionFilter : ExceptionFilterAttribute
{
    private IDictionary<Type, HttpStatusCode> map = null;

    public ExceptionFilter()
    {
        map = new Dictionary<Type, HttpStatusCode>();
        map.Add(typeof(ArgumentException), HttpStatusCode.BadRequest);
        map.Add(typeof(SecurityException), HttpStatusCode.Unauthorized);
        map.Add(typeof(NotImplementedException), HttpStatusCode.NotImplemented);
    }

    public override void OnException(HttpActionExecutedContext context)
    {
        if (!(context.Exception is HttpException))
        {
            context.Response = new HttpResponseMessage(map[context.Exception.GetType()])
                               {
                                   Content = new StringContent(context.Exception.Message)
                               };
        }
    }
}
```

▪ **Note** For those with an eye for details, I use 400 – Bad Request to denote the condition that a passed in ID is not a valid one or a bad one. This can be handled well with a 404, which means there is no employee for the incoming ID.

Response Headers

The response headers enable the server to pass any additional information about the response that belongs neither to the status line nor to the response body. For example, the Content-Type header has the MIME or media type of the response content. As another example, the Date header, which HTTP/1.1 mandates the servers to send with every response, contains the date and time the response was generated (in GMT).

The response headers look exactly like the request headers shown in Figure 4-3, in that the header fields are colon-separated key–value pairs terminated by a CRLF. The end of the header fields is indicated by an empty field: two consecutive CRLF pairs.

One of the important response headers from the security standpoint is the WWW-Authenticate header. When a request to ASP.NET Web API comes in with an invalid credential or if the required credential is missing, the standard response status code is 401 – Unauthorized. In such a case, as per the HTTP specification, the WWW-Authenticate header must be included in the response. This header denotes the authentication scheme supported by the web API.

Request for Comments (RFC) 2617 (HTTP Authentication: Basic and Digest Access Authentication) provides the specification for the HTTP authentication framework, the original Basic Access Authentication scheme and a scheme based on cryptographic hashes referred to as the Digest Access Authentication. The basic authentication scheme is based on the model that requires the client to authenticate itself with a user ID and a password for each realm. For example, a web API requiring basic authentication will send the following header if the authentication header is absent in the request or if the credential specified is invalid.

```
WWW-Authenticate: Basic
```

In addition to the scheme information, the WWW-Authenticate header can contain additional information for the client such as the realm.

```
WWW-Authenticate: Basic realm="GreenPlanet"
```

Like the basic access authentication, the digest access authentication verifies that both parties to a communication know a shared secret (a password). Unlike basic authentication, this verification is done without sending the password in the clear, which is the biggest weakness of basic authentication. The digest scheme uses a nonce. A client does not send the password at all. Instead, it sends a digest or a hash (an MD5 hash to be specific) of the username, the password, the given nonce, the HTTP method, and the requested URI. The nonce is generated by the server and sent with the WWW-Authenticate header, as shown in the following example.

```
WWW-Authenticate: Digest realm="MagicalRealm", qop="auth", nonce="abcd98b7102ee2f0e9f26d0d600bfb0c562"
```

A web API can simultaneously support both the basic and the digest authentication schemes. In such a case, as part of the 401 – Unauthorized response, two WWW-Authenticate headers will be sent to the client, as shown in the following example.

```
WWW-Authenticate: Basic realm="MagicalRealm"
WWW-Authenticate: Digest realm="MagicalRealm", qop="auth", nonce="abcd98b7102fd600bfb0c562"
```

When a client receives these two headers, it can choose to use the scheme that best suits its capability. If a client is capable of using both schemes, then digest authentication can be chosen because it is more secure. As an example, if Internet Explorer has an option of both the basic and digest schemes, it automatically picks digest over basic. We cover both the basic and digest authentication schemes in more detail in Chapter 8.

Response Body

The response body has the representation of the resource, as defined by the Content-Type header. For a web page, this will be the HTML. For ASP.NET Web API, this could be JSON, XML, or whatever format represents the response returned.

Putting all these pieces of the HTTP response together, the Figure 4-7 shows what a typical response message looks like. Some of the headers have been removed for brevity.

Status Line

HTTP/1.1 200 OK

Response Headers

Date: Thu, 27 Sep 2012 09:00:19 GMT
Cache-Control: no-cache
Content-Type: application/json; charset=utf-8
Content-Length: 122

Response Body

[{"Id":12345,"Name":"John Q Law","Department":"Enforcement"},
{"Id":45678,"Name":"Jane Q Taxpayer","Department":"Revenue"}]

Figure 4-7. *Response message*

Web Caching

A web cache is a cache of the web server responses—such as the web pages, the images, and the style sheets—for later use. Web caching can reduce the round trips, the network bandwidth, and the web server resource utilization. End users also perceive a better performance. The cache can be in a web browser, if one is involved, or any of the intermediate servers such as the ISP or any proxy servers in between. Nothing gets cached if HTTPS is used.

Expiration and validation are the two primary mechanisms associated with caching. The expiration mechanism allows a response to be reused without checking with the server, thereby reducing the round trip and the validation mechanism minimizes the bandwidth usage.

What is cached need not always be a file such as an image or a Cascading Style Sheet (CSS). Even ASP.NET Web API responses can be cached. An example for such a scenario is a web API returning any master list, such as a list of codes that hardly change or even changes less frequently. By default, the ASP.NET Web API framework marks the response to be not cached by setting the value of the Cache-Control header to no-cache.

The Cache-Control: max-age directive specifies the duration in seconds a cache can be used before it expires. To look at this response header in action, go back to the `ApiController` - `EmployeesController` used in Chapter 2. The `GetAllEmployess` method returns the employees list resource in the JSON representation, which is consumed by an MVC view through JQuery Ajax. You can override the default behavior of the response getting marked to be not cached by returning the cache-control response header with a specific value. In Listing 4-6, we use the max-age value of six seconds. As you probably know, the six seconds expiry time is too low for any practical implementation; it is used here only for illustration purposes.

Listing 4-6. Cache-Control: max-age

```
public class EmployeesController : ApiController
{
    public HttpResponseMessage GetAllEmployees()
    {
            var employees = new Employee[]
            {
                    new Employee()
                    {
                            Id = 12345,
                            Name = "John Q Law",
                            Department = "Enforcement"
                    },
```

```
                new Employee()
                {
                        Id = 45678,
                        Name = "Jane Q Taxpayer",
                        Department = "Revenue"
                }
        };

        var response = Request.CreateResponse<IEnumerable<Employee>>
                                                    (HttpStatusCode.OK, employees);

        response.Headers.CacheControl = new CacheControlHeaderValue()
        {
            MaxAge = TimeSpan.FromSeconds(6),
            MustRevalidate = true,
            Private = true
        };

        return response;
    }
}
```

Listing 4-7 shows a /Home/Index view to call the web API shown in the preceding example. Against each of the unordered list items, current date and time is provided to prove that JavaScript runs and updates the unordered list items with each click of the button.

Listing 4-7. Home/Index View

```
@section scripts{
    <script type="text/javascript">
        $(document).ready(function () {
            $('#search').click(function () {
                $('#employees').empty();
                $.getJSON("/api/employees", function (data) {
                    $.each(data, function (i, employee) {
                        var now = new Date();
                        var ts = now.getHours() + ':' + now.getMinutes() + ':' + now.getSeconds();

                        var content = employee.Id + ' ' + employee.Name;
                        content = content + ' ' + employee.Department + ' ' + ts;

                        $('#employees').append($('<li/>', { text: content }));
                    });
                });
            });
        });
    </script>
}
```

```
<div>
    <div>
        <h1>Employees Listing</h1>
        <input id="search" type="button" value="Get" />
    </div>
    <div>
        <ul id="employees" />
    </div>
</div>
```

When the Get button is clicked the first time, a request is made to the web API. For the next six seconds, which is the expiration time chosen for the cache, regardless of the number of times you click the button, no request is made to the web API; the data from the cache is used to rebuild the list.

Only the JSON representation is cached. JQuery runs and builds the unordered list each time the button is clicked. As you can see, the date and time stamp against the items changes every time you click the button, which is proof that the script is running for each click event. By using a tool like Fiddler, covered in more detail later in this chapter, you can verify that JQuery builds the list out of the web cache rather than making a call to the web API.

Once the cache becomes stale (i.e., after six seconds) the client can check with the server if the cache is still valid through the validation mechanism and get a new lease for another six seconds. We look at the ETag (entity tag) from the validation perspective in the next section.

BALANCING SPEED AND SECURITY

Take the case of the corporate networks with multiple users behind a proxy server. Alice, a legitimate user, issues a request to a web API on the Internet through the proxy server and gets the response back. If the web API denotes in the header that the response can be cached, the proxy will cache the response.

What if Mallory, a malicious user who is behind the same proxy, replays Alice's request? If Mallory's request makes it to the web API, the authentication message handler will fail the request, sensing replay. But will this request be serviced by proxy through its cache? The answer is yes if the cache control denotes it is public.

By specifying private, we are "requesting" intermediaries such as proxies to not cache, allowing only the browser of the end user to cache. It does not offer your data any protection because the intermediaries, both good and evil, can still see the response. Any intermediary who is either not willing to play by the rules or is ignorant of the rules can cache and do anything with the data in your web API response.

Before making a decision to cache your web API responses from a performance standpoint, review the security implications. As a general rule, allow only data that is generic and not specific to a user and data that is not sensitive to be cached public.

Entity Tag

An entity tag (ETag) is a unique identifier assigned by the web server to identify a specific version of a resource representation. If the representation changes at any time, a new ETag is assigned.

As shown in Figure 4-8, the server sends the ETag header along with the response. The client caches the response and the ETag. Subsequently, when the client makes a request for the same resource, the server will send the previously saved ETag in the If-None-Match request header.

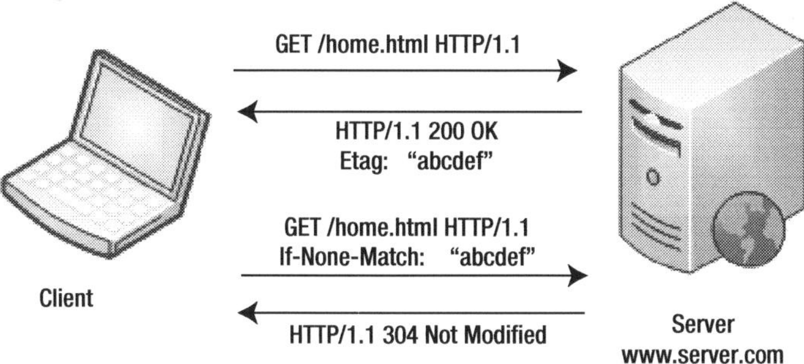

Figure 4-8. *ETag*

If the resource has not changed in the server, the server can simply respond with a status code of 304 – Not modified without sending the full response back. When the resource representation has changed, the server sends the new representation with the new ETag corresponding to the changed representation.

The basic idea behind sending the 304 – Not modified status is to save network bandwidth. If the response has not changed, there is no need to resend the entire response back. The server can simply return the status code and tell the client that what you got last time is still valid. The important thing here is that the response must be cached at the client side for this to work. Although it is possible to use the ETag without web caching (as in the case of implementing the optimistic concurrency that you will see next), the ETags and web caching go hand in hand.

With caching in the mix, the sequence is just the same as in the preceding, for the most part. When the ETag is sent in the 200 – OK response, the Cache-Control header also gets sent back. Assume the max age of six seconds, just as in the earlier example. That is, for the next six seconds until the time the cache expires, the browser does not send any request to the server. After the six-second period, post the cache expiry, the browser sends a request that contains the If-None-Match request header. If the resource representation has not changed, the server responds with a 304 status code. For the next six seconds, the browser will work off the cache and does not issue any more requests to the server.

Implementing ETag in ASP.NET Web API

The ETag capabilities can be added to a web API through an `ActionFilter`, as shown in Listing 4-8. I'm opting for an `ActionFilter` for the following two reasons.

1. `ActionFilter` makes sure the ETag-related code runs as close as possible to the actual action method. Assuming that authentication and authorization are implemented in the message handlers, the security-related code will have already run by the time execution comes to the filter and unauthorized requests will have failed earlier in the pipeline.

2. `ActionFilter` gives us the ability to specify the inclusion of the ETag in the response for specific action methods. Typically, you don't want to be caching everything. Data that hardly changes or that changes less frequently, such as the master list of codes, are good candidates. However, not every single action method of your web API can be cached.

Listing 4-8. ETag Action Filter

```
public class EnableETag : ActionFilterAttribute
{
    private static ConcurrentDictionary<string, EntityTagHeaderValue> etags = new
    ConcurrentDictionary<string, EntityTagHeaderValue>();

    public override void OnActionExecuting(HttpActionContext context)
    {
        var request = context.Request;

        if (request.Method == HttpMethod.Get)
        {
            var key = GetKey(request);

            ICollection<EntityTagHeaderValue> etagsFromClient = request.Headers.IfNoneMatch;

            if (etagsFromClient.Count > 0)
            {
                EntityTagHeaderValue etag = null;
                if (etags.TryGetValue(key, out etag) && etagsFromClient.Any(t => t.Tag == etag.Tag))
                {
                    context.Response = new HttpResponseMessage(HttpStatusCode.NotModified);
                    SetCacheControl(context.Response);
                }
            }
        }
    }

    public override void OnActionExecuted(HttpActionExecutedContext context)
    {
        var request = context.Request;
        var key = GetKey(request);

        EntityTagHeaderValue etag;

        if (!etags.TryGetValue(key, out etag) || request.Method == HttpMethod.Put ||
                                                        request.Method == HttpMethod.Post)
        {
            etag = new EntityTagHeaderValue("\"" + Guid.NewGuid().ToString() + "\"");
            etags.AddOrUpdate(key, etag, (k, val) => etag);
        }

        context.Response.Headers.ETag = etag;
        SetCacheControl(context.Response);
    }

    private string GetKey(HttpRequestMessage request)
    {
        return request.RequestUri.ToString();
    }
```

```
    private void SetCacheControl(HttpResponseMessage response)
    {
        response.Headers.CacheControl = new CacheControlHeaderValue()
        {
            MaxAge = TimeSpan.FromSeconds(6),
            MustRevalidate = true,
            Private = true
        };
    }
}
```

ETag ActionFilter

The ETag `ActionFilter` needs to keep track of the ETags it generates to validate the same if the client sends an ETag back in the request. For this purpose, I'm using `ConcurrentDictionary`. The key is the URI and the value is the ETag sent with the response. For example, if you make a GET for `http://server.com/api/employees/12345`, the web API sends back an ETag that says 123456789 in the response, after making an entry in the dictionary with the key as `http://server.com/api/employees/12345` and 123456789 as the value. The value is EntityTagHeaderValue, but I'm simply making an approximation here for the sake of brevity.

There are two major components of the `ActionFilter:` the `OnActionExecuted` and `OnActionExecuting` methods.

1. `OnActionExecuted` runs after the action method. If the HTTP method is a PUT or a POST, a new ETag is generated. I'm using a GUID as an ETag here. The generated ETag gets stored in the dictionary and gets sent in the ETag response header. The dictionary storage operation is an `AddOrUpdate`. The old tag gets updated and the new tag just gets inserted.

2. `OnActionExecuting` runs before the action method. It looks for an ETag in the If-None-Match request header. If the ETag value passed by the client in this header matches the one stored in the dictionary against the request URI, a 304 – Not modified status code is returned and the action method execution is short-circuited.

The ETag `ActionFilter` is based on the assumption that all the updates and the inserts go through the web API so that `OnActionExecuted` adjusts the ETag correctly. If the entity is stored in a database and someone directly updates the database, the web API will not know that the underlying data has changed. In that case, it is better to base the ETag off the version or timestamp associated with the database record. The web API must get the version from the database and compare it with the version corresponding to the ETag.

If you ask the web API for a JSON response and make a subsequent request with the ETag you got in the previous JSON response in the If-None-Match header, but you smartly ask for an XML representation the second time through Accept header, the web API will still send you a 304 and not an XML response!

Testing ETag ActionFilter

To test the preceding filter, you can apply it on the `Get(int id)` action method, as shown in Listing 4-9. Also, you can modify the Home/Index view to include another button and JavaScript to call this method (see Listing 4-10).

Listing 4-9. ETag Filter in Action

```
[EnableETag]
public Employee Get(int id)
{
    return new Employee()
    {
        Id = id, Name = "John Q Human", Department = "Enforcement"
    };
}
```

Listing 4-10. Home/Index View Changes to Call Get Method

```
@section scripts{
    <script type="text/javascript">
        $(document).ready(function () {
            $('#search').click(function () {
                // Removed for brevity
            });

            $('#details').click(function () {
                $('#employee').empty();
                $.getJSON("/api/employees/12345", function (employee) {
                    var now = new Date();
                    var ts = now.getHours() + ':' + now.getMinutes() + ':' + now.getSeconds();

                    var content = employee.Id + ' ' + employee.Name;
                    content = content + ' ' + employee.Department + ' ' + ts;

                    $('#employee').append($('<li/>', { text: content }));
                });
            });
        });
    </script>
}
<div>
    <div>
        <h1>Employees Listing</h1>
        <input id="search" type="button" value="Get" />
        <input id="details" type="button" value="Details" />
    </div>
    <div>
        <ul id="employees" />
    </div>
    <div>
        <ul id="employee" />
    </div>
</div>
```

ETags for Managing Concurrency

ETags can also be used for managing concurrency in an optimistic fashion, without combining with web caching. Concurrency management is essential to ensure data integrity in the case of multiuser environments such as the web. Because HTTP is stateless, locking a resource before the update is not a feasible option. The optimistic approach ensures that there will be no intermediate changes between the time of read and the subsequent update. The update will fail if there is an intermediate change. This is the best approach for the stateless HTTP services. As part of a GET response, the web API sends an ETag. Subsequent to this, if the same resource has to be updated through a PUT, the client sends the same ETag in the If-Match request header. Figure 4-9 shows this process.

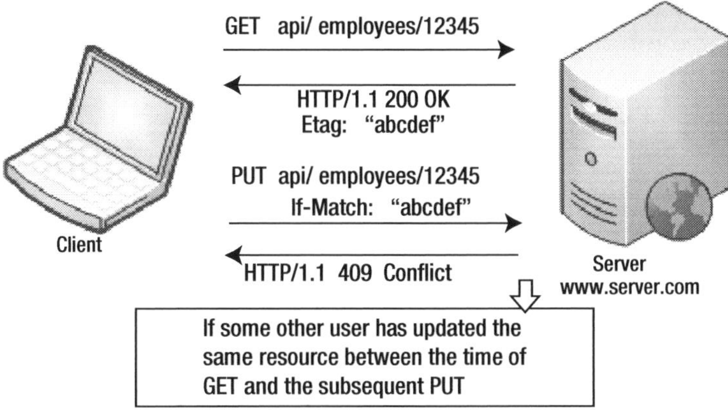

Figure 4-9. *ETag for managing concurrency*

If the ETag sent by the client matches the ETag in the persistence store, such as the database or a concurrent dictionary, the store is updated with the new value. If there is a mismatch, a status code of 409 - Conflict gets sent back to the client. The client can follow this with a fresh GET and retry the update. Listing 4-11 shows the code for an action filter that is very similar to the `EnableETag` filter in the preceding section.

Listing 4-11. ETag for Managing Concurrency

```
public class ConcurrencyChecker : ActionFilterAttribute
{
    private static ConcurrentDictionary<string, EntityTagHeaderValue> etags = new
    ConcurrentDictionary<string, EntityTagHeaderValue>();

    public override void OnActionExecuting(HttpActionContext context)
    {
        var request = context.Request;

        if (request.Method == HttpMethod.Put)
        {
            var key = request.RequestUri.ToString();

            EntityTagHeaderValue etagFromClient = request.Headers.IfMatch.FirstOrDefault();
```

```
            if (etagFromClient != null)
            {
                EntityTagHeaderValue etag = null;
                if (etags.TryGetValue(key, out etag) && !etag.Equals(etagFromClient))
                {
                    context.Response = new HttpResponseMessage(HttpStatusCode.Conflict);
                }
            }
        }
    }

    public override void OnActionExecuted(HttpActionExecutedContext context)
    {
        var request = context.Request;
        var key = request.RequestUri.ToString();

        EntityTagHeaderValue etag;

        if (!etags.TryGetValue(key, out etag) || request.Method == HttpMethod.Put ||
                                                  request.Method == HttpMethod.Post)
        {
            etag = new EntityTagHeaderValue("\"" + Guid.NewGuid().ToString() + "\"");
            etags.AddOrUpdate(key, etag, (k, val) => etag);
        }

        context.Response.Headers.ETag = etag;
    }
}
```

To test this filter, follow these steps.

1. Add the action method `public void Put(Employee employee) {}` to `EmployeesController`.
2. Apply the `ConcurrencyChecker` filter on this `Put()` method.
3. Click the Details button of the /Home/Index view to issue a GET and obtain the ETag.
4. Use the same ETag in the If-Match header and issue a PUT request from Fiddler. If PUT is successful, the web API returns 204 - No content because we have left `Put()` empty.
5. Replay the same PUT request and you will get a 409 - Conflict.

■ **Caution** *EnableETag* filter in Listing 4-8 and *ConcurrencyChecker* in Listing 4-11 use a concurrent dictionary, which is at the App domain level, to store the ETags. In a real production situation, especially when it involves a web garden or a web farm deployment, the tags must be retrieved from the database or some other place common to all servers. Otherwise, the dictionaries in the different app domains will not be in sync to implement this ETag or concurrency check in a meaningful way.

■ **Tip** If you try this example in Cassini, the web server that ships with Microsoft Visual Studio 2010, the ETag header does not get written on to the response. The previous filter works because we are also writing the cache-control, which is absent in this filter. For that reason, Cassini is suppressing the ETag header. IIS Express or IIS must be used to run this example.

Cross-Origin Resource Sharing

Cross-Origin Resource Sharing (CORS) is a specification that defines the ways for a web server (read ASP.NET Web API) to allow its resources to be accessed by the script running in a web page from a different domain. The server and the client work together, using HTTP headers to make accessing cross-origin resource possible.

The same origin policy, an important security concept relevant to the browser-side scripting languages such as JavaScript, restricts the scripts from accessing resources from a different origin. An origin is defined by the scheme, host, and port of a URL. For example, a web page from server.com cannot run a JavaScript and access a page from anotherserver.com. This policy has a direct impact on scenarios that involve the web pages accessing a shared or public ASP.NET Web API on the Internet.

In Chapter 2, we looked at an ASP.NET MVC view accessing a web API hosted in the same server. In Visual Studio, if I separate out the web API piece into an individual application running in a port different from the port where the MVC application runs, JQuery AJAX would stop working. There are a few workarounds for this problem. One workaround is CORS. Of course, CORS is not the only solution for cross-origin resource access. There are other mechanisms such as JSONP, proxying, and message passing via IFRAME, but CORS is a modern and better alternative. For example, JSONP supports only GET methods.

One key consideration if you choose CORS is the possible lack of support for CORS in older browsers. CORS is supported by the following browsers: Firefox 3.5+, Internet Explorer 10+, Google Chrome 4.0+, Safari 4.0+, Opera 12.0+, and Opera Mobile 12.0+ (Source: `http://caniuse.com/cors`).

Simple CORS

For a nullipotent method like GET, the client sends the Origin request header with the origin value. The web API checks to see if that origin can be allowed access to a resource. With the response, the web API returns the Access-Control-Allow-Origin header with the same value sent by the client or *, if this resource is available to all with no restriction. If the web API sends the response but does not send the header or the origin sent does not match the origin received, the client-side browser drops the response and does not proceed.

To understand CORS, you need to first understand how browsers enforce the same origin policy. The following steps illustrate the same origin policy at work.

1. Configure the earlier project, 'TalentManager,' that we worked on in Chapter 2 to use Visual Studio Development Server and run on a specific port 5214. Go to the project properties 'Web' tab, and specify the port as shown in Figure 4-10.

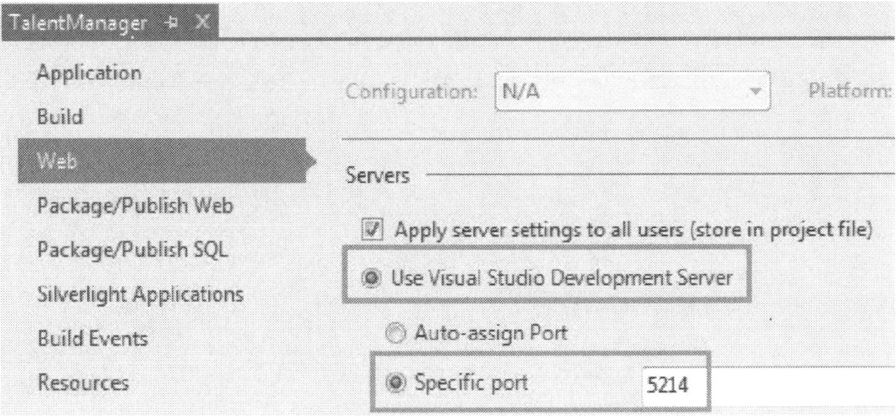

Figure 4-10. *Specifying a port for Visual Studio Development Server*

2. Create a new Web API project. Here we create it with the name 'Cors' and configure it to use Visual Studio Development Server and run on port 6504. Accessing the web API in Cors from a web page in TalentManager is a cross-origin request. That is what you are trying to test.

3. Take the MVC view from Listing 4-10 and change the URL of the `getJSON()`, making the GET request of a specific employee to an absolute path of `http://localhost:6504/api/employees/12345`, as shown in Listing 4-12.

Listing 4-12. CORS GET – MVC View

```
@section scripts{
    <script type="text/javascript">
        $(document).ready(function () {
            $('#search').click(function () {
                // Removed for brevity
            });

            $('#details').click(function () {
                $('#employee').empty();
                $.getJSON("http://localhost:6504/api/employees/12345", function (employee) {
                    var now = new Date();
                    var ts = now.getHours() + ':' + now.getMinutes() + ':' +
                                                                        now.getSeconds();

                    var content = employee.Id + ' ' + employee.Name;
                    content = content + ' ' + employee.Department + ' ' + ts;
```

```
                        $('#employee').append($('<li/>', { text: content }));
                    });
                });
            });
        </script>
    }
    <div>
        <div>
            <h1>Employees Listing</h1>
            <input id="search" type="button" value="Get" />
            <input id="details" type="button" value="Details" />
        </div>
        <div>
            <ul id="employees" />
        </div>
        <div>
            <ul id="employee" />
        </div>
    </div>
```

4. Add a new ApiController with the name EmployeesController to the 'Cors' project and implement the Get(int id) action method, exactly the same as 'TalentManager' for the view in Listing 4-12 to use. With this change, the Home/Index view of the project 'TalentManager' running on port 5214 will try to consume the web API running on port 6504 of the same localhost.

5. Run 'TalentManager' in Internet Explorer and in the /Home/Index page click the Details button. The button click appears to have no effect and nothing gets displayed in the unordered list. That is, Internet Explorer enforces the same origin policy.

6. If you want to be sure that the same origin policy enforcement by Internet Explorer is the real reason for the employees list not displaying, you can roll back the URL change so that the URL for getJSON is /api/employees/12345. The web API is in the same project and hence the same port gets exercised. It thus should begin to work this time, after the URL change rollback.

7. Finally, instead of using Internet Explorer, use the Mozilla Firefox browser. Go to `http://localhost:5214` and click the Details button. Firefox does not budge either. No browser allows cross-origin requests to work by default, for security reasons.

To get this working, change the Get(int) action method as shown in Listing 4-13.

Listing 4-13. CORS GET – Web API

```
public class EmployeesController : ApiController
{
    public HttpResponseMessage Get(int id)
    {
        var employee = new Employee()
        {
            Id = id,
            Name = "John Q Human",
            Department = "Enforcement"
        };
```

```
        var response = Request.CreateResponse<Employee>(HttpStatusCode.OK, employee);
        response.Headers.Add("Access-Control-Allow-Origin", "*");

        return response;
    }
}
```

With this change, rebuild the 'Cors' project and give it a try one more time, with Firefox (not Internet Explorer). It works this time! This is CORS in action.

The response header Access-Control-Allow-Origin with value of * is the secret sauce that gets the cross-origin request working. Of course, in Listing 4-13 the response header is blindly sent back with a *. However, it is typical to inspect the Origin header, which is available through `Request.Headers.GetValues("Origin").FirstOrDefault()`, and decide to allow the request or not. In the preceding example, the Origin header has a value of `http://localhost:5214` from where the request originates.

■ **Note** Validating the Origin header in the request and setting the Access-Control-Allow-Origin header in the response can be moved to an action filter. Only those GET methods that are potential candidates for CORS can be decorated with the filter attribute.

CORS SUPPORT IN THINKTECTURE.IDENTITYMODEL

In the preceding examples, I returned * in the Access-Control-Allow-Origin response header, which means that the resource can be accessed by any domain. However, it is typical to inspect several parameters including the Origin header and decide to allow the request or not.

`Thinktecture.IdentityModel`, for example supports a rich configuration API to control the access in a more granular way: the resources you want to allow access; which origins, HTTP methods, and request or response headers are allowed; and if cookies are allowed.

```
// Allow all CORS requests to the Employees controller from the http://foo.com origin.
corsConfig.ForResources("Employees")
              .ForOrigins("http://foo.com")
                  .AllowAll();

// Allow http://foo.com to use any method, pass cookies, send the request headers
// of Content-Type, Foo and Authorization and read the Foo response header for
// the Employees and Products controllers
corsConfig
        .ForResources("Employees", "Products")
            .ForOrigins("http://foo.com")
                .AllowAllMethods()
                    .AllowCookies()
                        .AllowRequestHeaders("Content-Type", "Foo", "Authorization")
                            .AllowResponseHeaders("Foo");
```

The CORS implementation of `Thinktecture.IdentityModel` will be part of the `System.Web.Cors` namespace in ASP.NET Web API. (`http://aspnetwebstack.codeplex.com/SourceControl/changeset/4284ca5270b9`).

Preflighted Request

Next, we see how CORS works with a method with a side effect such as PUT. It gets slightly complicated with the browser making an additional request, called a preflight request. This special request uses the HTTP OPTIONS method and sends two headers.

1. The **Origin** request header (same as the Simple CORS involving GET).
2. The **Access-Control-Request-Method** header with the method that the client wants to use, in this case a PUT.

The OPTIONS method response has two headers.

1. The **Access-Control-Allow-Methods** header has the comma-separated value of methods supported by the server.
2. The **Access-Control-Allow-Origin** header, with a value same as origin or a *.

Based on the preflight response, the browser goes ahead with the actual PUT request. Of course, the PUT action method has to return the Access-Control-Allow-Origin header for the script running in the browser to display any data returned by the PUT action method. The following sequence shows the HTTP transactions with the headers.

1. The client sends the preflight request, the JQuery explicit PUT request, which gets translated to an implicit OPTIONS issued by Firefox.

```
OPTIONS http://localhost:6504/api/employees HTTP/1.1
Access-Control-Request-Method: PUT
Origin: http://localhost:5214
```

2. The web API responds to the OPTIONS request with the appropriate headers. There is no response body.

```
HTTP/1.1 200 OK
Access-Control-Allow-Origin: *
Access-Control-Allow-Methods: PUT
```

3. Because the web API allows PUT, as indicated by the Access-Control-Allow-Methods response header in the OPTIONS response, the Firefox browser sends a PUT request to the web API.

```
PUT http://localhost:6504/api/employees HTTP/1.1
Origin: http://localhost:5214
```

4. The web API responds to PUT.

```
HTTP/1.1 200 OK
Access-Control-Allow-Origin: *
```

Implementing Preflighted CORS in ASP.NET Web API

Following are the steps to implement the preflighted CORS in ASP.NET Web API.

1. Add a new action method to the `HomeController` in the 'TalentManager' project.

```
public ActionResult Preflight()
{
        return View();
}
```

2. Right-click the action method created in the previous step and add a view. Copy and paste the code in Listing 4-14.

   Listing 4-15 shows the web API code with the action methods to handle the PUT and the OPTIONS requests.

   Listing 4-14. CORS Preflight - JQuery

```
@section scripts{
    <script type="text/javascript">
        $(document).ready(function () {
            $('#details').click(function () {
                $('#employee').empty();

                $.ajax({
                    type: "PUT",
                    url: "http://localhost.:6504/api/employees/12345",
                    data: { "Name": "John Q Law", "Department": "Legal" },
                    success: function (data) {
                        $('#employee').append($('<li/>', { text: data }));
                    },
                    error: function (error) {
                        console.log("ERROR:", error);
                    }
                });
            });
        });
    </script>
}
<div>
    <div>
        <input id="details" type="button" value="Details" />
    </div>
    <div>
        <ul id="employee" />
    </div>
</div>
```

■ **Note** Because CORS is related to the client side or the browser, you can open a local HTML file from your file system in Firefox and test this out. The MVC application is not mandatory. However, the Origin header will be null or absent in the OPTIONS request message in that case.

Listing 4-15. CORS Preflight – Web API

```
public HttpResponseMessage Put(Employee employee)
{
    // Update logic goes here

    var response = Request.CreateResponse<Employee>(HttpStatusCode.OK, employee);
    response.Headers.Add("Access-Control-Allow-Origin", "*");
    return response;
}

public HttpResponseMessage Options()
{
    var response = new HttpResponseMessage();
    response.StatusCode = HttpStatusCode.OK;
    response.Headers.Add("Access-Control-Allow-Origin", "*");
    response.Headers.Add("Access-Control-Allow-Methods", "PUT");
    return response;
}
```

3. With these changes in place, go to the `http://localhost.:5214/Home/preflight` URL in Firefox. Click the Details button.
4. The JSON response returned by the `Put(Employee)` action gets displayed in the unordered list. This is CORS preflight in action. Firefox issues an OPTIONS request, the preflight request followed by the actual PUT request behind the scenes. You can verify this using the Fiddler tool or the Firefox Web Console, which is available under the Web Developer menu.

The preceding code example showed you the code to add the headers inside the action methods, just to keep the code simple and hence easier to understand. Just as the CORS GET, a filter can be created to support request header checking and the response header addition. However, the Option method cannot be handled through a filter. Earlier in the pipeline, if the action method is not available to handle HTTP OPTIONS, a 405 – Method Not Allowed is sent back to the client.

The best bet is to use a message handler, similar to the one in Listing 4-16. One thing to keep in mind while designing a message handler for CORS preflight is that the message handlers run for all the requests (or at least all the requests in the route), unlike the filters, which run only for the action methods to which the filter is applied. The response headers are hard-coded in the following example, but in the real world they have to be based on the requirements at hand. Some configuration-based data along with `ApiExplorer` can be used to create the handler generically to handle the OPTIONS method for the multiple controllers. If the message handler does not fit the bill, only those controllers needing to support CORS can individually implement the action method to handle OPTIONS.

Listing 4-16. CORS Preflight Delegating Handler

```
public class CorsPreflightHandler : DelegatingHandler
{
    protected override async Task<HttpResponseMessage> SendAsync(HttpRequestMessage request,
                                                                  CancellationToken cancellationToken)
    {
        if (request.Headers.Contains("Origin") && request.Method == HttpMethod.Options)
        {
            var response = new HttpResponseMessage(HttpStatusCode.OK);

            response.Headers.Add("Access-Control-Allow-Origin", "*");
            response.Headers.Add("Access-Control-Allow-Methods", "PUT");
```

```
            return response;
        }

        return await base.SendAsync(request, cancellationToken);
    }
}
```

INTERNET EXPLORER

The CORS-related examples we have seen so far will not work with Internet Explorer 9 or earlier versions. For the cross-origin requests, you must use the `XDomainRequest` object that was introduced with Internet Explorer 8. XMLHttpRequest in Internet Explorer does not support CORS and hence JQuery AJAX will not work with Internet Explorer. With Internet Explorer 10, this situation is likely to change and JQuery $.ajax should work, too. However, using XDomainRequest is very simple, as shown in the following HTML/JavaScript code. Our modified version of the action method `Get(int id)` returning the Access-Control-Allow-Origin header in the response is all it needs to work.

```
<!DOCTYPE html>
<html>
        <head>
                <title>XDR</title>
                <script type="text/javascript">
                        var xdr = new XDomainRequest();
                        xdr.open("get", "http://localhost:6504/api/employees/12345");
                        xdr.onload=function()
                        {
                                alert(xdr.responseText);
                        }

                        xdr.send();
                </script>
        </head>
<body>
</body>
</html>
```

`XDomainRequest` supports only POST and GET. The concept of preflighting requests does not exist with Internet Explorer. Also, the MVC view that we have been using with Firefox can work equally well even if the HTML generated, along with JavaScript, is saved as a local HTML file. But XDR is strict about the URL prefix being the same. Hence, from a local HTML file, AJAX requests will not work.

HTTP Cookies

HTTP is stateless, but the HTTP specification does include a state management mechanism that uses the headers to transport data back and forth between the server and the client with a user agent (read browser). The user agent performs this action seamlessly, giving a stateful feeling to the whole stateless model. The underpinning of this mechanism is a cookie.

A cookie is data in the form of the key–value pairs sent by a web server to the client in the Set-Cookie response header. The client that supports the cookie mechanism starts sending this data back in the Cookie request header in every single request made from the same user agent from that point onward, until the time the cookie expires. The expiry of a cookie is determined by the server when it creates the cookie.

To set a cookie, the server sends the Set-Cookie header in the response, similar to this:

```
Set-Cookie: sesstoken=token=12345&token-type=general; expires=Wed, 26 Sep 2012 15:35:17 GMT
```

To send the cookie back, the client sends the Cookie header in the request, similar to this:

```
Cookie: sesstoken=token=12345&token-type=general
```

Cookies and ASP.NET Web API

A cookie is more relevant to a web application with the pages that a user navigates using a user agent such as a browser. If the server returns a cookie as part of the response to the first request, the user agent keeps sending the same data to the server until the time at which the cookie expires. There is nothing that needs to be done programmatically in the web pages in the client side, because the cookie implementation is standardized by the HTTP specification and the browser knows how to deal with the cookies.

On the other hand, ASP.NET Web API powered RESTful services are not navigated using a user agent and there is not lot of value in terms of implementing cookie support, although it is possible to do so. If a web API is hosted on the same domain as the web pages and the web pages hit the web API through AJAX, the web page cookie containing the authentication ticket, as in the case of the Forms Authentication, can be shared with the web API. In other words, the web API can piggyback on the session or authentication mechanism of the web application.

This is a marginal benefit and the risk is far more significant, irrespective of the cookie being an in-memory cookie that expires when the browser is closed or a persistent cookie that gets stored in the disk of the end user's computer. The persistent cookies continue to remain alive until the time of expiry, even if the browser window is closed. Compared to this, a normal HTTP header never outlives a transaction. A cookie, in memory or otherwise, that is used to store sensitive information such as a session makes an application susceptible to Cross-Site Request Forgery (CSRF), which is covered in depth in Chapter 15. Additionally, the cookies are generally frowned on in the REST style architecture.

In both cases of the plain HTTP header and the cookie, if the unencrypted text is sent, it will be visible to the malicious users with the ability to sniff the traffic. If a cookie must be used for a reason, data sent in the cookie must be encrypted and the expiry limit set judiciously so that the chance of misuse is minimized.

The web API design should take into account the fact that cookie data can be tampered with and that cookies can be deleted altogether. Thus, the cookie data must not be trusted. There must be a fallback mechanism in case a cookie goes missing.

Listing 4-17 shows how to set and get a cookie from a message handler in ASP.NET Web API.

Listing 4-17. Setting and Getting a Cookie

```
public class CookiesHandler : DelegatingHandler
{
    protected override async Task<HttpResponseMessage> SendAsync(HttpRequestMessage request,
                                                            CancellationToken cancellationToken)
    {
        // Getting a cookie
        CookieHeaderValue cookie = request.Headers.GetCookies("sesstoken").FirstOrDefault();
        if (cookie != null)
        {
            CookieState cookieState = cookie["sesstoken"];

            string token = cookieState["token"];
            string tokenType = cookieState["token-type"];
        }
```

```
        var response = await base.SendAsync(request, cancellationToken);

        // Setting a cookie
        var pairs = new NameValueCollection();
        pairs["token"] = "12345";
        pairs["token-type"] = "general";

        response.Headers.AddCookies(new CookieHeaderValue[]
        {
            new CookieHeaderValue("sesstoken", pairs)
            {
                Expires = DateTimeOffset.Now.AddSeconds(30),
                Path = "/"
            }
        });

        return response;
    }
}
```

HttpOnly Cookies

A cookie that is created by ASP.NET Web API can be read by JavaScript running in the browser. If a cookie contains critical security information, it becomes an important threat to deal with. HttpOnly cookies are transmitted by a browser only with HTTP and HTTPS requests that restrict access from JavaScript, thereby mitigating the threat of cookie theft via cross-site scripting (XSS).

To understand the security risk of JavaScript accessing a cookie, let's create an MVC controller `CookieReaderController` with an action method of `Read()`. We'll create the view for `Read()`, as shown in Listing 4-18.

Listing 4-18. JavaScript Accessing Cookie

```
@section scripts{
    <script type="text/javascript">
        $(document).ready(function () {
            $('#details').click(function () {
                $('#employee').empty();

                $.ajax({
                    type: "GET",
                    url: "/api/employees/12345",
                    success: function (response) {
                        alert(document.cookie);
                        $('#employee').append($('<li/>', { text: response.Id + ' ' + response.Name }));
                    }
                });
            });
        });
    </script>
}
```

```
<div>
    <div>
        <input id="details" type="button" value="Details" />
    </div>
    <div>
        <ul id="employee" />
    </div>
</div>
```

Click the Details button and you see an alert box with the cookie details. Thus, JavaScript from the MVC view page is able to access the cookie created by the web API. Of course, when you create the cookie in the preceding code listing, a path of "/" is specified, which opens up the cookie for both web API and MVC applications. The point I'm trying to illustrate, though, is that the doors are open for possible cookie theft through XSS.

If the web application that is consuming the web API has an XSS hole, the same hole can be used by a malicious user to inject some script that opens up a pop-up with an external URL passing `document.cookie` as the query string. Seamlessly posting the cookie to some other origin will not be possible because of same origin policy restrictions, though.

To mitigate this problem, set the `HttpOnly` property to true when creating the cookie. In this case, `document.cookie` will not be able to read the cookie created by the web API. However, the best approach is to avoid cookies altogether unless there is a really strong need.

NONBROWSER CLIENT

Cookies are not limited only to web browsers. Any HTTP-aware client that supports cookies can deal with a cookie sending ASP.NET Web API. The following code example shows a class extended from `WebClient`. It overrides the virtual method `GetWebRequest` to attach an instance of `CookieContainer` to the request. The `CookieContainer` object instance has to be reused across the requests to let it push cookies in the subsequent requests. For this reason, it is a class-level field and the same instance of the web client is used to send multiple requests. Here we use a proxy of address localhost and port 8888, that of Fiddler, to inspect requests and responses.

```
public class CookieWebClient : WebClient
{
    private CookieContainer jar = new CookieContainer();

    protected override WebRequest GetWebRequest(Uri address)
    {
        WebRequest request = base.GetWebRequest(address);

        HttpWebRequest webRequest = request as HttpWebRequest;
        if (webRequest != null)
            webRequest.CookieContainer = jar;

        return request;
    }
}

string url = "http://localhost:7077/api/employees/12345";
```

```
CookieWebClient client = new CookieWebClient()
{
    Proxy = new WebProxy("localhost", 8888)    // Fiddler
};

Console.WriteLine(client.DownloadString(url)); // Cookie is created here
Console.WriteLine(client.DownloadString(url)); // In this request, the cookie gets sent back
                                                  to the web API
```

Proxy Server

Typical corporate networks include a web proxy server through which all Internet traffic is directed. When a user inside the network makes a request for a resource on a web server hosted on the Internet, the request first goes to the proxy server. The proxy makes the request to the web server on behalf of the user, gets the response back, and returns the same to the user who initiated the request.

The web server will see only the IP address of the proxy and not the IP address of the individual users behind the proxy. The proxy server can cache responses and use the same to service the subsequent requests.

The proxy servers typically require a user to be authenticated to enforce corporate policies on Internet usage. In such a scenario, when a request with missing or invalid credentials is received by the proxy server it sends back a 407 - Proxy Authorization Required status code and starts a process, as shown in the following sequence of steps.

1. Client sends the initial request.

   ```
   GET /Protocols/rfc2616/rfc2616.html HTTP/1.1
   Host: www.w3.org
   ```

2. Proxy responds with a 407 status code.

   ```
   HTTP/1.1 407 Proxy Authorization Required
   Date: Thu, 27 Sep 2012 08:05:47 GMT
   Proxy-Authenticate: NTLM
   Proxy-Authenticate: Basic realm="Magical"
   Content-Length: 322
   Proxy-Support: Session-Based-Authentication
   ```

3. Client sends the credentials.

   ```
   GET /Protocols/rfc2616/rfc2616.html HTTP/1.1
   Host: www.w3.org
   Proxy-Authorization: NTLM TlRMTVNTUAABAAAAB7IIogACbdOxU2MTg5Q1RT
   ```

4. Proxy sends the NTLM challenge.

   ```
   HTTP/1.1 407 Proxy Authorization Required
   Date: Thu, 27 Sep 2012 08:05:47 GMT
   Proxy-Authenticate: NTLM TlRMTVNTUAACAAAFggAAUsIPcwnFBiwAAAAA==
   Content-Length: 322
   Proxy-Support: Session-Based-Authentication
   ```

5. Client sends the challenge response.

```
GET /Protocols/rfc2616/rfc2616.html HTTP/1.1
Proxy-Authorization: NTLM TlRMTVNTUhWRXsX+BwCt918SLJSdOzv8KAuloqVcQhWRXsX+BwCt918Q=
Host: www.w3.org
```

6. Finally, the response is sent.

```
HTTP/1.1 200 OK
Date: Thu, 27 Sep 2012 08:05:47 GMT
```

If a browser is used, it seamlessly performs the preceding steps and gets back the response. If a nonbrowser client is used, the 407 status needs to be handled. This generally occurs in the case of accessing a web API hosted on the Internet from behind the proxy.

The .NET Framework has the classes to handle this case quite easily. Listing 4-19 shows how to use the `WebClient` class to communicate to a web API through a proxy server. `DefaultCredentials` uses the account running the code as the account to authenticate against proxy. This means if you run this as a console application, the account under which you have logged into Windows is used. If this is run in an ASP.NET application, the account under which the worker process runs is used. Instead of `CredentialCache.DefaultCredentials`, the `new NetworkCredential("userId", "p@s5w0rd", "MyDomain")` can be used as well, in case a specific account must be used.

Listing 4-19. Client Communicating to a Web API Through a Proxy

```
WebClient client = new WebClient()
{
    Proxy = new WebProxy("proxy.server.com", 6666)
    {
        Credentials = CredentialCache.DefaultCredentials
    }
};

var response = client.DownloadString("http://localhost:12532/api/employees");
```

Of course, there is an element of security risk involved here, because the application has to store the Windows account credentials. If storing the Windows credentials absolutely must be done by an application for a reason, care must be taken to ensure credentials are protected. In the case of applications built using the .NET Framework, data such as application-level credentials typically are stored in a configuration file. In such a case, encrypting the configuration section is one effective way to ensure the credentials are safe. Chapter 15 provides details on encrypting the configuration file.

HTTPS

One of the great things about HTTP is that it is human friendly: The request and response messages are in plain text that is easier to read. On the flip side, it makes the HTTP less secure and is an easy target for man-in-the-middle (MITM) and eavesdropping attacks. HTTPS is designed to make HTTP secure by letting it operate on top of the SSL/TLS protocol. HTTPS URLs begin with "`https://`" and use port 443 by default.

There are two important aspects related to using HTTPS: First, it guarantees the user communicates with the web site that she intends to and that the site to which the user is connected is not masquerading itself as some other site that the user trusts.

Second, it prevents anyone in the middle from reading or modifying the messages exchanged. HTTPS accomplishes the latter by encrypting the entire message, including the request URI, headers, and cookies. For this reason, some of the things we examined earlier like caching will not work with HTTPS.

HTTPS was developed to be used with a web browser, but it can be used with other clients as well. Similarly, HTTPS is not limited only to web applications that serve up HTML web pages. HTTPS can secure ASP.NET Web API as well. First, you will see how HTTPS works with the web browsers. Some of the key concepts introduced here, such as encryption, are elaborated in much more detail in later chapters, specifically Chapter 6.

For the purpose of understanding this section, just assume that encryption is sort of a function that takes in two arguments: a key and the plain text that returns the encrypted text or the cipher text as the output. The plain text here is the message exchanged and the key is some random text that both the server and the browser share but no one else will have. Decryption is simply the reverse of encryption. Given the key and the encrypted text, decryption produces the plain text.

One problem you can sense right away is that a user would like to go to more than one web site and that a web site cannot have one common key for all users; it has to be handled per user. Otherwise, it is very easy for a malicious user to simply pick up the key for a web site, decrypt the message, and look at the messages exchanged.

It is not feasible for a web site, especially public-facing ones, to track all the users and assign and maintain keys for individual users. Similarly, it is not practical for a user to have and manage dedicated keys for all the web sites that he or she would like to visit. So, a random key has to be generated on the fly at the point when a user tries to connect to an HTTPS web site. This process is called a handshake and is the most important part of HTTPS communication. Once the web site and the browser have a shared key, it is easier to exchange the encrypted messages. The following steps summarize the handshake process.

1. Browser issues a request over HTTPS to a web site.
2. Web site sends a certificate containing its public key.
3. Browser generates a random key, encrypts it using the web site's public key, and sends it to the web site.
4. Both web site and browser now have a shared key to proceed with the encrypted message exchange.

I introduced a couple of new terms in the preceding steps that I have not touched on until now: the certificate and the public key.

A certificate is issued to a web site by a well-known agency, and it can be traced back to the site to which it was issued. No one can tamper with a certificate. If a certificate is issued to my-server.com, no one can tamper with it and make it look like it is issued to another-server.com.

A certificate has two mathematically linked keys, a private key and a public key. A public key of a certificate can be shared with anyone. A private key is secretly held by the web site to which the certificate was issued. Plain text that was encrypted with a public key can be decrypted only with the private key.

With that understanding, let's now revisit the preceding steps. The web site sends the public key down to the browser. It is acceptable to give it to anyone; it is a public key after all. Even a malicious user can have the same public key, but it cannot be used for decryption. The private key, which is within the safe custody of the web site, is a must for decryption. Only the web site can decrypt and get the key sent by the browser.

One loophole you might anticipate is a malicious user getting a valid certificate with both the public and private keys and sending the public key to the browser acting as a man-in-the-middle. Will the browser happily encrypt the random key it just generated and send it off for the malicious user to intercept and decrypt using his private key?

The answer is no. This loophole is prevented by a browser making the following two checks.

1. The browser checks the web site to which it is connecting against the web site to which the certificate (containing the public key that it received) has been issued.
2. The certificate must be issued by a certification authority (CA) it trusts, such as VeriSign, Thawte, or GeoTrust.

If the malicious user sends a valid certificate that is issued to his domain, as if the web site to which the user is connecting to is sending it, the first validation step will fail. If the malicious user creates a certificate as if it is issued to a popular e-commerce web site, the browser will still fail the validation step because the certificate is not issued by one of the CAs the browser trusts.

If there is a failure in any of these checks, the browser complains and alerts the user, as shown in Figure 4-11.

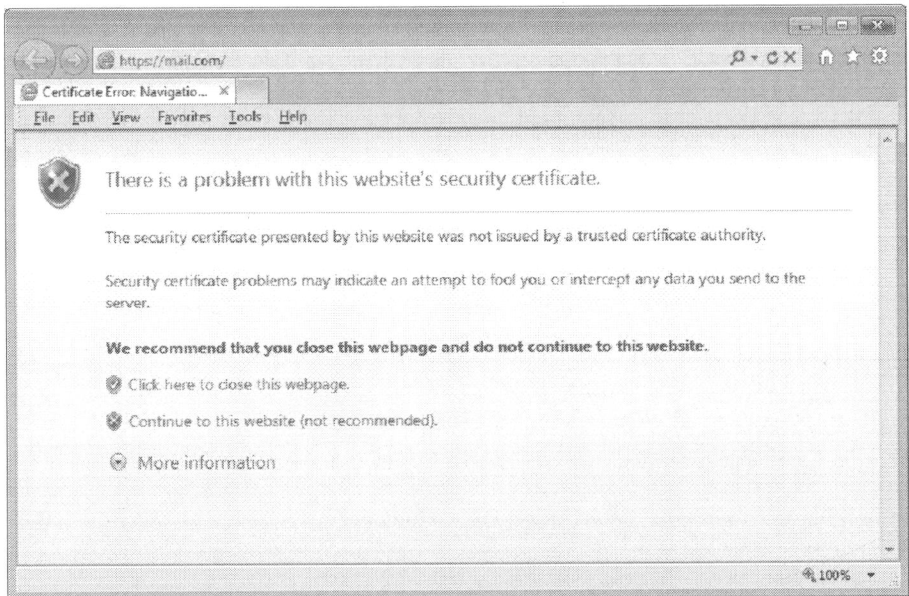

Figure 4-11. *Browser warning*

Configuring HTTPS for ASP.NET Web API Hosted in IIS

Configuring HTTPS for web-hosted ASP.NET Web API is the same as HTTPS enabling any other ASP.NET application. From the client side, any HTTPS-capable device or application can consume the web API. There is nothing special there as well.

Now, to mandate HTTPS for specific action methods that deal with the sensitive data, you can use an action filter like the one shown in Listing 4-20. If you require HTTPS for all the methods, this filter can be configured as a global filter. As another option, you can write a message handler that uses the preceding code or simply configure IIS to mandate HTTPS if your web API is web-hosted.

Listing 4-20. HttpsOnly Filter

```
public class HttpsOnly : ActionFilterAttribute
{
    public override void OnActionExecuting(HttpActionContext context)
    {
        var request = context.Request;

        if (request.RequestUri.Scheme != Uri.UriSchemeHttps)
        {
            var response = request.CreateResponse(HttpStatusCode.Forbidden);
```

```
                response.Content = new StringContent("HTTPS Required");
                context.Response = response;
            }
        }
    }
```

■ **Note** You have seen cookies in a previous section and you have just seen HTTPS. It is possible to specify at the time of the creation of a cookie that it must be transmitted only through HTTPS. By setting the boolean *Secure* property of the *CookieHeaderValue* object to true, you can create a secure cookie.

Fiddler: A Tool for Web Debugging

Fiddler, a web debugging proxy, is a useful tool to capture and analyze HTTP as well as the HTTPS traffic between the computer running Fiddler and the outside. Fiddler also has a feature to build a complete request with headers, send it to an HTTP endpoint such as the web API, and inspect the response returned by the web API. It is virtually impossible to develop a production-grade web API without using a debugger like Fiddler. Based on the version you use, the Fiddler user interface could be slightly different from the one shown in Figure 4-12.

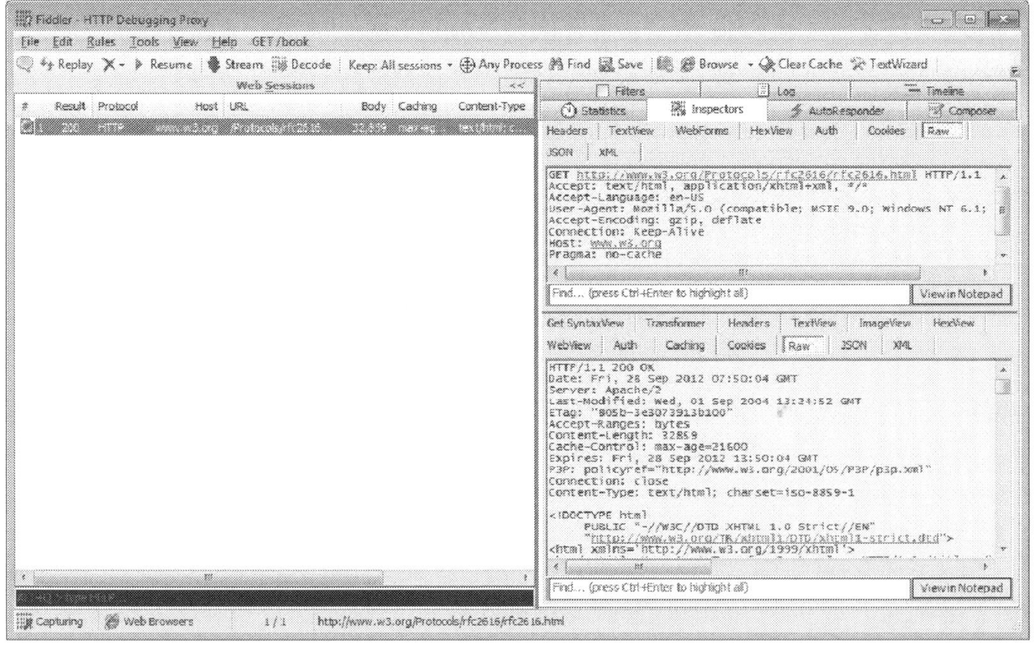

Figure 4-12. *Fiddler (4.4.1.1 beta)*

The left pane lists the requests captured. When a specific request is selected, the Inspectors tab on the right pane shows the request on the top and the corresponding response on the bottom. The Composer tab allows the requests to be hand-crafted and submitted with the HTTP method of your choice.

The older versions of Fiddler do not capture the traffic from localhost. One common workaround is to use localhost with a dot suffix (`http://localhost.:<port>`), use the machine name instead of localhost, or add an entry to the C:\Windows\System32\drivers\etc\hosts file for 127.0.0.1 and use the same.

The following list details how Fiddler can be configured to capture the traffic with different types of applications. Any application can consume a web API. Hence, learning to configure Fiddler to capture the traffic for all of the following scenarios is important.

1. **Internet Explorer:** When the Fiddler tool is launched, it registers itself as the system proxy. For this reason, requests from the applications that use WinInet such as Internet Explorer are automatically intercepted by Fiddler. No setting or configuration changes are needed.
2. **Other browsers like Firefox:** Fiddler can be configured as the web proxy with the browser so that Fiddler can start intercepting the requests. Fiddler runs on port 8888, so the proxy can be configured as localhost:8888 or 127.0.0.1:8888.
3. **Nonbrowser applications such as a .NET Framework WPF application:** Typically, these applications use the `WebClient` for HTTP communication. The `Proxy` property of the `WebClient` must be set to an instance of the `WebProxy` with the host as localhost and port as 8888 like this: `Proxy = new WebProxy("localhost", 8888)`.
4. **ASP.NET web application:** If you need to look at the HTTP client requests made by your code in an ASP.NET application or maybe a third-party library you are using in your ASP.NET application, it is possible to configure Fiddler as the proxy in the web.config file, as shown in Listing 4-21.

Listing 4-21. Web.config Configuring Fiddler as Proxy

```
<configuration>
        <system.net>
            <defaultProxy>
                  <proxy usesystemdefault="False" bypassonlocal="True"
                                         proxyaddress="http://127.0.0.1:8888" />
            </defaultProxy>
        </system.net>
</configuration>
```

Capturing and Decrypting HTTPS Traffic

Fiddler can capture and even decrypt HTTPS traffic. To enable that option, select Tools ➤ Fiddler Options... and select the Decrypt HTTPS traffic check box as shown in Figure 4-13.

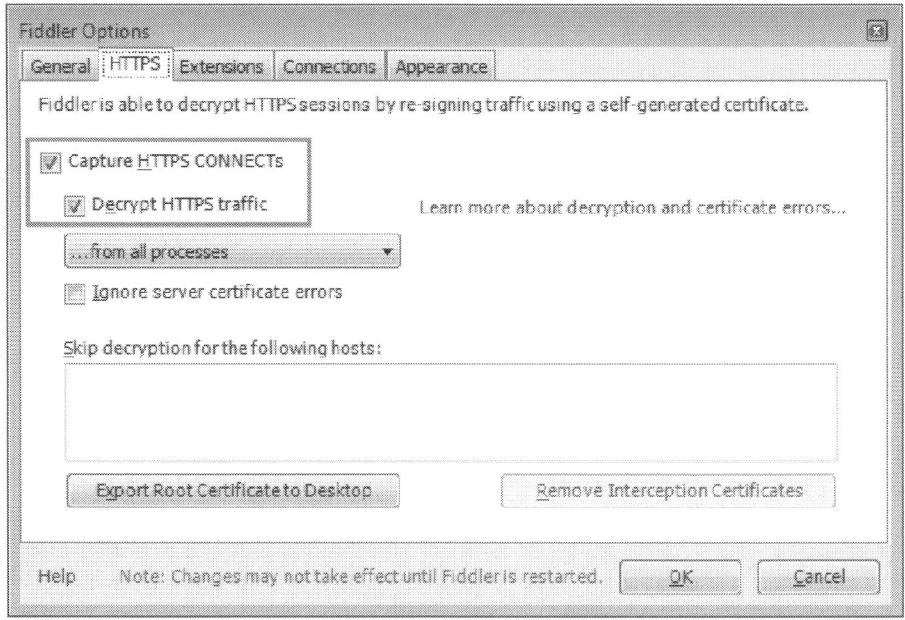

Figure 4-13. *Fiddler options*

When you select the Decrypt HTTP traffic check box, Fiddler asks you if you would like to add the Fiddler-generated root certificate to the trusted CA list in your machine. Select No and click OK. Fiddler is now all set to capture and decrypt HTTPS traffic.

To see Fiddler in action capturing the HTTPS traffic, go to `https://www.google.com` in Internet Explorer, with Fiddler running. As part of the capture, Fiddler sends the public key of a certificate it just generated to Internet Explorer, as if it is the certificate from `www.google.com`. Internet Explorer promptly shows "There is a problem with this website's security certificate."

If you go to the site without heeding Internet Explorer's warning, Internet Explorer goes ahead and shows the page. If you now go to Fiddler, you can see the traffic it has captured in all clear text, although sent over HTTPS. Internet Explorer shows the URL bar in red. If you look at the certificate error, it shows that the certificate is issued to `www.google.com`, but it was issued by DO_NOT_TRUST_Fiddler_Root, which is not a CA that Internet Explorer trusts (see Figure 4-14).

Certificate Information
This certificate cannot be verified up to a trusted certification authority.
Issued to: www.google.com
Issued by: DO_NOT_TRUST_FiddlerRoot
Valid from 9/ 21/ 2012 to 9/ 20/ 2022

Figure 4-14. *Certificate error*

Fiddler as Man-in-the-Middle

Fiddler's HTTPS capture and decryption functionality can be used to simulate an MITM attack on ASP.NET Web API secured by transport security (HTTPS). The preceding section covered how a browser reacts to Fiddler's attempt to capture HTTPS traffic. In this section, we use a nonbrowser client, a C# console application that uses the `WebClient` class for HTTP communication. The objective of this section is to understand how critical it is to pay attention to the errors that result in HTTPS and to emphasize the importance of not ignoring or bypassing these errors just to get things working. The following steps show how to simulate the MITM attack.

1. Deploy the 'TalentManager' ASP.NET Web API application that we created in Chapter 2 in the local IIS. IIS Express does not support HTTPS.

2. Launch Visual Studio as an administrator. Select the Use Local IIS Web Server option on the Web tab of the ASP.NET Web API application in Visual Studio and let it create the virtual directory for you.

3. Using IIS Manager, create a self-signed certificate (from the root node corresponding to that of your machine, IIS > Server Certificates).

4. Using this certificate, create an HTTPS binding to the web site the web API application is part of. With that, you are ready to submit the requests to the web API through HTTPS. See the section "Enabling HTTPS in IIS through Self-Signed Certificates" in Chapter 9 for more information as well as screenshots.

5. Create a console application and make a request to our web API, as shown in Listing 4-22. Because the certificate used to create HTTPS binding in the preceding step is issued to the local machine name, you need to use the machine name to connect instead of `https://localhost`.

Listing 4-22. Client Communicating to HTTPS Web API (Console App)

```
WebClient client = new WebClient();
var response = client.DownloadString
("https://mymachine/talentmanager/api/employees/1234");
```

6. At this point, your console application must be successfully making the web API call with no errors. Now include a line in the preceding code to let Fiddler intercept the calls through HTTPS: `client.Proxy = new WebProxy("localhost", 8888);`

7. Ensure Fiddler is capturing the traffic from all the processes, not just the web browsers. If you look at the task bar, Fiddler must show "Capturing All Processes." If Fiddler shows "Web Browsers" in the task bar, click on the same and change it to "All Processes."

8. With Fiddler running and Decrypt HTTPS traffic selected, run the console application. An exception gets thrown: "The underlying connection was closed: Could not establish trust relationship for the SSL/TLS secure channel." There is an inner exception, too: "The remote certificate is invalid according to the validation procedure." Clearly, `WebClient` is able to sense something is wrong with the certificate Fiddler has cooked up to decrypt the HTTPS traffic.

9. In the case of a web browser, you can go ahead and view the page, despite the browser's warning. What about `WebClient`? Yes, it is possible. You will need to modify the code, as shown in Listing 4-23.

Listing 4-23. Modified Client Communicating to HTTPS Web API (1Console)

```
ServicePointManager.ServerCertificateValidationCallback =
(object sender, X509Certificate cert, X509Chain chain, SslPolicyErrors error) =>
{
        Console.WriteLine(chain.ChainStatus.First().StatusInformation);
        return true;
};

WebClient client = new WebClient();
var response = client.DownloadString("https://mymachine/talentmanager/api/
employees/1234");
```

10. Now the `ServicePointManager` callback prints, "A certificate chain processed, but terminated in a root certificate which is not trusted by the trust provider." Obviously, root certificate is the DO_NOT_TRUST_FIDDLER_ROOT. Because true is returned, it continues to process. However, bypassing the certificate check like this is not good practice. The exception gets thrown because of a bad certificate as well as when someone mounts an MITM attack on your web API. Simply ignoring the error makes your web API vulnerable to MITM attacks.

■ **Caution** Bypassing the certificate checks in a production environment with code like that of Listing 4-23 is highly risky. We tend to take the path of least resistance, especially under the influence of a stressful project schedule. It is acceptable to take shortcuts like the preceding code during development, but you must have sound software development processes in place to ensure this code does not get promoted to production and become a big risk for your users.

Here is a small tip on web debugging: The web browsers do have built-in tools to look at the requests and the responses. For example, as shown in Figure 4-15, Internet Explorer has F12 Developer Tools available on the Tools menu. If you want to quickly inspect the request and response, when your client is the web browser you can use a tool like this without having to run Fiddler.

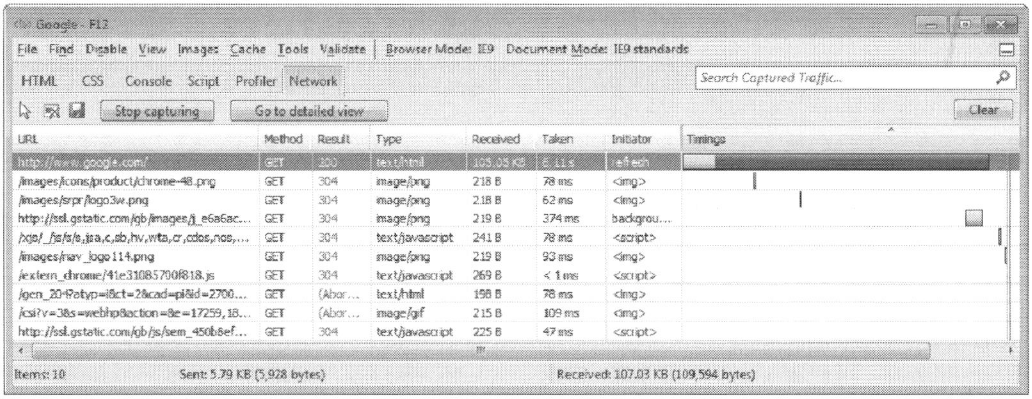

Figure 4-15. *Internet Explorer F12 Developer Tools*

Summary

In this chapter, we looked at the basics of HTTP from the point of view of building a web API that complies with the HTTP specification through ASP.NET Web API. By sticking to the HTTP specification, we ensure that any device or software that is HTTP compliant can use the service.

We also examined some advanced HTTP concepts, such as caching, ETags, and CORS. Caching is preferred for speed but not for security, depending on the data that is cached. ETags, when used with caching, can reduce bandwidth usage. Without caching, ETags can be used for concurrency checking.

CORS is a specification that helps us overcome the constraints imposed by same origin policy. CORS is supported only in modern browsers. There are still dinosaurs left out there in the wild with no CORS support. Use CORS only when absolutely needed.

We then looked at HTTPS or secure HTTP, the transport layer security. Finally, we explored how to use Fiddler, the ultimate tool for HTTP debugging, to capture and decrypt HTTPS traffic.

CHAPTER 5

Identity Management

In this chapter, I cover an important aspect of securing an application: identity management. The term has a broader meaning but our focus is limited to how a subject or an entity gets authenticated and how the actions an entity attempts to perform are authorized by an application in the context of the .NET Framework.

An entity, which can be a human being, an organization, a hardware device, or application software, makes a request to access a resource. A resource can be a web service, a web site, a web page in a web site or even a UI element in a web page, depending on the context of the application. Unless the resource is public and is available to everyone, some kind of access control will be implemented by the application owning the resources. To enforce access control, the entity that is issuing the request must first be identified and authenticated.

Authentication and Authorization

Identity management has two important facets: authentication and authorization.

- Authentication is the process of discovering the identity of an entity through an identifier and verifying the identity through validating the credentials provided by the entity against an authority.
- Authorization is the process of determining whether an identity is allowed to perform a requested action.

An application identifies an entity, or user, through an identifier, or user ID. For example, assume you are a user trying to establish an identity with an application. Suppose you inform the application your identifier is lbadri (which is actually my identifier). At this point, the system can establish an identity for you, based on the identifier you have provided. But to be a trustworthy application, it must validate that you really are who you claim to be. That process is called authentication, which is sometimes abbreviated to AuthN. It is accomplished by accepting a credential (typically a password) and validating it against the password stored against the user ID in the application data store. Hopefully you will not know my password and will not be able to guess it, and thus your attempt to authenticate using my credentials will be failed by the application. This is one of the most fundamental building blocks of the application security.

The user can be authenticated through three types of credentials.

1. Based on what a user knows (knowledge); for example, a password or PIN.
2. Based on what a user owns (ownership); for example, a certificate or USB dongle.
3. Based on what the user is (inherence); for example, a fingerprint or DNA sequence.

It is typical for an application to implement the authentication mechanism based on one of the three factors from the preceding list, the knowledge factor being the most frequently used. An application with higher security needs implements an authentication mechanism based on two factors from the list; this kind of mechanism is called two-factor authentication (TFA or 2FA). An example of TFA is a corporate network that requires the use of a hardware token or a USB dongle along with a password. Another well-known example is an ATM: An ATM requires the debit card that you own and the PIN that you know before it allows you to complete a transaction. It is uncommon to see an application implementing three-factor security, at least in the enterprise landscape.

Once an authenticated identity is established, the application can control the access to the application resources based on this identity. This process is called authorization, which is sometimes abbreviated to AuthZ. An extremely simple and trivial application might authorize resource access purely based on the identity. But most practical applications authorize access based on attributes, such as roles, that are associated with the identity.

Role-Based Security

Role-based security is the most commonly used security model in the business or enterprise applications. The major benefit of using a role-based security model is the ease of security administration. The access rights are not given to an individual user, but to an abstraction called a role. A user gets assigned to one or more roles, through which the user gets access rights.

With this model, the security administration becomes a matter of managing the roles (typically far fewer than users) by assigning and unassigning roles to the users. By assigning an access right to a role, an administrator can assign the same access right to hundreds of users in a single operation. Also, by assigning a user to a role, the user immediately gets all the access rights defined for that role. The same ease of administration is applicable to the unassignment operations as well.

Role-based security has been around for a long time in the .NET Framework, starting with version 1.0. Identity and principal are the two abstractions provided by the .NET Framework for implementing role-based security.

Identity and Principal

In the .NET Framework, an identity object represents the user on whose behalf the code runs. A principal object represents the security context of the user on whose behalf the code runs, including the user's identity and the roles to which that user has been assigned. The `IIdentity` and `IPrincipal` interfaces form the basis of Role-Based Access Control (RBAC) implementation in the .NET Framework. `IIdentity` represents the identity of the user. `IPrincipal` represents the identity and the roles associated with the user. `IPrincipal` has the `Identity` property and the `IsInRole(string)` method that accepts a role and returns true if the principal is a member of the role.

Figure 5-1 shows the `IIdentity and IPrincipal` interfaces.

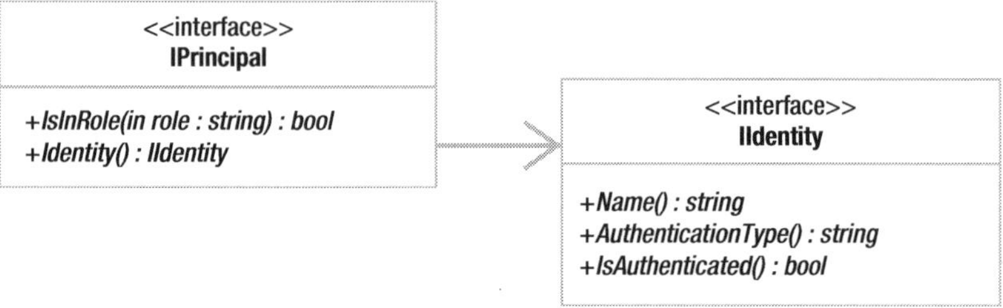

Figure 5-1. *IIdentity and IPrincipal*

Every thread in the .NET Framework has the `CurrentPrincipal` property, which is of type `IPrincipal`. The `CurrentPrincipal` property is more like a key hanger on which to hang the principal object. If there is a key hanger in the house, it is easy to hang the key there so that whoever needs the key can easily locate it.

Typically, the module that is responsible for authentication creates the principal object and hangs the principal on the key hanger, which is `Thread.CurrentPrincipal`. This is typically done in the main thread and any new thread created automatically gets the same principal. The principal object is fundamental to role-based security as implemented by the .NET Framework.

There are two out-of-box implementations available for the identity and principal abstractions in the .NET Framework.

1. `GenericIdentity` and `GenericPrincipal`, for the custom scenarios.
2. `WindowsIdentity` and `WindowsPrincipal`, for Windows authentication-based scenarios.

The `GenericIdentity` and `WindowsIdentity` classes implement the `IIdentity` interface, whereas the `GenericPrincipal` and `WindowsPrincipal` classes implement the `IPrincipal` interface.

Using Generic Identity in a WinForms Application

The `GenericIdentity` and `GenericPrincipal` classes represent a generic user and a generic principal, respectively. Although the .NET Framework allows custom classes to be created implementing the `IIdentity` and `IPrincipal` interfaces, when the application-specific data and behavior are not required to be a part of the identity and principal objects, it is more convenient to use the out-of-the-box generic implementations instead of creating custom classes. I'll now show you how these classes can be used in a simple WinForms application. I've chosen WinForms only to keep the example easy to understand at a glance. The concepts you see here apply to any .NET Framework application.

As shown in Listing 5-1, Program.cs has the `Main` method as the entry point. The `Main` method pops a modal dialog LoginForm, which authenticates and sets `Thread.CurrentPrincipal` for the other application parts to exercise RBAC. The `Main` method requires the user to be in the 'General User' role to show the main screen. `MainForm` is the main screen and it has the delete functionality, which requires the user to be in the 'Admin' role.

Listing 5-1. Program.cs

```
static void Main()
{
    Application.EnableVisualStyles();
    Application.SetCompatibleTextRenderingDefault(false);

    DialogResult result = DialogResult.None;
    using (var loginForm = new LoginForm())
        result = loginForm.ShowDialog();

    if (result == DialogResult.OK)
    {
        // By the time execution comes here, user has been shown the login screen, authentication
        // process completed and principal object created and set in Thread.CurrentPrincipal
        var permission = new PrincipalPermission(null,"General User");
        permission.Demand();

        Application.Run(new MainForm());
    }
}
```

The Login screen has two text boxes, txtUserId and txtPassword, to receive credentials from the user. If you click the Login button, the Login screen authenticates the credentials (I haven't implemented this in the example for brevity), creates a generic principal, and hangs that in the Thread.CurrentPrincipal key hanger for other classes to use. Listing 5-2 shows the LoginForm code.

Listing 5-2. LoginForm.cs

```
public partial class LoginForm : Form
{
    public LoginForm()
    {
        InitializeComponent();
    }

    private void btnLogin_Click(object sender, EventArgs e)
    {
        // Authenticate using this.txtUserId and this.txtPassword

        Thread.CurrentPrincipal = new GenericPrincipal
        (
            new GenericIdentity(this.txtUserId.Text),
            new[] { "General User", "Admin" } // roles hard-coded for the purpose of illustration
        );

        this.DialogResult = DialogResult.OK;
        this.Close();
    }
}
```

MainForm, on load, disables the Delete button if the current principal is not in the 'Admin' role. In addition, the event handler is decorated with the PrincipalPermission attribute that demands the 'Admin' role. The prior step is for the visual clue and the latter step is to make sure the delete code executes only for the 'Admin' role even if some other part of the application calls the method directly. Using the attribute is the declarative way of doing RBAC. The same can also be done in the code, just as how it is done in the Main method, and that is the imperative way of doing RBAC.

Listing 5-3 shows the MainForm code.

Listing 5-3. MainForm.cs

```
public partial class MainForm : Form
{
    public MainForm()
    {
        InitializeComponent();
    }

    private void MainForm_Load(object sender, EventArgs e)
    {
        btnDelete.Enabled = Thread.CurrentPrincipal.IsInRole("Admin");
    }
```

```
    [PrincipalPermission(SecurityAction.Demand, Role="Admin")]
    private void btnDelete_Click(object sender, EventArgs e)
    {
        // Do some important admin stuff here
    }
}
```

In the preceding example, I used a generic principal with a generic identity that gets authenticated on the successful login at the application startup, which is then used by the downstream classes to enforce RBAC. Even if your application has hundreds of forms, access control will be simply a matter of specifying the roles against the actions, as shown in the example declaratively using the `PrincipalPermission` attribute.

Using Windows Identity in a Console Application

Similar to the `GenericIdentity` and `GenericPrincipal` classes, the `WindowsIdentity` and `WindowsPrincipal` classes implement `IIdentity` and `IPrincipal`, respectively, and are part of the .NET Framework library. However, `WindowsIdentity` and `WindowsPrincipal` are specific to Windows authentication.

`WindowsIdentity` represents a Windows user or account and `WindowsPrincipal` allows access control through Windows groups. I use a console application in Listing 5-4 to show these two classes in action.

Listing 5-4. WindowsIdentity and WindowsPrincipal Console App

```
WindowsIdentity id = WindowsIdentity.GetCurrent();
Console.WriteLine(id.Name);
Console.WriteLine(id.User);

foreach (var group in id.Groups)
    Console.WriteLine(group.Value);

foreach (var group in id.Groups.Translate(typeof(NTAccount)))
    Console.WriteLine(group);

WindowsPrincipal principal = new WindowsPrincipal(id);
Console.WriteLine(principal.IsInRole("Builtin\\Users"));
```

The code in Listing 5-4 can run as part of any application: console, WinForms, Windows Service, or even a web application. Ultimately, it executes in a process space created under a Windows account. The static method `WindowsIdentity.GetCurrent()` returns the identity represented by this Windows account. If you have this code running in a console application on a computer to which you have logged in as MyDomain\Myself, then `WindowsIdentity` represents this account. The Name property is just that: MyDomain\Myself.

I use the static method `GetCurrent()` to get the Windows account under which the code currently runs. It is also possible to use the `WindowsIdentity` of some other Windows account, different from the account under which the application runs, by creating an instance of the `WindowsIdentity` class using a Windows account token. The token can be obtained by calling the Win API `LogonUser()` passing the user name, domain, and password.

Listing 5-5 shows how to manually create a `WindowsIdentity` instance.

Listing 5-5. WindowsIdentity Creation Using a Token

```
[DllImport("advapi32.dll", SetLastError = true)]
public static extern bool LogonUser(String lpszUsername, String lpszDomain, String lpszPassword,
    int dwLogonType, int dwLogonProvider, ref IntPtr phToken);
```

```
[DllImport("kernel32.dll", CharSet = CharSet.Auto)]
public extern static bool CloseHandle(IntPtr handle);

static void Main(string[] args)
{
    string userName = "jqhuman";
    string password = "p@ssw0rd!";
    string domain = "Magic";
    IntPtr token = IntPtr.Zero;

    try
    {
        if (LogonUser(userName, domain, password, 3, 0, ref token))
        {
            using (var idBasedonToken = new WindowsIdentity(token))
            {
                // We now have the WindowsIdentity for username here!
            }
        }
    }
    finally
    {
        if (token != IntPtr.Zero)
            CloseHandle(token);
    }
}
```

You can use `WindowsIdentity` in this way to create `WindowsPrincipal`, which can be used for access control. As part of the `LogonUser()` call, the user's credentials are authenticated. In some situations, that is not required. Simply creating a `WindowsPrincipal` instance for RBAC alone is sufficient. For these cases, `WindowsIdentity` supports a constructor that takes in the User Principal Name (UPN), as shown in Listing 5-6.

Listing 5-6. WindowsIdentity Creation Using UPN

```
var idUpn = new WindowsIdentity("Myself@MyDomain.com");
var principalUpn = new WindowsPrincipal(id);
bool isInRole = principalUpn.IsInRole("MyDomain\\SomeGroup");
```

IMPERSONATION

Impersonation is the ability of a thread to execute in a security context that is different from the context of the process that owns the thread. Under the hood, the `WindowsIdentity` constructor that accepts the UPN calls `LsaLogonUser()`, which uses Kerberos S4U. As part of the `LsaLogonUser()` call, no authentication happens. Hence, the token returned by `LsaLogonUser()` will have the impersonation level of 'Identification' as against the level of 'Impersonation' returned by `LogonUser()`. This can be verified by looking at the `ImpersonationLevel` property of the `WindowsIdentity` object created using the token. It is possible to impersonate a user, as shown in Listing 5-7, by using the `WindowsIdentity` object created using the token return by `LoginUser()`.

Listing 5-7. Impersonation

```
Console.WriteLine("Before: " + WindowsIdentity.GetCurrent().Name);

using (WindowsIdentity id = new WindowsIdentity(token)) // LogonUser() token
{
    using (WindowsImpersonationContext impersonatedUser = id.Impersonate())
    {
        // WindowsIdentity.GetCurrent().Name will be that of impersonated identity
        Console.WriteLine("After: " + WindowsIdentity.GetCurrent().Name);

        impersonatedUser.Undo(); // Undo the impersonation, once done
    }
}
```

The Curious Case of Thread.CurrentPrincipal

Typically, the module that is responsible for authentication creates the principal object and hangs the principal on the key hanger, which is `Thread.CurrentPrincipal`. This is typically done in the main thread and any new thread created automatically gets the same principal. The principal object is fundamental to role-based security as implemented by the .NET Framework.

What if you don't use these interfaces or `Thread.CurrentPrincipal` at all and simply use your own custom objects? Although you are reinventing the wheel, that approach can work. However, some of the .NET Framework and third-party components will expect to retrieve the principal object from `Thread.CurrentPrincipal` because that is the standard. As an example, the property User in `ApiController` returns `Thread.CurrentPrincipal`. If your authentication mechanism does not set it, the User property will return the generic dummy principal set by `HttpServer` in the ASP.NET Web API pipeline.

However, setting your principal object in `Thread.CurrentPrincipal` alone is not sufficient, if you web host your ASP.NET Web API. ASP.NET Web API can be web hosted using the IIS/ASP.NET infrastructure or self-hosted on any process such as a Windows service. In either case, you must set the principal in `Thread.CurrentPrincipal`. For web hosting, you must also set the principal in `HttpContext.Current.User`. If you expect to host your code both ways, you must check `HttpContext.Current.User` for `null`, before accessing the User property, because it will be null in the case of self-hosting.

There is another important scenario in ASP.NET Web API related to `Thread.CurrentPrincipal`. It is possible to return `IQueryable<T>` from the ASP.NET Web API action method. If you refer to the identity set in `Thread.CurrentPrincipal` in the query, the principal will not be on the thread anymore when the deferred execution of the query happens, leading to unexpected results. By the time media type formatter runs, where the query is actually executed, the principal set in `Thread.CurrentPrincipal` by a message handler would have been already cleaned up. This behavior could change for the better in the future releases of ASP.NET Web API. One potential workaround, meanwhile, is to retrieve the identity-related information out of `Thread.CurrentPrincipal` and store it locally. For example, you can use the following snippet to retrieve the list of employees based on the reporting manager, who is the authenticated user.

```
public IQueryable<EmployeeDto> GetEmployees()
{
        string manager = User.Identity.Name;
        return context.Employees
                                .Where(e => e.ManagerId == manager)
                                    .Select(e => new EmployeeDto(e));
}
```

Do not use `Thread.CurrentPrincipal` or the User property of `ApiController` that internally returns `Thread.CurrentPrincipal`, in your expression tree directly like this: `Where(e => e.ManagerId == User.Identity.Name)`.

For more information related to `Thread.CurrentPrincipal`, go to Dominick Baier's blog: "Important: Setting the Client Principal in ASP.NET Web API" (`http://leastprivilege.com/2012/06/25/important-setting-the-client-principal-in-asp-net-web-api/`) and "Alternative to Thread.CurrentPrincipal in ASP.NET Web API" (`http://leastprivilege.com/2013/03/11/alternative-to-thread-currentprincipal-in-asp-net-web-api/`).

Claims-Based Security

The identity model covered so far focuses on a user presenting the identifier and the credentials to an application and the application establishing an identity to the user. Based on the credentials presented, if the application is able to authenticate that the user is what he is claiming to be, the identity becomes an authenticated identity. The user is authorized to have access to resources, based on the roles of which the user is part.

Another way to model the security is based on claims. The most fundamental aspect of a claims-based identity is the set of claims. A claim is just a claim—it is a statement that an entity (a user or another application) makes about itself. The following list shows examples of claims.

- This user's name is Badri.
- Badri's e-mail is evelyn.mallory@evilandmalicious.com.
- Badri's age is four and a half.
- Badri can delete users.

Compared to the earlier model in which a user presents the credentials directly to the application, in the claims-based model the user presents only the claims and not the credentials to the application. For a claim to be of any practical value, it must come from an entity the application trusts.

The underpinning of claims-based architecture is trust. If I present a claim that my e-mail is `evelyn.mallory@evilandmalicious.com`, a human being will know right away that my claim is not a valid one. An application does not have the intelligence to make this determination, so it must rely on trust. If I present to an application the claims created by an entity that the application trusts, then the application goes by the trust and accepts the claim. In this case, the application relies on the other entity. This kind of application is known as a relying party (RP) application.

The entity that the RP application relies on is called the issuing authority. The issuing authority issues security tokens (which are different from the Windows tokens covered in the preceding section). I provide more details on security tokens in the last section of this chapter, but for now just imagine a token as a container holding a set of claims together for secure transport.

The endpoint of an issuing authority that accepts requests for tokens and issues the same is called a Security Token Service (STS). When a user requests a token, the issuing authority must make sure the user is what she claims to be. In other words, the issuing authority must authenticate the user based on the credentials. Thus, authentication happens even in claims-based security, but the difference is that the authentication responsibility is delegated to the issuing authority and is no longer with the application.

STS can choose to keep the responsibility of authentication within itself (based on how it is designed) or delegate that to another entity called an identity provider (IdP). The IdP validates the user credentials and communicates the validity of the credentials back to STS. If the credentials are valid, STS issues a token with claims. The user presents the token to the RP application, which validates the token, extracts the claims, establishes the identity based on the claims, and subsequently controls the access based on the claims. Because claims are the foundation for this model, it is known as claims-based security.

Figure 5-2 illustrates the sequence of steps that happen in a claims-based security model.

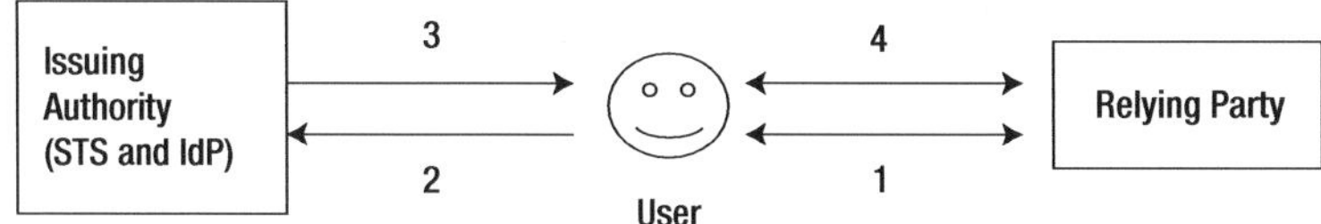

Figure 5-2. *Claims-based security*

1. The user requests an action. The RP asks for a token.
2. The user presents the credentials to the issuing authority that the RP application trusts.
3. The issuing authority issues a signed token with claims, after authenticating the user's credentials.
4. The user presents the token to the RP application. The application validates the token signature, extracts the claims, and—based on the claims—either accepts or denies the request.

Real-World Analogy

Claims-based security is different from the way security is modeled traditionally, but it is more natural because it is very analogous to what we do in the real world.

Take the case of air travel. I book my flight through a web site and check in online. I arrive at the airport, proceed to the boarding counter, and claim that I am the one who is supposed to travel as per the ticket and boarding pass that I have in my hand. The airline agent at the boarding counter has the responsibility to check that I am indeed the person who can travel with that ticket. The agent doesn't verify it himself. Instead he asks for my driver's license, which is issued by the Department of Motor Vehicles (DMV), an entity the airline trusts. The DMV has already authenticated my credentials and issued a license valid until a specific date. I present my license to the airline agent. He accepts it, validates the license for authenticity by ensuring the license is not tampered with, and reviews the license details, all before letting me board.

In this example, the airline is the RP that relies on the DMV, which is the issuing authority. The DMV issues the license, which is the token. The license includes information like my photo, name, and age that represent the claims that the airline or the RP is interested in. In addition, my driver's license contains mechanisms such as a hologram to make sure someone does not tamper with the license information. The hologram is the equivalent of the issuing authority's signature, to ensure that the token cannot be forged.

In the real world, RPs typically trust government agencies. Such agencies issue documents like a driver's license, a state ID, or a passport. There are many other kinds of real-world scenarios that involve RPs, such as restaurants or bars serving alcoholic beverages that are restricted to a certain age group, retail stores selling goods that can be sold only to people above a certain age, or movie theaters screening movies that are not suitable for all.

I've provided the preceding real-world examples to illustrate the main concepts of claims-based security. Of course, the examples do not strictly correspond to the actual process of claims-based security in web-based software applications. For example, in a claims-based security model the security token typically is requested and obtained almost immediately, at the point when the RP application asks for it. In the airline scenario, a person doesn't go to an airline boarding counter, receive a request for an ID, and then jump into his car and drive to the DMV to get his driver's license. Another difference is that a driver's license is issued with a validity period of several years, but no security token has such a long life.

Claims-Based Access Control vs. Role-Based Access Control

The fundamental difference between RBAC and claims-based access control is the criterion necessary to get authorized to perform an action.

- In RBAC, being in a role is the necessary criterion to get authorized.
- In claims-based access control, having a claim with the correct value as expected by the application is the necessary criterion to get authorized.

Take the case of a business requirement that states only store managers can make discounts to the list price of the items sold in the store. If the discounting logic is implemented in a method, say `MakeDiscount()`, then the role-based approach of access control is to check if the user is in a role, say 'StoreManager,' to allow or deny the method call. In the case of the claims-based approach, a call to the method `MakeDiscount` is allowed only if the user presents a valid claim with a type, such as 'canMakeDiscount' and a value of 'true.'

What is the basis for the issuing authority to create a 'canMakeDiscount' claim with a value of 'true'? It can be anything, including the user being in the role of 'StoreManager'! If the claim ultimately is going to depend on the role, what value does claims-based security bring to the table? Well, by adding a level of abstraction over roles, access control checking logic in the application is simplified. Also, the application does not need to change when the access control logic changes. This is similar to the benefit you get for accessing a database from your application through an ODBC driver. Even if the underlying database engine changes, say from Oracle Server to Microsoft SQL Server, your application code will not be impacted by the change.

There are other benefits to gain from implementing a claims-based model. The application is outsourcing authentication and the related modules to the issuing authority. Hence, the application need not provide the mechanisms for account management, such as account and password creation, reset, and other related features. Also, the application can support multiple identity providers (e.g., Windows Live, Google, Yahoo!, and Windows Authentication). The users need not create an account specific to the application and can reuse their existing accounts.

Using Claims-Based Security

Claims are at the very core of the .NET Framework 4.5. The base claim classes such as `Claim`, `ClaimsIdentity`, and `ClaimsPrincipal` are all part of mscorlib. Identity is claims based, by default. `WindowsIdentity` and `GenericIdentity` inherit from `ClaimsIdentity`. The principal objects inherit from `ClaimsPrincipal`. Figure 5-3 illustrates this inheritance in the .NET Framework 4.5.

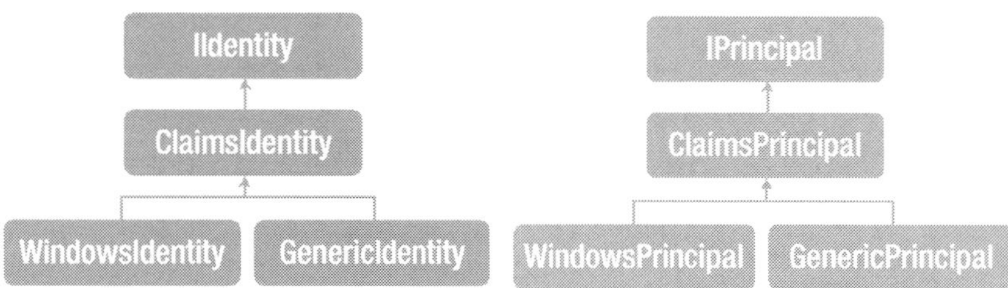

Figure 5-3. *Identity and principal classes in the .NET Framework 4.5*

The classes from Windows Identity Foundation (WIF) are all absorbed into the .NET Framework 4.5. The WIF classes mainly are spread across three assemblies: `System.Security.Claims`, `System.IdentityModel`, and `System.IdentityModel.Services`.

Implementing Role-Based Access Control Using Claims

The changes made to the identity and principal classes in the .NET Framework 4.5 are meant to be backward compatible and work very well with the traditional RBAC, as long as there are role claims available. You can continue to call the `IsInRole()` method even on a principal object that has an underlying `ClaimsIdentity` object. You are free to use `PrincipalPermission` both imperatively and declaratively. In Listing 5-8, I show an example of implementing RBAC using claims-based identity.

Listing 5-8. Claims-Based Identity and RBAC

```
static void Main(string[] args)
{
    var claims = new List<Claim>()
    {
        new Claim(ClaimTypes.Name, "badri"),
        new Claim(ClaimTypes.Email, "badri@nowhere.com"),
        new Claim(ClaimTypes.Role, "StoreManager"),
        new Claim(ClaimTypes.Role, "BackOfficeClerk")
    };

    var id = new ClaimsIdentity(claims, "Dummy"); // Non-empty string is needed as authentication type
    var principal = new ClaimsPrincipal(new[] { id });
    Thread.CurrentPrincipal = principal;

    MakeDiscount(); // Call the method that needs authorization
}

[PrincipalPermission(SecurityAction.Demand, Role = "StoreManager")] // Declarative
private static void MakeDiscount()
{
    new PrincipalPermission(null, "BackOfficeClerk").Demand();      // Imperative
    Console.WriteLine(Thread.CurrentPrincipal.IsInRole("StoreManager"));
    Console.WriteLine("Discount of 10% has been applied");
}
```

In the preceding code, a `ClaimsPrincipal` object is created with claims and not roles and gets set in `Thread.CurrentPrincipal`. Yet RBAC (both declarative and imperative) works and the method outputs True and "Discount of 10% has been applied".

■ **Note** In the .NET Framework 4.5, when you create a new `ClaimsIdentity` you must set the authentication type to a non-empty string with the method you used to authenticate. In Listing 5-8, I use "Dummy". This sets the `IsAuthenticated` property of `ClaimsIdentity` to true. Without this, all access control checks will fail.

Implementing Claims-Based Access Control Using Claims

Claims-based access control allows better separation of authorization rules from the core business logic. When authorization rules need to change, the core business logic remains unaffected. To perform claims-based access control, use the subclass `ClaimsAuthorizationManager` and configure it for use with the application. Then, instead of using `PrincipalPermission`, use `ClaimsPrincipalPermission`. You have the freedom to use it declaratively or imperatively. Listing 5-9 shows how you can modify the same code I showed you in Listing 5-8 to use claims-based access control.

Listing 5-9. Claims-Based Identity and Claims-Based Access Control

```
static void Main(string[] args)
{
    var claims = new List<Claim>()
    {
        new Claim(ClaimTypes.Name, "badri"),
        new Claim(ClaimTypes.Email, "badri@nowhere.com"),
        new Claim(ClaimTypes.Role, "StoreManager"),
        new Claim(ClaimTypes.Role, "BackOfficeClerk")
    };

    var id = new ClaimsIdentity(claims, "Dummy");
    var principal = new ClaimsPrincipal(new[] { id });
    Thread.CurrentPrincipal = principal;

    MakeDiscount(); // Call the method that needs authorization
}

[ClaimsPrincipalPermission(SecurityAction.Demand, Operation = "MakeDiscount", Resource =
"ListPrice")]
private static void MakeDiscount()
{
    Console.WriteLine("Discount of 10% has been applied");
}
```

To use the `ClaimsPrincipalPermission` attribute for claims-based access control, you need to subclass `ClaimsAuthorizationManager` and plug it into the claims pipeline by making a configuration change. Following are the two steps involved.

1. Create a subclass of `ClaimsAuthorizationManager`, as shown in Listing 5-10.

   Listing 5-10. ClaimsAuthorizationManager Subclass

```
public class AuthorizationManager : ClaimsAuthorizationManager
{
    public override bool CheckAccess(AuthorizationContext context)
    {
        string resource = context.Resource.First().Value;
        string action = context.Action.First().Value;
```

```
            if (action == "MakeDiscount" && resource == "ListPrice")
            {
                ClaimsIdentity id = (context.Principal.Identity as ClaimsIdentity);

                if (id.Claims.Any(c => c.Type == ClaimTypes.Role &&
                                                c.Value.Equals("StoreManager")))
                    if (id.Claims.Any(c => c.Type == ClaimTypes.Role &&
                                                c.Value.Equals("BackOfficeClerk")))
                        return true;
            }

            return false;
        }
    }
```

2. Configure it in app.config, as shown in Listing 5-11.

Listing 5-11. App.config

```
<?xml version="1.0" encoding="utf-8" ?>
<configuration>
        <configSections>
            <section name="system.identityModel"
                    type="System.IdentityModel.Configuration.SystemIdentityModelSection,
                    System.IdentityModel, Version=4.0.0.0, Culture=neutral,
                                            PublicKeyToken=B77A5C561934E089"/>
        </configSections>
        <system.identityModel>
            <identityConfiguration>
                <claimsAuthorizationManager
                    type="ClaimsBasedIdentityConsoleApp.AuthorizationManager,
                                                    ClaimsBasedIdentityConsoleApp"/>
            </identityConfiguration>
        </system.identityModel>
</configuration>
```

Subclassing `ClaimsAuthorizationManager` involves one main task: Override the `CheckAccess(AuthorizationContext)` method and provide your implementation to return true if access is allowed or false otherwise. The input parameter is an object of type `AuthorizationContext`. It has all the necessary data for you to make the authorization decision in terms of three properties: `Principal`, `Action`, and `Resource`. `Principal` represents the subject for which the authorization is getting requested. `Action` and `Resource` are a set of claims representing the action that the subject would like to perform and the resource that is to be acted on.

In Listing 5-10, the logic assumes the count of the resource and action claims will be one each. To authorize, it checks if the identity of the principal has two role claims, one for StoreManager and another one for BackOfficeClerk.

With the preceding two steps, claims-based access control is implemented in the console application. Similar to the preceding role-based example, the authorization is purely based on two roles, StoreManager and BackOfficeClerk. The important point to note is, unlike RBAC, which specifies the roles directly in the code that implements business rules, in claims-based access control the authorization rules are moved over to the `ClaimsAuthorizationManager` subclass. The only reference to authorization is the usage of the `ClaimsPrincipalPermission` attribute and the resource name and operation name that are passed in. However, roles can change over the time with new rules coming in from the business users, impacting the code time and again.

As an illustration of how resilient the claims-based model is, let's assume a new rule comes in: The current month must be factored into the authorization logic; that is, no discount is allowed in the months of September through December. To handle that rule change, only two changes are required in the code: Get an additional season claim and check that claim in the `ClaimsAuthorizationManager` subclass. The core business logic does not change at all, as `CheckAccess()` continues to return a true or false.

Implementing Claims-Based ASP.NET Web API

In this section, I show you how to implement a claims-aware ASP.NET Web API. I use the example API I have been using all along, the Employee API. The business rule here is that to delete an employee the user must be in the 'Human Resources Manager' role and must be from the same department and country as the employee who is getting deleted. This rule is comparatively complex, because it depends not only on the user claims but also on the resource claims (the attributes of the employee, which is the resource).

1. As shown in Listing 5-12, create a global message handler and add it to the message handlers collection in WebApiConfig under the App_Start folder. A claim is hard-coded here for illustration. Getting the claims from a token issued by STS is covered in Chapter 7. A claims principal is created using this single hard-coded claim, which is a name claim, and passed to the `Authenticate()` method of `ClaimsAuthenticationManager`. The principal object returned by the `Authenticate()` method is set in `Thread.CurrentPrincipal` and `HttpContext.Current.User`.

   Listing 5-12. Authentication Handler

```
public class AuthHandler : DelegatingHandler
{
    protected override async Task<HttpResponseMessage> SendAsync(
                                HttpRequestMessage request,
                                CancellationToken cancellationToken)
    {
        // Pretend this claim comes from a token minted by an STS
        var claims = new List<Claim>() { new Claim(ClaimTypes.Name,
                                          "jqhuman") }; // User Id of John Q Human

        var id = new ClaimsIdentity(claims, "dummy");
        var principal = new ClaimsPrincipal(new[] { id });

        var config = new IdentityConfiguration();
        var newPrincipal = config.ClaimsAuthenticationManager
                                          .Authenticate(request.RequestUri.ToString(),
                                                                      principal);
        Thread.CurrentPrincipal = newPrincipal;

        if (HttpContext.Current != null)
            HttpContext.Current.User = newPrincipal;

        return await base.SendAsync(request, cancellationToken);

    }
}
```

2. Create a subclass of `ClaimsAuthenticationManager` so that the initial principal object created with the hard-coded claim can be enriched with more local claims. In this example, the claim is hard-coded. However, even if an STS is used it might not have access to the human resources database. So, based on the value of the name claim, get the department, country, and the role and add those as additional claims. Of course, for brevity, values of those three additional claims are hard-coded in Listing 5-13.

Listing 5-13. ClaimsAuthenticationManager

```
public class AuthenticationManager : ClaimsAuthenticationManager
{
    public override ClaimsPrincipal Authenticate(string resourceName,
                                                ClaimsPrincipal incomingPrincipal)
    {
        if (incomingPrincipal == null ||
                String.IsNullOrWhiteSpace(incomingPrincipal.Identity.Name))
            throw new SecurityException("Name claim missing");

        // Go to HR database and get the department to which user is assigned
        // Also, get the role of the user and the country user is based out of
        string department = "Engineering";
        var deptClaim = new Claim("http://badri/claims/department", department);
        var roleClaim = new Claim(ClaimTypes.Role, "Human Resources Manager");
        var countryClaim = new Claim(ClaimTypes.Country, "US");

        ClaimsIdentity identity = (ClaimsIdentity)incomingPrincipal.Identity;
        identity.AddClaim(deptClaim);
        identity.AddClaim(roleClaim);
        identity.AddClaim(countryClaim);

        return incomingPrincipal;
    }
}
```

3. Create a subclass of `ClaimsAuthorizationManager` and implement the authorization rules in the `CheckAccess()` method in Listing 5-14. This is similar to the previous subclass in Listing 5-10, but this code handles multiple resource and action claims. You will need two resource claims in addition to the name claim: the department claim of the resource (read employee) and the country claim of the resource.

Listing 5-14. ClaimsAuthorizationManager

```
public class AuthorizationManager : ClaimsAuthorizationManager
{
    public override bool CheckAccess(AuthorizationContext context)
    {
        var resource = context.Resource;
        var action = context.Action;

        string resourceName = resource.First(c => c.Type == ClaimTypes.Name).Value;
        string actionName = action.First(c => c.Type == ClaimTypes.Name).Value;
```

```
            if (actionName == "Delete" && resourceName == "Employee")
            {
                ClaimsIdentity identity = (context.Principal.Identity as ClaimsIdentity);
                if (!identity.IsAuthenticated)
                       return false;

                var claims = identity.Claims;

                string employeeDepartment = resource.First(c => c.Type ==
                                                        "http://badri/claims/department").Value;
                string employeeCountry = resource.First(c => c.Type == ClaimTypes.Country).Value;

                if (claims.Any(c => c.Type == "http://badri/claims/department" &&
                                                    c.Value.Equals(employeeDepartment)))
                    if (claims.Any(c => c.Type == ClaimTypes.Country &&
                                                    c.Value.Equals(employeeCountry)))
                        if (claims.Any(c => c.Type == ClaimTypes.Role &&
                                                    c.Value.Equals("Human Resources Manager")))
                            return true;
            }
            return false;
        }
    }
```

4. Register the ClaimsAuthenticationManager subclass and the ClaimsAuthorizationManager subclass in web.config, as shown in Listing 5-15.

Listing 5-15. Web.config Entries

```
<configuration>
        <configSections>
        ...
        <section name="system.identityModel"
                 type="System.IdentityModel.Configuration.SystemIdentityModelSection,
                               System.IdentityModel, Version=4.0.0.0, Culture=neutral,
                               PublicKeyToken=B77A5C561934E089"/>
        </configSections>
        ...
        <system.identityModel>
                <identityConfiguration>
                        <claimsAuthenticationManager
                                type="ClaimsBasedWebApi.AuthenticationManager,
                                                                ClaimsBasedWebApi"/>
                        <claimsAuthorizationManager
                                type="ClaimsBasedWebApi.AuthorizationManager,
                                                                ClaimsBasedWebApi"/>
                </identityConfiguration>
        </system.identityModel>
```

5. Implement the ApiController action method, as shown in Listing 5-16. Because the ClaimsAuthorizationManager subclass needs the resource claims to implement the authorization logic, the ClaimsPrincipalPermission attribute cannot be used. Create an instance of AuthorizationContext, attach resource claims to it, and call the CheckAccess() method, explicitly passing the context (done in the extension method defined in the PrincipalHelper class for the IPrincipal type). Unlike the case of using ClaimsPrincipalPermission, flow is controlled through a logical bool check and not by catching a SecurityException.

Listing 5-16. EmployeesController Delete

```
public HttpResponseMessage Delete(int id)
{
    // Based on ID, retrieve employee details and create the list of resource claims
    var employeeClaims = new List<Claim>()
    {
        new Claim(ClaimTypes.Country, "US"),
        new Claim("http://badri/claims/department", "Engineering")
    };

    if (User.CheckAccess("Employee", "Delete", employeeClaims))
    {
        //repository.Remove(id);
        return new HttpResponseMessage(HttpStatusCode.NoContent);
    }
    else
        return new HttpResponseMessage(HttpStatusCode.Unauthorized);
}

public static class PrincipalHelper
{
    public static bool CheckAccess(this IPrincipal principal, string resource, string action,
                                                            IList<Claim> resourceClaims)
    {
        var context = new AuthorizationContext(principal as ClaimsPrincipal,
        resource, action);
        resourceClaims.ToList().ForEach(c => context.Resource.Add(c));

        var config = new IdentityConfiguration();
        return config.ClaimsAuthorizationManager.CheckAccess(context);
    }
}
```

6. To test the security implementation, submit a DELETE request to EmployeesController. You can either use Fiddler to do that or have the /Home/Index view changed to the code shown in Listing 5-17.

Listing 5-17. Index View

```
@section scripts{
    <script type="text/javascript">
        $(document).ready(function () {
            $('#delete').click(function () {
                $.ajax({
                    type: "DELETE",
                    url: "api/employees/12345",
                    success: function (data) {
                        alert('Employee deleted');
                    }
                });
            });
        });
    </script>
}
<div>
        <input id="delete" type="button" value="Delete" />
</div>
```

The important takeaway here is that code-based access control is elegant to write and easier to maintain. Unless the authorization can be enforced purely through being in a role or not, which is unlikely for practical scenarios, the authorization logic lies scattered all around with RBAC.

Security Token

The missing piece in the preceding claims-based ASP.NET Web API implementation is the security token containing the claims issued by an STS. In this section, I cover what a security token is and the different types of tokens at a high level. Tokens and creating a custom STS are covered in depth in the upcoming chapters.

A security token is basically a set of claims. In the .NET Framework 4.5, a claim is represented by the `System.Security.Claims.Claim` class, the properties of which are shown in Listing 5-18.

Listing 5-18. Claim Properties

```
public string Type { get; }
public string Value { get; }
public string ValueType { get; }
public string Issuer { get; }
public string OriginalIssuer { get; }
public ClaimsIdentity Subject { get; internal set; }
public IDictionary<string, string> Properties { get; }
```

- Type property is a string, typically a URI. For example, the name claim type is `http://schemas.xmlsoap.org/ws/2005/05/identity/claims/name`. A claim type can be one of the well-known claim types defined in the `ClaimTypes` class, or it can be a custom URI as defined by the issuing authority. In the preceding examples, the name claim's type is the well-known claim type `ClaimTypes.Name`. The department claim added by `AuthenticationManager` is of custom type. I have used the URL `http://badri/claims/department`.

- `Value` property contains the actual value of the claim such as 'Engineering' for the department claim. It is a string, so even a claim that is a number such as an age will also be a string—"32" instead of 32.
- `ValueType` property, as the name suggests, is the type of the claim value, which will help in deserializing complex types.
- `Subject` property is a `ClaimsIdentity` object that represents the subject of the claim—the entity (typically the user) about which the claim has been issued.
- `Issuer` property has the name of the issuing authority and `OriginalIssuer` has the name of the original issuing authority and holds importance in the case of a claim passing through multiple issuers. `Issuer` is important from the point of view of asserting that the issuing authority that has issued this claim is someone the RP application trusts.

The claims typically come in groups. For a bunch of claims to be sent over the network, they need to be serialized. A security token is a container of a serialized set of claims. To ensure the claims stay secure—that is, not seen by anyone other than the intended or tampered with while in transit—claims get digitally signed and encrypted. Figure 5-4 shows an illustration of a token.

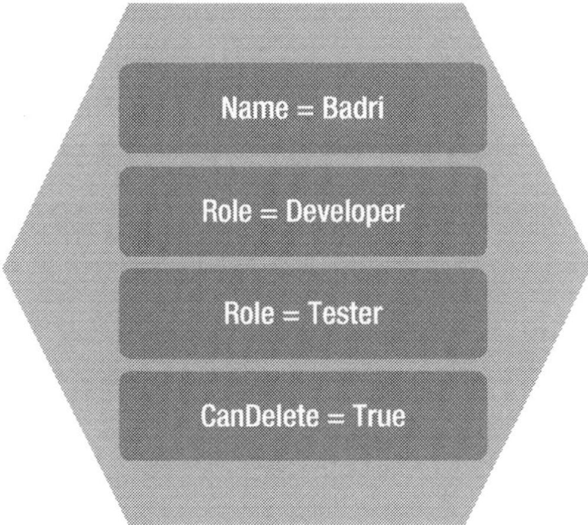

Figure 5-4. *Security token*

Token Formats

There are three standard token formats: Security Assertion Markup Language (SAML), Simple Web Token (SWT), and JSON Web Token (JWT). Table 5-1 shows a comparison of these formats.

Table 5-1. *Token Formats Comparison*

	SAML	SWT	JWT
Representation	XML	HTML Form encoding	JSON
Geared Toward	SOAP	REST	REST
Out-of-the-Box WIF Support	Yes	No	No
Protocols	WS-Trust and WS-Federation	OAuth 2.0	OAuth 2.0
Typical Carrier	HTTP body or URL	HTTP Auth header (Bearer)	HTTP Auth header (Bearer)
Support for Signing	Yes, asymmetric key - X509 certificate	Yes, HMAC SHA-256 using symmetric key	Yes, both symmetric and asymmetric signing
Support for Encryption	Yes	No	Yes

Listing 5-19 shows a sample SAML token containing just one claim, a name claim. The token contains the signature and the public key of the issuing authority as well, for the RP to validate the authenticity of the token.

Listing 5-19. SAML Token

```
<saml:Assertion MajorVersion="1" MinorVersion="1"
                AssertionID="_05d9930e-a4d0-4678-bcc1-7b754223fb71"
                Issuer="PassiveSigninSTS" IssueInstant="2012-10-03T03:58:20.018Z"
                xmlns:saml="urn:oasis:names:tc:SAML:1.0:assertion">
  <saml:Conditions NotBefore="2012-10-03T03:58:20.018Z" NotOnOrAfter="2012-10-03T04:58:20.018Z">
    <saml:AudienceRestrictionCondition>
            <saml:Audience>http://localhost:62177/</saml:Audience>
    </saml:AudienceRestrictionCondition>
  </saml:Conditions>
  <saml:AttributeStatement>
    <saml:Subject>
      <saml:SubjectConfirmation>
        <saml:ConfirmationMethod>
          urn:oasis:names:tc:SAML:1.0:cm:bearer
        </saml:ConfirmationMethod>
      </saml:SubjectConfirmation>
    </saml:Subject>
    <saml:Attribute AttributeName="name" AttributeNamespace="http://schemas.xmlsoap.org/ws/2005/05/
                                                                                identity/claims">
      <saml:AttributeValue>jqhuman</saml:AttributeValue>
    </saml:Attribute>
  </saml:AttributeStatement>
  <ds:Signature xmlns:ds="http://www.w3.org/2000/09/xmldsig#">
    <ds:SignatureValue>G5GXu+D/zPRvTSPRA/Z04WjeD7UK28o...7v4afGo=</ds:SignatureValue>
    <KeyInfo xmlns="http://www.w3.org/2000/09/xmldsig#">
      <X509Data>
          <X509Certificate>MIIBrTCCAVugAwIBAgIQ2eYG/dM...kKjNV6A==</X509Certificate>
      </X509Data>
    </KeyInfo>
  </ds:Signature>
</saml:Assertion>
```

The following sample SWT shows two role claims. Unlike SAML, which is XML, this is just a bunch of key-value pairs that are form encoded. The RP that receives this token can validate the authenticity by comparing the value of the HMACSHA256 key against the one it can generate using the shared key. We look at SWT in depth in Chapter 10.


```
Audience=http%3a%2f%2flocalhost%2fmyservice&ExpiresOn=1255913549&Issuer=https%3a%2f%2fmyservice.
accesscontrol.windows.net%2f&role=Admin%2cUser&&HMACSHA256=sT7Hr9z%2b3t1oDFLpq5GOToVsu6Dyxpq7hHsSAz
nmwnI%3d
```


The following sample JWT is basically JSON. In the sample, the first part is the header, followed by the payload with claims. Although the token is shown in JSON format below for readability, the actual representation of a JWT consists of three parts separated by a period (.). The first part is the base64-encoded header, the second part is the base64-encoded payload, and the third part is the signature, which is the encoded header and the encoded payload signed with the SHA-256 algorithm. We look at JWT in depth in Chapter 10.s


```
{"typ":"JWT", "alg":"HS256"}
{
    "aud":"https://my-server.com/relyingparty", "iss":"https://my-server.acs.windows.net/",
    "nbf":1336067338,
    "exp":1336070938,
    "nameid":"jqhuman", "identityprovider":"idp.com",
    "role": [ "admin", "user" ]
}
```


Summary

Authentication and authorization are the two important aspects of identity management. Authentication is the process of discovering the identity of an entity and verifying the identity through validating the credentials. Authorization is the process of determining whether an identity is allowed to perform a requested action.

Role-based security is the most commonly used security model in business or enterprise applications for access control. Identity and principal are the two abstractions provided by the .NET Framework for implementing role-based security. You can use the `GenericIdentity` and `GenericPrincipal` classes in the .NET Framework 4.5 for custom scenarios. For Windows authentication, you can use the `WindowsIdentity` and `WindowsPrincipal` classes.

Compared to the traditional model in which a user presents the credentials directly to the application, in the claims-based security model the user presents only the claims and not the credentials to the application. The fundamental difference between role-based access control and claims-based access control is that for role-based control a user must be assigned to a role to be authorized to perform an action, whereas for claims-based control a user must have a claim with the correct value, as expected by the application, to be authorized. Claims-based access control is elegant to write and easier to maintain.

Claims are issued to an application by an issuing authority in the form of a security token. A security token basically is a set of claims signed and possibly encrypted for secure transport. There are three types of security tokens: SAML, SWT, and JWT.

CHAPTER 6

Encryption and Signing

Encryption is the process of transforming data in plain text and making it unreadable to all except those who are meant to read the data, with the goal of confidentiality. Signing, or more specifically digital signing, is the process by which a digital signature is created to demonstrate the authenticity and integrity of data. A valid signature gives the recipient the confidence that the data received is indeed from the correct sender and that the data is not tampered with in any way during transit.

For example, let's say I want to send a confidential message exclusively to Alice. I encrypt the message so that only she can decrypt and read the data. Now I want to send a message to Bob. I sign the message because Bob is concerned about the authenticity of data; that is, he wants to be sure the message is from me and not an impostor and that the original message from me is not altered in transit.

Encryption and signing are not mutually exclusive. A message can be both encrypted and digitally signed. For example, let's say I want to send a confidential message to Charlie so that only he can read the message. I also want to ensure that Charlie accepts the message only if it is from me and not an imposter. In this case, I encrypt the message as well as sign it.

If a message is encrypted on one end of the communication channel, it is decrypted on the other end. If a message is signed on one end of the channel, the signature is validated on the other end.

In this chapter, I show you how to manually encrypt and sign data using symmetric and asymmetric keys. I also show you how Windows Identity Foundation (WIF) encrypts and signs tokens, to help you appreciate the cryptographic heavy lifting WIF does for you. If you work outside the realm of WIF, as often is the case with the web tokens used with REST, you need a solid understanding of the concepts of encryption and signing to build a secure ASP.NET Web API.

Cryptography

Cryptography helps secure data in motion. It helps provide secure means of communication by preventing unintended parties from viewing confidential data (encryption/decryption) and providing ways for the intended receiving party to detect if the data has been tampered with in transit (signing/validation). Apart from the confidentiality and integrity aspects, cryptography also helps in the process of authentication and nonrepudiation.

A cryptographic key, which is randomly generated data, is an important input to the cryptographic algorithms in addition to the actual data that the algorithm is trying to secure. Depending on how the key is used, cryptographic algorithms can be divided into two main areas.

1. Symmetric key or secret key cryptography that employs one key, the same key used at both the sending and receiving ends.

2. Asymmetric key or public key cryptography that uses a pair of mathematically linked keys, with one key used at the sending end and the other used at the receiving end.

The defining characteristic of symmetric key cryptography is that the same key is used at both ends, the sender and receiver. A symmetric key is also called a secret key because this mechanism requires the key to be a secret shared by only the sender and the receiver. In the case of symmetric key encryption, the key that is used to encrypt is used to decrypt as well. Similarly, the key that is used to sign is used to validate the message. The symmetric-key-based approach sounds more natural because we use a key to lock a door and use the same key to unlock the door. You can use the `RNGCryptoServiceProvider` class of the .NET Framework to generate keys to be used with symmetric algorithms.

For asymmetric cryptography there are two keys, a public and a private key. The keys are mathematically linked. To encrypt a message, the public key of the receiver is used by the sender. The message thus encrypted can be decrypted only with the private key of the receiver. To sign a message, the private key of the sender is used by the sender. The message thus signed can be validated by the receiver using the public key of the sender. A private key must never be shared, whereas a public key can be shared with anyone.

You can use the `RNGCryptoServiceProvider` class of the .NET Framework to generate the asymmetric keys as well. Also, the public-private key pair from an X.509 digital certificate can be used for this purpose. A certificate is more than a container for the keys. It is issued by a certificate authority (CA) and it ensures the key contained within it belongs to the entity to which the certificate was issued; therefore, it is a means to prove one's identity. This is an important aspect of consideration for the nonrepudiation requirements. To repudiate is to deny. The origin of a message signed with the private key of an X.509 certificate can be traced to the sender's identity, satisfying nonrepudiation requirements. Compared to this, a public-private key pair generated using `RNGCryptoServiceProvider` cannot be used for the purpose of nonrepudiation.

Table 6-1 shows the comparison of symmetric and asymmetric key algorithms.

Table 6-1. *Symmetric vs. Asymmetric Keys*

Factor	Symmetric Key Algorithm	Asymmetric Key Algorithm
Performance	Much faster compared to asymmetric algorithms.	Comparatively slower.
Data volume	Can deal with large amount of data.	Mathematical limitation in terms of the volume of data that can be handled.
Key secrecy	Key must be shared between the sender and the receiver and both parties must safeguard the key, which is generally harder and doubly risky compared to only one party having to keep a secret.	You must rigorously safeguard your private key but can freely distribute the same public key to all your communication partners. The safety of your key is not in others' hands.
Lifetime	In practice, symmetric keys are rotated on a regular basis. There is administrative and operational overhead to replacing the old key with a new one, communicating to the relevant parties about the change, and having the communicating parties adjust to the change.	Asymmetric keys are generally long-lived. There is overhead to maintaining asymmetric keys, but the keys generally are not changed as frequently as symmetric keys.
Susceptibility to brute-forcing	Key size chosen determines the susceptibility, but symmetric keys are comparatively more susceptible.	Range of possible values for an asymmetric key is much larger compared to a symmetric key, so an asymmetric key is less susceptible to brute-force attacks.
Cost	No external agency like a CA is involved and hence there is no cost involved for acquiring keys needed for the algorithms.	Although it is possible to generate the keys, in practice asymmetric algorithms are used with X.509 digital certificates. It does cost money to acquire them from a CA as well as to subsequently renew and manage them.

It is interesting to note that both symmetric and asymmetric keys can be used together, especially when the symmetric key must be generated on the fly at the time communication is initiated. In such a case, one party can generate a symmetric key, encrypt it using an asymmetric key encryption algorithm, and securely share it with the other party. Once shared, further message exchanges can be secured by symmetric key algorithms.

Encrypting a Message Using Symmetric Keys

To illustrate the process of encryption using symmetric keys, let's say I have to send a message that includes my credit card details to Alice, a customer service representative, to make a payment. I don't want anyone but Alice to read the message because it includes sensitive data. To ensure confidentiality, I encrypt the message. However, before Alice and I can start exchanging any encrypted messages, we must agree on two things.

1. The key to be used to encrypt and decrypt a message. Alice and I share the key, and the same key is used to encrypt and decrypt; hence, it is a symmetric key.

2. The encryption algorithm to use. Because we use a symmetric key, a symmetric algorithm must be used. The .NET Framework supports several algorithms out of the box, as shown in Table 6-2.

Table 6-2. *Symmetric Encryption Classes Provided by the .NET Framework*

Class	Description
`RC2CryptoServiceProvider`	RC2 is a block cipher designed by Ron Rivest in the late 1980s. This is a weak cipher and must not be used.
`DESCryptoServiceProvider`	Data Encryption Standard, from the 1970s, with a key size of 56 bits, is also not suitable for today's encryption needs.
`TripleDESCryptoServiceProvider`	As the name indicates, this is DES run three times. Even by today's standards, this is a strong encryption.
`RijndaelManaged`	Rijndael (pronounced rain-dahl) is the algorithm selected by the U.S. National Institute of Standards and Technology (NIST) as the candidate for the Advanced Encryption Standard (AES), the official replacement for DES and eventually Triple DES. The .NET Framework also has an `AesManaged` class, which is essentially the Rijndael algorithm with a block size of 128 bits, and does not allow the feedback modes.

Alice and I decide to use Rijndael with a block size of 128 bits and a key size of 256 bits, the default values of the `RijndaelManaged` class. The following steps show how to implement the encryption.

1. Listing 6-1 shows the code to generate a random key of size 256 bits and an initialization vector (IV) of size 128 bits using `RNGCryptoServiceProvider`. The IV is just a random input with a fixed size, generally the same as the block size. The randomness of the IV allows the same key to be used to encrypt the messages repeatedly, even the messages with sequences of repeating bytes, preventing an attacker from inferring relationships between segments of the encrypted message. For illustration purposes, the code in Listing 6-1 shows the generation of the key and IV. In practice, the shared key is typically generated and shared between the communicating parties out of band and not as part of the message exchange.

Listing 6-1. EncryptionKey Generation

```
using (RijndaelManaged provider = new RijndaelManaged())
{
    byte[] initVector = new byte[provider.BlockSize / 8]; // Converting 128 bits to bytes
    byte[] key = new byte[provider.KeySize / 8];          // Converting 256 bits to bytes

    using (var rngProvider = new RNGCryptoServiceProvider())
    {
        rngProvider.GetBytes(initVector);
        rngProvider.GetBytes(key);
    }

    // Encryption code goes here - See Listing 6-2.
}
```

■ **Caution** The `RNGCryptoServiceProvider class` provided by the .NET Framework implements a cryptographic Random Number Generator (RNG) and is the best fit to generate random keys for cryptography. Never use `System.Random` for this purpose. It could be faster but is not geared for the specialized job of key generation.

---

2. Listing 6-2 shows the code for encrypting my message to Alice. My plain text message of "1234 5678 9012 3456 06/13" contains the credit card number and the expiry date. My message is a string or text. I get the byte array representation of this string by calling `Encoding.UTF8.GetBytes()` and pass the resulting byte array onto the `Transform` method. The input to an encryption or a decryption function is an array of bytes and so is the output.

Listing 6-2. Shared Key or Symmetric Key Encryption

```
// Credit card data that I want to send Alice
string creditCard = "1234 5678 9012 3456 06/13";
byte[] clearBytes = Encoding.UTF8.GetBytes(creditCard);

byte[] foggyBytes = Transform(clearBytes,
                        provider.CreateEncryptor(key, initVector));
```

3. The `Transform` method shown in Listing 6-3 is used for both encryption and decryption. It encrypts or decrypts based on the cryptographic transformation object that is passed in. For encryption, I pass the encryptor object returned by the `CreateEncryptor` method, which is used to create a `CryptoStream` object, the contents of which are returned as a byte array. This is the cipher text or the encrypted message.

Listing 6-3. Transform Method

```
private byte[] Transform(byte[] textBytes, ICryptoTransform transform)
{
    using (var buf = new MemoryStream())
```

```
        {
            using (var stream = new CryptoStream(buf, transform,
                                                        CryptoStreamMode.Write))
            {
                stream.Write(textBytes, 0, textBytes.Length);
                stream.FlushFinalBlock();
                return buf.ToArray();
            }
        }
    }
```

4. Convert the cipher text to a base64-encoded string. This is necessary in scenarios like sending cipher text as part of HTML, such as in a hidden field, a cookie, or in an HTTP header. See Listing 6-4. The cipher text in base64 encoding that gets written to the console is "naoJ1WaoyI8Ra0bviykBT23o5M0iEWhF56ojcJskQ/8=". Of course, this output will not be same as yours, if you run this code, because the key generated in the first step for me will be different from yours.

Listing 6-4. Sending the Cipher Text

```
// This is the string that gets sent to Alice
string encryptedData = Convert.ToBase64String(foggyBytes);
Console.WriteLine(encryptedData);
```

5. Finally, Listing 6-5 shows the code Alice runs to decrypt my message and extract the credit card. Note that the same `Transform` method is used here as well. However, by passing in the decryptor object created by `CreateDecryptor`, I instruct the method to assume the input as cipher text and decrypt to clear text.

Listing 6-5. Shared Key or Symmetric Key Decryption

```
var foggyBytes = Convert.FromBase64String(messageFromBadri);

Console.WriteLine(
    Encoding.UTF8.GetString(
        Transform(foggyBytes, provider.CreateDecryptor(key, initVector))));
```

Signing a Message Using Symmetric Keys

Now that we have seen encryption in action, let's move on to digital signing. The objective of signing is to ensure authenticity (the data received is from someone the receiver believes it is from) and integrity (the data is not tampered with in transit).

Let's say I have to send a message to Bob asking him to meet me in the town square. Bob is concerned about the authenticity of the data. He wants to be sure the message is from me and not an impostor. In this example, I'm not concerned with confidentiality because I'm not sending any confidential data. Sending plain text is acceptable to me.

As with encryption, Bob and I have a shared secret key. The key can be generated just as in the previous section. However, only a key is needed and not an IV, as an IV is a requirement for encryption but not signing. I create a hash-based code using the shared key and send it as my signature.

Hashing is the transformation of a string or textual data into a shorter fixed-length string that represents the original string. I cover hashing in detail in Chapter 15, as a mechanism to secure data in REST. A hash-based message authentication code (HMAC) can be used as a signature, which is the focus of this section.

In cryptography, a message authentication code (MAC) is calculated using a hash function in combination with a secret key. It is used to verify both the data integrity and the authenticity of a message. If I create an HMAC for the message I plan to send to Bob using a key, it results in a hash code. I'll send the message along with this code (my signature) to Bob. On receipt, Bob can also create the HMAC for the message using the key he has, which is of course the same as mine. If the message is not tampered with in transit, the code Bob created and the one I sent will exactly match. Also, because Bob and I share the key the only other person who could have created the same code from the message has to be me. By comparing the code, Bob can ascertain both the authenticity and the integrity of the message. Just like encryption, several hashing algorithms are supported by the .NET Framework to produce an HMAC code (shown in Table 6-3).

Table 6-3. *Classes Provided by the .NET Framework for HMAC Creation*

Class	Description
HMACMD5	Uses the Message Digest Algorithm 5 (MD5) hash function. The output hash is 128 bits in length. The MD5 algorithm was designed by Ron Rivest in the early 1990s and is not a preferred option today.
HMACSHA1	Uses Security Hash Algorithm (SHA1) hash published in 1995. The output hash is 160 bits in length. Although most widely used, this is not a preferred option today.
HMACSHA256, HMACSHA384 and HMACSHA512	Use the functions SHA-256, SHA-384, and SHA-512 of the SHA-2 family. SHA-2 was published in 2001. The output hash lengths are 256, 384, and 512 bits, respectively, as the hash functions' names indicate.

The following steps show how to implement signing and validation.

1. Similar to encryption, the participants (Bob and I) agree on the algorithm to be used and the key. We decide to use the hashing algorithm SHA256. Listing 6-6 shows the code to generate a 32-byte key. As with encryption, the generation code is shown here for illustration purposes. In practice, it is created and shared out of band.

   Listing 6-6. Signing Key Generation

   ```
   using (var provider = new RNGCryptoServiceProvider())
   {
       byte[] secretKeyBytes = new byte[32];
       provider.GetBytes(secretKeyBytes);

       return Convert.ToBase64String(secretKeyBytes);
   }
   ```

2. The message for which I need to create the HMAC signature is "Meet me in the town square." I use the secret key generated in the previous step to create an instance of the `HMACSHA256` class. I convert the text message into a byte array by calling `Encoding.UTF8.GetBytes` and pass that on to the `ComputeHash` method of the `HMACSHA256` object. The result of the method call is the signature, which is a byte array. See Listing 6-7. It prints FI0rhihM5nVisyT6X8TrtifBbbl4xGx6wxm4m9MmdVs=, which is the base64-encoded representation of the signature.

Listing 6-7. Symmetric Key Signing

```
byte[] dataToJoe = Encoding.UTF8.GetBytes("Meet me in the town square");
using (HMACSHA256 hmac = new HMACSHA256(secretKeyBytes))
{
    byte[] signatureBytes = hmac.ComputeHash(dataToJoe);

    string signature = Convert.ToBase64String(signatureBytes);
    Console.WriteLine(signature);
}
```

3. Now that I have the signature, I can send the message “Meet me in the town square” in clear text and the corresponding signature to Bob. Bob knows the message is from me. Thus, he knows the specific secret key to use because we have a common shared key. He uses the key and creates the HMAC256 signature himself, corresponding to the message that I have sent him. If the signature he creates matches the signature that I've sent along with the message, Bob knows that the data has not been tampered with in transit. Because only Bob and I know this shared secret key, he is convinced that the data is from me. Of course, for this to work the shared key must remain a secret between Bob and me.

4. Finally comes the validation. Listing 6-8 shows the code that Bob can use to validate the message and signature.

Listing 6-8. Symmetric Key Signing Verification

```
string signatureOfBadri = "FIOrhihM5nVisyT6X8TrtifBbbl4xGx6wxm4m9MmdVs=";
byte[] dataFromBadri = Encoding.UTF8
                                .GetBytes("Meet me in the town square");

using (HMACSHA256 hmac = new HMACSHA256(secretKeyBytesOfBadri))
{
    byte[] signatureBytes = hmac.ComputeHash(dataFromBadri);
    string computedSignature = Convert.ToBase64String(signatureBytes);

    if (computedSignature.Equals(signatureOfBadri,
                                      StringComparison.Ordinal))
        Console.WriteLine("Authentic");
}
```

■ **Note** Simple Web Token (SWT), which you will see in Chapter 10, uses the same HMAC SHA256 hash that we are using here to ensure authenticity.

Encrypting a Message Using Asymmetric Keys

In this section I show you how to perform encryption and signing through asymmetric keys (a public and a private key pair) from an X.509 certificate. To illustrate the encryption process, I use the earlier scenario where I send credit card data to Alice.

The easiest way to make a certificate is to use a tool like Makecert.exe. It generates the X.509 certificates with a public and private key pair for testing purposes, but this is acceptable for illustration purposes. You can run Makecert.exe from the Visual Studio command prompt under Visual Studio Tools in Visual Studio 2010 or the Developer command prompt for Visual Studio 2012. You must launch the Visual Studio Command Prompt as an administrator for Makecert to work. Once you are ready, you can run the tool with the command-line arguments in Listing 6-9.

Listing 6-9. Certificate Generation Through Makecert

```
makecert.exe -sr LocalMachine -ss My -a sha1 -n CN=Badri -sky exchange -pe
makecert.exe -sr LocalMachine -ss My -a sha1 -n CN=Alice -sky exchange -pe
```

The following steps show how to view the certificates generated by Makecert.exe.

1. Run the Microsoft Management Console by typing mmc in the run box.
2. Select File ➤ Add/Remove snap-in, followed by the Certificates snap-in on the left side under Available snap-ins.
3. Click Add and subsequently select Computer account, local computer to see the certificates on your computer.

Figure 6-1 shows the result after Makecert is run twice. Two certificates, Badri and Alice, are created, and both have private keys. I have opted to use the SHA1 algorithm for these certificates, which is the default option and is better than MD5, the only other option. By specifying "exchange" for the sky switch, as shown in Listing 6-9, I ensure that the certificates can be used for both encryption and signing.

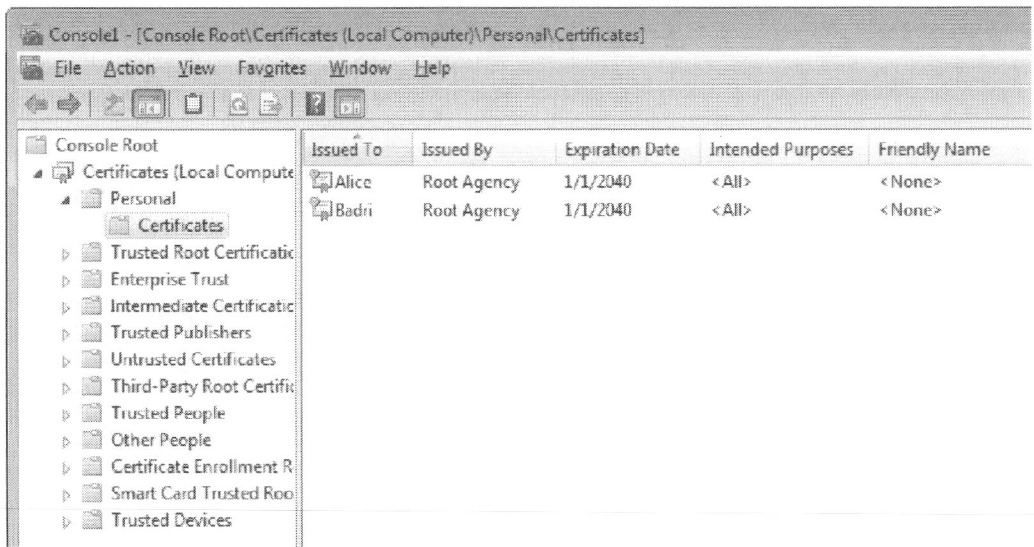

Figure 6-1. *MMC Certificates snap-in*

Now that we've created the necessary certificates, we can encrypt the message containing the credit card data using the new certificate. Because we are going to do asymmetric encryption and decryption, let's use the RSA algorithm, which is the algorithm for public-key cryptography. The class that implements this algorithm in the .NET Framework is `RSACryptoServiceProvider`.

1. The `X509Certificate2` class in the .NET Framework represents an X.509 certificate. I use an extension method to the string to create an X509Certificate2 instance from the subject name (see Listing 6-10). We locate a certificate in the certificate store using the subject name. First create and open an `X509Store` object. Using the `Certificates` collection of the store object, narrow down to the certificate you are looking for, using the subject name. The final result will be an `X509Certificate2` object.

Listing 6-10. Get Certificate

```
static class CertificateHelper
{
    public static X509Certificate2 ToCertificate(
                                this string subjectName,
                                   StoreName name = StoreName.My,
                                      StoreLocation location = StoreLocation.LocalMachine)
    {
        X509Store store = new X509Store(name, location);
        store.Open(OpenFlags.ReadOnly);

        try
        {
            var cert = store.Certificates.OfType<X509Certificate2>()
                        .FirstOrDefault(c => c.SubjectName.Name.Equals(subjectName,
                                                            StringComparison.OrdinalIgnoreCase));

            return (cert != null) ? new X509Certificate2(cert) : null;
        }
        finally
        {
            store.Certificates.OfType<X509Certificate2>().ToList().ForEach(c => c.Reset());
            store.Close();
        }
    }
}
```

2. Let's go ahead and encrypt the data "1234 5678 9012 3456 06/13" just as we did for the symmetric key. I'm encrypting the message to be read by Alice. It is important that I use Alice's public key. Alice could have given her public key to many, but her private key is a secret and only Alice has it. She will use the private key to decrypt my message. By using Alice's public key, I'm making sure only Alice, who has the private key, can read the data and not anyone else. This is the most important part of the asymmetric key encryption: The sender uses the public key of the receiver's certificate to encrypt and the receiver uses the private key of their own certificate to decrypt. See Listing 6-11.

Listing 6-11. Asymmetric Key Encryption

```
string dataToAlice = "1234 5678 9012 3456 06/13";
var cert = "CN=Alice".ToCertificate();
var provider = (RSACryptoServiceProvider)cert.PublicKey.Key; // Note the use of public key

byte[] cipherText = provider
                        .Encrypt(Encoding.UTF8
                            .GetBytes(dataToAlice), true);

Console.WriteLine(Convert.ToBase64String(cipherText));

// What gets sent to Alice is cipherText
```

3. Listing 6-12 shows the code Alice can use to decrypt the message and get the credit card information. Alice uses the private key of her certificate.

Listing 6-12. Asymmetric Key Decryption

```
// Alice receives cipherText here

// Alice decrypts the cipherText using her private key
var cert = "CN=Alice".ToCertificate();
var provider = (RSACryptoServiceProvider)cert.PrivateKey;

Console.WriteLine(
    Encoding.UTF8.GetString(
        provider.Decrypt(cipherText, true)));
```

I generated both certificates on my machine and hence I have the private key of both certificates. However, practically speaking that will not be the case. I'll have both certificates but the certificate with CN=Badri will have a public key as well as the private key. The certificate with CN=Alice will have only the public key. It is the other way around with Alice, as shown in Figure 6-2.

Figure 6-2. *Certificate and key distribution:sender and receiver machines*

■ **Note** In Listing 6-11, I'm encrypting data using Alice's public key and Alice uses her private key to decrypt, which is the typical method. What if I have access to Alice's private key and use the same to encrypt the data? Can Alice now use her public key to decrypt? The answer is no. Regardless of the use of a public or a private key in asymmetric key encryption, only a private key can be used for decryption. However, using a private key for encryption is not the right way. The correct implementation of asymmetric key encryption uses the receiver's public key for encryption at the sender's end and the receiver's private key for decryption at the receiver's end.

It is possible to encrypt and decrypt using asymmetric keys generated by the `RSACryptoServiceProvider` class without employing an X.509 certificate. Unlike the previous section, where we generated two certificates along the exact lines of how they must be used in real life, we will now generate just a key pair to keep things simple. Listing 6-13 shows the code to generate the keys and Listing 6-14 shows the encryption and decryption.

Listing 6-13. RSACryptoServiceProvider Generating Private-Public Key Pair

```
string publicKey = String.Empty;
string privateKey = String.Empty;

using (RSACryptoServiceProvider rsa = new RSACryptoServiceProvider())
{
        publicKey = rsa.ToXmlString(false);
        privateKey = rsa.ToXmlString(true);
}
```

■ **Caution** Keys generated through the `ToXmlString()` method are in plain text XML format, but you should not store these in the file system for security reasons. A key container must be used instead. `System.Security.Cryptography.CspParameters` can help you use the key container to store the keys.

Listing 6-14. Encryption Using the Keys Generated by RSACryptoServiceProvider

```
byte[] encryptedData = null;
byte[] secretData = Encoding.UTF8.GetBytes("1234 5678 9012 3456 06/13");

// Sender's end
using (RSACryptoServiceProvider rsa = new RSACryptoServiceProvider())
{
        rsa.FromXmlString(publicKey); // encrypt using public key
        encryptedData = rsa.Encrypt(secretData, true);
}

// Receiver's end
using (RSACryptoServiceProvider rsa = new RSACryptoServiceProvider())
{
        rsa.FromXmlString(privateKey); // decrypt using private key
        Console.WriteLine(Encoding.UTF8.GetString(rsa.Decrypt(encryptedData, true)));
}
```

Signing a Message Using Asymmetric Keys

Now that we have seen how encryption/decryption is done using asymmetric keys, let's move on to signing. The main difference with respect to key usage is that I sign the data using my private key. The receiver, who in our example is Bob, uses the public key of my certificate to verify the signature. I pass SHA1 while signing the data because that is the algorithm I chose when I created the certificate using Makecert. Listing 6-15 shows the code to sign the message using my private key.

Listing 6-15. Asymmetric Key Signing

```
byte[] dataFromBadri = Encoding.UTF8.GetBytes("Meet me in the town square");
var cert = "CN=Badri".ToCertificate();

var provider = (RSACryptoServiceProvider)cert.PrivateKey; // Note the use of private key here
byte[] signatureOfBadri = provider.SignData(dataFromBadri,
                                                CryptoConfig.MapNameToOID("SHA1"));

Console.WriteLine(Convert.ToBase64String(signatureOfBadri));

// What gets sent to Bob are the data and signature
// dataFromBadri and signatureOfBadri
```

Listing 6-16 shows the code Bob can use to verify the authenticity of the data. Bob knows the data is from me, so he will use the certificate with the subject name of CN=Badri. He will have only the public key for my certificate, and that is what he will use to verify the data and signature.

Listing 6-16. Asymmetric Key Signing Verification

```
// Bob receives my data and signature here
// dataFromBadri and signatureOfBadri

// Bob validates the signature using my public key
var cert = "CN=Badri".ToCertificate();
var provider = (RSACryptoServiceProvider)cert.PublicKey.Key; // Note the use of public key here

if (provider.VerifyData(dataFromBadri,
                            CryptoConfig.MapNameToOID("SHA1"),
                                signatureOfBadri))
    Console.WriteLine("Verified");
```

Here is a quick recap of how the keys were used in our scenario:

- For encryption, I used the public key of the certificate CN=Alice.
- For decryption, Alice used the private key of the certificate CN=Alice.
- For signing, I used the private key of the certificate CN=Badri.
- For validating the signature, Bob used the public key of the certificate CN=Badri.

NONREPUDIATION

Take the scenario of Bob receiving the message from me and validating my signature using the public key of my certificate. This scenario involves only two individuals, but the scenario holds for organizations as well.

If two organizations use the real X.509 certificates issued by a CA (as against the usage of test certificates generated by Makecert), once the receiver validates the message using the public key of the sender's certificate it will not be possible for the sender to deny that the message did not originate from their organization. The message had to have been signed using the private key of the sender, which must have been securely kept by the sender. For this reason, signatures created using X.509 certificates help with nonrepudiation aspects.

It is possible to sign using the asymmetric keys generated by the class RSACryptoServiceProvider (see Listing 6-17). Key generation logic is shown in Listing 6-13 in the preceding section.

Listing 6-17. Signing Using the Keys Generated by RSACryptoServiceProvider

```
byte[] signature = null;
byte[] secretData = Encoding.UTF8.GetBytes("Mum's the word");

// Sender's end
using (RSACryptoServiceProvider rsa = new RSACryptoServiceProvider())
{
        rsa.FromXmlString(privateKey); // sign using private key
        signature = rsa.SignData(secretData, "SHA256");
}

// Receiver's end
using (RSACryptoServiceProvider rsa = new RSACryptoServiceProvider())
{
        rsa.FromXmlString(publicKey);  // validate using public key
        Console.Write(rsa.VerifyData(secretData, "SHA256", signature)); // Outputs True, if
        signature is valid
}
```

Token Encryption and Signing

In this chapter so far, we have been encrypting and signing data just as a precursor to understanding how a token issuer encrypts and signs a security token.

My role in the preceding examples is the same as that of a token issuer, because I encrypt and sign messages before sending them out. Alice and Bob, the cryptographic stereotypes, represent the relying parties because they decrypt and validate messages sent by me. The message exchanged in the preceding examples is analogous to a token that is exchanged between a token issuer and the relying party (RP).

Typically, a token issuer is a Security Token Service (STS) endpoint, as specified by the WS-Trust protocol. It is possible to create our own custom STS by using WIF, which we look at in depth in Chapter 7.

Comparison to Cryptographic Handling in WIF

If you leverage the classes provided by WIF, the nuts and bolts of encryption and signing are taken care for you. All you need to do is specify an encrypting and a signing credential. Figure 6-3 illustrates a scenario that uses X.509 encrypting and signing credentials; in other words, X.509 certificates.

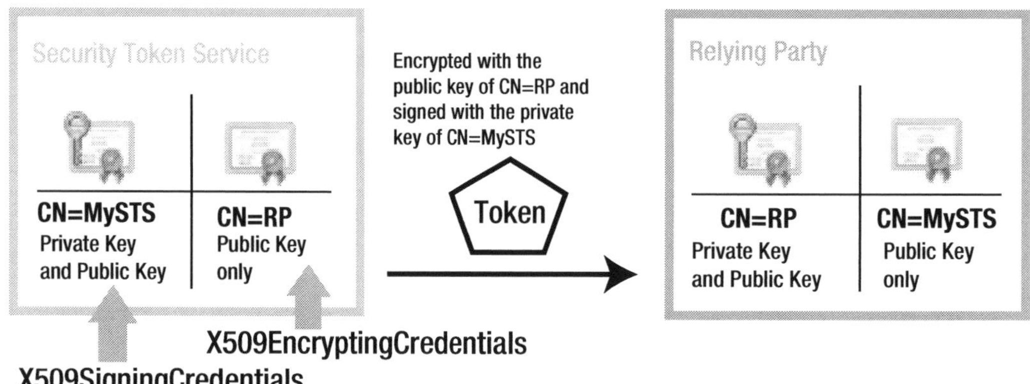

Figure 6-3. *Certificate and key distribution: STS and RP application*

In the next sections I provide a quick overview of how WIF helps us accomplish the same encryption and signing that we have done manually so far. If you are not familiar with the classes and properties in the following sections, don't worry. I cover the creation of a custom STS in detail in Chapter 7. In the scenario of a custom STS implemented through WIF, data is the token that needs to be encrypted and signed. The roles of Alice, Bob, and I are all played by WIF. WIF knows what needs to be done based on where it runs—the sender side or the receiver side. The sender is the STS and the receiver is the RP application.

Token Encryption

STS: WIF uses the RP application's certificate. This is analogous to me using Alice's certificate to encrypt. In practice, there can be more than one relying RP using the same STS. In our previous encryption example, where communication is only between Alice and me, I have no dilemma in choosing the right certificate because the only certificate available to me is that of Alice, in addition to my own. However, in the case of an STS there can be multiple RP applications. So, an STS must be designed to be intelligent enough to pick the right certificate for encryption.

In the `GetScope` method overridden in the STS class, based on the `RequestSecurityToken` object passed in, STS can pick up the certificate corresponding to the RP that has issued the token request and set the certificate in the `EncryptingCredentials` property of the scope. WIF does the rest by encrypting the token using the public key of the certificate assigned into `EncryptingCredentials`.

RP Application: WIF decrypts the token using the private key of the RP application's certificate. This is similar to what Alice did to read the encrypted data I sent her in the scenario earlier in this chapter. WIF picks up the certificate based on the `<serviceCertificate>` element of the `<system.serviceModel>` section of the application's config file, as shown in Listing 6-18.

Listing 6-18. Application Config ServiceCertificate

```
<serviceCertificate>
        <certificateReference x509FindType="FindBySubjectName"
                findValue="RP"
                storeLocation="LocalMachine" storeName="My" />
</serviceCertificate>
```

Token Signing

STS: STS uses its own certificate, just like I used my own certificate when I had to sign the data to be sent to Bob. Unlike the encryption certificate, there is no scope for any confusion here. The certificate to be used is the STS certificate, which is not going to change on a request basis. The certificate to be used is the same for all the requests. Hence it is set in the constructor of SecurityTokenServiceConfiguration.

By the time the GetScope() method is called, the scope object's signing credentials will already be set with the certificate passed into the SecurityTokenServiceConfiguration constructor. WIF jumps in and signs the token with the private key of the STS certificate. This is similar to what I did while signing the data to be sent to Bob.

Relying Party Application: WIF validates the signature using the public key of the STS. WIF picks up the certificate based on <trustedIssuers> in the config file (shown in Listing 6-19) and uses the public key to validate the signature. This is similar to how Bob validated my signature using the public key of my certificate.

Listing 6-19. Web.config Trusted Issuers

```
<issuerNameRegistry type="System.IdentityModel.Tokens.ConfigurationBasedIssuerNameRegistry,
            System.IdentityModel, Version=4.0.0.0, Culture=neutral, PublicKeyToken=b77a5c561934e089">
        <trustedIssuers>
                <add thumbprint="A6155968B7BBB9C35421B19FA9E14D4DCEF3FC5A"

name="http://mysts" />
        </trustedIssuers>
</issuerNameRegistry>
```

Similar to how Alice and I exchanged public keys but kept a private key secret, the STS certificate with the private key will be kept only on the server running the STS and the certificate with only the public key published to the RP applications. Similarly, an RP application keeps its own certificate with the private key secret and publishes only the public key to STS.

Summary

Encryption and signing are two important facets of cryptography. Encryption is the process of transforming data in plain text and making it unreadable to all except those who are meant to read the data, with the goal of confidentiality. Signing or, more specifically, digital signing is the process by which a digital signature is created to demonstrate the authenticity of data to the recipients.

Based on how the keys are used, encryption and signing can be performed using symmetric keys or asymmetric keys. In the former case, the same key is shared between the sender and the receiver. In the case of the latter, there are two mathematically linked keys: a public key and a private key. A private key is kept secret and a public key is shared with all.

If you leverage the classes provided by WIF, the nuts and bolts of encryption and signing of the security tokens are taken care of automatically for you. All you need to do is to specify an encrypting and a signing credential. WIF does the cryptographic heavy lifting by encrypting and signing the tokens on the STS side and decrypting and validating the tokens on the RP application side.

By understanding the underlying concepts of encryption and signing, you can confidently work outside the realm of WIF when needed, such as when dealing with REST-friendly web tokens.

CHAPTER 7

Custom STS through WIF

A Security Token Service (STS) is a web service that issues security tokens. The concept of STS is defined in a web service specification called WS-Trust, which specifies how a security token must be requested and issued. Creating an STS from scratch involves a fair bit of work. Windows Identity Foundation (WIF), a framework from Microsoft, does all the work for you by abstracting away the nuts and bolts of WS-Trust and presenting a nice API surface for you to work on as you build an STS.

In a typical enterprise, the business drivers to build a custom STS are very few, if any. Because STS is a pure security infrastructure, a typical business tends to focus its IT resources on providing IT solutions of business value rather than using those resources to build a production-grade STS.

From a technology standpoint, the mechanisms defined by WS-Trust are SOAP based. The REST world, where ASP.NET Web API lives, cannot relate to these mechanisms. Even so, it is worthwhile to cover the subjects of STS and WS-Trust in this book on ASP.NET Web API. In an enterprise that has invested in an STS-based infrastructure, leveraging the existing investment could come as a technology mandate for the REST-style architectures involving ASP.NET Web API. A good example for such an STS-based infrastructure is Active Directory Federation Services (AD FS) 2.0. AD FS 2.0 is part of Windows Server and is an STS that uses Active Directory as the identity provider. AD FS 2.0 issues Security Assertion Markup Language (SAML) tokens.

In this chapter, I show you how to create a custom STS purely from the perspective of enhancing your understanding of STS and the WS-Trust specification that defines it. Creating a production-grade STS is outside the scope of this book. In Chapter 9, where I cover SAML tokens as ownership factors for security, I use the same custom STS to mint SAML tokens for ASP.NET Web API to consume.

However, if you intend to create a production-grade STS, before you roll your own implementation, review Thinktecture.IdentityServer v2 (`https://github.com/thinktecture/Thinktecture.IdentityServer.v2`). IdentityServer is a lightweight STS built with .NET 4.5, MVC 4, Web API, and WCF. It supports multiple protocols (both WS-Trust, which I cover in this chapter, and OAuth 2.0, which I cover in Chapters 11, 12, and 13). IdentityServer can mint tokens of different formats (SAML 1.1/2.0, JWT) and integrates with ASP.NET membership, roles, and profile out-of-the-box.

Starting with the .NET Framework 4.5, WIF has been fully integrated into the .NET Framework. Hence, the term WIF as used here simply represents the .NET Framework classes related to WS-Trust. The content and code in this book target the .NET Framework 4.5.

WS-Trust

There are a variety of web service specifications built on top of the XML and SOAP standards to address different areas such as security, reliable messaging, and transactions. These specifications are collectively referred to as WS-* (WS-STAR).

WS-Security, one such specification, is an extension to SOAP for securing web services. WS-Security describes how to attach signature and encryption headers as well as security tokens (including X.509 certificates and Kerberos tickets) to SOAP messages for assuring message authenticity, integrity, and confidentiality. WS-Trust, another WS-* specification, defines extensions that build on WS-Security to provide a framework for requesting, issuing, and validating security tokens. The core of this protocol is the STS and the protocol to request a token by means of the request-response message pairs of a Request Security Token (RST) and a Request Security Token Response (RSTR). The format of the security token issued by an STS is typically a SAML token.

Trust Brokering

Direct authentication is a common security pattern in which a client presents its credentials to a service directly. There is a trust relationship between the client and the service. Building a trust relationship between a client and a service is done out of band. For example, before using a service, a user registers with the entity hosting the service and uses the credentials created in this process to authenticate from the client application. Direct authentication is a simple pattern, but when the number of services a client has to interact with increases, the overall process gets really complex. Out-of-band registration has to happen for each service and credentials must be maintained as well.

Brokered authentication, on the other hand, is a pattern that introduces an entity that centralizes authentication. Even if no trust is established between the client and the service, a trust relationship is established between the client and the central authentication broker and the service and the broker.

The STS forms the basis of trust brokering, as stated in the WS-Trust specification. A client trusts the STS. It provides the credentials to STS and gets a token. The relying party application trusts the STS as well. If a client presents a token from the STS it trusts, the relying party application honors the token as long as it is satisfied the token is valid. STS is what makes the brokered authentication possible and is an important piece in the WS-Trust machinery. Figure 7-1 illustrates brokered authentication achieved through STS, as specified by WS-Trust.

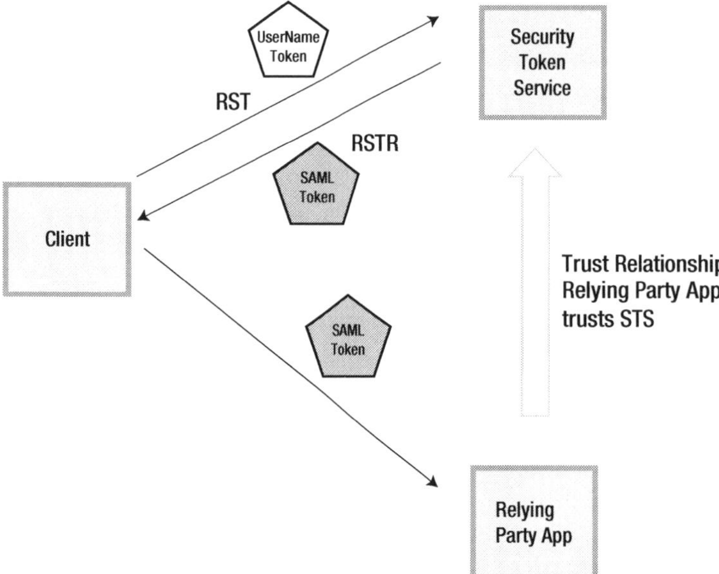

Figure 7-1. *WS-Trust*

The Request-Response Pair of RST and RSTR

WS-Trust specifies a framework for requesting and returning security tokens using RST and RSTR messages. RST provides the means for requesting a security token from an STS. RSTR contains the requested token and other related information. For an RST, there is an RSTR and there are no intermediate steps in trust message exchanges. The RST message body contains exactly one `<RequestSecurityToken>` element and the RSTR message contains exactly one `<RequestSecurityTokenResponse>` element.

Listing 7-1 has a simple RST with some of the elements edited to improve readability. It is XML, as you would expect in any WS-* protocol. The XML namespace of `http://schemas.xmlsoap.org/ws/2005/02/trust` indicates WS-Trust 1.2. The key elements of the RST shown in Listing 7-1 are the following:

1. `<RequestType>`, which in this example is Issue, denoting the request for STS to issue a new token.
2. `<UsernameToken>` containing the user credentials.
3. `<AppliesTo>` indicating the relying party application to which the token needs to be issued.

Listing 7-1. Request for Security Token (RST)

```
<t:RequestSecurityToken
        xmlns:t=http://schemas.xmlsoap.org/ws/2005/02/trust
        xmlns:wsse="http://docs.oasis-open.org/wss/2004/01/oasis-200401-wss-wssecurity-secext-1.0.xsd"
        xmlns:wsu="http://docs.oasis-open.org/wss/2004/01/oasis-200401-wss-wssecurity-utility-1.0.xsd">
        <wsp:AppliesTo xmlns:wsp="http://schemas.xmlsoap.org/ws/2004/09/policy">
                <wsa:EndpointReference xmlns:wsa="http://www.w3.org/2005/08/addressing">
                        <wsa:Address>http://my-server.com/</wsa:Address>
                </wsa:EndpointReference>
        </wsp:AppliesTo>
        <t:Base>
                <wsse:UsernameToken wsu:Id="SecurityToken-369f98c0a-234c-1568-abc1-f96512eb2628">
                        <wsse:Username>jqhuman</wsse:Username>
                        <wsse:Password Type="...#PasswordDigest">AC2jkCf6Tu456bufThXKlF=</wsse:Password>
                        <wsse:Nonce>5kMy6oS6yF98vweJPkeofs==</wsse:Nonce>
                        <wsu:Created>2012-10-10T11:03:10Z</wsu:Created>
                </wsse:UsernameToken>
        </t:Base>
        <t:RequestType>http://schemas.xmlsoap.org/ws/2005/02/trust/Issue</t:RequestType>
</t:RequestSecurityToken>
```

On receiving a request for a security token, STS validates the credentials in the `<UsernameToken>` element and creates a token, which is a SAML token in this case, and sends back an RSTR. Listing 7-2 shows a typical response, edited for brevity. Some of the key elements of RSTR are as follows:

1. `<Lifetime>` element with the token creation timestamp and the time the token will expire.
2. `<RequestedSecurityToken>` element in the response contains the SAML token, which in turn contains the claims and the STS signature. For the sake of readability, the token shown in Listing 7-2 is not encrypted.
3. `<TokenType>` is the type of the token, which is SAML 1.1.
4. `<RequestType>`, which is Issue, the same as the request.
5. `<KeyType>`, which is the symmetric key.
6. `<RequestProofToken>` element containing the proof key, which the client uses to demonstrate to the relying party application that the client is the rightful owner of the token. In other words, it is used to prove to the relying party application that the client directly received the token from the issuing authority and that it did not steal it or find it somewhere! This element warrants a bit more discussion and is covered in depth in the following subsection.

Listing 7-2. Request for Security Token Response (RSTR)

```
<t:RequestSecurityTokenResponse
     xmlns:t="http://schemas.xmlsoap.org/ws/2005/02/trust"
     xmlns:wsu="http://docs.oasis-open.org/wss/2004/01/oasis-200401-wss-wssecurity-utility-1.0.xsd">
     <t:Lifetime>
          <wsu:Created>2012-10-10T09:39:49.400Z</wsu:Created>
          <wsu:Expires>2012-10-10T10:39:49.400Z</wsu:Expires>
     </t:Lifetime>
     <t:RequestedSecurityToken>
          <!-- SAML Token -->
          <saml:Assertion MajorVersion="1" MinorVersion="1"
               xmlns:saml="urn:oasis:names:tc:SAML:1.0:assertion">
               <saml:AttributeStatement>
                    <saml:Subject>
                         <saml:SubjectConfirmation>
                              <saml:ConfirmationMethod>
                                        urn:oasis:names:tc:SAML:1.0:cm:holder-of-key
                              </saml:ConfirmationMethod>
                              <KeyInfo xmlns="http://www.w3.org/2000/09/xmldsig#">
                                   <trust:BinarySecret
                                        xmlns:trust="http://docs.oasis-open.org/ws-sx/ws-trust/200512">
                                        AcNrXK+wW9QOpynB/5uYHprtafX2S2ELbNimapbiygY=
                                   </trust:BinarySecret>
                              </KeyInfo>
                         </saml:SubjectConfirmation>
                    </saml:Subject>
               </saml:AttributeStatement>
               <!-- Rest of SAML Token contents -->
          </saml:Assertion>
     </t:RequestedSecurityToken>
     <t:RequestedProofToken>
          <t:BinarySecret>AcNrXK+wW9QOpynB/5uYHprtafX2S2ELbNimapbiygY=</t:BinarySecret>
     </t:RequestedProofToken>
     <t:TokenType>urn:oasis:names:tc:SAML:1.0:assertion</t:TokenType>
     <t:RequestType>http://schemas.xmlsoap.org/ws/2005/02/trust/Issue</t:RequestType>
     <t:KeyType>http://schemas.xmlsoap.org/ws/2005/02/trust/SymmetricKey</t:KeyType>
</t:RequestSecurityTokenResponse>
```

Proof of Possession

STS issues a token to a client after authenticating its credentials, for the client to present this token to a relying party application. Apart from the aspects of authenticity, integrity, and confidentiality, there is the aspect of ownership. A proof key, or more formally a proof-of-possession key, is used to demonstrate the token ownership.

Ownership is about ensuring the token presented to the relying party application by a client is indeed issued to the client by the STS. In other words, the client presenting the token is the rightful owner of that token. Based on the ownership concern, the tokens can be classified into two categories: bearer tokens and holder-of-key tokens.

A **bearer token** is like cash: finders, keepers. A **holder-of-the-key token** contains cryptographic material for the entity to which it was issued to prove the ownership of the token. This is more like a credit card, with your name and signature.

To demonstrate ownership, I use the same techniques of signing and encryption that I used in Chapter 6; however, in this chapter the way I show you how to use the proof key to accomplish the objective is different and the process is a bit more involved.

When an RST is sent by a client to an STS, one of the elements in the request is the `<KeyType>`. It is not shown in Listing 7-1 to keep the example request simple. Also, it is an optional element. There are three possible values for this element.

1. **Public key:** An asymmetric public key is used as the proof key. The proof key can be from an X.509 certificate or can be an ephemeral RSA public key that is just generated on the fly.
2. **Symmetric key:** A symmetric key is used as the proof key. This is the default option when the key type is not specified in the request.
3. **Bearer:** There is no proof key. A bearer token contains no proof key for the obvious reason that the entity bearing the token is considered the owner and there is no need to prove ownership. A client asks for this token when it does not need to demonstrate proof of possession to the relying party application.

In the case of public and symmetric key types, the SAML token returned by the STS has the subject confirmation type of **holder-of-key**, as shown in bold in Listing 7-2. For the bearer key type, the SAML token has the subject confirmation of bearer. Let us now see how a symmetric proof key is used to establish the token ownership. The following steps show the process of checking the proof of possession of the token.

1. STS, at the time of token creation for an RST with `<KeyType>` of symmetric key, generates a symmetric key as the proof key. It is possible for the client to specify a `<KeySize>` (in bits) in RST indicating the size of the symmetric key that would need to be generated. If not specified, the STS generates a 256-bit symmetric key.
2. STS stuffs the generated key into the SAML token and encrypts the token with the public key of the relying party. Because the private key of the relying party is not available to the client, the proof key inside the SAML is unknown to the client.
3. STS signs the SAML token with its private key.
4. STS includes the proof key in the RSTR in the `<RequestedProofToken>` element, as shown in Listing 7-2 in bold. As you can see, the proof key inside the SAML token and the one in the `<RequestedProofToken>` element are exactly the same. It is very important to understand that the client must not be able to get the key inside the token. For this reason the SAML token requested using the symmetric key type must always be encrypted with the public key of the relying party.
5. The client receives the encrypted and signed SAML token and the `<RequestedProofToken>` element. It creates a new message including the SAML token for the relying party application, signs this message with the key from `<RequestedProofToken>`, and sends it. The proof key is never sent in the message to the relying party. Only the message with the encrypted and signed SAML token and the signature the client has created using the proof key in `<RequestedProofToken>` are sent.
6. The relying party application receives the message and retrieves the SAML token out of the message payload.

7. The relying party application validates the STS signature in the SAML token using the public key of STS. Once satisfied with the integrity and authenticity of the SAML token, it decrypts the token using its own private key because STS has encrypted the token with the corresponding public key. If there are no failures up to this point, the token is deemed authentic. It has not been tampered with by anyone in the middle and the token contents are confidential.
8. The relying party application picks up the proof key from inside the SAML token.
9. The relying party application computes the signature of the message from the client using this proof key retrieved from the SAML token.
10. The signature thus created is compared to the signature sent by the client. If they match, it proves to the relying party application that the client application that presented the token is the owner of the token.

Figure 7-2 illustrates this process of ownership verification.

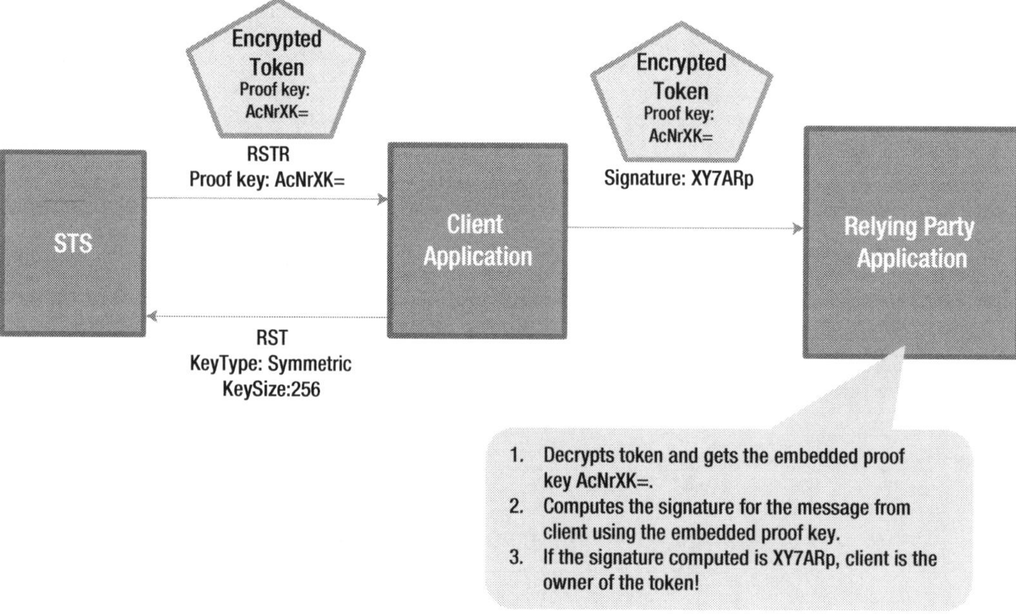

Figure 7-2. *Proof key used for confirming token ownership*

In the case of asymmetric keys, the steps involved are similar to the preceding steps. The main difference, however, is that the proof key used in the case of the asymmetric keys is the public key provided to STS by the client. Only the client has access to the corresponding private key. STS creates the SAML token, embedding the public key instead of the symmetric key that we saw in the preceding scenario, and sends the token in the RSTR. The client creates a message to the relying party with this token and signs it with the private key, whose corresponding public key is the proof token. The relying party application, on receiving the SAML token, can directly validate the client signature using the public key embedded in the SAML token as the proof key. Because the proof key inside the SAML token is a public key, encryption of the SAML token is not mandatory.

WS-FEDERATION

WS-Federation is another WS-* protocol. It extends WS-Trust to support federation of identity across trust domains, typically the organizational boundaries. WS-Federation enables a common model for performing federated identity operations for both web services (SOAP clients) and web applications (browsers). SOAP clients are typically capable of performing the complex cryptographic operations that WS-Trust requires. Such a client is defined as an **active client**, whereas one that is not capable, such as a web browser, is known as a **passive client**.

WS-Federation describes how to use the mechanisms available in HTTP (GET, POST, redirects, query strings, cookies, etc.) for requesting and obtaining tokens, sending them to relying parties, and in general handling sign-in, sign-out, and similar operations from a web browser. This is what WS-Federation is well known for. The term WS-Federation has become associated with the passive case through common usage by developers. In this book, I focus on the active case of a client application using RST and RSTR of WS-Trust to directly request and obtain a token from an STS and present the SAML token thus obtained to the relying party application of ASP.NET Web API.

Building a Custom STS

In this section, I demonstrate how to build a custom STS using the WIF classes. Our STS will be a simple console application. At a high level, building a custom STS entails subclassing the abstract class `System.IdentityModel.SecurityTokenService` provided by WIF and hosting it using `ServiceHost` provided by Windows Communication Foundation (WCF). The following steps show how to build the STS.

1. Create a subclass of `System.IdentityModel.SecurityTokenService`, with a name of `MySecurityTokenService`. In this subclass, you will override the `GetScope()` and `GetOutputClaimsIdentity()` methods for the custom STS to issue tokens (shown in the next steps in detail). To renew, cancel, or validate tokens, appropriate methods must be overridden and implemented. However, we focus only on the token issuance part.

2. As shown in Listing 7-3, use the Makecert tool to generate two X.509 certificates to be used with the custom STS: one for STS and one for the relying party application, named MySTS and RP, respectively.

Listing 7-3. Certificate Generation through Makecert

```
makecert.exe -sr LocalMachine -ss My -a sha1 -n CN=MySTS -sky exchange -pe
makecert.exe -sr LocalMachine -ss My -a sha1 -n CN=RP -sky exchange -pe
```

We saw in Chapter 6 how these two certificates will be used by STS and the relying party application to encrypt/decrypt and sign/validate the token. STS encrypts the token using the public key of CN=RP and signs the token using the private key of CN=MySTS. The RP decrypts the token using the private key of CN=RP and validates the token signature using the public key of CN=MySTS. Because I run the STS, the client, and the relying party application on the same machine, both the certificates CN=MySTS and CN=RP will have the private key on my machine. In a production scenario, a certificate with a private key will be strictly in possession of an entity to which the certificate has been issued.

3. In the MySecurityTokenService class, override the GetScope method, as shown in Listing 7-4. GetScope() returns the configuration for RST, represented by the Scope class. Following are the steps.

Listing 7-4. GetScope Method

```
public class MySecurityTokenService : SecurityTokenService
{
        public MySecurityTokenService(SecurityTokenServiceConfiguration configuration)
                                                                      : base(configuration) { }

        protected override Scope GetScope(ClaimsPrincipal principal, RequestSecurityToken request)
        {
                if (request.AppliesTo == null)
                        throw new InvalidRequestException("Specify RP in AppliesTo");

                if (!request.AppliesTo.Uri.Equals(new Uri("http://my-server.com")))
                {
                        Console.WriteLine("Invalid Relying party Address ");
                        throw new InvalidRequestException("Invalid Relying party Address ");
                }

                var encryptingCredentials = new X509EncryptingCredentials("CN=RP".ToCertificate());

                Scope scope = new Scope(
                                    request.AppliesTo.Uri.AbsoluteUri,
                                       SecurityTokenServiceConfiguration.SigningCredentials,
                                         encryptingCredentials);

                return scope;
        }

        // GetOutputClaimsIdentity goes here
}
```

a. First, I verify AppliesTo against a hard-coded URI of the relying party application. In the case of this example, there is only one relying party and the URI of the same is hard-coded in the check.

b. I create an instance of X509EncryptingCredentials using the certificate CN=RP and set that in the scope. Because we have only one RP, I'm simply creating a new instance. If there are multiple RP applications, based on AppliesTo, I have to pick the right certificate for encrypting the token. Note the usage of the extension method ToCertificate that I created in Chapter 6.

c. I also pass in signing credentials to the Scope constructor, but I take it from the configuration. This credential, which is for signing, is that of the STS itself and does not change for each request. Hence, I take it from the config.

4. In the MySecurityTokenService class, override the GetOutputClaimsIdentity method, as shown in Listing 7-5. GetOutputClaimsIdentity() creates and returns a new ClaimsIdentity. In this case, I use the name claim from the incoming principal and add an additional e-mail claim.

Listing 7-5. GetOutputClaimsIdentity Method

```
protected override ClaimsIdentity GetOutputClaimsIdentity(ClaimsPrincipal principal,
                                                        RequestSecurityToken request, Scope scope)
{
            string userName = principal.Identity.Name;
            string authenticationType = principal.Identity.AuthenticationType;

            var outputIdentity = new ClaimsIdentity(authenticationType);

            Claim nameClaim = new Claim(System.IdentityModel.Claims.ClaimTypes.Name, userName);
            Claim emailClaim = new Claim(ClaimTypes.Email, userName + "@somewhere.com");

            outputIdentity.AddClaim(nameClaim);
            outputIdentity.AddClaim(emailClaim);

            return outputIdentity;
}
```

5. Now, the question you might have is where this incoming principal gets the identity and the name claim. As shown in Listing 7-6, `CustomUsernameTokenHandler`, which is a subclass of `UserNameSecurityTokenHandler`, performs that function of validating the credentials in the incoming `UserNameSecurityToken` and creating an identity corresponding to the credentials. In this example, I simply check that the user name and password are the same for the credentials to be considered authentic. Create a subclass and override the `CanValidateToken` method, also shown in Listing 7-6.

Listing 7-6. CustomUsernameTokenHandler

```
public class CustomUsernameTokenHandler : UserNameSecurityTokenHandler
{
        public override bool CanValidateToken { get { return true; } }

        public override ReadOnlyCollection<ClaimsIdentity> ValidateToken(SecurityToken token)
        {
                UserNameSecurityToken userNameToken = token as UserNameSecurityToken;

                if (!userNameToken.UserName.Equals(userNameToken.Password))
                        throw new SecurityTokenValidationException("Invalid credentials");

                var claim = new Claim(System.IdentityModel.Claims.ClaimTypes.Name,
                                                                        userNameToken.UserName);
                var identity = new ClaimsIdentity(new Claim[] { claim }, "NameToken");

                return new ReadOnlyCollection<ClaimsIdentity>(
                                                                new ClaimsIdentity[]
                                                                {
                                                                        identity
                                                                });
        }
}
```

6. I use WCF `ServiceHost` to host our custom STS. Let us first look at the app.config file (see Listing 7-7). There is nothing special here. It's a configuration any WCF service will have. The key point to note is the service contract implementation. The implementation typically is provided by the developer, but in this example I use the `System.ServiceModel.Security.WSTrustServiceContract` object provided by the .NET Framework 4.5. For the endpoint contract, I use the `IWSTrust12SyncContract` interface provided by the .NET Framework 4.5. Message security is configured to be used with the credential type of the username. For service credentials, the CN=MySTS certificate that was generated was specified.

***Listing** 7-7.* App.config File of the Custom STS Console Application

```
<?xml version="1.0" encoding="utf-8" ?>
<configuration>
  <system.serviceModel>
    <services>
      <service name="System.ServiceModel.Security.WSTrustServiceContract"
              behaviorConfiguration="myStsBehavior">
        <endpoint address=""
                 contract="System.ServiceModel.Security.IWSTrust13SyncContract"
                 binding="ws2007HttpBinding"
                 bindingConfiguration="myStsBinding"/>
      </service>
    </services>
    <bindings>
      <ws2007HttpBinding>
        <binding name="myStsBinding">
          <security mode="Message">
            <message clientCredentialType="UserName"
                    establishSecurityContext="false"
                    negotiateServiceCredential="true"/>
          </security>
        </binding>
      </ws2007HttpBinding>
    </bindings>
    <behaviors>
      <serviceBehaviors>
        <behavior name="myStsBehavior">
          <serviceCredentials>
            <serviceCertificate findValue="CN=MySTS" storeLocation="LocalMachine"
                    storeName="My" x509FindType="FindBySubjectDistinguishedName"/>
          </serviceCredentials>
        </behavior>
      </serviceBehaviors>
    </behaviors>
  </system.serviceModel>
</configuration>
```

7. For the purpose of hosting, I use the WSTrustServiceHost class in the System.ServiceModel.Security namespace. The WSTrustServiceHost constructor expects an instance of SecurityTokenServiceConfiguration. The SecurityTokenService property of the configuration is where the type of our custom STS is set. Just like any self-hosted WCF, once the Open() method of the host instance is called, the service is ready to accept requests. In our case, the RST requests through the IWSTrust12SyncContract endpoint. Listing 7-8 shows the Main method, the entry point of the console application we have been building hosting the STS. The logic of the code in the Main method can be broken down into the following steps.

Listing 7-8. Main Method

```
class Program
{
    static void Main(string[] args)
    {
        SigningCredentials signingCreds = new X509SigningCredentials("CN=MySTS".ToCertificate());

        SecurityTokenServiceConfiguration config =
                      new SecurityTokenServiceConfiguration("http://MySTS", signingCreds);

        config.SecurityTokenHandlers.AddOrReplace(new CustomUsernameTokenHandler());
        config.SecurityTokenService = typeof(MySecurityTokenService);

        // Create the WS-Trust service host with our STS configuration
        var host = new WSTrustServiceHost(config, new Uri("http://localhost:6000/MySTS"));

        try
        {
            host.Open();
            Console.WriteLine("STS is ready to issue tokens... Press ENTER to shutdown");
            Console.ReadLine();
            host.Close();
        }
        finally
        {
            if (host.State != CommunicationState.Faulted)
                host.Close();
            else
                host.Abort();
        }
    }
}
```

a. Create an object of type SecurityTokenServiceConfiguration by passing the signing credentials created using the STS certificate CN=MySTS into the SecurityTokenServiceConfiguration constructor. What is passed gets set as the signing credential in every Scope object returned by the GetScope method of our custom STS.

b. Add the CustomUsernameTokenHandler to the security token handler collection of the config object. Next, set the SecurityTokenService property of the config object to the type of our custom STS. All the individual pieces created thus far are brought together in the Main method.

c. Finally, create a host instance passing this config object and call Open(). STS is now ready to issue tokens!

Figure 7-3 shows the classes that are involved in the creation of the custom STS. MySecurityTokenService and CustomUsernameTokenHandler are the classes we created by subclassing the WIF classes. Other classes are used as is from WIF.

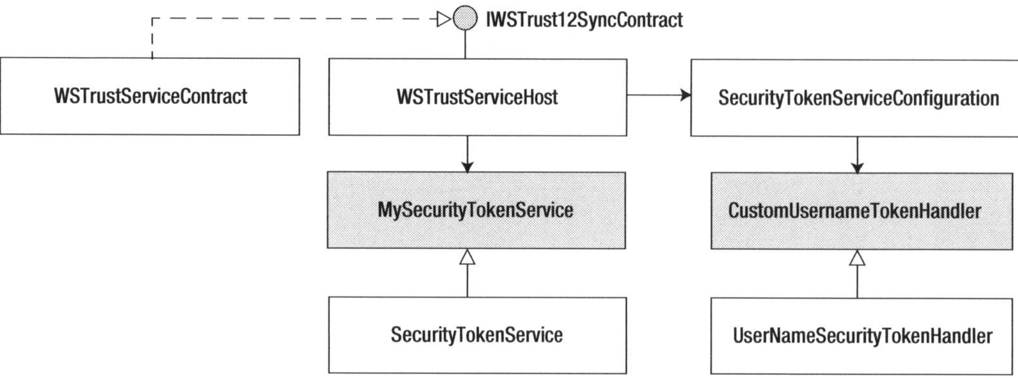

Figure 7-3. *Custom STS classes*

Requesting a Token from a Custom STS

In the soapy world of WCF, an endpoint configured to use ws2007FederationHttpBinding can make use of our custom STS in a seamless way. Almost solely through the configuration and a few supporting classes, a WCF service can send metadata to a client, at the time of client proxy generation, instructing it how to go about getting the token from the STS it trusts. While adding the service reference to this WCF service, the client config file is updated with all the necessary information. But we live in a world outside of that!

Fear not, it is very easy to talk to our STS through some standard C# code and get it to issue a token. The following steps show how to complete this task.

1. Create WS2007HttpBinding with message security. Of course, transport security can be used, but it involves HTTPS and hence more complexity in terms of the setup. I just use message security using user name client credentials, as shown in Listing 7-9.

Listing 7-9. Binding with Message Security

```
private static string GetToken()
{
    var binding = new WS2007HttpBinding(SecurityMode.Message);
```

```
    binding.Security.Message.ClientCredentialType = MessageCredentialType.UserName;
    binding.Security.Message.NegotiateServiceCredential = true;
    binding.Security.Message.EstablishSecurityContext = false;

    // Rest of the code is covered in the following steps

}
```

2. Create an endpoint address with that of STS. Note that I use a certificate generated through Makecert, and I give a name that is not in line with the domain name of the STS address. So, I have to explicitly specify the DNS name to match the subject name of the STS certificate, as shown in Listing 7-10.

Listing 7-10. Endpoint Creation

```
var address = new EndpointAddress(new Uri(@"http://localhost:6000/MySTS"),
                                                    new DnsEndpointIdentity("MySTS"));
```

3. Using the binding and the endpoint address, create a `WSTrustChannelFactory` instance and set the user credentials here, as shown in Listing 7-11.

Listing 7-11. Channel Factory Creation

```
WSTrustChannelFactory factory = new WSTrustChannelFactory(binding, address);
factory.TrustVersion = TrustVersion.WSTrust13;

factory.Credentials.ServiceCertificate
        .Authentication.CertificateValidationMode = X509CertificateValidationMode.None;

factory.Credentials.ServiceCertificate.Authentication.RevocationMode =
X509RevocationMode.NoCheck;
factory.Credentials.UserName.UserName = "jqhuman";
factory.Credentials.UserName.Password = "jqhuman"; // got to be same as user name in our example
```

4. As shown in Listing 7-12, request the factory to create a channel for us and call the `Issue` method on the channel, passing in the RST. That returns our SAML token.

Listing 7-12. Request for Token

```
WSTrustChannel channel = (WSTrustChannel)factory.CreateChannel();

var request = new RequestSecurityToken(System.IdentityModel.Protocols.WSTrust.RequestTypes.Issue)
{
    AppliesTo = new EndpointReference("http://my-server.com")
};

RequestSecurityTokenResponse response = null;
var token = channel.Issue(request, out response) as GenericXmlSecurityToken;

return token.TokenXml.OuterXml;
```

The token thus returned is a SAML token. It is just XML in the form of a string and can be used with any .NET Framework application, including ASP.NET Web API. Unfortunately, the token is all encrypted and hardly pleasing to our eyes, but that is okay. We look at how to extract the claims out of this encrypted blob in Chapter 9, when we use this SAML token with ASP.NET Web API.

■ **Note** It is possible for the client application to retrieve the proof token using code like this: `response.RequestedProofToken.ProtectedKey.GetKeyBytes()`. We use the proof key to validate token ownership in Chapter 9.

Summary

There are a variety of web service specifications built on top of the XML and SOAP standards that are collectively referred to as WS-*. WS-Security, one such specification, is an extension to SOAP for securing web services. WS-Trust, another WS-* specification, defines extensions that are built on WS-Security to provide a framework for requesting, issuing, and validating security tokens. The core of this protocol is the STS and the protocols to request a token by means of the request–response message pairs of RST and RSTR.

Creating an STS from scratch involves a fair bit of work. WIF, a framework from Microsoft, does all the work for you by abstracting away the nuts and bolts of WS-Trust and provides classes for you to help with the creation of STS. There are two main steps in the creation of STS using WIF classes:

1. Create a subclass of `System.IdentityModel.SecurityTokenService`, overriding the `GetScope()` and `GetOutputClaimsIdentity()` methods.
2. Host the STS with the .NET Framework `System.ServiceModel.Security.WSTrustServiceContract` class as the service contract implementation and the interface of `IWSTrust12SyncContract` as the endpoint contract.

I demonstrated STS creation in this chapter to help you understand STS and the WS-Trust specification. I use the STS I created here in Chapter 9, where we look at consuming SAML tokens from ASP.NET Web API. This is the case with organizations that have already invested in an STS-based infrastructure such as AD FS 2.0, where leveraging such an existing infrastructure will be a technology mandate for even the REST-style architectures involving ASP.NET Web API.

CHAPTER 8

Knowledge Factors

In Chapter 5, I covered one of the key and fundamental aspects of security: authentication. Authentication is the process of discovering the identity of a user and verifying the same through validating the user-supplied credentials against an authority. The credential can be a knowledge factor based on what a user knows, such as a password, or an ownership factor based on what a user owns, such as a security token, or an inherence factor based on what the user is, such as fingerprints. The focus of this chapter is on the knowledge factor.

RESTful services, such as the ones created using ASP.NET Web API, have a unique consideration regarding the design of the authentication mechanism. In web applications, authentication happens when a user starts using the application. During the session that is subsequently established, the user is not authenticated again. One of the REST constraints—the statelessness constraint that we saw in Chapter 2—prohibits any client state data on the server. This means authentication needs to happen in every service call for RESTful services.

With the direct authentication pattern, where a client trusts a service and hence presents the credentials directly to the service, the credential such as a password (or a hash based on the password) is sent in every request. In this area, HTTP authentication schemes hold sway. Request for Comments (RFC) 2617, "HTTP Authentication: Basic and Digest Access Authentication," provides the specification for the HTTP's authentication framework, the original **Basic Access Authentication** scheme, and a scheme based on cryptographic hashes referred to as **Digest Access Authentication**. The basic authentication scheme is based on the model that the client must authenticate itself with a user ID and a password. Unlike basic authentication, in digest authentication password verification is done through a digest or a hash created from the password. I cover both basic and digest authentication in depth in this chapter.

In the case of the brokered authentication pattern where a broker such as an STS that we saw in Chapter 7 issues a token to a client application, the token is sent in every request. In this area, the security tokens hold sway. We looked at the three major formats—Security Assertion Markup Language (SAML), Simple Web Token (SWT), and JSON Web Token (JWT)—in Chapter 5. I cover SAML in depth in Chapter 9 and web tokens in Chapter 10. In this chapter, we look at **Windows authentication**, a scheme that uses the Microsoft technology stack of IIS and Internet Explorer to authenticate a user's Windows account credentials against Active Directory (AD) using Kerberos/NTLM protocols.

Basic Authentication

Basic authentication is a part of the HTTP specification. As the name indicates, it is a basic or simple scheme and works as follows.

1. The client asks for a resource in the server.

2. If the resource requires the client to be authenticated, the server sends back a 401 - Unauthorized status code in the response and the response header **WWW-Authenticate: Basic**. This response header can also contain a realm, which is a string that uniquely identifies an area within the server for which the server needs a valid credential to successfully process the request.

3. The client now sends the authorization header **Authorization: Basic YmFkcmk6U2VjcmV0U2F1Y2U=** that contains the credentials. The authorization request header value is just a base64-encoded string of the user ID and password separated by a colon in between and is not encrypted in any way.

4. If the credentials are valid, the server sends back the response and a 200 - OK status code, as illustrated in Figure 8-1.

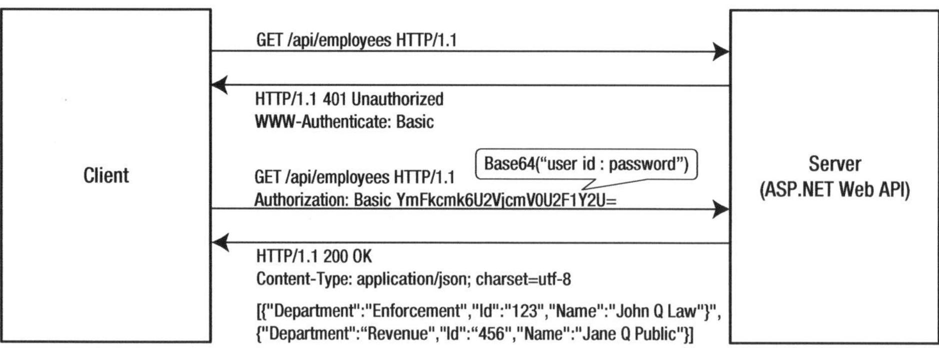

Figure 8-1. *Basic authentication*

Implementing Basic Authentication in ASP.NET Web API

As you start implementing basic authentication, you might wonder where to implement the logic to return the HTTP status codes, response headers, and the actual authentication logic. As we have seen in Chapter 3, there are some options available. Most notably, you can write a filter, which might be a custom authorization filter, or you can write a message handler.

We have also seen in Chapter 3 that filters, in contrast to message handlers, run much later in the ASP.NET Web API pipeline. Because basic authentication establishes identity, it is a good practice to establish identity early in the pipeline so that requests are authenticated and bad or malicious requests get rejected as soon as possible.

A message handler runs for every request and a filter can be used selectively on required action methods. If your web API requires authentication for only a few action methods, then a filter makes more sense. However, in most cases a web API enforces authentication for most, if not all, requests. For these cases, it is better to use a message handler.

In this chapter, I use a message handler to perform the authentication. We authenticate only when the credentials are supplied in the Authorization request header. The output of the authentication process is that `Thread.CurrentPrincipal` is set to a `ClaimsPrincipal` instance with an authenticated `ClaimsIdentity`. We will use the out-of-box `Authorize` filter to decorate the action methods for which we would like to force authentication.

When an action method with the `Authorize` filter is called without setting the Authorization header in the request, the message handler will not set `Thread.CurrentPrincipal` and hence the `Authorize` filter will return a 401 - Unauthorized response. The message handler has to do a little bit of clean up as well, because the filter does not set the WWW-Authenticate response header. So, our message handler has to look for the 401 status and add the response header, indicating the basic scheme to the client. With this design in place, let's start coding the message handler. I show you a template in Listing 8-1.

Listing 8-1. Basic Authentication Message Handler

```
public class AuthenticationHandler : DelegatingHandler
{
    private const string SCHEME = "Basic";

    protected async override Task<HttpResponseMessage> SendAsync(HttpRequestMessage request,
                                                        CancellationToken cancellationToken)
    {
        try
        {
            // Perform request processing here

            var response = await base.SendAsync(request, cancellationToken);

            // Perform response processing here

            return response;
        }
        catch (Exception)
        {
            // Perform error processing here
        }
    }
}
```

We now add code to the three appropriate places in the preceding listing to handle the request, response, and error.

1. **Request processing:** Retrieve the user ID and password from the HTTP Authorization header and perform the authentication, as shown in Listing 8-2. Following are the steps:

   Listing 8-2. Request Processing

```
var headers = request.Headers;

if (headers.Authorization != null && SCHEME.Equals(headers.Authorization.Scheme))
{
        Encoding encoding = Encoding.GetEncoding("iso-8859-1");

        string credentials = encoding.GetString(Convert.FromBase64String(
                                                headers.Authorization.Parameter));
        string[] parts = credentials.Split(':');
        string userId = parts[0].Trim();
        string password = parts[1].Trim();

        // TODO - Do authentication of userId and password against your credentials store here
        if (true)
        {
                var claims = new List<Claim>
                {
                        new Claim(ClaimTypes.Name, userId),
                        new Claim(ClaimTypes.AuthenticationMethod, AuthenticationMethods.Password)
                };
```

```
                var principal = new ClaimsPrincipal(
                                    new[] { new ClaimsIdentity(claims, SCHEME) });

                Thread.CurrentPrincipal = principal;

                if (HttpContext.Current != null)
                    HttpContext.Current.User = principal;
        }
}
```

a. Get the payload of the HTTP Authorization request header, if the header is present.

b. Split the payload by semicolon and take the trimmed first part as the user ID and the trimmed second part as the password.

c. Perform the actual authentication. I skip this part in Listing 8-2 for the sake of brevity. Here is where you will authenticate the credentials against an authority such as a membership store.

d. Gather the claims, create a principal, and set it in `Thread.CurrentPrincipal`. If you web-host, you must also set the principal in `HttpContext.Current.User`.

2. **Response processing:** Check if the HTTP status code is 401 Unauthorized; if so, add the corresponding WWW-Authenticate header, as shown in Listing 8-3. Per the HTTP specification, when a 401 status code is sent back to the client, the response must include the WWW-Authenticate header specifying the schemes the server supports for the client to authenticate itself. We accomplish the same as part of this step.

Listing 8-3. Response Processing

```
if (response.StatusCode == HttpStatusCode.Unauthorized)
{
        response.Headers.WwwAuthenticate.Add(
                                    new AuthenticationHeaderValue(SCHEME));
}
```

3. **Error processing:** If there is any exception in the message handler flow, set the status code to 401 Unauthorized and set the WWW-Authenticate header, just as in the previous step, and return the response short-circuiting the pipeline. See Listing 8-4.

Listing 8-4. Error Processing

```
var response = request.CreateResponse(HttpStatusCode.Unauthorized);
response.Headers.WwwAuthenticate.Add(new AuthenticationHeaderValue(SCHEME));

return response;
```

■ **Note** Using `ClaimsIdentity` is not mandatory to implement basic authentication, but it is highly recommended from a cleaner design point of view. Using `ClaimsAuthenticationManager` to add additional claims and using `ClaimsAuthorizationManager` for access control are covered in Chapter 5.

The preceding code is a great example for illustrating the power of message handlers. The HTTP status code can be set to 401 Unauthorized by any component in the pipeline, including the Authorize filter. By registering AuthenticationHandler as the first handler to execute after HttpServer, we get the opportunity to inspect the response as late as possible and add the necessary WWW-Authenticate header(s).

To demonstrate the capability of a message handler to completely stop the pipeline processing, you can discard whatever response has been created thus far and send a new response. I'm catching the exception and starting a new response with the 401 Unauthorized status code. Of course, I set the WWW-Authenticate response header here as well, to comply with the HTTP specification. Starting a new response need not happen only inside the catch block. It can be done any time while processing the request or the response, depending on the need.

Finally, AuthenticationHandler has to be registered in the WebApiConfig file under the App_Start folder, as shown in Listing 8-5. The handler is registered as an all-route handler, which makes more sense for a handler that deals with authentication because authentication is typically a common aspect for all the routes.

Listing 8-5. Delegating Handler Registration

```
public static class WebApiConfig
{
    public static void Register(HttpConfiguration config)
    {
        config.Routes.MapHttpRoute(
            name: "DefaultApi",
            routeTemplate: "api/{controller}/{id}",
            defaults: new { id = RouteParameter.Optional }
        );

        config.MessageHandlers.Add(new AuthenticationHandler());
    }
}
```

■ **Caution** It is important to understand the sequence in which delegating handlers run in your application. The sequence is based on how you configure the handlers in Global.asax.cs. It is typical for the handler that deals with authentication to run immediately after HttpServer, because this is where identity is established. Hence, this handler must be the first handler, even if you have to register multiple handlers in your application.

With this, we now have the infrastructure in place to mandate that only authenticated users can make specific requests. Of course, if the need is to enforce authenticated users for all requests, it can be easily done in the handler itself.

Because we decided to enforce selectively, we will use the out-of-the-box Authorize filter, as shown in Listing 8-6. We use the filter without specifying any roles. Thus, it will make sure only that the identity is an authenticated identity. The Authorize filter can be at the controller level as well. Another point to note is that it is possible to subclass the Authorize filter and add more functionality, as covered in Chapter 3.

Listing 8-6. Authorize Filter

```
public class EmployeesController : ApiController
{
    [Authorize]
    public Employee Get(int id)
```

```
    {
        return new Employee()
        {
            Id = id,
            Name = "John Q Human"
        };
    }

    [Authorize]
    public Employee Post(Employee human)
    {
        human.Id = 12345;
        return human;
    }
}
```

Testing Basic Authentication

We can write a simple C# program to test an ASP.NET Web API implementing basic authentication. We just need to prepare a base64-encoded string of user ID and password separated by a colon and put in the Authorize request header before making the request to the web API, as shown in Listing 8-7. We use `System.Net.Http.HttpClient` in this example.

Listing 8-7. Testing Basic Authentication Through a C# Client

```
class Program
{
    static void Main(string[] args)
    {
        // Testing Basic Authentication
        using (HttpClient client = new HttpClient())
        {
            string creds = String.Format("{0}:{1}", "badri", "badri");
            byte[] bytes = Encoding.ASCII.GetBytes(creds);
            var header = new AuthenticationHeaderValue("Basic", Convert.ToBase64String(bytes));
            client.DefaultRequestHeaders.Authorization = header;

            var postData = new List<KeyValuePair<string, string>>();
            postData.Add(new KeyValuePair<string, string>("Name", "John Q Human"));

            HttpContent content = new FormUrlEncodedContent(postData);

            string response = String.Empty;
            var responseMessage = client.PostAsync("http://localhost:29724/api/employees/12345", content)
                                    .Result;

            if(responseMessage.IsSuccessStatusCode)
                response = responseMessage.Content.ReadAsStringAsync().Result;
        }
    }
}
```

I'm passing the user credentials in that listing. If you know beforehand that the service supports basic authentication, the credentials can be passed proactively. Or the credentials can be sent to the service reactively, based on the supported schemes specified in the WWW-Authenticate header in the 401 Unauthorized response. Because basic authentication is an HTTP standard, the web browsers know how to package the Authorize header and put it in the request on receipt of 401 Unauthorized. When a browser such as Internet Explorer makes a request to our web API, it first gets a 401 response with WWW-Authenticate: Basic header.

Nobody knows HTTP better than a web browser! The web browser now knows that it has to send the credentials in the HTTP request header using the basic authentication scheme. First, the web browser pops up a dialog box, as shown in Figure 8-2.

Figure 8-2. *Browser dialog box for basic authentication*

Next, the web browser gets the credentials, packages the same in the correct format, and sends it to the web API. Because I don't use HTTPS in my example, the web browser warns that the user name and password are about to be sent in an insecure manner.

The WWW-Authenticate header does not contain a realm and Internet Explorer is showing null in its place. If I press ahead and enter the credentials and click OK, it submits the credentials and our message handler gets the credentials in the format expected. Without writing a single line of code, we can use the browser as the test harness.

Merits and Demerits of Basic Authentication

The biggest advantage of basic authentication is its simplicity. It is probably the easiest, most lightweight way to secure ASP.NET Web API. It requires nothing special. There is no need for hashing, encryption, or anything complex. Basic authentication requires just the base64-encoded value to be put into the standard HTTP request header.

Another advantage of basic authentication is that it is a standard HTTP scheme. The HTTP standard goes a long way in reaching out to devices and clients in any kind of platform you can imagine.

On the flip side, it is too simple for most of the production scenarios. First and foremost, it will require transport security to make sure the credentials transported are not exposed to those with malicious intentions. This means the client consuming the service must be capable of communicating using HTTPS. Although complexity in the message is reduced with this scheme, complexity in the transport is increased.

Fortunately, HTTPS is a standard. Clients that are capable of dealing with complexity in the transport through some underlying helping mechanism, but are not capable of dealing with cryptographic things like hashing, encrypting, and signing can themselves leverage this scheme.

The greatest disadvantage of basic authentication is that the credentials are cached by the browser until you close the browser. If you make a request to a URI for which you are already authenticated, the browser sends the credentials in the Authorize header, making it susceptible to cross-site request forgery (CSRF) attacks. Read the CSRF section of Chapter 15 for more details.

■ **Caution** Do not use basic authentication without SSL/TLS. HTTPS is a must for this scheme, without which anyone can sniff the traffic and get the credentials.

Digest Authentication

Digest authentication is part of the HTTP specification, just like basic authentication. Unlike basic authentication, digest authentication is comparatively safer to use with plain HTTP. One important point to note about digest authentication is that the actual password is not sent to the server. Only an MD5 hash or a digest is sent.

Technology choice is all about trade-offs. There is no such thing as a free lunch! Digest authentication shifts the transport complexity to the message. Unlike basic authentication, digest authentication is more complex and needs support from the client as well as the human end users to make the scheme work efficiently. The client needs to increment a nonce counter for every request to prevent replay attacks. That means the client needs to be tracking the requests made. Also, the client needs to have the capability to create MD5 hashes. Finally, the whole scheme's effectiveness banks on the strength of the password chosen by the human user.

The Nuts and Bolts

Digest authentication is slightly complicated. In the following steps, I show you the digest authentication process. This will prepare you for the details you need to understand to implement digest authentication, which can be quite overwhelming for most of us!

1. Server responds with a 401 Unauthorized response on finding that the credentials are invalid or missing, as shown in Listing 8-8.

   Listing 8-8. Unauthorized Response

   ```
   HTTP/1.1 401 Unauthorized
   WWW-Authenticate: Digest realm="RealmOfBadri",
                                    nonce="dcd98b7102dd2f0e8b11d0f600bfb0c093", qop="auth"
   ```

2. In the WWW-Authenticate header, the server indicates the scheme involved, which is the digest scheme, and sends a randomly generated number called a nonce. A nonce is a number used once. It is not exactly use and throw. The same nonce gets passed along in subsequent requests until the nonce expires. At that time, the server sends back a 401 response along with a fresh nonce. The expiration time for a nonce is set to prevent replay attacks. However, there is a possibility that a malicious user could obtain and send the nonce within the expiration time. For example, if the expiration time is one minute, a malicious user could send the nonce within that minute and the server will accept the nonce. Fortunately, there are other mechanisms in place to prevent those attacks. The main point is that a nonce with a definite lifetime is better than a nonce that is valid forever. For the purposes of this example, assume the nonce is **dcd98b7102dd2f0e8b11d0f600bfb0c093**.

3. The other parameter sent in addition to the nonce is a Quality of Protection (QOP) value. I have mentioned previously that a hash or a digest is sent to the server. QOP is basically the recipe for cooking the hash. It determines how other parameters are combined and hashed to get the final digest value. I limit the discussion to "**auth**", which denotes authentication only. The other value is "**auth-int**", denoting authentication with integrity protection.

4. With a QOP value of "auth", a client nonce **cnonce** and a client nonce counter **nc** comes into the picture. Just like the server nonce, which is sent by the server to the client, the cnonce is a nonce generated by the client and sent to the server. The nc is the counter that typically starts off with 00000001. The next request from the same client will have the same server nonce and client nonce, but now the nc will be 00000002. It need not always increment by 1, but it has to be greater than the previous nc.

5. The client, on receiving the WWW-Authenticate header, knows based on the QOP value how it must create the hash. Because it is "auth" in our case, it generates a cnonce, say **0a4f113b**. For the first time, it uses an nc of **00000001**. The hash is computed through the following steps, for QOP of "auth". The hash values in this illustration are all truncated for brevity.

    a. Compute the MD5 hash of `username:realm:password`. Example: MD5 hash of the string `jqhuman:RealmOfBadri:abracadabra`. Let's call it HA1 and say it is **aa71f01f351**.

    b. Compute the MD5 hash of `method:uri`. Example: MD5 hash of the string `GET:/api/employees`. Let's call it HA2 and say it is **939e7552ac**.

    c. Compute the MD5 hash of `HA1:nonce:nc:cnonce:qop:HA2`. Say, a hash of `aa71f01f351:dcd98b7102dd2f0e8b11d0f600bfb0c093:0a4f113b:auth:939e7552ac` is **6629fae49393a05397450978507c4ef1**.

6. The final MD5 hash or the digest calculated in Step 5c is sent by the client in the response field of the authorization header, as shown in Listing 8-9.

Listing 8-9. Digest Header

```
Authorization: Digest username="jqhuman", realm="RealmOfBadri",
nonce="dcd98b7102dd2f0e8b11d0f600bfb0c093", uri="/api/employees", qop=auth,
nc=00000001, cnonce="0a4f113b", response="6629fae49393a05397450978507c4ef1"
```

7. The server receives all these values and gets the user name from the request header value. It pulls up the password for this user name from the credentials store. The server then proceeds to cook up the MD5 digest by itself, exactly along the same lines of how the client created it, using the same exact ingredients or the values through the same exact well-known recipe. If the client has put in the right password or, in other words, used the authentic credentials, the digest cooked up and sent by the client must exactly match the digest the server has just cooked up. If the incoming digest and generated digest are the same, the user is deemed an authentic user. That is the essence of digest authentication, as illustrated in Figure 8-3.

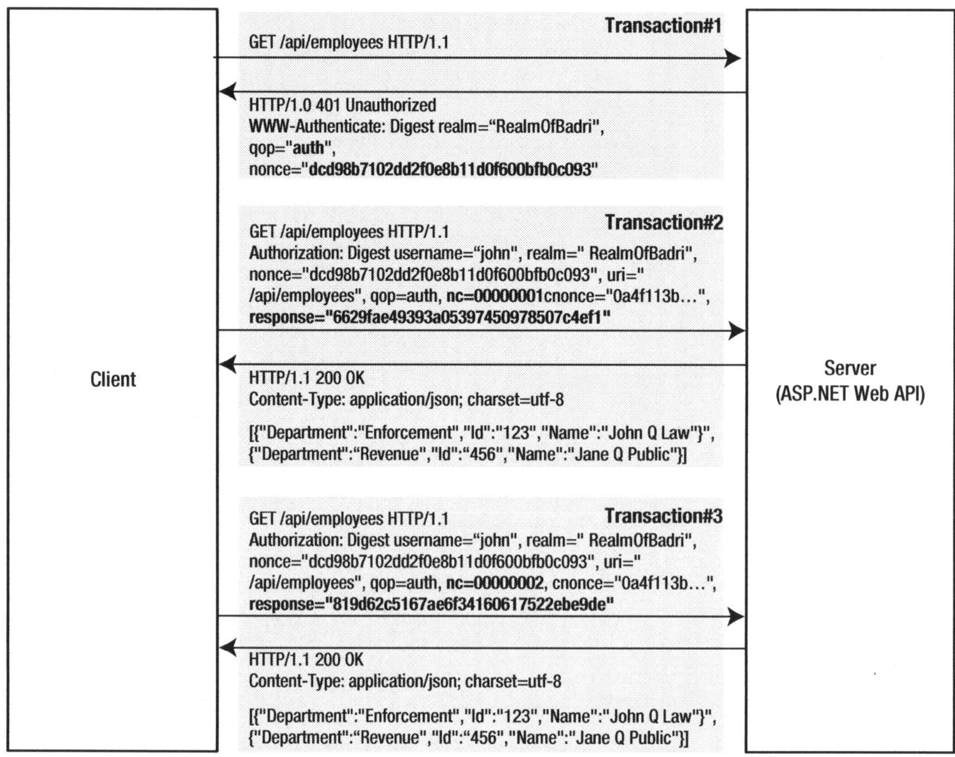

Figure 8-3. *Digest authentication*

▒ **Caution** Basic authentication absolutely needs transport security. Digest authentication does not need transport security—mostly! Here is a word of caution. Although the password is not sent at all, with only a digest being sent, the user name does get sent as plain text in the request header, as you can see in Listing 8-9. For the scenarios where a malicious user knowing the user name is half the battle lost or worse, digest authentication over plain HTTP might not be appropriate.

Security Defenses

Digest authentication is designed to survive in the open wilderness without HTTPS protection. For this reason, digest authentication protected services operating on HTTP are good targets for man-in-the-middle (MITM) attacks. MITM is a form of active eavesdropping in which the attacker holds two independent connections with the victims and relays messages between them, making them believe they are talking directly to each other. The attacker in such a case can pass the message from one victim to another as is, tamper with it to his liking, or completely replace the original message with his own and completely control the exchange of messages.

To counteract the MITM threat, several checks are built into the digest authentication scheme. On receiving the authorization header shown in Listing 8-9, the server runs through the following checks.

1. The first and the most basic validation is checking if the nonce is something the server generated in the recent past by looking at the nonce store the server maintains.
2. If the nonce exists in the store, it checks the freshness of the nonce against the expiration date stored in the nonce store against the nonce. If the nonce has expired, the server immediately sends back a 401 and a fresh nonce for the client to restart the digest authentication process once again.
3. If the nonce is fresh, the server gets the nc that it received last time corresponding to this server nonce, which is also stored in the nonce store against the server nonce. If the nc in this request is lesser or equal to the value it has on record, the request is rejected with a 401.
4. If not, the server retrieves the password for the user (jqhuman, in this case) from some place such as a database and computes the MD5 hash by following the three steps we saw in the preceding section.
5. If the client has sent the right password, the MD5 hash the server has just calculated will exactly match the hash sent by the client in the response field. If there is any difference, the hashes will not match and the server rejects the request again with a 401.

Let's say Mallory, the cryptographic stereotype for a malicious user, gets the digest header from Listing 8-9. The options Mallory has and the corresponding defense the digest mechanism has are listed here.

1. The first and foremost option is for Mallory to replay the old request. If the server nonce expiration time is up, the server will reject the request and send a fresh nonce. Mallory cannot use the new nonce to create a valid request, because she does not know the password.
2. Before expiry, Mallory must use a client counter that is greater than the current one. It is easier to add one and come up with a new one, but then this value is part of the MD5 digest. So, without knowing the password, the hash cannot be calculated correctly and the server will reject the request.
3. Mallory can mount a chosen plain text attack by presenting the client a server nonce of her liking to make the cryptanalysis easier, but the client nonce is randomly generated by the client and hence it allows the client to vary the input to the hashing process in a way not determined by the attacker. Thus, the purpose of the client nonce and the counter is to prevent replay and chosen plain text attacks.
4. The final option Mallory has is to use a brute force attack; that is, to do exactly what the server does, which is to compute the MD5 hash by following the three steps. Of course, the password is not available but by using one password after another, Mallory can compute the hash and compare it with the value in the response field of the header to guess the password. First, Mallory tries all the individual alphabets and then combinations. If the hash matches for any combination, that is the password. This technique is called a brute-force attack. A dictionary can also be used to guess passwords because most of the time human beings prefer words or a sequence of them for their passwords. Passwords are stronger, of course, if users use a combination of upper and lower case, numbers, and special characters. A password of apple can be easily cracked compared to P0larbe@RinDFr!dg3. Even so, a determined hacker with resources can guess the password. To be exact, the password is the weakest link. Thus, digest authentication is not infallible, but it's a better alternative than basic authentication over HTTP.

■ **Note** From a pure statelessness perspective, digest authentication's suitability to be used with REST-based services is left to the designer's REST affinity. First of all, the service must keep track of the server nonce it generates. Worse, it must keep track of the nonce counter last used by the client to prevent replay attacks.

Implementing Digest Authentication

Similar to basic authentication, we will use message handler `AuthenticationHandler` to implement digest authentication with ASP.NET Web API because it runs earlier in the ASP.NET Web API pipeline and is an appropriate place to implement authentication logic. It is a good practice to have authentication logic running as early as possible in the pipeline to reject the bad requests as soon as possible. There are four classes involved in the implementation. Table 8-1 provides a quick introduction to the classes.

Table 8-1. *Classes in the Digest Authentication Implementation*

Class	Purpose
`AuthenticationHandler`	The message handler that implements the authentication logic. It reads the Authorize request header using the `Header` class and sets the WWW-Authenticate response header by generating a nonce using the `Nonce` class.
`Header`	The CLR representation of the HTTP Authorize request header in digest authentication. A new `Header` object can be created by passing the Authorize header payload into the constructor. A `Header` instance can be serialized back into the Authorize header payload by calling the `ToString` method.
`Nonce`	The class that can generate a nonce as well as validate a nonce sent by the client.
`HashHelper`	An extension to the type of byte[], an array of bytes to create the corresponding MD5 hash.

Implementation Overview

The different methods in the classes listed in Table 8-1 get called at different points in time of the authentication process. Before we get to the implementation, let's take a look at an overview of the sequence that shows the functionality at different steps.

1. The client sends a request without the Authorization header.
2. `AuthenticationHandler`, as part of the request processing, inspects the request for the authorization header. Because it is absent, it does not establish an authenticated identity.
3. Because the action method of `ApiController` is decorated with the `Authorize` attribute, it checks if the identity established is an authenticated identity. That not being the case, the `Authorize` attribute sets the response status code to 401 - Unauthorized and short-circuits the action method execution.
4. `AuthenticationHandler`, as part of the response processing, inspects the response status code. Because it is 401, it proceeds to set the WWW-Authenticate response header.
5. `AuthenticationHandler` calls `Nonce.Generate()` to create a new nonce. Along with QOP and the realm, it sets the nonce in the WWW-Authenticate response header.
6. The client reads the server nonce from the WWW-Authenticate header and resubmits the request with an authorization header containing all the necessary fields.

7. AuthenticationHandler, as part of the request processing, inspects the request for the authorization header. It finds the header this time. The message handler creates an instance of the Header class by passing in the authorize header payload.

8. AuthenticationHandler, continuing with the request processing, calls Nonce.IsValid() passing in the nonce value and the nonce counter retrieved from the authorization header through the Header object. If the nonce is valid, the handler computes the MD5 hash and compares it with the hash sent in by the client. If there is a match, the handler creates a principal and sets it in Thread.CurrentPrincipal.

Implementation Details

Finally, you get to see some code! The flow touches different points of different classes. In line with the flow sequence, I show only the related code under each step. If you need the individual classes as a whole, you can find the code samples for this chapter in the Source Code/Download area of the Apress web site (www.apress.com). Also, the steps in the preceding overview section do not correspond exactly to the steps in the detailed implementation shown in this section. The sequence is the same but the correspondence is not one-to-one.

1. Steps 1 and 2 in the preceding overview happen implicitly with our code. We start off with the process outlined in Step 3, which is done in the response handling portion of the message handler, as shown in Listing 8-10.

Listing 8-10. Unauthorized Status Code Generation

```
public class AuthenticationHandler : DelegatingHandler
{
    protected async override Task<HttpResponseMessage> SendAsync(HttpRequestMessage request,
                                                    CancellationToken cancellationToken)
    {
        try
        {
            // Request handling goes here

            var response = await base.SendAsync(request, cancellationToken);

            if (response.StatusCode == HttpStatusCode.Unauthorized)
            {
                response.Headers.WwwAuthenticate.Add(new AuthenticationHeaderValue("Digest",
                                            Header.UnauthorizedResponseHeader.ToString()));
            }

            return response;
        }
        catch (Exception)
        {
            var response = request.CreateResponse(HttpStatusCode.Unauthorized);
            response.Headers.WwwAuthenticate.Add(new AuthenticationHeaderValue("Digest",
                                            Header.UnauthorizedResponseHeader.ToString()));
```

```
                return response;
            }
        }
    }
```

2. The message handler calls the static property `UnauthorizedResponseHeader` of the `Header` class, which returns an instance of `Header` that corresponds to the WWW-Authenticate header payload in a 401 Unauthorized response. See Listing 8-11.

Listing 8-11. Unauthorized Response Header Generation

```
public static Header UnauthorizedResponseHeader
{
        get
        {
            return new Header()
            {
                Realm = "RealmOfBadri",
                Nonce = <Put your namespace here>.Nonce.Generate()
            };
        }
}
```

3. The static method `Generate` of the Nonce class, shown in Listing 8-12, gets called. This method uses the `RNGCryptoServiceProvider` class provided by the .NET Framework to generate a byte array of size 16 and creates an MD5 hash of the same. The nonce thus produced is added to a `ConcurrentDictionary` before being returned to the caller. I use `ConcurrentDictionary` for illustration. In reality, this will most likely be a table in a database. Because the dictionary is in the application domain, this logic will not work in case of a pure stateless web farm that does not implement sticky sessions. Also, the `Nonce` class keeps adding nonces to the dictionary. There is no code to purge the stale nonces out of the dictionary in the example.

Listing 8-12. Nonce Generation

```
public class Nonce
{
        private static ConcurrentDictionary<string, Tuple<int, DateTime>>
                        nonces = new ConcurrentDictionary<string, Tuple<int, DateTime>>();

        public static string Generate()
        {
                byte[] bytes = new byte[16];

                using (var rngProvider = new RNGCryptoServiceProvider())
                {
                    rngProvider.GetBytes(bytes);
                }

                string nonce = bytes.ToMD5Hash();
```

```
                nonces.TryAdd(nonce, new Tuple<int, DateTime>(0, DateTime.Now.AddMinutes(10)));

                return nonce;
        }

        // IsValid method removed for brevity
}
```

4. Listing 8-13 shows the extension method that creates the MD5 hash. I use the .NET Framework class of MD5 to create the MD5 hash. It is important to note that the byte array returned by the ComputeHash method of MD5 is converted to a hex string before getting returned by the method.

Listing 8-13. MD5 Hash Creation

```
public static class HashHelper
{
    public static string ToMD5Hash(this byte[] bytes)
    {
        StringBuilder hash = new StringBuilder();
        MD5 md5 = MD5.Create();

        md5.ComputeHash(bytes)
              .ToList()
                     .ForEach(b => hash.AppendFormat("{0:x2}", b));

        return hash.ToString();
    }

    public static string ToMD5Hash(this string inputString)
    {
        return Encoding.UTF8.GetBytes(inputString).ToMD5Hash();
    }
}
```

5. At this point, the WWW-Authenticate header gets sent back with the nonce and the QOP of auth. Listing 8-14 shows the ToString method of the Header class that serializes the Header object into a string representation that can be stuffed into the WWW-Authenticate header.

Listing 8-14. ToString Method of Header Class

```
public override string ToString()
{
        StringBuilder header = new StringBuilder();
        header.AppendFormat("realm=\"{0}\"", Realm);
        header.AppendFormat(", nonce=\"{0}\"", Nonce);
        header.AppendFormat(", qop=\"{0}\"", "auth");
        return header.ToString();
}
```

6. The client reads the response header, gets the nonce and the QOP, formats a proper Authenticate header containing all the necessary data, and resubmits the request. One such example request is shown in Listing 8-15.

Listing 8-15. Example Authorization Header

```
Authorization: Digest username="aaa", realm="RealmOfBadri", nonce="5039c371d8eed05f0166d6
1e629e9e40", uri="/api/employees", cnonce="0a4f113b., nc=00000001, response="6629fae49393
a05397450978507c4ef1", qop="auth"
```

7. The request from the previous step comes to the request handling portion of the message handler, shown in Listing 8-16.

Listing 8-16. Message Handler Request Handling

```
var headers = request.Headers;
if (headers.Authorization != null)
{
        Header header = new Header(request.Headers.Authorization.Parameter,
                                                            request.Method.Method);

        if (Nonce.IsValid(header.Nonce, header.NounceCounter))
        {
                // Just assuming password is same as username for the purpose of illustration
                string password = header.UserName;

                string ha1 = String.Format("{0}:{1}:{2}", header.UserName, header.Realm,
                                                                   password).ToMD5Hash();

                string ha2 = String.Format("{0}:{1}", header.Method, header.Uri).ToMD5Hash();

                string computedResponse = String
                                    .Format("{0}:{1}:{2}:{3}:{4}:{5}",
                                        ha1, header.Nonce, header.NounceCounter,
                                                header.Cnonce, "auth", ha2).ToMD5Hash();

                if (String.CompareOrdinal(header.Response, computedResponse) == 0)
                {
                        // digest computed matches the value sent by client in the response field.
                        // Looks like an authentic client! Create a principal.
                        var claims = new List<Claim>
                        {
                                    new Claim(ClaimTypes.Name, header.UserName),
                                    new Claim(ClaimTypes.AuthenticationMethod,
                                                        AuthenticationMethods.Password)
                        };

                        var principal = new ClaimsPrincipal(
                                                new[] { new ClaimsIdentity(claims, "Digest") });

                        Thread.CurrentPrincipal = principal;
```

```
                    if (HttpContext.Current != null)
                        HttpContext.Current.User = principal;

                }
            }
}
```

a. The Authorize request header payload is converted into a CLR object `Header` by passing the header payload into the constructor.

b. The `IsValid` static method of the `Nonce` class is called by passing the nonce and nonce counter.

c. If valid, ha1 and ha2 are computed and based on that the digest is calculated, as we discussed in the preceding section. In practice, the actual password will be retrieved from the membership store at this point. For brevity, I do not show any code related to database access and just consider the password to be the same as the user ID.

d. If the computed digest matches the digest sent by the client, authentication is deemed successful and `Thread.CurrentPrincipal` gets set with an instance of `ClaimsPrincipal`.

8. Listing 8-17 shows the `Header` class with the properties and the constructor that sets these properties based on the header payload passes into the constructor. The header payload is split by a comma and each token is parsed as a key-value pair based on the '=' character. Based on the key, the corresponding property of the `Header` object is set.

Listing 8-17. Header Constructor

```
public class Header
{
    public Header() { }

    public Header(string header, string method)
    {
        string keyValuePairs = header.Replace("\"", String.Empty);

        foreach (string keyValuePair in keyValuePairs.Split(','))
        {
            int index = keyValuePair.IndexOf("=");
            string key = keyValuePair.Substring(0, index);
            string value = keyValuePair.Substring(index + 1);

            switch (key)
            {
                case "username": this.UserName = value; break;
                case "realm": this.Realm = value; break;
                case "nonce": this.Nonce = value; break;
                case "uri": this.Uri = value; break;
                case "nc": this.NounceCounter = value; break;
                case "cnonce": this.Cnonce = value; break;
```

```
                case "response": this.Response = value; break;
                case "method": this.Method = value; break;
            }
        }

        if (String.IsNullOrEmpty(this.Method))
            this.Method = method;
    }

    public string Cnonce { get; private set; }
    public string Nonce { get; private set; }
    public string Realm { get; private set; }
    public string UserName { get; private set; }
    public string Uri { get; private set; }
    public string Response { get; private set; }
    public string Method { get; private set; }
    public string NounceCounter { get; private set; }

}
```

9. The message handler uses the properties of the Header object to retrieve the nonce and nonce counter, which are passed to the IsValid static method of the Nonce class (see Listing 8-18). The IsValid method returns true if the nonce is found in the store, which is a ConcurrentDictionary, if the nonce is fresh, and if the corresponding client nonce counter is greater than the value in the store.

Listing 8-18. Nonce Validation

```
public class Nonce
{
    // Generate method goes here

    public static bool IsValid(string nonce, string nonceCount)
    {
        Tuple<int, DateTime> cachedNonce = null;
        nonces.TryGetValue(nonce, out cachedNonce);

        if (cachedNonce != null) // nonce is found
        {
            // nonce count is greater than the one in record
            if (Int32.Parse(nonceCount) > cachedNonce.Item1)
            {
                // nonce has not expired yet
                if (cachedNonce.Item2 > DateTime.Now)
                {
                    // update the dictionary to reflect the nonce
                    // count just received in this request
                    nonces[nonce] = new Tuple<int,
                                          DateTime>(Int32.Parse(nonceCount),
                                              cachedNonce.Item2);
```

```
                        // Every thing looks ok - server nonce is fresh
                        // and nonce count seems to be
                        // incremented. Does not look like replay.
                        return true;
                    }
                }
            }

            return false;
        }
    }
```

Testing Digest Authentication

Writing a C# test harness for testing digest authentication is a slightly more involved process than the one we wrote for basic authentication. The main reason is that the client must generate the client nonce and keep incrementing the nonce counter for every request.

Instead of going through that hassle, we will instead use Internet Explorer as the test harness, although any modern browser can be used for this purpose. The web browser will do all the heavy lifting for us. Just like basic authentication, digest authentication is part of the HTTP specification, so the browser knows exactly what needs to be done right from the moment it receives a 401 - Unauthorized status code and a WWW-Authenticate header with the digest scheme.

Internet Explorer pops up a window to get the user name and password (see Figure 8-4).

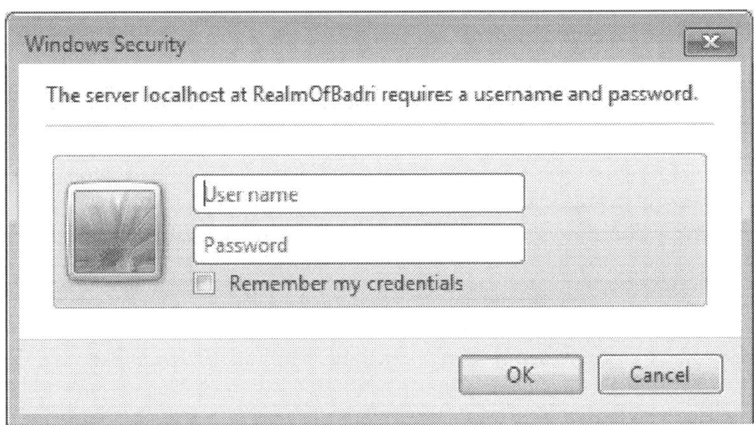

Figure 8-4. *Internet Explorer pop-up box*

Because we have sent a realm in the WWW-Authenticate header, it shows the realm name correctly this time in the pop-up box. After receiving the credentials from the user, Internet Explorer uses the server nonce and rigorously follows all the steps in using the exact ingredients and the recipe to cook up the MD5 digest and then puts that in the Authorize header.

For subsequent requests, Internet Explorer continues to use the same server nonce but does increment the nonce count every time a new request is sent. Excellent! You can fire up the Fiddler tool that we discussed in Chapter 4 to inspect all the requests going back and forth between Internet Explorer and ASP.NET Web API.

You can directly issue GET requests to a web API from the browser by typing the URI or you can have JQuery `getJSON()` do that at the click of a button, like we have been doing in previous chapters.

Merits and Demerits of Digest Authentication

The biggest advantage of digest authentication is that the password is not transmitted in any form. Also, digest authentication does not need transport security in most cases. Clients that are capable of creating MD5 hashes, even if they are not HTTPS enabled, can talk to a web API using digest authentication in a secure manner.

Digest authentication is slightly complex and needs support from the client as well as human users to make the scheme work efficiently. The client needs to increment a nonce counter for every request and that means the client needs to be tracking the requests made.

Digest authentication employs hashing based on the nonce that is just generated as part of the first request, thereby making the rainbow tables useless. A rainbow table is a precomputed table used to crack hashes. It is essentially a dictionary of precomputed hashes and the corresponding passwords from which they were calculated. By precomputing and storing the hashes, the rainbow table achieves efficiency in time by trading off space or storage efficiency. A generated nonce is used to compute hash and hence rainbow tables cannot be used; precomputation becomes a moot point.

Yet, it is possible for anyone to get the server nonce and start creating digests and compare against the digest sent by a client through a brute force attack. Weak passwords can be easily retrieved through such brute force attacks. We will look at brute force attacks in depth in the next section.

ASP.NET Web API or any HTTP service, for that matter, can support both basic and digest authentication at the same time. It is all about negotiation. A smart piece of software such as a browser, on receiving both WWW-Authenticate: Basic and WWW-Authenticate: Digest as part of a 401 - Unauthorized response, will pick digest authentication because it is comparatively stronger. Of course, a client that cannot participate in digest authentication can use basic authentication. One possible problem with the freedom to choose is that a man in the middle can remove the WWW-Authenticate: Digest header, tricking a client to send the credentials in the basic scheme and picking up the same from the header.

Trying to Break Digest Authentication

Digest authentication provides the nonce counter to counteract replay attacks. To test this, let's replay a previous successful request through Fiddler. Fire up Fiddler and capture the traffic to your ASP.NET Web API.

Now, after managing to capture a few requests, select a successful ASP.NET Web API request with a 200 OK response in the web sessions pane on the left. Right-click Replay > Reissue Unconditionally (see Figure 8-5).

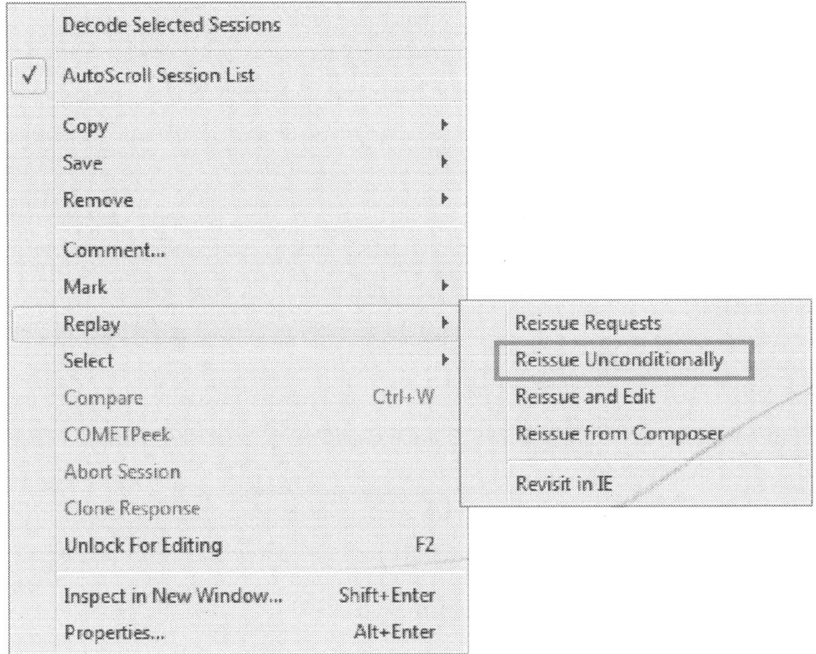

Figure 8-5. *Replaying requests through Fiddler*

If you do this, you will not get another 200 - OK but a 401 - Unauthorized, along with a fresh server nonce. What is preventing the replay is the check we are doing with the nonce counter to see that it should always be greater than the previous one. Of course, you can copy and paste the request into 'Composer,' edit the nc so that the value is incremented, and resubmit. Again, it will be a 401. This time, by tinkering with the nc, we have ensured that the calculated hash does not match the hash in the response field.

Let's shift our focus toward attacking digest authentication with brute force. In the response field of the authorization header, the client sends the digest or MD5 hash. There is no way we can recover the password from the digest, but we can assume the password is one letter 'a' and compute the MD5 hash. If the hash thus computed matches the response field, we have a winner! If not, we don't lose heart and move on with the next letter, 'b.' Once we reach 'z,' we start with 'aa' and then 'ab' and so on until the hashes match or, in other words, we know the password.

Before we move forward with this, I want to repeat that rainbow tables are of no use with digest authentication. The digest is computed using both the server nonce and the client nonce. It is not possible to precompute the hashes in advance and create a dictionary to look up. So, let's try to muscle our way out of digest authentication using brute CPU power. First, we need a method to generate combinations of letters. To keep this simple, let's generate the passwords based on lowercase letters only—a through z—as shown in Listing 8-19.

Listing 8-19. Password Generator

```
static IEnumerable<string> GeneratePassword(IEnumerable<string> input = null)
{
    // ASCII a is 97 and I need the next 26 letters for a - z
    var range = Enumerable.Range(97, 26);

    input = input ?? range.Select(n => char.ConvertFromUtf32(n));
```

```
    foreach (var password in input)
        yield return password;

    var appendedList = input.SelectMany(x => range.Select(n => x + char.ConvertFromUtf32(n)));

    foreach (var password in GeneratePassword(appendedList))
        yield return password;
}
```

Next, we need a method to calculate the hash (see Listing 8-20). It is pretty much the same logic in the handler. One important thing to note is that ha2 need not be computed every time. Because it is based only on the HTTP method and URI, it can be computed once and reused. So, I'm hard-coding it in Listing 8-20, for GET and the URI. The `Header` class, which is passed into `IsMatch()`, can be just a collection of properties, as shown in Listing 8-21.

Listing 8-20. Hash Calculator

```
static bool IsMatch(Header header, string password)
{
    string ha1 = String.Format("{0}:{1}:{2}",
        header.UserName,
        header.Realm,
        password).ToMD5Hash();

    string ha2 = "347c9fe6471afafd1ac2c5551ada479f";

    string computedResponse = String.Format("{0}:{1}:{2}:{3}:{4}:{5}",
        ha1,
        header.Nonce,
        header.NounceCounter,
        header.Cnonce,
        "auth",
        ha2).ToMD5Hash();

    return (String.CompareOrdinal(header.Response, computedResponse) == 0);
}
```

Listing 8-21. Header Class

```
class Header
{
    public string Cnonce { get; set; }
    public string Nonce { get; set; }
    public string Realm { get; set; }
    public string UserName { get; set; }
    public string Uri { get; set; }
    public string Response { get; set; }
    public string Method { get; set; }
    public string NounceCounter { get; set; }
}
```

With that, we are almost ready. Let's say we have the ability to sniff a network and we caught a request with a valid authorization header, like the one shown in Listing 8-22.

Listing 8-22. Authorization Header

```
Authorization: Digest username="john", realm="RealmOfBadri", nonce="932444f708e9c1e5391aad0e849ea201",
uri="/api/values", cnonce="968ffba69bfc304eabaebffc10d56a0a", nc=00000001, response="4d0b1211f1024ec
616d55ac8312f5f46", qop="auth"
```

Let's create an instance of the header and load the values from the header into the properties. I call `IsMatch()` in a loop (PLINQ) and when there is a match, I come out after printing the password. I just use `DateTime` to time this, although I could have used a `StopWatch` (see Listing 8-23).

Listing 8-23. Brute Force Attacker

```
static void Main(string[] args)
{
    Header header = new Header()
    {
        UserName = "john",
        Realm = "RealmOfBadri",
        Nonce = "932444f708e9c1e5391aad0e849ea201",
        Uri = "/api/values",
        Cnonce = "968ffba69bfc304eabaebffc10d56a0a",
        NounceCounter = "00000001",
        Response = "4d0b1211f1024ec616d55ac8312f5f46",
        Method = "GET"
    };

    DateTime start = DateTime.Now;

    Parallel.ForEach<string>(GeneratePassword(), (password, loopState) =>
    {
        if (IsMatch(header, password))
        {
            Console.WriteLine("Gotcha ---> " + password);
            loopState.Break();
        }
    });

    DateTime end = DateTime.Now;
    Console.WriteLine((end - start).TotalSeconds + " seconds");

}
```

The laptop I use has two cores with 2.26 GHz and 2 GB RAM. It's not especially powerful, but even with this I'm able to figure out the password of apple in about 46 seconds. But if the password is strong (in other words, longer and using a mix of uppercase, numbers, and special characters) and not straight out of an English dictionary, it is going to be very tough to crack!

As they say, any security mechanism can be breached. It is only a time-resource trade-off. The time factor is very important. What harm is it if someone gets your current online banking password 10 years from now? You will have changed it more than 100 times by then.

Windows Authentication

Integrated Windows Authentication (IWA), better known by the slightly shorter name of Windows authentication, is definitely not as far-reaching a mechanism as basic or digest authentication. Unlike basic and digest authentication, which are backed by the HTTP specification and hence can work on any platform that supports HTTP, Windows authentication has dependencies on a specific technology stack. As the name indicates, Windows authentication is all about the Windows platform. The term is used typically to indicate the authentication scheme that makes use of the Windows account and the associated Microsoft technologies such as Active Directory (AD), Internet Information Services (IIS), and Internet Explorer (IE).

However, Windows authentication does have a role to play in intra-network scenarios. Imagine users with Windows AD accounts working on Windows workstations using Internet Explorer to access an intranet web application running in IIS. This is a frequent scenario in enterprises, and Windows authentication is very relevant for this type of scenario.

From a developer perspective, Windows authentication is even simpler to implement than basic authentication. Assuming that using AD for authentication and IIS for hosting the web API are acceptable to you, without writing any code you can establish the user identity. The `WindowsPrincipal` object with `WindowsIdentity` is automatically created for you by the collaborative effort of IIS, ASP.NET, and Internet Explorer, at times without requiring end users to input their credentials.

Configuring Windows Authentication

There are two main configuration changes that we need to do to get Windows authentication going.

1. Add the <authentication> element to the Web.config file.
2. Configure the ASP.NET application to use Windows authentication through IIS Manager.

The first change is for the ASP.NET pipeline to bring in the two modules that establish the `WindowsPrincipal` object in `Thread.CurrentPrincipal`: `WindowsAuthenticationModule` and `DefaultAuthenticationModule`. The second change is for IIS to get the token from Internet Explorer. Web.config is pretty simple. We need to simply add an element under system.web, as shown in Listing 8-24.

Listing 8-24. Web.config Change

```
<system.web>
    ...
    <authentication mode="Windows" />
    ...
<system.web>
```

To make the change to the ASP.NET application in IIS, open Internet Information Services (IIS) Manager (`InetMgr.exe`).

In Windows 7, you can just type **iis** in the Search programs and files text box in the Start pop-up box to get to IIS Manager. Locate the application in the left tree and double-click the Authentication icon to get to the Authentication screen shown in Figure 8-6.

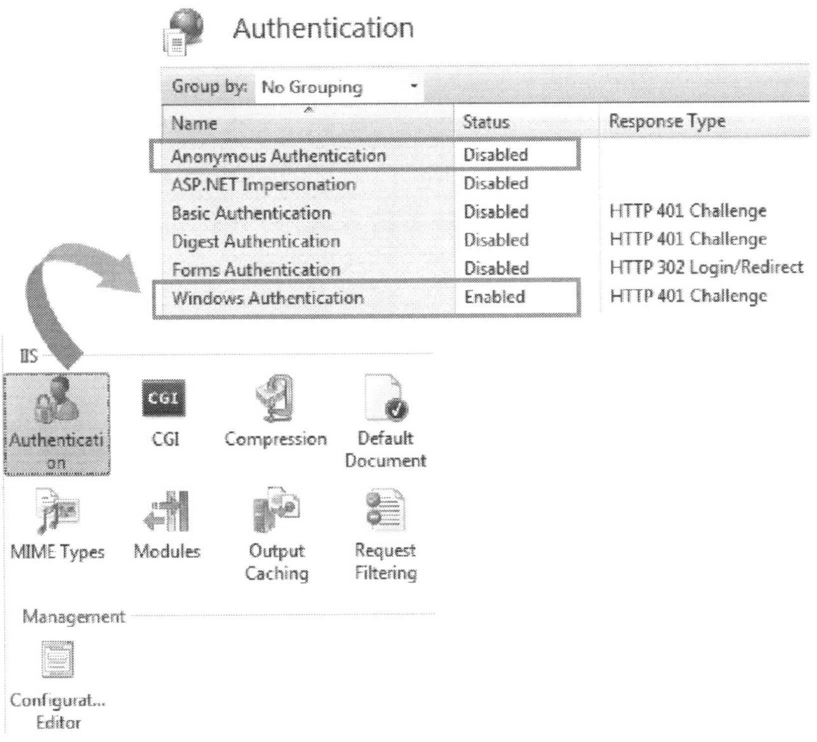

Figure 8-6. IIS Manager change

Right-click the Windows Authentication item and select Enable in the pop-up menu to enable Windows authentication. Also, disable anonymous authentication the same way. This is to make sure the identity established is an authenticated identity; in other words, valid credentials must be supplied by the client to access this web application.

Windows Authentication in Action

We now have our web API secured by Windows authentication, hosted in IIS, with the URI of a resource hosted by our web API being `http://server.com/api/Employees/12345`. Suppose a user types this URI in the Internet Explorer address bar and presses Enter. This is not a likely action for most users, but let's pretend our user is a developer who wants to go to the web API directly to see the sequence of steps as the action unfolds.

1. The user issues a GET request using IE from a workstation in the same local network as server.com. The user has logged into the workstation using her Windows network credential.

2. IIS is the first one to receive the request. Because the web application is set up for Windows authentication, IIS knows how to go about handling this request: It asks IE for authentication credentials.

3. Typically, the browser will not present the credentials with the initial GET request and hence gets back a 401 - Unauthorized. As with the case of any other schemes, the WWW-Authenticate header gets sent. In this case, two such headers are sent back: WWW-Authenticate: Negotiate and WWW-Authenticate: NTLM.

4. Just as IE acted smart on receiving the WWW-Authenticate header with basic or digest schemes, it now goes about doing what the server needs. IE sends a token representing the Windows user account of the user. Compared to basic and digest authentication, where IE had to prompt the user to enter credentials in a pop-up box, IE acts even smarter in this scenario. It is already running under a Windows account and it silently sends the token for this account without troubling the user. If IIS is not satisfied with the credentials for whatever reason, a window similar to the earlier ones pops up and prompts the user to enter the credentials.

5. IE does not send the user name or password to IIS directly. It uses Kerberos or NTLM authentication, depending on the server and client capabilities. The two options available with Windows authentication are NTLM and Negotiate. NTLM just uses NTLM authentication. With Negotiate, there is a level of indirection. Kerberos is attempted first, and only when it is not possible to use Kerberos, NTML is selected. So, it is pretty much NTLM or Kerberos, with Kerberos as the first choice.

6. In the case of NTLM, IE gets AD to send the authentication information to IIS. For Kerberos, IE gets a ticket from AD and sends that to IIS. Kerberos is chosen for Windows 2000 or later running on both the workstation and IIS, with both machines in the same domain. This is typically the case today with corporate networks. If the conditions are not satisfied, NTLM is chosen.

7. Ultimately, the token received by IIS is passed onto ASP.NET. As part of the ASP.NET pipeline processing, the token gets converted into a `WindowsPrincipal` object and is made available to API controllers through the `User` property or through `Thread.CurrentPrincipal` by two modules.

    a. The first module, `WindowsAuthenticationModule`, which is activated by the presence of the element `<authentication mode="Windows"/>` in the Web.config file, creates `WindowsPrincipal` and `WindowsIdentity` objects to represent the authenticated user and attaches the principal to the current web request.

    b. `DefaultAuthenticationModule` ensures `Thread.CurrentPrincipal` is set with the same principal, which the `User` property of `ApiController` returns. The great thing is that the identity established by these modules contains the AD group information ready to run RBAC off these AD groups, if that is sufficient for the web API business needs.

Getting into the details of NTLM or Kerberos is not practical for a book dedicated to ASP.NET Web API security. These topics merit dedicated books, not just sections in a chapter. But I show the HTTP transactions associated with a typical Negotiate scheme (with Kerberos chosen as a result of the negotiation) in Listing 8-25. Of course, the messages are touched up for brevity reasons.

Listing 8-25. Windows Authentication: HTTP Transactions

```
Transaction 1
GET http://server.com/api/employees/12345 HTTP/1.1
User-Agent: Mozilla/5.0 (compatible; MSIE 9.0; Windows NT 6.1; Trident/5.0)

HTTP/1.1 401 Unauthorized
WWW-Authenticate: Negotiate
WWW-Authenticate: NTLM
```

Transaction 2

```
GET http://server.com/api/employees/12345 HTTP/1.1
User-Agent: Mozilla/5.0 (compatible; MSIE 9.0; Windows NT 6.1; Trident/5.0)
Authorization: Negotiate YHUGBisGAQUFAqBrMGmgMDAuBgorBgEEAYI3AgIKBgkqhkiC9xIBAgIGCSqGSIb3EgEC
AgYKKwYBBAGCNwICHqI1BDNOVExNU1NQAAEAAACXsgjiAwADADAAAAAIAAgAKAAAAAYBsBOAAAAPTFQwMDYxODlDVFM=

HTTP/1.1 401 Unauthorized
WWW-Authenticate: Negotiate oYHQMIHNoAMKAQGhDAYKKwYBBAGCNwICCqKBtwSBtE5UTE1TU1AAAgAAAAYABg
A4AAAAFcKJ4oz7beEq6PhxAIFyAQAAAAB2AHYAPgAAAAYBsBOAAAAPQwBUAFMAAgAGAEMAVABTAAEAEABMAFQAMAAw
ADYAMQA4ADkABAAOAGMAdABzAC4AYwBvAGOAAwAgAEwAVAAwADAANgAxADgAOQAuAGMAdABzAC4AYwBvAGOABQAO
AGMAdABzAC4AYwBvAGOABwAIAPp2snlKqcOBAAAAAA==
```

Transaction 3

```
GET http://server.com/api/employees/12345 HTTP/1.1
User-Agent: Mozilla/5.0 (compatible; MSIE 9.0; Windows NT 6.1; Trident/5.0)
Authorization: Negotiate oXcwdaADCgEBoloEWE5UTE1TU1AAAwAAAAAAAABYAAAAAAAAAFgAAAAAAAAAWAAAAAAAA
ABYAAAAAAAAAFgAAAAAAAAAWAAAABXCiOIGAbAdAAAAD2MaSBcRsZyiME2Njmbv/ISjEgQQAQAAAPUXp1AtIpqEAAAAAA==

HTTP/1.1 200 OK
Persistent-Auth: true
WWW-Authenticate: Negotiate oRswGaADCgEAoxIEEAEAAABDh+CIwTbjqQAAAAA=
```

This exchange of messages is done as per the SPNEGO (Simple and Protected GSS-API Negotiation) mechanism, pronounced *spen-go,* that defines how IE and IIS use Kerberos in web transactions. The URL of the SPNEGO memo is `http://tools.ietf.org/html/rfc4559`.

Impersonation

Generally speaking, impersonation is the ability of a thread to execute in a security context that is different from the context of the process that owns the thread. When an ASP.NET Web API is secured by Windows authentication, the `WindowsPrincipal` object corresponding to the Windows user account under which IE runs is set to the `Thread.CurrentPrincipal` or the `User` property of the controller. This is mainly from an authentication and authorization point of view. That is, we now know the following: (1) what the user identity is, (2) if the identity is an authenticated identity, and (3) the AD groups to which the user belongs. The last one is important if web API authorization is going to be based on the AD groups.

Windows authentication brings to the table an important dimension of security, which is otherwise not possible in other methods. In basic or digest authentication, we do get a user name from the identity. But this user is only an application-level user. From the Windows operating system (OS) point of view, the user is not a Windows account or OS-level user. Hence, the Windows privilege checks—for example, checking if a user can access a directory or if a user can modify a file, and so on—cannot be applied. However, in the case of Windows authentication an authenticated user does mean something to the Windows OS. The user is a Windows account that has privileges to do certain things and vice versa. With Windows authentication, it is possible to let the thread that is servicing the request to our web API assume the context of the Windows account of the user and perform the actions on behalf of the user's account.

This is a huge thing for a corporate scene. For example, any local resource can be access controlled through the existing AD groups in the corporate domain. Now, if we can simply make the thread running our web API inherit the privileges of the user, we don't need to perform any access control checks programmatically. If the user is not in the AD group that has the privileges to access a resource, the request to access the resource is going to fail anyway for the want of privilege. We just need to handle the failure. Examples of a resource are a local file or the private key of an X.509 certificate. If a user SomeDomain\jqhuman does not have privileges to access a specific certificate, when the web API code runs in the context of SomeDomain\jqhuman the code execution will automatically fail.

To enable the impersonation, we just need to add another line to Web.config, in addition to the authentication mode, as shown in Listing 8-26.

Listing 8-26. Impersonation

```
<system.web>
  ...
    <authentication mode="Windows" />
    <identity impersonate="true" />
  ...
<system.web>
```

With this configuration, ASP.NET will impersonate the authenticated user, and all resource access is performed under the security context of the authenticated user. There are cases where you would like to impersonate on a specific case-by-case basis and not on a blanket basis. For those cases, we can impersonate the user temporarily, as shown in Listing 8-27. I want to bring to your attention the concept of impersonation I covered in Chapter 5. It is almost exactly the same here but with a slight difference, which is that I am impersonating the `WindowsIdentity` of what is set in `Thread.CurrentPrincipal`. In Chapter 5, I showed you how to impersonate an identity that I created from the token I got from `LogonUser()`.

Listing 8-27. Temporary Impersonation

```
WindowsIdentity id = (WindowsIdentity)User.Identity;
using (WindowsImpersonationContext impersonatedUser = id.Impersonate())
{
        // WindowsIdentity.GetCurrent().Name will be that of the user
        // All actions executed here will be under the context of the Windows account of the user

        impersonatedUser.Undo(); // Undo the impersonation, once done
}

// At this point, we are back to executing under the context of default ASP.NET process account
```

▒ **Note** Impersonation gives access to only local resources. If we have to extend this capability to access network resources such as a file share, delegation is the answer. Kerberos authentication lets us use Kerberos delegation to pass the user's identity to access network resources. Delegation can be a constrained one; administrators can specify the resources another server or domain account can access while impersonating.

Testing Windows Authentication

Testing a web API secured by Windows authentication using Internet Explorer is the most convenient way. IE does all the heavy lifting. In reality, no one is going to hit the web API directly from IE. However, in the case of another ASP.NET Web application using our web API, if the web application is also secured by Windows authentication, the web API will be passed the same token and hence get the same `WindowsPrincipal`, even when accessed by AJAX through JQuery. One thing to note here is the same origin policy. As long as the web API and the web application are considered to be in the same origin, JQuery will have nothing to complain about.

What if we have to test the web API through a nonbrowser client? A simple C# console application can communicate to our web API. Listing 8-28 shows the C# code, using `System.Net.Http.HttpClient` to communicate to our API. Although I use `HttpClient`, other classes in the .NET Framework such as `WebClient` can also be used.

Listing 8-28. Windows Authentication Web API Test Client

```
using (var handler = new HttpClientHandler() { Credentials = CredentialCache.DefaultCredentials })
{
        using (var httpClient = new HttpClient(handler))
        {
                var result = httpClient.GetStringAsync("http://localhost/webapi/api/employees/12345").Result;
        }
}
```

Merits and Demerits of Windows Authentication

The first and foremost advantage in using Windows authentication is the convenience or simplicity in getting the identity established by the .NET Framework without having to write a line of code. IIS, ASP.NET, AD, and IE do all the heavy lifting and give you an authenticated `WindowsPrincipal` to work with.

From an IT administration point of view, the user management is outsourced internally to the Windows administration team that administers the user accounts. Windows authentication uses the Windows accounts from AD and hence the application is relieved of the burden of user management—not just the initial overhead to create user IDs, but also ongoing tasks like resetting a password if a user forgets his password and so on. Piggybacking on the corporate AD has security benefits as well. As soon as a Windows account is deactivated, the application access will also get revoked automatically. In addition, the corporate-level security policies of enforcing password strength and resets are automatically inherited by the application using Windows authentication.

Another advantage worth mentioning is the impersonation capabilities. In some cases, it will be a huge advantage if we need to strictly execute under the context of each of the individual user accounts. Without Windows authentication, it is still technically possible to impersonate, provided we get the Windows account credentials of individual users. In a practical sense, though, it is not possible to do this unless you are willing to live with the nightmares of maintaining and protecting Windows credentials in your system. For most enterprise-grade production systems, Windows authentication is the only way to implement impersonation.

The major disadvantage is there is too much reliance on the Microsoft technology stack, especially given the nature of ASP.NET Web API in embracing HTTP, which is a standard that cuts across platforms. Using Windows authentication goes in the opposite direction with respect to the reach.

Clients must use Windows and users need to have Windows accounts. Kerberos requires the client to have direct connection to the domain controller, which is generally the case only with an intranet. NTLM is generally stopped by proxy servers. For these reasons, Windows authentication is best suited for intranet usage.

Apart from the technology stack, the nature of the application can also limit the choice of Windows authentication. For example, although it makes sense to create an AD account for a new employee, it might not make the same sense to create an AD account for each potential candidate who applies for the position. In some cases, the security policies related to the creation of Windows accounts might prohibit account creation for the entire user base.

Just like basic authentication and cookies-based mechanisms such as forms authentication, browsers tend to cache authenticated credentials, thereby making the Windows authentication susceptible to CSRF.

Summary

Authentication is the process of discovering the identity of a user and verifying the same by validating the user-supplied credentials against an authority. The credential can be a knowledge factor that the user knows, such as a password. It can also be an ownership factor that the user owns or an inherence factor that the user is.

RFC 2617, "HTTP Authentication: Basic and Digest Access Authentication" provides the specification for HTTP's authentication framework, which comprises basic access authentication and digest access authentication. Both mechanisms are password-based. Whereas a password is sent in clear text in basic authentication, only a hash created that is based on the password is sent in the case of digest authentication.

The biggest advantage of basic authentication is its simplicity, whereas sending the password in clear text is its biggest weakness. For this reason, basic authentication must always be implemented with HTTPS. Basic authentication is susceptible to CSRF attacks because a web browser caches the authenticated credential and sends it to the server automatically, whenever the browser makes a subsequent request to the same server and realm combination.

Digest authentication is comparatively safer to use with plain HTTP. On the flip side, digest authentication is complex and needs support from the client as well as human users to make the scheme work efficiently.

IWA or Windows authentication is another password-based authentication mechanism that relies on the Windows infrastructure. It is a good fit mainly for intranet scenarios. Windows authentication is very simple to implement from a developer's point of view, but it is not platform-agnostic. It also has CSRF risks similar to basic authentication.

CHAPTER 9

Ownership Factors

As you saw in Chapter 5, authentication is a fundamental aspect of security that involves verifying credentials supplied by a user to establish an identity for the user in an application. A credential can be a knowledge factor that the user knows, an ownership factor that the user owns, or an inherence factor that the user is. I covered knowledge factors in Chapter 8. In this chapter, I focus on ownership factors.

An ownership factor is an element that a user owns or possesses, such as a key, certificate, or token. Unlike a knowledge factor, which can be passed on to others easily, intentionally or otherwise, it is difficult to share an ownership factor. An employee can share a knowledge factor, such as his password, with a coworker and ask her to submit the timesheet that he forgot to submit on Friday evening, despite the fact that it is against his company's policy. Worse yet, an employee could write his password on a sticky note and leave it next to a keyboard. An ownership factor such as an X.509 client certificate installed in the certificate store of a machine is much safer, and exporting it is generally beyond the technical prowess of most typical business users. Also, Windows-based privileges can be used to make the sharing harder or even impossible.

In this chapter, we look at securing ASP.NET Web API through ownership factors such as a preshared key, an X.509 client certificate, and a SAML token. I dedicate the next chapter to web tokens, which are another kind of ownership factor. Web tokens are a good fit for RESTful services. Specifically, I cover the Simple Web Token (SWT) and the JSON Web Token (JWT).

Preshared Key

A preshared key (PSK), also known as an API key, is a secret that is shared between two parties out-of-band prior to the actual usage. The out-of-band sharing typically happens over a channel more secure than the channel through which the communication of the actual messages is meant to happen subsequently. Security based on PSKs typically uses a symmetric key cryptographic algorithm similar to what we saw in Chapter 6.

At a fundamental level, a PSK can be used like a secret handshake or shibboleth. If a client sends 'the' PSK, which is, of course, common to all who are supposed to use the service, the request is serviced. If not, a status code of 401 - Unauthorized Response is sent back.

For this kind of rudimentary scheme, transport security is a must. Otherwise, anyone who can sniff the traffic could get the key and use your web API. You might wonder if there is any real use case for this kind of security arrangement. Devices, such as Internet of Things (IOT) devices, need to communicate to a central server, such as a web API, through HTTP. These devices might not have the resources to store individual keys. At the time the devices were produced (typically mass-produced), they were given one common shared key that was probably cast in stone at that time. This is better than no security at all. A web API can at least look for one of these keys burned in at the time of manufacturing to see if the request is from one of the legitimate devices.

At the next level are clients capable of sending the individual PSK. The advantage is that the web API can now individually identify the client. Suppose I sniff the traffic and get a bunch of requests. Next, I make up a request of my own, using a shared key that I obtained in the traffic capture. The web API will process my request because there is no way for it to differentiate between a genuine request and a fake one. In this case, as with the earlier case, transport security is a must.

Is this mechanism similar to the case of basic authentication, or perhaps a stripped-down version of it, sending only the username without sending the password? It's similar, but not exactly the same. The username and password are knowledge factors. This basically means you know them. You can remember them or maybe look at a sticky note and type in what was written there into a system. Even worse, you can tell your friend what your username and password are and she can type them in and impersonate you.

Ownership factors, such as PSKs, are different. A PSK is typically a big bunch of bytes appearing in base64-encoded format, or perhaps a hex string that is impossible for even the brightest person to memorize and remember. It is not just about being able to remember, but also is about how it is used. PSKs are typically saved somewhere in a system. The key is used by an application on the user's behalf in transactions, precluding the need for a user to enter the key manually.

A great example for this type of a PSK is a key created through Windows Azure Tools for Microsoft Visual Studio. You can use the Windows Azure Storage node in Server Explorer to look at blob and table data from your Windows Azure storage accounts. When you add a storage account to Server Explorer, the application creates a lengthy key as the input. Visual Studio uses this key to communicate with a web service.

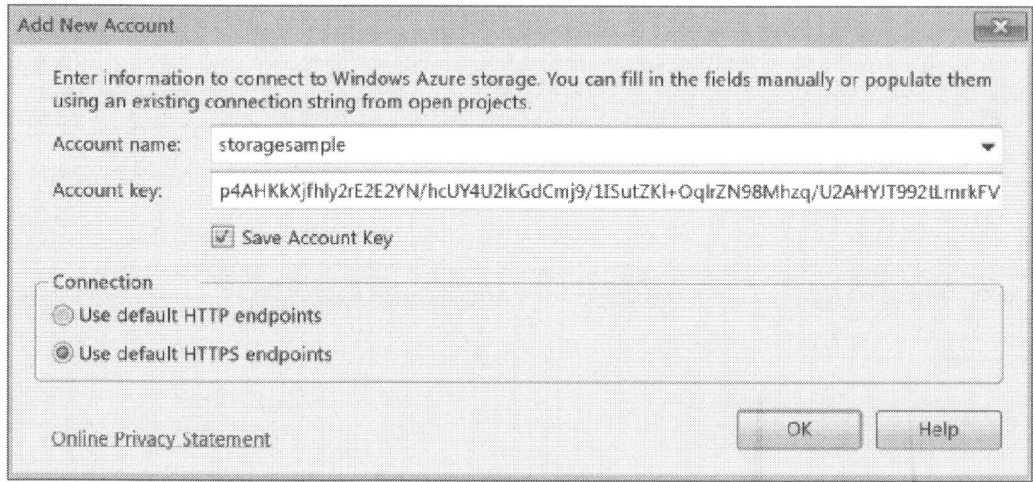

Figure 9-1. *PSK example using Visual Studio and Azure*

Designing a Preshared Key Security Mechanism

A PSK in its simplest form is a key that is exchanged between two parties out-of-band with the sender using the shared key as is in the messages as the credential. For this reason, HTTPS generally is a must for PSKs. Without help from transport security, it is easier for a malicious user to get the PSK and use it in a malicious request, just like a legitimate request.

The greatest advantage of a PSK is that it is exchanged out of band. In digest authentication, which I covered in Chapter 8, a server nonce is generated on the fly and shared with the client as part of the transaction. This means a malicious user can see the nonce. Despite that, the advantage associated with the server nonce is that a malicious user cannot anticipate the nonce and prepare for it ahead of the transaction because it is randomly generated at the time the transaction is initiated. But with a PSK, we are in an even stronger position. A PSK will not be known to the malicious user. However, we need to be aware of possible security weaknesses and defend against those weaknesses. We examine the most common security risks in the following sections. Later in the chapter, we'll build a secure PSK mechanism that does not require HTTPS.

Defense Against Replay Attacks

Suppose we design our security mechanism to transmit the credentials not in plain text but encrypted using the PSK. The encrypted credential is sent in the message, typically in the HTTP request header. A malicious user cannot decrypt the header and extract the credentials but can replay the earlier request as is. Worse, a malicious user can frame a new request and use only the header value containing the valid credentials from the previous successful request.

This type of replay attack is a form of attack in which a valid message exchange that was previously successful is maliciously repeated as is or repeated with a tampered message body retaining the bits containing the credentials. Imagine that you making a service request with your encrypted credentials asking the service to transfer $500 from your bank account to a utility company. A malicious user does not need to decrypt the ciphertext to get your password. He can simply submit a request like your previous request but change the recipient details to his account and change the amount to $50,000. The service will accept that request because the decrypted header value contains authentic credentials.

We need to acknowledge the fact that a security mechanism built on a PSK will be susceptible to a replay attack and guard against it. For example, a timestamp is a relatively effective way to defend against a replay attack. A timestamp can be added to the message and encrypted along with the rest of the message content. The service can retrieve the timestamp after decrypting the message and fail the request if the timestamp is too old for the threshold that is already agreed on. This cuts down on the window of opportunity to replay a request.

However, there is a small downside to the timestamp approach. For the timestamp to work, the client's clock and the server's clock must be in sync to a reasonable extent. If we set the time window to three seconds, within that time the request must get processed by the web API. If the clocks are not exactly in sync, the window of three seconds can further shrink, failing even the genuine requests, or grow and accommodate malicious replay requests.

An alternative to a timestamp is a counter such as the nonce counter that we saw with digest authentication. With a counter, we don't need to be concerned about the skew between the clocks. However, clients must implement a counter to ensure the count sent in a request is greater than the count in the previous request at least by one, and the server must keep a record of the last received counter. Of course, the message has to be signed so that a malicious user does not increment the counter and replay the rest of the request.

Defense Against Identifier Misuse

In its simplest form, a PSK is both the user identifier and the credential. For this reason, PSKs must be unique. Given a key, an application must be able to identify the corresponding user without any ambiguity. The basic premise that we are working on is the avoidance of HTTPS. For this reason, the PSK cannot be transmitted as is.

We need to have two keys: one acting as the identity of the user and the other acting as the credential. I call the former a public key and the latter a private key, similar to the keys we saw in Chapter 6 with asymmetric algorithms. However, these keys are not mathematically linked. Also, the same key used to sign on the sender's end is used to validate the signature on the receiver's end; hence, this is just a symmetric shared key. But similar to public key cryptography, only the private key must be guarded.

As we saw in Chapter 8, in digest authentication a username is transmitted, although the password is not sent. In contrast, when we use two keys, the username or user ID is not transmitted. Only the identifier key is sent. By also making the identifier a key, we strengthen the mechanism and prevent identifier misuse by the users sharing the ID. A user must "possess" both the public key (identifier) and the private key (credential), not just know them, to access the web API.

Defense Against Man-in-the-Middle Attacks

With no HTTPS, a man-in-the-middle (MITM) attack is one of the most significant threats. The primary mechanism to ensure data integrity of messages is a Hash-Based Message Authentication Code (HMAC). HMAC is just a piece of data created through a cryptographic hashing algorithm and a shared secret key. In this section, I show you how to create an HMAC using the SHA256 algorithm. For the purpose of this implementation, I ignore confidentiality requirements. However, if the message needs to be encrypted for confidentiality, you can easily add that functionality using the same private key we use for HMAC or you can introduce a new key specifically for encryption.

When a user sends a request, it includes three important parameters.

1. The public key, which is the key associated with the user. The public PSK is transmitted, not the actual identifier or username.

2. The counter, which is the same as the nonce counter that we saw with digest authentication in Chapter 8. This is just a number that the client application keeps incrementing with each request.

3. The timestamp or simply the stamp, with a number representing the seconds elapsed since midnight of January 1, 1970 UTC, also known as UNIX time.

In addition to the parameters, the request includes a signature that ensures that none of the parameters are tampered with. It is possible to create the signature based not only on the three parameters but also on the entire body of the request if the objective is to make sure nothing in the request gets modified.

To make sure no one tampers with the parameters, we can include an HMAC-SHA256 of all three values plus the request URI and HTTP method. Listing 9-1 shows an HTTP request secured by the PSK mechanism. Figure 9-2 shows the PSK design.

Listing 9-1. HTTP Request Message

```
GET http://localhost.:12536/api/values/7 HTTP/1.1
X-PSK: DpLMCOihcYI2i6DaMbso9Dzo1miy7OG/3+UibTccoKaen3Fecywdf7DrkcfkG3KjeMbZ6djBihD/4A==
X-Counter: 33
X-Stamp: 1350214768
X-Signature: 9D2rq7KuFh9KxvibgT3bLNIFAm3HFWLD1Adn/KyagIY=
Host: server.com
```

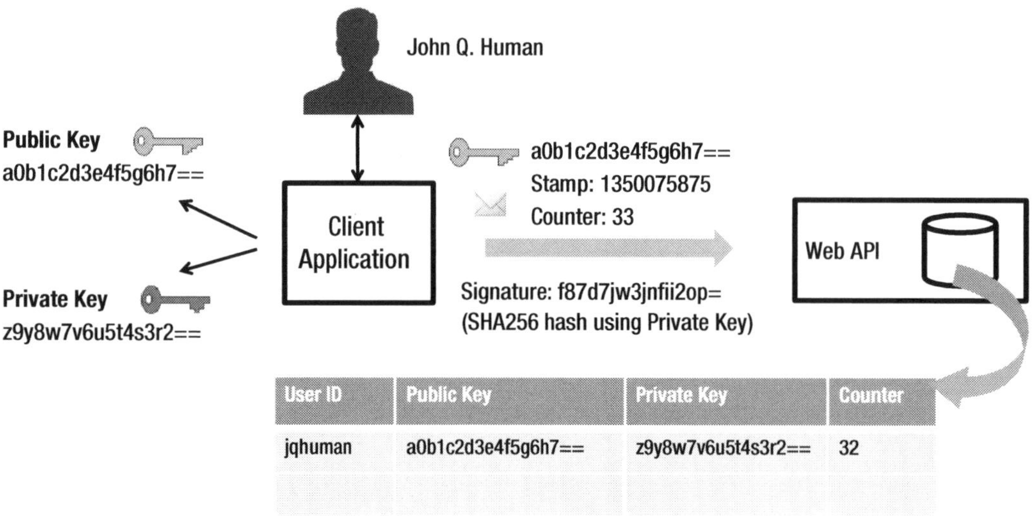

Figure 9-2. *PSK pair*

Table 9-1 shows the custom headers we use and describes how the values in the headers are used in the validation to counteract replay and MITM attacks.

Table 9-1. *Custom Headers*

Custom Header	Purpose
X-PSK	The public shared key used as the user identifier.
X-Signature	If the value sent by the client application in the X-Signature matches the HMAC-SHA256 of the values of X-PSK, X-Counter, X-Stamp, request URI, and the HTTP method, we can safely conclude that nothing was altered in transit.
X-Stamp	The value sent by the client and the UNIX time of the current time are compared. If the skew between these two are within the allowable tolerance limit, the request is not a replay. UNIX time is the number of seconds elapsed since midnight of January 1, 1970 Coordinated Universal Time (UTC).
X-Counter	If the value sent by the client is greater than the last received counter in the record kept by the server, the request is not a replay. Although I use both the timestamp and counter in the implementation example in this chapter, one typically is good enough, depending on your needs. If clock times are reasonably in sync, a timestamp is the best approach because there is no overhead in terms of storing the counter in the web API side or incrementing it in the client side.

Implementing the Preshared Key Design

In this section, I show you how to implement PSK-based authentication in ASP.NET Web API. I start by implementing my design on the client side. First, I need a mechanism to generate keys. I use the same mechanism involving `RNGCryptoServiceProvider` that I used in Chapter 6 to generate shared keys (see Listing 9-2). I use a key size of 64 bytes here.

Listing 9-2. Shared Key Generation

```
using (var provider = new RNGCryptoServiceProvider())
{
    byte[] secretKeyBytes = new byte[64];
    provider.GetBytes(secretKeyBytes);

    Console.WriteLine(Convert.ToBase64String(secretKeyBytes));
}
```

For the obvious reason that I am making up my own security mechanism here using PSKs, I will not get any help from a browser out of the box. The following steps show how to create a console application in C#.

1. I start with a typical console application with a `Program` class containing a `Main` method. For the purpose of illustration, I hard-code a public and a private key. The public and private keys are cut in half and then joined together in the code listing for cosmetic reasons because the keys are too long to fit into a single line (see Listing 9-3).

   Listing 9-3. PSK Client: Console Application

   ```
   class Program
   {
       static void Main(string[] args)
       {
           string publicKey = "DpLMCOihcYI2i6DaMbso9Dzo1miy7OG/3+UibTttjLSiJ3cco";
           publicKey += "Kaen3Fecywdf7DrkcfkG3KjeMbZ6djBihD/4A==";
   ```

```
            string privateKey = "W9cE42m+fmBXXvTpYDa2CXIme7DQmk3FcwXOzqR7fmj";
            privateKey += "D6PHHliwdtRb5cOUaxpPyh+3C6Y5Z34uGb2DWD/Awiw==";

            // The code to use HttpClient to make a web API request goes here

            Console.Read();
        }
    }
```

2. I use HttpClient to set the headers and make a GET request (see Listing 9-4).

Listing 9-4. Client: Console Application

```
using (HttpClient client = new HttpClient())
{
        // Step 2-a
        int counter = 33;
        Uri uri = new Uri("http://localhost:54400/api/employees/12345");

        client.DefaultRequestHeaders.Add("X-PSK", publicKey);
        client.DefaultRequestHeaders.Add("X-Counter", String.Format("{0}", counter));

        // Step 2-b
        DateTime epochStart = new DateTime(1970, 01, 01, 0, 0, 0, 0, DateTimeKind.Utc);
        TimeSpan ts = DateTime.UtcNow - epochStart;
        string stamp = Convert.ToUInt64(ts.TotalSeconds).ToString();
        client.DefaultRequestHeaders.Add("X-Stamp", stamp);

        string data = String.Format("{0}{1}{2}{3}{4}", publicKey, counter, stamp,
                                                        uri.ToString(), "GET");

        // Step 2-c
        byte[] signature = Encoding.UTF8.GetBytes(data);
        using (HMACSHA256 hmac = new HMACSHA256(Convert.FromBase64String(privateKey)))
        {
                byte[] signatureBytes = hmac.ComputeHash(signature);
                client.DefaultRequestHeaders.Add("X-Signature",
                                                Convert.ToBase64String(signatureBytes));
        }

        var httpMessage = client.GetAsync(uri).Result;
        if(httpMessage.IsSuccessStatusCode)
            Console.WriteLine(httpMessage.Content.ReadAsStringAsync().Result);
}
```

a. I'm hard-coding a counter here and not incrementing it with every request, just to keep the example code simple. The counter value is sent in the X-Counter header.

b. For UNIX time, I create a new DateTime object of type UTC corresponding to January 1, 1970. I get the current time in UTC using DateTime.UtcNow and compute the difference between these two dates in seconds. That is the UNIX time.

c. The signature or HMAC is computed for the public key, two headers, and the resource URI and HTTP method concatenated as one single string, with no delimiters. Finally, I'm using HMACSHA256 to compute the signature, which is stuffed into the X-Signature header. I'm simply following the convention of using the X- prefix to indicate that these are our own custom headers.

In the server side, which as usual is ASP.NET Web API, I write a message handler to check the PSK (see Listing 9-5).

Listing 9-5. PSK Delegating Handler

```
public class PskHandler : DelegatingHandler
{
    protected override async Task<HttpResponseMessage> SendAsync(HttpRequestMessage request,
                                                      CancellationToken cancellationToken)
    {
        string privateKey = "W9cE42m+fmBXXvTpYDa2CXIme7DQmk3FcwXOzqR7fmj";
        privateKey += "D6PHHliwdtRb5cOUaxpPyh+3C6Y5Z34uGb2DWD/Awiw==";

        var headers = request.Headers;

        if (headers.Contains("X-PSK") && headers.Contains("X-Counter") &&
                headers.Contains("X-Stamp") && headers.Contains("X-Signature"))
        {
            string publicKey = headers.GetValues("X-PSK").First();
            string counter = headers.GetValues("X-Counter").First();
            ulong stamp = Convert.ToUInt64(headers.GetValues("X-Stamp").First());
            string incomingSignature = headers.GetValues("X-Signature").First();

            string data = String.Format("{0}{1}{2}{3}{4}", publicKey, counter, stamp,
                                                    request.RequestUri.ToString(),
                                                    request.Method.Method);

            byte[] signature = Encoding.UTF8.GetBytes(data);
            using (HMACSHA256 hmac = new HMACSHA256(Convert.FromBase64String(privateKey)))
            {
                byte[] signatureBytes = hmac.ComputeHash(signature);
                if (incomingSignature.Equals(
                                Convert.ToBase64String(signatureBytes), StringComparison.Ordinal))
                {
                    DateTime epochStart = new DateTime(1970, 01, 01, 0, 0, 0, 0, DateTimeKind.Utc);
                    TimeSpan ts = DateTime.UtcNow - epochStart;

                    if (Convert.ToUInt64(ts.TotalSeconds) - stamp <= 3)
                        return await base.SendAsync(request, cancellationToken);
                }
            }
        }

        return request.CreateResponse(HttpStatusCode.Unauthorized);
    }
}
```

The signature computation is the same as what is done on the client side. After all, that is the idea. If there is any problem in the validation, I send back a 401 - Unauthorized Response.

To keep this code example lean, I intentionally skip the following steps in the message handler.

1. I don't check to see if the counter is incremented from the previous request, and for that reason I don't maintain a record of the counters. If you want to see this implementation, please refer to digest authentication in Chapter 8, where I show how the nonce counter is stored and checked.

2. I don't retrieve the private key corresponding to the public key. I simply hard-code the private key I use in the client (the console app).

3. I don't create an object of type `IPrincipal` and set it to `Thread.CurrentPrincipal` for other components down the pipeline to use. When you implement this mechanism with the backup from a persistence store such as a database, while retrieving the private key from the data store for the incoming public key you can retrieve the corresponding username as well. Based on that, claims such as the username claim and other relevant claims can be built and the principal created.

In the preceding code, I check for freshness of the request by looking at the timestamp. If the timestamp was made only 3 seconds ago, I accept the request. It could be too close for some scenarios, and it does demand that the client and server clocks are closely synchronized. However, it does a good job of preventing replays.

You can test this by using the Fiddler tool, the same tool we used in Chapter 4. Launch Fiddler and make sure it is capturing "All Processes." From the console app, make a request and ensure you get 200 - OK. As soon as you see the result column in the web sessions list on the left pane change from a dash to 200, right-click and select Replay ➤ Reissue Unconditionally from the shortcut menu. You should get a 401 - Unauthorized status code.

Merits and Demerits of a Preshared Key

If we implement a PSK by using a key pair, we ensure that the PSK is not sent in the messages exchanged. Because the secret key is not sent, we can use HTTP. Because we implement message security and not transport security, the need for the server-side X.509 certificate is obviated. For this reason, the message-security-based PSK is relatively cost effective. Of course, we generate the random keys ourselves to be used as the symmetric PSK. The message-security-based mechanisms generally are considered superior to transport security because message security guarantees security despite the presence of intermediaries.

On the flip side, PSKs are based on the assumption that both parties involved will keep the keys secure. If it is compromised on one end, it affects both parties. Also, the message security mechanism is slightly complex to implement. Even so, it is a smaller price to pay than the cost of implementing transport security. Another disadvantage of PSKs is that they can cause overhead for IT departments because the keys need to be rotated regularly as a countermeasure to the security risk involved with two parties having to keep a shared key secret.

X.509 Client Certificate

A digital X.509 certificate, when used as a credential to authenticate an entity to a service, is called an X.509 client certificate. The entity to which the certificate is issued could be an application or an end user. Unlike the server certificates that are issued to an entity such as a company, a client certificate can be issued to individual end users to be used as their credential to authenticate into an application. In the context of a web application, the user agent (the web browser) can automatically pick up the client certificate from the local store and present it to the server as the user's credential, on whose behalf it transacts with the server.

A digital certificate binds an identity to a pair of keys that can be used to encrypt and sign data. In Chapter 6, we saw encryption and signing in action using the pair of public and private keys from a digital certificate as well as without a certificate. Obviously, the sole purpose of existence of a digital certificate is not for providing a public-private key pair for public key cryptography. It is more than that, because a digital certificate ensures that the public key contained in the certificate belongs to an entity to which the certificate was issued. A digital certificate is an identity. In this section, we focus specifically on the client certificate, which is the digital certificate issued to an end user to be used as a credential for authentication.

A digital certificate is issued by a certification authority (CA). A certificate typically contains the following items:

- Public key
- Name of the entity to which the certificate is issued
- Date of expiry
- CA who has issued the certificate
- Serial number associated with the certificate
- Digital signature created using the CA's private key
- Algorithm used to create the signature

The most widely accepted format for digital certificates is defined by the CCITT X.509 international standard. When someone mentions a digital certificate, he typically is referring to a X.509 certificate. Sometimes, people do refer to a certificate by the name of "SSL certificate" because the major use for X.509 certificates is with the SSL/TLS protocol.

Server Certificate vs. Client Certificate

An X.509 certificate that is used by a server as a credential to prove its identity to the end user (or the user agent the user uses) is called a server certificate. An X.509 certificate that is used by an end user through the user agent to prove her identity to a server is called a client certificate.

An X.509 certificate as a credential to prove one's identity is relevant for the communication involving transport layer security (TLS). In our case, it is TLS with HTTP, known more commonly as HTTPS. We saw in Chapter 4 how the X.509 certificate issued to a server is used and checked by browsers when HTTPS is used. During the TLS handshake process the web server sends the X.509 certificate (with the public key only), which is issued to the entity that owns the web site, to the user agent (web browser). This certificate is called a server certificate. The browser validates it against the list of CAs it trusts. If the certificate is in the trusted CA list and the certificate is issued to the web site to which the browser currently connects, the web browser is convinced about the server's identity. So far, this check is done from the perspective of ascertaining the authenticity of the web server's identity. In other words, the server certificate is the means to prove the identity of the server to the end user. Of course, the end user does not check the certificates during the TLS handshake. The user agent or the web browser does it, on behalf of the user.

TLS allows mutual validation. Just like a web browser validating the authenticity of the server credential, a server can validate the authenticity of the user credential. A browser can be configured to send an X.509 certificate of the end user to the web server when it establishes the secure connection through a TLS handshake. Such an X.509 certificate, which is sent by the browser to the web server as a means to prove the identity of the end user to the server, is called a client certificate (not a user certificate, although it basically is a user credential). A client certificate is generally issued to a user.

An X.509 certificate can be used as both a server certificate and a client certificate. What really differentiates a certificate is the end of the communication channel where it is used. The extended key usage indicates how a certificate is supposed to be used, as shown in Figure 9-3. A server certificate, when configured to be used as client certificate, will never work and vice versa.

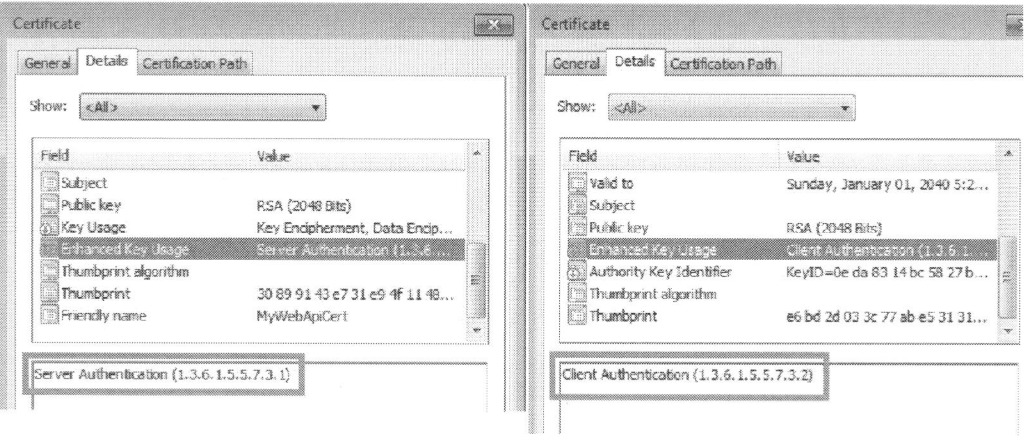

Figure 9-3. *Server certificate vs. client certificate*

Using Client Certificate for Authentication in ASP.NET Web API

In this section, I implement authentication in ASP.NET Web API using an X.509 client certificate. There are several steps, which are mostly configuration-related steps that I need to perform to implement client certificate-based security in ASP.NET Web API. For this purpose, I use web-hosted ASP.NET Web API, which uses IIS. For the client side, I use Internet Explorer. But I do show you how to consume a web API outside of a browser, through a C# console application. Following is an overview of the steps to implement client certificate-based authentication in ASP.NET Web API.

1. Enable HTTPS in IIS. Although you must use a CA-issued certificate for this purpose in production, I use a self-signed certificate. Make HTTPS and the client certificate mandatory in IIS.

2. Create a self-signed certificate to be used as a client certificate and package it for distribution using the PVK2PFX tool. Configure this certificate in Internet Explorer.

3. Implement a message handler in ASP.NET Web API to retrieve the client certificate from the request, validate the same, and set the principal object.

SELF-SIGNED CERTIFICATE

A self-signed certificate is signed by the same entity for whose identity it stands. A self-signed certificate is signed with its own private key! In short, this is similar to me certifying myself. In the real world, unless you are someone who everyone else trusts, no one is going to believe the certificate you give to yourself. A third party that is trusted by both the first and second party is needed to complete the circle of trust. In the world of digital certificates, that trusted third party is a certification authority (CA) such as VeriSign. A certificate issued by a CA is trusted by all, but it does cost money. A self-signed certificate, such as the one created by the tool Makecert that we saw in Chapter 6, costs nothing but is trusted by no one. It can be used for testing purposes only.

Enabling HTTPS in IIS through Self-Signed Certificates

To enable HTTPS in IIS, I use Visual Studio 2012 to create the application in IIS and IIS Manager (InetMgr.exe) to do the rest. The following steps show the process.

1. Launch Visual Studio an as administrator.
2. Create a new ASP.NET MVC 4.0 project with the Web API template. In Solution Explorer, double-click the Properties node under the project (see Figure 9-4).

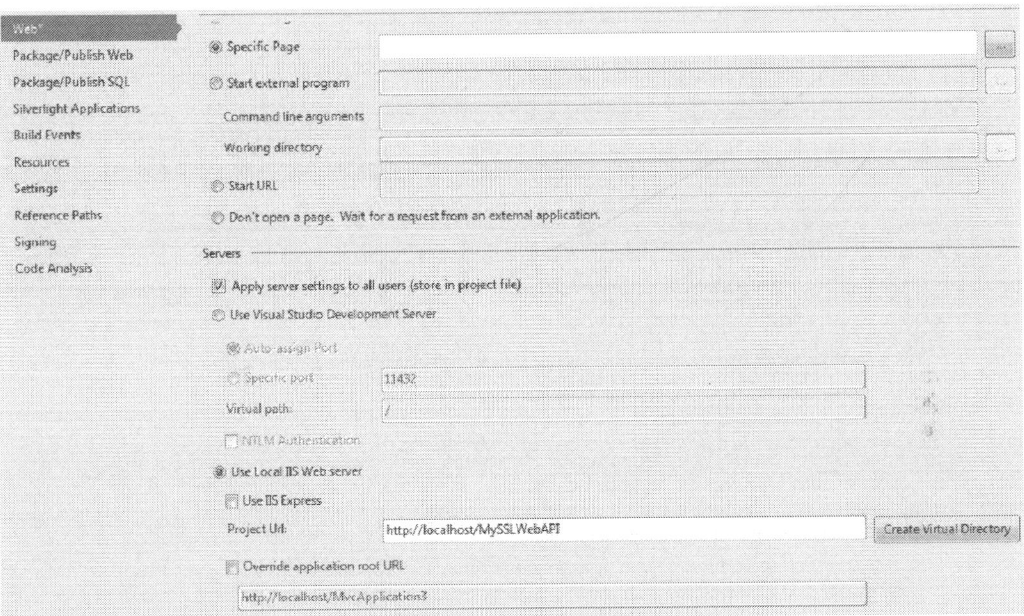

Figure 9-4. *Running a web API application in IIS*

3. Select Use Local IIS Web server and make sure the Use IIS Express check box remains cleared. Click Create Virtual Directory so that Visual Studio creates a virtual directory for you as part of the Default Web Site.
4. Next, use IIS Manager to generate a server certificate, as shown in Figure 9-5. I use IIS 7.5. Depending on the version you use, what you see on your machine could be different from the screenshots. Click on the root machine node in tree view in the left pane and double-click the Server Certificates icon in the right pane. On the resulting screen, click the Create Self-Signed Certificate. . . link. Enter a friendly name such as MyWebApiCert in the pop-up and click OK to complete the server certificate generation.

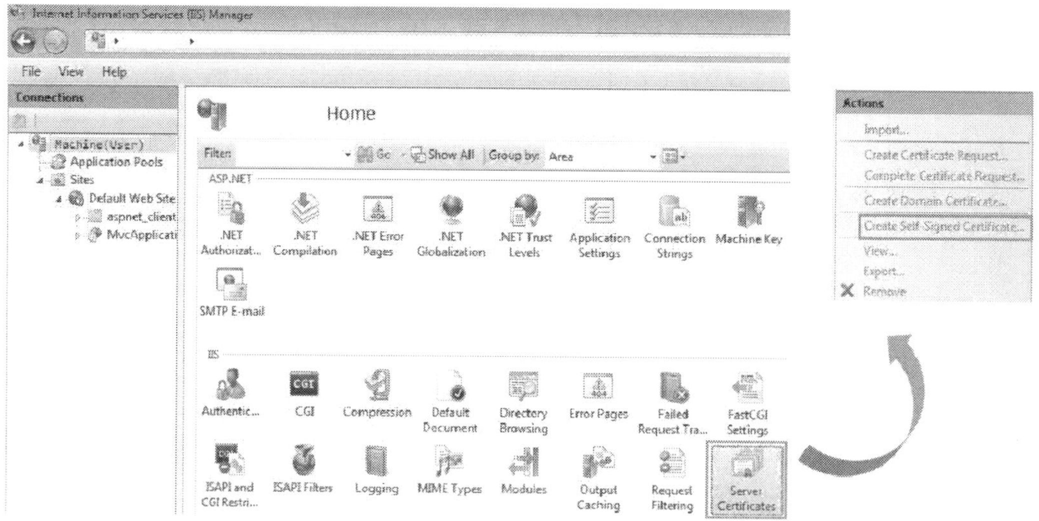

Figure 9-5. *IIS Manager: Certificate generation*

5. Now that we have the server certificate, we need to let IIS use it. Click the Default Web Site node of the tree view in the left pane. In the Actions pane on the right, click Bindings. . . . Click Add (see Figure 9-6). In the Add Site Binding dialog box, select https as Type and select the certificate we just generated, which is MyWebApiCert. Click OK to finish creating the binding.

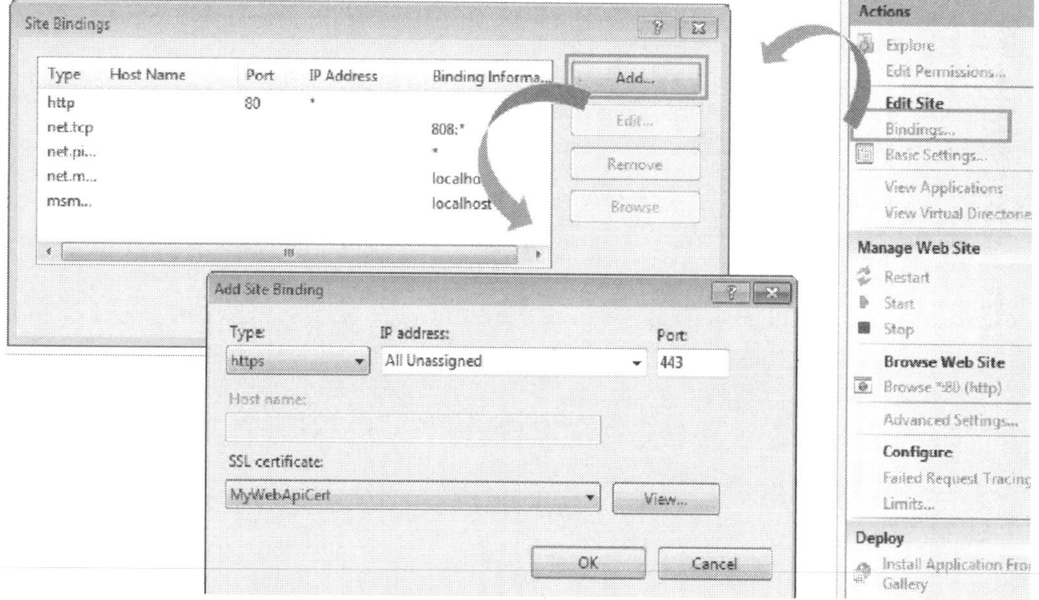

Figure 9-6. *IIS Manager: Configuring HTTPS binding*

6. Now we are all set to invoke our web API using HTTPS. When we do so directly through a browser, IIS will send the public key of the self-signed server certificate we just generated to the browser. Because this is a self-signed certificate, the browser will not be happy and will show a warning that the certificate is not something it trusts. But it works!

7. We will now configure IIS to mandate a client certificate. It is just a configuration change. Click the virtual directory of the tree view in the left pane. As shown in Figure 9-7, double-click SSL Settings, select the Require SSL check box, and select the Require radio button. That completes the configuration changes we need to make in IIS.

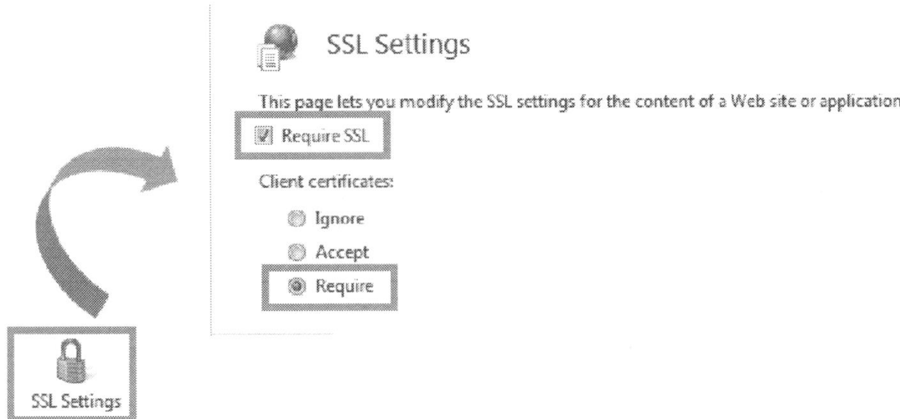

Figure 9-7. *IIS Manager: Configuring to mandate a client certificate*

Creating and Configuring the Client Certificate

IIS 7.0 helps us generate the server-side certificate, but when it comes to the client-side certificate, we are on our own. Of course, we can use the Makecert tool to create a self-signed certificate. Following are the steps to generate a client certificate using Makecert, package the certificate using PVK2PFX, and configure the same in Internet Explorer.

1. Before we generate the client certificate, we need a root certificate on which we will base our client certificate. In an ideal world, this will be a CA like VeriSign. In this scenario, though, we will create the root certificate using Makecert, as shown in Listing 9-6. The command-line parameter of cy is what makes this certificate a special CA certificate.

Listing 9-6. Makecert Command to Create a Root Certificate

```
makecert.exe -r -n "CN=WebApiCA" -pe -sv WebApiCA.pvk -a sha256  -cy authority WebApiCA.cer
```

■ **Note** To run the Makecert commands, use the Developer command prompt for Visual Studio 2012, available under All Programs ➤ Microsoft Visual Studio ➤ Visual Studio Tools. If you use Visual Studio 2010, it will be a Visual Studio command prompt. In either case, you must run the prompt as an administrator.

---

2. Type in a password when prompted. Once Makecert completes execution successfully, you will have two files created.

   a. A PVK file that contains the certificate's private key. Because this file contains the private key, this file must be appropriately safeguarded.

   b. A CER file that contains the public key.

3. In Chapter 6, we used Makecert to generate and add the certificate to the local store directly. In this case, it just generates the certificate files. Because we plan to use this certificate as the root certificate for the client certificates, this certificate needs to be sent to the users and ultimately get added to the certificate store on their machines. We need to add this certificate to the Trusted Root CA in both IIS and the machine where the client will run. We can use the Microsoft Management Console (MMC) for this purpose.

   a. The executable corresponding to MMC is `C:\Windows\System32\mmc.exe`. You can also run MMC by typing **mmc** in the Run box.

   b. Once MMC is launched, select File ➤ Add/Remove snap-in or press Ctrl+M to bring up Add or Remove Snap-ins.

   c. Select Certificates from the Available snap-ins list view on the left and click Add.

   d. In the resulting dialog box, choose the Computer account radio button, click Next, select Local computer, and click Finish.

   e. Finally, click OK to see the certificates on your computer, as shown in Figure 9-8.

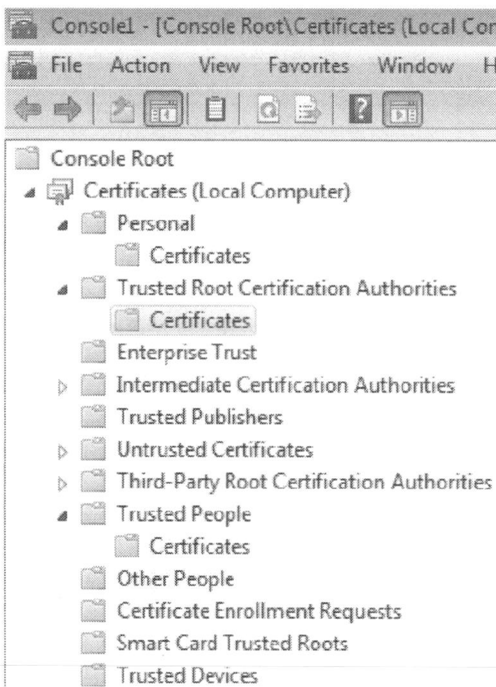

Figure 9-8. *Microsoft Management Console*

f. Expand the tree view on the left and go to Trusted Root Certification Authorities. Right-click the Certificates folder and select All Tasks... ➤ Import. Select the WebApiCA.CER and complete the process to add the certificate to the Trusted Root CA.

You need to perform these steps only in IIS (server). Of course, you can do the same on client machines as well, but there is an additional step involved in creating and packaging client certificates.

4. Next, we need to create the client certificate. We will use the same Makecert command that we used to create the root certificate. The command to run is shown in Listing 9-7.

Listing 9-7. Makecert Command to Create a Client Certificate

```
makecert.exe -iv WebApiCA.pvk -ic WebApiCA.cer -n "CN=jqhuman" -pe -sv jqhuman.pvk -a sha256 -sky
exchange jqhuman.cer -eku 1.3.6.1.5.5.7.3.2
```

5. Makecert again creates two files: one each for the public and private key. As a general rule, all private keys must be safely kept and only public keys can be distributed. The client certificate CN=jqhuman is issued by WebApiCA. The parameter of eku is what makes this certificate a client certificate. If you plan to use the web API from a browser, say JQuery calling the web API, unless the certificate is specifically marked as a client certificate the browser will not send the certificate to IIS. Basically, it will not work!

6. A client certificate has been created, but the certificate needs packaging for delivery. PVK2PFX is another command-line tool we will use to package the certificate (public and private keys) into a Personal Information Exchange (.pfx) file. See Listing 9-8 for the command to use to create the .pfx file.

   Listing 9-8. PVK2PFX Command-Line Tool

   ```
   pvk2pfx.exe -pvk jqhuman.pvk -spc jqhuman.cer -pfx jqhuman.pfx -po p@ssw0rd!
   ```

7. Now, we can send the two files, `jqhuman.pfx` and `WebApiCA.cer`, to the user John Q. Human to be installed into the personal certificate store and Trusted Root CA, respectively. John can simply double-click the files and provide the password of p@ssw0rd! when prompted to complete the installation. Note this password is for the .pfx file only and can be different from the password entered at the time the certificate was generated by Makecert.

8. To verify the client certificate installed successfully, John can open Internet Explorer and go to Tools ➤ Options, click the Content tab, and click the Certificates button to confirm the certificate is installed, as shown in Figure 9-9.

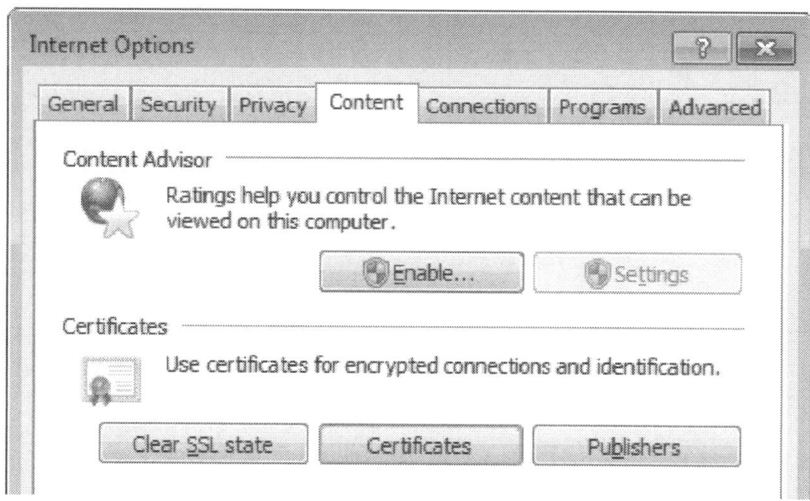

Figure 9-9. *Internet Explorer*

With the setup complete, if you go directly to an API, say /api/employees from Internet Explorer, nothing special will appear to have happened. However, Internet Explorer is silently picking the certificate CN=jqhuman and sending it to IIS.

We configured IIS to require this certificate, so it will fail all the requests without a client certificate. Once the certificate is received, it verifies that the issuer of the certificate is in the Trusted CA list on the server running IIS. If all is well, the request goes through to our web API pipeline.

Here is a quick summary of the setup we have accomplished.

1. We created a self-signed server certificate using IIS Manager and used it to create an HTTPS binding.
2. We made HTTPS and the client certificate mandatory in IIS.
3. We then created a root certificate using Makecert.
4. Using this root certificate, we created a client certificate.
5. We used the PVK2PFX tool to package the client certificate for distribution.

Ultimately, the end user's machine's trusted CA and the server—in this case, the machine running IIS that has the Trusted CA list—must include our root certificate for this whole thing to work. Additionally, from the client side, the browser must have the client certificate configured. If you double-click the .pfx file, Windows configures the client certificate for you automatically.

If you have control over what can be added to the Trusted CA list on the client machines, you can get away with generating your own client certificates using Makecert, even for production use. Although using certificates issued by a CA for all production needs is a good practice, our self-signed certificate will work just fine for client certificates. By providing an individual certificate to a user, we get enhanced security. Because a certificate is an ownership factor, you can restrict access to the web API only from machines where the certificates are installed. This is the great differentiating point of ownership-factor-based security over knowledge-factor-based security.

Using an X.509 Certificate in ASP.NET Web API

Finally, we get to write some code to use the client certificate that has come our way. It is really up to us to have the validations in place and the subsequent process to establish the identity based on the certificate. I generated the client certificate with the common name representing some kind of an identifier, jqhuman, representing the user John Q. Human. First, I need a database or a store where I track the certificates I have issued, against which I can validate the client certificate when it comes in the request. Second, I can go to some other store to get the claims or roles to be associated with this user identity. With these two, I can establish an authenticated identity with roles or claims that can be used for access control. I use a message handler here (see Listing 9-9), just as I have demonstrated in previous chapters.

Listing 9-9. X.509 Client Certificate Message Handler

```
public class X509ClientCertificateHandler : DelegatingHandler
{
    protected override async Task<HttpResponseMessage> SendAsync(HttpRequestMessage request,
                                                            CancellationToken cancellationToken)
    {
        var cert = request.GetClientCertificate();

        X509Chain chain = new X509Chain();
        chain.ChainPolicy.RevocationMode = X509RevocationMode.NoCheck;

        if (chain.Build(cert) && cert.Issuer.Equals("CN=WebApiCA"))
        {
            var claims = new List<Claim>
            {
                    new Claim(ClaimTypes.Name, cert.Subject.Substring(3)), // ignoring CN=
            };

            var principal = new ClaimsPrincipal(new[] { new ClaimsIdentity(claims, "X509") });

            Thread.CurrentPrincipal = principal;

            if (HttpContext.Current != null)
                HttpContext.Current.User = principal;

            return await base.SendAsync(request, cancellationToken);
        }

        return request.CreateResponse(HttpStatusCode.Unauthorized);
    }
}
```

The client certificate is pulled out of the request using the `GetClientCertificate()` method. The `X509Chain` class is used to validate the certificate by building the chain. In the example, I'm ignoring the revocation list, but in production that line can be commented out, if a proper list is available. I'm also making sure the issuer of the client certificate is CN=WebApiCA.

Testing our ASP.NET Web API

If the web API is used from JQuery or something similar that runs under the context of the browser, the browser sends the client certificate to IIS.

Listing 9-10 shows the C# code for a non-browser scenario. The important point to note is I had to set the callback for server certificate validation and simply return true to get this to work. The main reason is that the server returns our self-signed certificate. **This is a strict no-no for production**. A certificate issued by a CA is needed.

Listing 9-10. C# Client for ASP.NET Web API

```
ServicePointManager.ServerCertificateValidationCallback =
(object sender, X509Certificate cer, X509Chain chain, SslPolicyErrors error) =>
{
    return true; // This is done because we are using a self-signed certificate in the server side,
    not production strength
};

var client = WebRequest.Create("https://server.com/api/employees/12345") as HttpWebRequest;
var cert = new X509Certificate2(File.ReadAllBytes(@"C:\Users\Me\Certs\TestCert.pfx"), "p@ssw0rd!");
client.ClientCertificates.Add(cert);

string response = new StreamReader(client.GetResponse().GetResponseStream()).ReadToEnd();
```

■ **Note** It is possible to combine other authentication methods such as basic authentication, which is a knowledge-factor-based authentication, with the client certificate, which is an ownership-factor-based authentication, and make it a strong two-factor authentication. Because the client certificate is based on HTTPS, sending the credentials in clear text, as needed by basic authentication, poses no security issues. Chapter 14 includes a sample Two-Factor Authentication (TFA) implementation along this line.

Merits and Demerits of a Client Certificate Mechanism

A client certificate-based authentication is a robust way of authenticating a user. When combined with Windows privileges, a certificate cannot be shared with others and misuse can be prevented, compared to a password-based mechanism. No one can prevent you from writing your username and password on a sticky note and handing it to someone else, but a certificate can be closely guarded by IT systems because it's a file.

A client certificate mechanism can be combined with other authentication mechanisms, such as basic authentication, to achieve two-factor authentication for enhanced security.

A certificate needs to be installed on a machine before a web API can be called from that machine. This is a double-edged sword. It can work to your advantage, if you intend to limit the machines from where the web API must be accessed. On the other hand, it can get really stifling, restricting the users to use the web API only from those machines where a client certificate is available. Depending on the needs, this quality of the client certificate can work for you or against you. On the flip side, the process to set up and maintain the infrastructure supporting the client certificate is a bit complex and needs support from the IT operations and administration team. Also, a client certificate piggybacks on HTTPS and hence HTTPS is a must to implement client certificate-based authentication.

■ **Note** It is possible to map a client certificate to an Active Directory account. If implemented, the client certificate alone is needed to establish the identity with all the Active Directory groups as roles. This topic pertains to IT administration rather than programming, which is what this book is all about. For that reason, except for this brief mention, there will not be any detailed coverage.

SAML Tokens

Any security token is an ownership factor. The token might be in computer memory or doing rounds in the network stream all the time, unlike a certificate that can be saved into a file system as a file. We reviewed the three major formats of security tokens in Chapter 5, namely the Security Assertion Markup Language (SAML) token, the Simple Web Token (SWT), and the JSON Web Token (JWT). SAML is XML-based and has SOAP affinity. Typically, it travels as part of the payload of a SOAP web service rather than in HTTP headers or the body of RESTful service messages.

In Chapter 7, we built a custom Security Token Service (STS) with a WS-Trust endpoint capable of issuing SAML tokens. In this chapter, we get a SAML token from that STS and will use it from ASP.NET Web API. When a RESTful service is being built from the ground up along with the security infrastructure, it is likely that RESTful-friendly tokens like SWT or JWT will get used. This is not a hard and fast rule, though.

The organizations that have already invested in SAML token issuing infrastructure will want to leverage the existing infrastructure with the new RESTful services they would like to build using the great ASP.NET Web API framework. That is the reason I provide this section on using SAML tokens with ASP.NET Web API. We look at web tokens in the next chapter, which is dedicated exclusively to SWT and JWT.

Figure 9-10 illustrates the overall setup. The STS used in this chapter will be straight from Chapter 7. It exposes a WS-Trust endpoint that issues a token in the RSTR response for the incoming RST request. STS can support both WS-Federation for passive clients and WS-Trust directly for active clients. In our case, we do not deal with passive clients; hence, the STS that we created will support WS-Trust only and more specifically, only the token issuance.

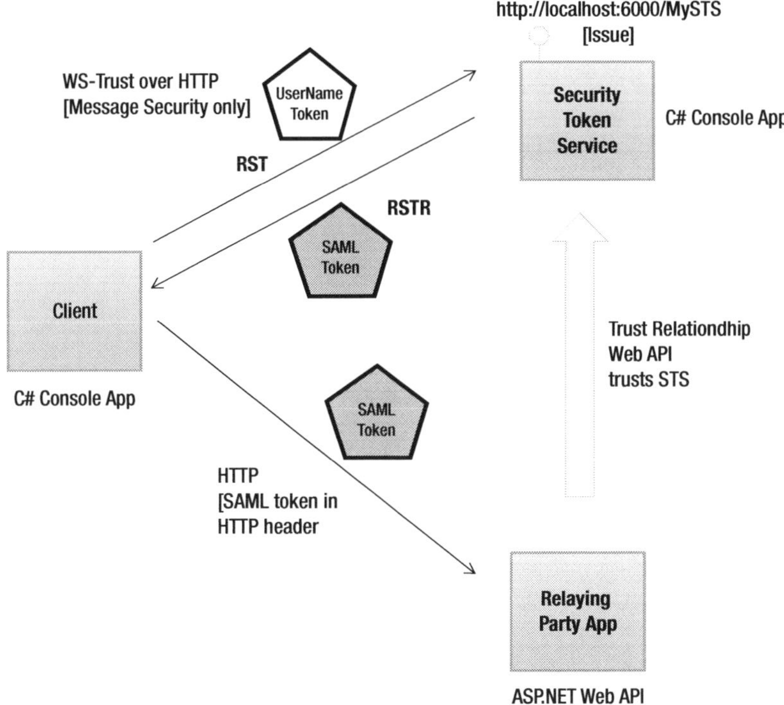

Figure 9-10. *Using a SAML token with ASP.NET Web API*

In this book, I do not intend to cover the topic of building a production-strength STS. Coverage is limited to building a basic STS, from which a token can be requested by the client (which is a console application) and ultimately presented as a credential to an ASP.NET Web API. The assumption here is that your IT security infrastructure already has something equivalent, such as an Active Directory Federation Services endpoint or a custom STS that you might have purchased in the past.

Implementing the Client Console Application

To implement the client console application, I build on the code from Chapter 7 that makes an RST request to the STS and gets the SAML token from the RSTR response. The `GetToken()` method described in the section "Requesting a Token from a Custom STS" in Chapter 7 does this and returns the token as a string. I modify the method to return a `Tuple` of a SAML token and the proof key. I use `System.Net.Http.HttpClient` to make a GET request to our web API, as shown in Listing 9-11. In this request, I put the SAML token as a base64-encoded string in the Authorization request header, using a custom scheme that I have named Saml. I use the proof key to sign the SAML token and send the signature separately in another header called X-ProofSignature.

Listing 9-11. Modifications to the GetToken Method

```
private static Tuple<string, byte[]> GetToken()
{
    var binding = new WS2007HttpBinding(SecurityMode.Message);

    binding.Security.Message.ClientCredentialType = MessageCredentialType.UserName;
    binding.Security.Message.NegotiateServiceCredential = true;
    binding.Security.Message.EstablishSecurityContext = false;

    var address = new EndpointAddress(new Uri(@"http://localhost:6000/MySTS"),
                                                        new DnsEndpointIdentity("MySTS"));

    WSTrustChannelFactory factory = new WSTrustChannelFactory(binding, address);
    factory.TrustVersion = TrustVersion.WSTrust13;

    factory.Credentials.ServiceCertificate.Authentication.CertificateValidationMode =
                                                                X509CertificateValidationMode.None;
    factory.Credentials.ServiceCertificate.Authentication.RevocationMode =
                                                                        X509RevocationMode.NoCheck;
    factory.Credentials.UserName.UserName = "jqhuman";
    factory.Credentials.UserName.Password = "jqhuman"; // has to be the same as username in our example

    WSTrustChannel channel = (WSTrustChannel)factory.CreateChannel();

    var request = new RequestSecurityToken(System.IdentityModel.Protocols.WSTrust.RequestTypes.Issue)
    {
        AppliesTo = new EndpointReference("http://my-server.com")
    };

    RequestSecurityTokenResponse response = null;
    var token = channel.Issue(request, out response) as GenericXmlSecurityToken;

    var proofKey = response.RequestedProofToken.ProtectedKey.GetKeyBytes();

    return new Tuple<string,byte[]>(token.TokenXml.OuterXml, proofKey);
}
```

The concept of checking the ownership of a SAML token using a proof key is part of the WS-Trust specification, which is for SOAP. In REST-based services, when a SAML token has to be used it is generally used as a bearer token rather than as a holder-of-key token. However, there is no hard and fast rule that holder-of-key tokens must not be used with ASP.NET Web API. The process is slightly more involved and has to be customized through the use of the X-ProofSignature custom HTTP header, but I decided to include the proof key validation. It is very easy to drop the same if you intend to deal with only bearer tokens. If you want the STS to issue a bearer token, ask for it explicitly by specifying the KeyType of `KeyTypes.Bearer` when you issue an RST. The following steps show how to complete the client application implementation.

1. Modify the `GetToken` method from Chapter 7 to return the SAML token (XML) as a string and the proof key as a byte array in a `Tuple`. See Listing 9-11. The modifications are shown in bold type.

2. Call the `GetToken` method from the `Main` method and receive the SAML token as XML and the proof key as a byte array, as shown in Listing 9-12.

Listing 9-12. Client Application

```
static void Main(string[] args)
{
    Tuple<string, byte[]> token = GetToken();

    string saml = token.Item1;
    byte[] proofKey = token.Item2;

    // Code to use HttpClient goes here
}
```

3. Use `HttpClient` to make an HTTP GET to ASP.NET Web API, passing the SAML token in the Authorization header (using a custom scheme that I call Saml). See Listing 9-13. Using the proof key returned by the `GetToken` method call, create an HMAC using the SHA256 algorithm for the SAML token XML and stuff it in the X-ProofSignature header before the call to ASP.NET Web API.

Listing 9-13. Calling ASP.NET Web API

```
using (HttpClient client = new HttpClient())
{
    byte[] bytes = Encoding.UTF8.GetBytes(saml);
    var header = new AuthenticationHeaderValue("Saml", Convert.ToBase64String(bytes));
    client.DefaultRequestHeaders.Authorization = header;

    using (HMACSHA256 hmac = new HMACSHA256(proofKey))
    {
        byte[] signatureBytes = hmac.ComputeHash(bytes);
        client.DefaultRequestHeaders.Add("X-ProofSignature", Convert.ToBase64String(signatureBytes));
    }

    var httpMessage = client.GetAsync("http://localhost:54400/api/employees/12345")
                              .Result;
    if (httpMessage.IsSuccessStatusCode)
        Console.WriteLine(httpMessage.Content.ReadAsStringAsync().Result);
}
```

■ **Note** At this point, the client console application has no visibility to the proof key inside the SAML token because the token is encrypted. HMAC is created using the proof key received in the RSTR from the STS. Also, note the client application computes the HMAC for the SAML XML and sends only the HMAC in the X-ProofSignature header. The proof key is never sent to the relying party (ASP.NET Web API).

Accepting a SAML Token in ASP.NET Web API

The client application, a console application in this case, requests a SAML token from our custom STS, stuffs the token and the signature it computed using the proof key in the Authorization and the custom headers, respectively, and makes a call to ASP.NET Web API. The following steps show how to implement the code in ASP.NET Web API to accept the SAML token as a client credential, validate it, extract the claims out, and establish the user identity.

1. In the ASP.NET Web API side, we use a message handler as shown in Listing 9-14 to read, validate the token, extract the claims out, and use the same to build a principal and set it in `Thread.CurrentPrincipal`. If there is no authorization header or the scheme does not match the name Saml, we don't send an unauthorized response. We simply do not set the `Thread.CurrentPrincipal` and any access control down the line depending on this will fail. This handler can short-circuit the pipeline and send an unauthorized response, if that is what is desired.

Listing 9-14. Message Handler to Read the SAML Token

```
public class AuthenticationHandler : DelegatingHandler
{
    protected override async Task<HttpResponseMessage> SendAsync(HttpRequestMessage request,
                                                                  CancellationToken cancellationToken)
    {
        var encoding = Encoding.GetEncoding("iso-8859-1");
        var headers = request.Headers;

        if (headers.Authorization != null && headers.Authorization.Scheme.Equals("Saml"))
        {
            string token = encoding.GetString(
                                    Convert.FromBase64String(headers.Authorization.Parameter));

            // Code to use the token goes here
        }

        return await base.SendAsync(request, cancellationToken);
    }
}
```

2. It is possible to parse the SAML just like any other XML, but there is a better alternative. We can use a security token handler to read and validate the token. Of course, we need to specify the X.509 certificate used by the STS as encrypting credentials so that the token handler can decrypt it correctly. In Listing 9-15, I use the certificate CN=RP. On a machine running STS, this certificate will contain only the public key. The machine running the web API must have the certificate with the private key. I reuse the extension method `ToCertificate` that we created in Chapter 6 here to read the certificates.

Listing 9-15. Reading a SAML Token

```
using (var stringReader = new StringReader(token))
{
        using (var samlReader = XmlReader.Create(stringReader))
        {
            var tokenHandlers = SecurityTokenHandlerCollection
                                                .CreateDefaultSecurityTokenHandlerCollection();
            SecurityTokenHandlerConfiguration config = tokenHandlers.Configuration;

            var securityTokens = new List<SecurityToken>()
            {
                new X509SecurityToken("CN=RP".ToCertificate())
            };

            config.ServiceTokenResolver = SecurityTokenResolver.CreateDefaultSecurityTokenResolver(
                                                        securityTokens.AsReadOnly(), false);
            config.CertificateValidator = X509CertificateValidator.None; // See the following caution
            config.IssuerTokenResolver = new X509CertificateStoreTokenResolver(StoreName.My,
                                                                StoreLocation.LocalMachine);
            config.IssuerNameRegistry = new TrustedIssuerNameRegistry();
            config.AudienceRestriction.AllowedAudienceUris.Add(new Uri("http://my-server.com"));

            SecurityToken samlToken = tokenHandlers.ReadToken(samlReader);

            // Proof checking logic goes here

        }
}
```

■ **Caution** In my examples here, I use self-signed certificates with both STS and the relying party (ASP.NET Web API). To ensure they work, I bypass the check, as I have done in other places. The following line bypasses the certificate validation.

```
config.CertificateValidator = X509CertificateValidator.None;
```

It is not production strength in most cases, and you should consider using it with care as you design the security mechanism.

---

3. To check the token ownership using the proof key, compute HMAC-SHA256 just like the client and compare the HMAC thus computed with the one sent by the client. If they match, the client is the rightful owner of the token. Note the proof key used to compute the HMAC is retrieved from the token. The client application uses the proof key from the RSTR, as sent by STS. So, if this client is the entity that received the token directly from STS, it will have received the same proof key that is baked into the SAML token. That is the basis for the ownership checking. After ensuring the token ownership, validate the token and extract out the identity, as defined by the claims contained in the token. Create a principal object for this identity and set it in `Thread.CurrentPrincipal` (see Listing 9-16).

Listing 9-16. Proof Checking

```
bool isOwnershipValid = false;
if (headers.Contains("X-ProofSignature"))
{
    string incomingSignature = headers.GetValues("X-ProofSignature").First();

    var proofKey = (samlToken.SecurityKeys.First() as InMemorySymmetricSecurityKey)
                                                                .GetSymmetricKey();

    using (HMACSHA256 hmac = new HMACSHA256(proofKey))
    {
        byte[] signatureBytes = hmac.ComputeHash(Encoding.UTF8.GetBytes(token));

        isOwnershipValid = incomingSignature
                                                .Equals(
                                                    Convert.ToBase64String(signatureBytes),
                                                        StringComparison.Ordinal);
    }
}

if (isOwnershipValid)
{
    var identity = tokenHandlers.ValidateToken(samlToken).FirstOrDefault();

    var principal = new ClaimsPrincipal(new[] { Identity });

    Thread.CurrentPrincipal = principal;

    if (HttpContext.Current != null)
        HttpContext.Current.User = principal;
}
```

4. As the last step, we use the `TrustedIssuerNameRegistry` class that we used in Listing 9-15. The most fundamental element of brokered authentication is the trust. ASP.NET Web API, which is the replying party application, trusts our custom STS and hence the tokens issued by the same STS. When a token is presented to ASP.NET Web API, it must ensure the token is minted by our custom STS. This logic is implemented in the class `TrustedIssuerNameRegistry`, which inherits `IssuerNameRegistry`. The logic just looks at the subject name of the X.509 certificate to ensure the token is issued by our custom STS. See Listing 9-17.

Listing 9-17. TrustedIssuerNameRegistry

```
public class TrustedIssuerNameRegistry : IssuerNameRegistry
{
    private const string THE_ONLY_TRUSTED_ISSUER = "CN=MySTS";

    public override string GetIssuerName(SecurityToken securityToken)
    {
        using (X509SecurityToken x509Token = (X509SecurityToken)securityToken)
```

```
        {
            string name = x509Token.Certificate.SubjectName.Name;

            return name.Equals(THE_ONLY_TRUSTED_ISSUER) ? name : String.Empty;
        }
    }
}
```

Active Directory Federation Services

Active Directory Federation Services (AD FS) is meant to simplify access to systems and applications across security realms. Take the scenario of an employee of Company A who has a Windows account within the AD of Company A. If this employee wants to access an application of the partner company Company B, it becomes a trust problem. The application in Company B trusts only the AD of Company B. The employee of Company A has the AD credentials only in the AD of Company A.

AD FS helps us solve such problems across organizational boundaries. Using AD FS, the employee of Company A can seamlessly access the application in Company B with his Company A Active Directory credentials, as long as he is authorized to do so.

AD FS typically uses an AD as the identity provider and issues SAML tokens. As you know, tokens are all about claims. ADFS issues tokens that contain claims, which an application uses to authenticate and authorize a user.

AD FS is not just for federation across organizational boundaries. Even outside of the federation capabilities, it is possible to simply set up an AD FS endpoint that issues tokens for incoming Windows credentials within the boundaries of an organization. By developing applications that depend on claims from the AD FS–issued tokens, single sign-on (SSO) can be achieved with browser-based applications within an organization.

We deal with ASP.NET Web API, which is all about active clients. Suppose an organization that has invested in AD FS would like to leverage AD FS–issued tokens with a web API as well. AD FS 2.0 does support a WS-Trust endpoint exactly the same as our custom STS. Well, our custom STS issues a token with just a name claim. But AD FS 2.0 can issue a SAML token with claims representing anything related to the AD account, such as AD groups the user is a part of, depending on how claims mapping is configured in AD FS.

Listing 9-18 shows the code to obtain a SAML token from an AD FS 2.0 WS-Trust endpoint.

Listing 9-18. SAML Token from AD FS 2.0 WS-Trust

```
private static string GetTokenFromAdfs20()
{

    var binding = new WS2007HttpBinding(SecurityMode.TransportWithMessageCredential);

    binding.Security.Message.ClientCredentialType = MessageCredentialType.UserName;
    binding.Security.Message.NegotiateServiceCredential = true;
    binding.Security.Message.EstablishSecurityContext = false;

    var address = new EndpointAddress(new Uri(
                                @"https://yourserver.com/adfs/services/trust/13/usernamemixed"));

    WSTrustChannelFactory factory = new WSTrustChannelFactory(binding, address);
    factory.TrustVersion = TrustVersion.WSTrust13;

    factory.Credentials.UserName.UserName = "You Active Directory User Id";
    factory.Credentials.UserName.Password = "Corresponding password";
```

```
    WSTrustChannel channel = (WSTrustChannel)factory.CreateChannel();

    var request = new RequestSecurityToken(System.IdentityModel.Protocols.WSTrust.RequestTypes.Issue)
    {
        AppliesTo = new EndpointReference("https://relyingparty"),
        KeyType = KeyTypes.Bearer
    };

    RequestSecurityTokenResponse response = null;
    var token = channel.Issue(request, out response) as GenericXmlSecurityToken;

    return token.TokenXml.OuterXml;
}
```

The code in Listing 9-18 is almost identical to the code we used to get a token from our custom STS. The reason for the similarity is that we are dealing with the same specification, which is WS-Trust. However, there are two differences in the way AD FS is used.

1. I use HTTPS and hence specify the same in the security mode, while creating the `ws2007HttpBinding`.
2. When this AD FS endpoint was configured, no encryption certificate was provided. For that reason, the token issued cannot be a holder-of-key token but can only be a bearer token. KeyType of the request (RST) reflects this fact.

This section on AD FS is just to prove the point that using the work we have already done, you will be able to obtain SAML tokens from the existing AD FS within your organization and use the same to secure ASP.NET Web API. A web API will not care how you mint the SAML token, whether from a custom STS or from an AD FS 2.0 endpoint, as long as it is set up to rely on one of these services correctly with all the cryptographic accessories intact to validate the signature and decrypt the token.

Merits and Demerits of SAML Tokens

The main advantage of using a SAML token to secure ASP.NET Web API is that it provides the opportunity to reuse existing token issuance infrastructure such as AD FS. The Windows Identity Foundation (WIF) classes support getting a SAML token through WS-Trust as well as parsing and validating SAML tokens, all out of the box. With the .NET Framework 4.5, WIF classes have been absorbed into the core namespaces.

The main downside to using SAML tokens using WS-Trust infrastructure is that this step forces you to go in the opposite direction of embracing a technology such as HTTP, which finds support in almost any platform. SAML is a standard and so is WS-Trust, which is the typical protocol used for requesting SAML tokens.

Yet, forcing clients to talk to WS-Trust endpoints to get a SAML token reduces the reach of the web API. A client that doesn't have the ability to talk WS-Trust protocol will pretty much not be able to use our web API. Reusing the existing WS-Trust endpoints is a major motivation for using SAML tokens. However, if there is a huge client base that lacks WS-Trust capabilities, it is better to use a web token format such as SWT or JWT instead of creating a token issuance authority capable of issuing SAML tokens outside of WS-Trust.

Also, SAML is XML and hence SAML tokens tend to get heavier. The web tokens such as SWT or JWT tend to be better fits for RESTful services than SAML.

Summary

Authentication is the process of discovering the identity of a user and verifying the same through validating the user-supplied credentials against an authority. The credential can be a knowledge factor that the user knows, an ownership factor that the user owns such as a token or an X.509 certificate, or an inherence factor that the user is. I covered three ownership factors in this chapter: PSKs (also known as API keys), X.509 client certificates, and SAML tokens.

Unlike a knowledge factor that can be easily passed on to others intentionally or otherwise, it is comparatively difficult to do the same with an ownership factor. For example, an X.509 client certificate installed in the certificate store of a machine is much safer, and exporting it is generally beyond the technical prowess of the typical business user. Also, Windows-based privileges can be used to make the sharing harder or impossible.

The most basic implementation of a PSK involves sending the key as is in the request. In this case, the key acts as both the identifier and the credential. This implementation requires transport-level security. An alternative to the basic implementation is using two keys, a public key and a private key. The public key is sent in the request and acts as the identifier of the user. The private key is not sent; instead, an HMAC computed for some of the key elements of the request using the private key is sent to prove the authenticity of the user owning the private PSK to the service. Because the private key is not sent in the message, the PSK implementation using key pairs does not need HTTPS.

An X.509 certificate is an identity. When a web server sends the public keys of an X.509 certificate to a client as part of the TLS handshake in HTTPS, it is used as a server credential. TLS does allow a client such as a web browser to send an X.509 certificate to the server to prove the identity of the user using the client. Using an X.509 certificate as a client credential with a web-hosted ASP.NET Web API running in IIS is mainly about configuring IIS to use HTTPS and require a client certificate. When configured correctly, a web browser automatically sends the user's X.509 certificate to the web API. As a developer, you need to validate the certificate once it is made available to you in the request object in the ASP.NET Web API pipeline and establish a principal corresponding to the client certificate.

A security token is also an ownership factor. There are three major formats: SAML, SWT, and JWT. I covered SAML in this chapter. The custom STS built in Chapter 7 is used as the token issuer to implement a SAML token-based security in ASP.NET Web API. A symmetric proof key is used to demonstrate the token ownership. Because a custom STS and an STS endpoint of AD FS can both use the WS-Trust protocol, I concluded the chapter by showing how to request and obtain a SAML token, similar to how it was with the custom STS example.

The web tokens—both SWT and JWT—are ownership factors as well, just like any other security token. But the web tokens are a better fit to RESTful services. For this reason, I dedicate Chapter 10 to them.

CHAPTER 10

Web Tokens

A security token is a container of claims packaged for secure transportation over the network. As the carrier of claims, security tokens have an important role to play in the claims-based security model covered in Chapter 5. A token issuance authority issues a token to a client application after authenticating the user credentials. The client application then presents this token to the relying party (RP) application as a user credential. The RP application verifies the token and establishes the identity for the user based on the claims contained in the token.

A security token is often short-lived compared to other ownership factors such as a preshared key or an X.509 certificate. Yet it is an ownership factor because the client application must own or possess the token to present it to an RP application to get authenticated and authorized. So, this chapter is an extension of the previous chapter on ownership-factor-based security.

A security token is fundamentally a bunch of bytes but based on the format, there are three major types: Security Markup Assertion Language (SAML) tokens, Simple Web Token (SWT), and JSON Web Token (JWT). The SAML tokens I covered in the previous chapter are XML based, closely related to SOAP and WS-* protocols. The endpoint of the token issuance authority, as defined in the WS-Trust specification, is a Security Token Service (STS). A client that needs a token from an STS makes a request for security token (RST) to STS and gets back the token in the request for security token response (RSTR), in accordance with the WS-Trust specification. I covered WS-Trust and STS in Chapter 7.

A SWT (pronounced *swot*) is just a collection of name–value pairs that are HTML form encoded, whereas a JWT is JSON-based. They are both web tokens because they are designed for the web (read HTTP). Compared to XML-based SAML, these tokens tend to be compact and hence better suited to travel in an HTTP header. For this reason, the web tokens are favored over SAML tokens in the world of REST, where ASP.NET Web API lives. Another important characteristic that differentiates the web tokens from SAML tokens is that the web tokens are bearer tokens and are typically used in the HTTP authorization header through the bearer scheme.

The rough equivalent for WS-Trust in the REST world is OAuth 2.0, the protocol that is typically used to request and obtain web tokens. OAuth 2.0 does not mandate a SWT or JWT to be used as token formats. However, in practice, when the OAuth 2.0 specification is used the tokens used are typically web tokens. I cover OAuth 2.0 in the next three chapters. Because of the web tokens' affinity to the REST world, I cover them here exclusively in this chapter.

Simple Web Token

Simple Web Token: The name says it all. It is a token, it is for the web (read HTTP), and it is simple! Because of the simplicity and compactness, a SWT is a good choice for ASP.NET Web API. Using OAuth 2.0, a client application can make a request for a SWT and use the token issued as a bearer token to authenticate to ASP.NET Web API. A bearer token gets sent in the HTTP authorization header through a bearer scheme. An example for the HTTP authorization header using a bearer scheme is `Authorization: Bearer <base64 encoded token bytes>`.

Anatomy of a SWT

In this section, I focus on explaining the anatomy of a SWT. A dissection, however, will not be needed, because what is inside a SWT is there for all to see. It is a simple token, after all!

A SWT is just HTML form encoded name-value pairs. The token issuer and the RP decide on the exact names and the values. However, there are a few name-value pairs that are important for a token to be functional: Issuer, Audience, and ExpiresOn. See Listing 10-1 for a sample SWT.

Listing 10-1. Sample SWT

```
Audience%3Dhttp%3A%2F%2Fserver.com%2Fapi%26ExpiresOn%3D1255913549%26Issuer%3Dhttps%3A%2F%2Fmyservice.
accesscontrol.windows.net%2F%26role%3DAdmin%2CUser%26HMACSHA256%3DsT7Hr9z%2B3t1oDFLpq5GOToVsu6Dyxpq
7hHsSAznmwnI%3D
```

The SWT in Listing 10-1 is not very pleasing to the eyes because it is encoded, but it is basically a bunch of name-value pairs. Listing 10-2 shows how it looks after I decode it, highlight field names, and put each name-value pair on a new line.

Listing 10-2. SWT Decoded Content

```
Audience=http://server.com/api&
ExpiresOn=1255913549&
Issuer=https://myservice.accesscontrol.windows.net/&
role=Admin,User&
HMACSHA256=sT7Hr9z+3t1oDFLpq5GOToVsu6Dyxpq7hHsSAznmwnI=
```

The following list explains each of the fields in Listing 10-2 in detail.

1. Audience is the RP application. When you use a SWT with ASP.NET Web API, the audience field will denote your ASP.NET Web API. A token issuing authority can issue tokens for multiple RPs. An RP application will honor only the tokens issued specifically to it.

2. ExpiresOn is the token expiration timestamp. For obvious reasons, tokens don't live forever and there is an expiry date and time. Some countries have daylight saving time. When the time is adjusted for this purpose, it can impact the token lifetime it was issued just before the time change. Also, different countries follow different formats. For example, 02/06 is June 2 in some countries, whereas in other countries it indicates February 6. To avoid this confusion and to simplify the representation, we follow UNIX time, which is the number of seconds elapsed since midnight of January 1, 1970 Universal Coordinated Time (UTC).

3. Issuer is the token issuing authority. A token and hence the claims it contains has no face value if it is from an issuer who the RP application does not trust. If the issuer is considered trustworthy, then the token has value, just like a currency note. A currency note can be simply a piece of crumpled, soiled paper, yet it has the power to buy things because it was issued by someone that people trust. It is important to note here that an RP must honor a SWT only if is it issued by an issuer it trusts and the token is issued specifically to it. For the first check the issuer field is important, whereas for the second check the audience field is important.

4. Role in Listing 10-2 is a custom name-value pair. It indicates the roles that the user is part of, mostly likely to be used in access control. A claim is also a name-value pair and hence it is very convenient to map a field's name to a claim type and value to a claim value. There can be more than one custom name-value pair.

5. HMACSHA256 is the most important name-value pair of all. As defined by the SWT specification, this is always the last name-value pair and the only mandatory name-value pair. The value of this name-value pair is the HMAC of all the other name-value pairs in the token. An HMAC is basically a code generated by hashing a message in combination with a key. In the case of a SWT, the name-value pairs in the token except HMACSHA256 are used for creating the HMAC. The key used in HMAC generation is a shared symmetric key that only the issuer and the RP application know. The purpose of an HMACSHA256 name-value pair is to ensure token integrity and authenticity. When the RP application receives the token, it computes the HMAC code and compares it with the value of the HMACSHA256 name-value pair. Matching values mean the token has not been tampered with in transit. The only other entity that could have created the HMAC the same as the RP application is the entity that holds the same key, which is the token issuer. This way it ensures token authenticity as well. However, a SWT does not ensure confidentiality of the token content. Sure enough, a SWT can be encrypted but that is not something defined by the SWT specification.

■ **Caution** The issuer and the RP to which a token is minted share a secret 256-bit key. Because the key is shared—in other words, the same key is used at both ends—it is a symmetric key. Because a symmetric key is known to two parties, the risk is twice as high that it will be compromised. For this reason, it is important to rotate symmetric keys by discarding a key after a certain time period and generating a new one.

Using a SWT in a Console Application

If you are reading this book on ASP.NET Web API security, it is highly likely that you are interested in securing ASP.NET Web API. Yet, I demonstrate a SWT using a console application. A console application is faster to write, run, debug, and understand. Besides, I do not believe in repeating the same code in the book in a different context. In Chapter 5, the section "Implementing Claims-Based ASP.NET Web API" clearly illustrates how to use claims using Windows Identity Foundation (WIF) classes in ASP.NET Web API. What is not implemented there is the code to deal with tokens and extract the claims. In this section, I cover that missing piece, of course from a SWT perspective. Hence, to keep the focus on a SWT, which is the core topic of the discussion here, I use a console application. The token issuer and the RP are all modeled as simple C# classes. In practice, these entities will be applications and not classes, just to state the obvious. The following are the four classes I cover in this section.

1. `Program` class with the `Main` method acting as the client application.
2. `TokenIssuer` class with the `GetToken` method that issues a SWT, which is just a string.
3. `RelyingParty` class has two methods.
    a. The `Authenticate` method that accepts the token and establishes the identity based on the claims in the token.
    b. `TheMethodRequiringAuthZ` method, as the name indicates, is an access-controlled method. The client application is allowed or denied the permission to call this method, based on the claims in the token.
4. `SimpleWebToken` class, which implements the SWT specification.

The Program Class

The Main method of the Program class of the console application acts as the client application. It calls the GetToken method on the TokenIssuer object and presents the token to the RelyingParty object and calls the TheMethodRequiringAuthZ method, as shown in Listing 10-3.

Listing 10-3. Client Application

```
class Program
{
    static void Main(string[] args)
    {
        // Token issuer
        TokenIssuer issuer = new TokenIssuer();

        // Relying party app
        RelyingParty app = new RelyingParty();

        // A client of the relying party app gets the token
        string token = issuer.GetToken("MyRelyingPartApp", "jqhuman:opensesame");

        // With the token, client now presents the token to Authenticate()
        // and calls the access protected method
        app.Authenticate(token);
        app.TheMethodRequiringAuthZ();
    }
}
```

The TokenIssuer Class

There are two methods in the TokenIssuer class: One is GetToken, which returns a SWT, and the second is GenerateKey, which generates a 256-bit key that can be used as the shared secret key by the TokenIssuer and RelyingParty. Listing 10-4 shows the GenerateKey method. I do not use this method in the illustration here; I just use a hard-coded key instead. I do show the code for key generation for the sake of completeness.

The GenerateKey() method generates and returns a 256-bit key using RNGCryptoServiceProvider. In practice, an issuer must store the generated key against the audience for later use to sign the generated token, but I don't do that here because I use a hard-coded key for illustration.

Listing 10-4. GenerateKey Method

```
public class TokenIssuer
{
    public string GenerateKey(string audience)
    {
        using (var provider = new RNGCryptoServiceProvider())
        {
            byte[] secretKeyBytes = new Byte[32];
            provider.GetBytes(secretKeyBytes);

            return Convert.ToBase64String(secretKeyBytes);
        }
    }
}
```

■ **Note** There is no mandate that a token issuing authority must also issue the shared secret key. It can be some other entity as well as the RP application. In the case of asymmetric keys involving X.509 certificates, the certificates are issued by a CA, which is different from an RP as well as an issuing authority. In the case of a SWT, the key is a shared symmetric key. There is not a lot of value in getting it from a third party and hence the issuing authority typically generates one.

Next up is the `GetToken` method, shown in Listing 10-5. It takes in two parameters: an audience and the credentials. An audience or the RP is needed so that the correct shared key corresponding to the RP is picked up for signing the token. The reason for passing in the credentials is obvious. The token is issued only if the credentials passed in are authentic. However, for the purpose of this example, I totally ignore both parameters and use a hard-coded key. The `GetToken()` method creates a new SWT, adds a few hard-coded claims, and sends back the string representation of the token.

Listing 10-5. TokenIssuer GetToken Method

```
public class TokenIssuer
{
    public string GetToken(string audience, string credentials)
    {
        // TODO - Authenticate credentials here
        // TODO - Based on the audience passed in, pick the shared key from key store
        // Just hard-coding a key here
        string key = "qqO5yXcbijtAdYmS2Otyzeze2XQedqy+Tp37wQ3sgTQ=";
        SimpleWebToken token = new SimpleWebToken(key)
                                    { Issuer = "TokenIssuer" };
        token.AddClaim(ClaimTypes.Name, "jqhuman");
        token.AddClaim(ClaimTypes.Email, "jqhuman@somewhere.world");
        token.AddClaim(ClaimTypes.Role, "Developer");
        token.AddClaim(ClaimTypes.Role, "Administrator");

        return token.ToString();
    }
}
```

The RelyingParty Class

`RelyingParty` accepts the token as a credential for authentication. It accepts the token through the `Authenticate()` method. The first thing it does with the token in the form of a string is to call the static method `Parse()`. If everything goes well with parsing, a SWT is created out of this string. The claims contained in the token are used to create a `ClaimsIdentity` and then a `ClaimsPrincipal`, which is set to `Thread.CurrentPrincipal`. Thus, as part of the call to the `Authenticate()` method, a SWT is read and validated, the claims are parsed out, and an identity is established based on this set of claims.

The `RelyingParty` class has a `TheMethodRequiringAuthZ()` method that is access controlled. I use `PrincipalPermission` to look for a specific role of Developer, which is not as good as using claims-based access control, but will help keep the code lean and the focus on the core topic of a SWT. See Listing 10-6.

Listing 10-6. RelyingParty Class

```
public class RelyingParty
{
    // RelyingParty and TokenIssuer share the secret key (symmetric key)
    private string key = "qqO5yXcbijtAdYmS2OtyzeZe2XQedqy+Tp37wQ3sgTQ=";

    public void Authenticate(string token)
    {
        try
        {
            SimpleWebToken swt = SimpleWebToken.Parse(token, key);
            Console.WriteLine(swt.ToString());

            // Now, swt.Claims will have the list of claims
            swt.Claims.ToList().ForEach(c => Console.WriteLine("{0} ==> {1}", c.Type, c.Value));

            Thread.CurrentPrincipal = new ClaimsPrincipal(new[] { new ClaimsIdentity(swt.Claims, "SWT") });
        }
        catch (Exception ex)
        {
             Console.WriteLine(ex.Message);
        }
    }

    [PrincipalPermission(SecurityAction.Demand, Role = "Developer")]
    public void TheMethodRequiringAuthZ()
    {
        Console.WriteLine("Remember what uncle Ben said...");
        Console.WriteLine("With great power comes great responsibility");
    }
}
```

■ **Caution** When creating the `ClaimsIdentity`, the second parameter of "SWT" that appears to be innocuous and rather unimportant is indeed very important in the .NET Framework 4.5. Without this, the `IsAuthenticated` property of the identity remains false and all your authorization will fail for no obvious reasons.

The SimpleWebToken Class

Last but not the least, I show you the code for `SimpleWebToken`. I intentionally stay away from WIF-related classes to keep the focus on a SWT. The preceding `TokenIssuer` class is not a subclass of `SecurityTokenService`. `SimpleWebToken` does not inherit from `SecurityToken` either. There is no real reason other than standardization or uniformity to use WIF classes for this. `SimpleWebToken` is a large class, which makes it difficult to show all the lines of code in one listing. For this reason, I divide the class into four logical parts, as follows.

1. The properties of the `SimpleWebToken` class: `Issuer`, `Audience`, `ExpiresOn`, and `Signature`. `ExpiresOn` is not a timestamp but is the number of seconds since midnight of January 1, 1970

UTC for the token to expire. It adds two minutes to the current date and time and computes the UNIX time for the same. I use two minutes as the lifetime for our SWT. `Signature` is just the value of the HMACSHA256 name-value pair. The constructor takes in the 256-bit code shared key of the audience for which this token is being created. See Listing 10-7.

Listing 10-7. Simple Web Token (Partial): Properties

```
public class SimpleWebToken
{
    private static readonly TimeSpan lifeTime = new TimeSpan(0, 2, 0);
    private static readonly DateTime epochStart = new DateTime(1970, 01, 01, 0, 0, 0, 0, DateTimeKind.Utc);
    private NameValueCollection nameValuePairs;
    private byte[] keyBytes = null;

    public SimpleWebToken(string key)
    {
        TimeSpan ts = DateTime.UtcNow - epochStart + lifeTime;
        this.ExpiresOn = Convert.ToUInt64(ts.TotalSeconds);
        this.nameValuePairs = new NameValueCollection();

        keyBytes = Convert.FromBase64String(key);
    }

    public string Issuer { get; set; }
    public string Audience { get; set; }
    public byte[] Signature { get; set; }
    public ulong ExpiresOn { get; private set; }
}
```

2. Now, let's get to the claims part. There is a method to add claims in the form of name-value pairs. There is a read-only property that returns the claims thus added in the form of `IList<Claim>` (see Listing 10-8). A little bit of complication here is that the property getter handles the case of multivalue claims such as role. There can be multiple claims with the same name; in such cases, the values for that name are grouped as comma-separated values. For example, role=role1&role=role2 will be role=role1,role2.

Listing 10-8. Simple Web Token (Partial): Claims Property and AddClaim Method

```
public IList<Claim> Claims
{
    get
    {
        return this.nameValuePairs.AllKeys
                 .SelectMany(key =>
                         this.nameValuePairs[key].Split(',')
                                 .Select(value => new Claim(key, value))
                                         ).ToList();
    }
}
```

```
public void AddClaim(string name, string value)
{
    this.nameValuePairs.Add(name, value);
}
```

3. The `ToString()` method of `object` is overridden to return the string representation of the SWT or the serialized token, as shown in Listing 10-9. Following are the steps.

    a. First, stuff the issuer in the corresponding field.

    b. Add the claims. The claim is just a name-value pair. So, just loop through the set of claims added to the token and add every claim to the serialized representation using the name and the value.

    c. Add the expiry stamp and audience.

    d. Finally, add the signature in the HMACSHA256 field. What gets hashed is the entire content of the SWT except the HMACSHA256 field. In other words, whatever has been added to `StringBuilder` up to this point is the data that must be signed. The signature is the HMAC-SHA256 hash of the data, created using the class `HMACSHA256`.

Listing 10-9. Simple Web Token (Partial): ToString Method

```
public override string ToString()
{
    StringBuilder content = new StringBuilder();

    content.Append("Issuer=").Append(this.Issuer);

    foreach (string key in this.nameValuePairs.AllKeys)
    {
        content.Append('&').Append(key).Append('=').Append(this.nameValuePairs[key]);
    }

    content.Append("&ExpiresOn=").Append(this.ExpiresOn);

    if (!string.IsNullOrWhiteSpace(this.Audience))
    {
        content.Append("&Audience=").Append(this.Audience);
    }

    using (HMACSHA256 hmac = new HMACSHA256(keyBytes))
    {
        byte[] signatureBytes = hmac.ComputeHash(Encoding.ASCII.GetBytes(content.ToString()));

        string signature = HttpUtility.UrlEncode(Convert.ToBase64String(signatureBytes));

        content.Append("&HMACSHA256=").Append(signature);
    }

    return content.ToString();
}
```

4. In the SimpleWebToken class, the Parse method creates back a SWT object from its string representation while validating the signature and token expiration at the same time. See Listing 10-10. The Parse method deserializes a SWT from its serialized representation. It is mostly a reverse of the earlier method of ToString().

    a. Use HttpUtility.ParseQueryString() to decode and extract the name-value pairs.

    b. Loop through all the names in the token. If a name-value pair is a predefined name-value pair such as audience, expiry stamp, issuer, or the signature, the corresponding value gets set in the relevant property of the SimpleWebToken object that gets returned. If a name-value pair is not one of these predefined ones, a claim object is created with the claim type as the name and the claim value as the value corresponding to the name.

    c. Signature validation is done as follows. (1) As part of the looping through names, the Signature property is set to the value of the field with the name HMACSHA256. This is the incoming signature. It needs to be compared with the computed signature. (2) The signature is computed by reusing the serialization logic that is already implemented in the ToString() method. I set the properties and call ToString(), thereby getting the computed signature in the string returned by the ToString() method. I simply extract out the computed signature using HttpUtility.ParseQueryString() to generate name-value pairs and pick up the computed signature using the HMACSHA256 name. (3) This computed signature is compared against the incoming signature held in the Signature property. If both signatures match, the token has not been tampered with in transit.

    d. Another validation done in the Parse method is the expiry check, which is self-explanatory. I compute the UNIX time of the current date and time and compare that against the UNIX time put in as the expiry at the time of the SWT creation. If the token has expired, I just throw a SecurityException.

    e. The validations related to checking the audience for the RP and the issuer for the issuing authority are left as an exercise to the reader! The basic idea behind this step is to ensure the token is created by an issuing authority that the RP trusts and the token is minted specifically for the RP application.

Listing 10-10. Simple Web Token (Partial): Parse Method

```
public static SimpleWebToken Parse(string token, string secretKey)
{
    var items = HttpUtility.ParseQueryString(token);
    var swt = new SimpleWebToken(secretKey);

    foreach (string key in items.AllKeys)
    {
        string item = items[key];
        switch (key)
        {
            case "Issuer": swt.Issuer = item; break;
            case "Audience": swt.Audience = item; break;
            case "ExpiresOn": swt.ExpiresOn = ulong.Parse(item); break;
            case "HMACSHA256": swt.Signature =
                                      Convert.FromBase64String(item); break;
```

```
            default: swt.AddClaim(key, items[key]); break;
        }
    }

    string rawToken = swt.ToString(); // Computes HMAC inside ToString()
    string computedSignature = HttpUtility.ParseQueryString(rawToken)
                                                        ["HMACSHA256"];

    if (!computedSignature.Equals(Convert.ToBase64String(swt.Signature),
                                                StringComparison.Ordinal))
        throw new SecurityTokenValidationException("Signature is invalid");

    TimeSpan ts = DateTime.UtcNow - epochStart;

    if (swt.ExpiresOn < Convert.ToUInt64(ts.TotalSeconds))
        throw new SecurityTokenException("Token has expired");

    return swt;
}
```

Thus, we used a SWT to supply a claim (role claim) to the RP application. We did not follow any protocol such as OAuth 2.0 to request and obtain the SWT. The token request and the subsequent presentation to the RP are all done through simple method invocations.

When you use a SWT in ASP.NET Web API, the RP application is your web API. The token issuer can be an outside entity such as Azure Access Control Service (ACS) or something that is internally available. If you implement your own token issuer, it can be along the lines of the `TokenIssuer` class in Listing 10-5. In ASP.NET Web API, you can implement the authentication logic in a message handler. The message handler will pull the serialized token from the authorization request header in the bearer scheme and call the `Parse` static method of `SimpleWebToken` passing the serialized token retrieved from the header. If the token is valid, claims can be extracted out and an identity created based on that, as shown in Listing 10-6.

JSON Web Token

JWT is a token, which means that the main purpose of its existence is to carry a set of claims from the issuing authority to the requestor and from the requestor to the RP. JWT (pronounced *jot*) is very much like a SWT, except that it is in JSON format. A SWT is made up of name-value pairs that are HTML form encoded, but a JWT is based on JSON, which is easier to use for JavaScript-based applications. An important difference to note is that a SWT does not support encryption. There is nothing that prevents us from encrypting a SWT, but it is not defined as part of the SWT specification. In contrast, a JWT comes in the following three flavors.

1. Plain text JWT: A JWT that is neither integrity-protected nor encrypted.
2. Signed JWT: A JWT with the claim set protected from tampering by an HMAC or a digital signature using a public key infrastructure (PKI) in accordance with a JSON Web Signature (JWS).
3. Encrypted JWT: A JWT with the claim set encrypted for confidentiality, as specified by JSON Web Encryption (JWE).

In the following sections, I cover signed JWT and encrypted JWT. A plain text JWT is just a subset of signed JWT (without the signature), and hence I do not specifically cover plain text JWT.

Base64 URL Encoding

Unlike XML-based SAML, the web tokens—both SWT and JWT—are compact and hence better suited to be used in an HTTP header for REST-based services. The web tokens can be sent even in the query string part of URLs. The JWT specification takes the last part into account while defining the encoding scheme to be used with JWT.

It is a standard practice to use base64 encoding to transmit binary data such as the byte array encrypted or a digital signature, which is again a byte array. When binary data has to be transmitted as part of textual data—for example, if we need to send a token containing a signature in an HTTP header that will accept only textual or string data—base64 encoding is used to make sure the binary data does not get corrupted in transit.

The .NET Framework has `Convert.ToBase64String(byte[])` and `Convert.FromBase64String(string)` to convert a byte array to a base64-encoded string and vice versa. Using standard base64 encoding in a URL requires encoding of some of the characters created by the standard base64 encoding such as '+', '/', or '=' characters into special encoding sequences, '%2B', '%2F', and '%3D', respectively. In place of one character, we now have three. This makes the payload bigger, which goes against the objective of making the payload as compact as possible, to be used in an HTTP header or a query string.

For this reason, the JWT specification specifies base64 URL encoding to be used. Base 64 URL encoding is a variation on top of the standard base64 encoding, where '+' and '/' characters are replaced with '-' and '_', respectively, and the padding '=' characters are removed so that the payload remains just the same, regardless of URL encoding or form encoding.

Before we dive deep into examining the JWT internals, let's take some time to review the logic to accomplish base64 URL encoding so that we can pay undivided attention to the core topic later.

Listing 10-11 shows the extension methods that help us perform base64 URL encoding on top of the standard base64 encoding.

Listing 10-11. Base64 URL Encoding Extensions

```
public static class EncodingHelper
{
    public static string ToBase64String(this byte[] bytes)
    {
        return Convert.ToBase64String(bytes).TrimEnd('=').Replace('+', '-').Replace('/', '_');
    }

    public static string ToBase64String(this string input)
    {
        return Convert.ToBase64String(Encoding.UTF8.GetBytes(input))
                       .TrimEnd('=').Replace('+', '-').Replace('/', '_');
    }

    public static byte[] ToByteArray(this string input)
    {
        input = input.Replace('-', '+').Replace('_', '/');

        int pad = 4 - (input.Length % 4);
        pad = pad > 2 ? 0 : pad;

        input = input.PadRight(input.Length + pad, '=');

        return Convert.FromBase64String(input);
    }
}
```

The ToBase64String() method is self-explanatory. It just performs the standard base64 encoding using Convert.ToBase64String(). In the resulting string, it replaces '+' with '-' and '/' with '-' and removes the trailing '='.

ToByteArray() does the decoding and is a bit more involved. First, it puts back the '+' and '/' it replaced while encoding. The dilemma while putting back the trailing '=' is how many to put back. We blindly removed the trailing '=' while encoding. Math comes to our rescue here. If the length is exactly divisible by 4, there would not have been any trailing '=' in the standard base64-encoded string. A valid base64-encoded string will have either one trailing '=' or two trailing '=', as in '=='. So, we get the modulus of four, which is the remainder when the length is divided by four, and subtract that from four to get the vacant spaces to pad. If it is a legal value of one or two, we pad the string with that many '=' at the end of the string. If it is a zero or any other value, we do nothing. Once this logic is applied, we get the standard base64-encoded string from the base64 URL encoded string, which we simply convert to a byte array using Convert.FromBase64String() provided in the .NET Framework.

With base64 URL encoding out of our way now, we are back to the main topic of JWT.

Anatomy of a Signed JSON Web Token

A signed JWT has its payload, which is the set of claims, protected from tampering by the help of a signature. A signature here represents both the HMAC as well as a signature created using a private key of the PKI. In this book, I use HMAC-SHA256 for the signature, the same as with a SWT.

Let's start with a review of a sample signed JWT, shown in Listing 10-12. It is worse than a SWT in terms of readability. A SWT is forms encoded, which makes it hard on the eyes, but a JWT is total gibberish because it is base64 URL encoded. Listing 10-12 shows what we get when dealing with JWT in C# code.

Listing 10-12. Sample JWT


```
eyJ0eXAiOiJKV1QiLCJhbGciOiJIUzI1NiJ9.eyJleHAiOiIxMzUwNzExNTI0IiwiaXNzIjoiVG9rZW5Jc3N1ZXIiLCJhdWQ
iOiJNeVJlbHlpbmdQYXJ0QXBwIiwiaHR0cDovL3Nja|GVtYXMueG1sc29hcC5vcmcvd3MvMjAwNS8wNS9pZGVudGl0eS9jbGF
pbXMvbmFtZSI6ImpxaHVtYW4iLCJodHRwOi8vc2NoZW1hcy5taWNyb3NvZnQuY29tL3dzLzIwMDgvMDYvaWRlbnRpdHkvY2x
haW1zL3JvbGUiOiJEZXZlbG9wZXIsQWRtaW4ifQ.3_TI8aTLcKHW17bpkZL2_-sngnQOuD86JQ-MtmZxeKM
```


Listing 10-13 shows a better looking decoded JWT. I not only decoded the content, but also put the separating dots (.) on new lines so you can see the segments of the token.

Listing 10-13. Decoded JWT for Your Reading Pleasure

```
{"typ":"JWT","alg":"HS256"}
.
{"exp":"1350711524","iss":"TokenIssuer","aud":"MyRelyingPartApp","http://schemas.xmlsoap.org/ws/
2005/05/identity/claims/name":"jqhuman","http://schemas.microsoft.com/ws/2008/06/identity/claims/
role":"Developer,Admin"}
.
[Signature - HMAC SHA256]
```

There are three segments in Listing 10-13.

1. First is the JWT header. Because this is a token protected by an HMAC created using SHA256, the algorithm field reflects that piece of information. The header segment is in JSON.
2. The segment following the first dot contains the set of claims. This is the actual payload. I use three reserved claims, namely expiration time claim (exp), issuer claim (iss), and audience claim (aud). A reserved claim, as the name indicates, is reserved by the specification. This is similar to certain keywords being reserved by a programming language for naming variables. The purpose of a reserved claim is to prevent ambiguity.

When there is an iss claim in JWT, you know for sure that it is an issuer claim. There also are private claims. You can put the claims that are meaningful to your application here. In the preceding example, I use the .NET Framework claim type and the claim value. The payload segment is also in JSON.

3. Because we are looking at a signed JWT, which is protected by an HMAC, I show the third segment containing the signature. I cannot meaningfully decode the signature into a string, and hence just show a placeholder.

■ **Note** If this is a plain text JWT, the header will have "alg":"none" and the third segment will be absent.

Using a Signed JSON Web Token in a Console Application

Similar to the way I demonstrated a SWT, I use a signed JWT in a console application here. To keep the focus on JWT, the token issuer and the RP are modeled as simple C# classes. In practice, these entities will be applications and not classes, just to state the obvious. The following are the four classes I cover in this section.

1. The `Program` class with the `Main` method acting as the client application.
2. The `KeyIssuer` class with the `GenerateSharedSymmetricKey` method to generate a symmetric key.
3. The `TokenIssuer` class with the `GetToken` method that issues a JWT, which is just a string. It also has a `ShareKeyOutofBand` to accept the shared key during out-of-band key exchange.
4. The `RelyingParty` class has three methods.
    a. The `ShareKeyOutofBand` method to accept the shared key during out-of-band key exchange.
    b. The `Authenticate` method that accepts the token and establishes the identity based on the claims in the token.
    c. The `TheMethodRequiringAuthZ` method, as the name indicates, is an access-controlled method. The client application is allowed or denied permission to call this method, based on the claims in the token.
5. The `JsonWebToken` class, which implements the JWT and JWS specifications.

The Program Class

The logic implemented in the `Main` method of the `Program` class shown in Listing 10-14 consists of two major parts.

1. The symmetric key generation followed by the key sharing between `TokenIssuer` and `RelyingParty`. The `GenerateSharedSymmetricKey` method on the `KeyIssuer` object is called to generate a shared key. It is then shared with the `TokenIssuer` and `RelyingParty` objects through the call to the `ShareKeyOutofBand` method. In practice, this part happens out of band.
2. The `GetToken` method on the `TokenIssuer` object is called and the token returned is presented to the `RelyingParty` object through the `Authenticate` method call followed by the call to the access-controlled `TheMethodRequiringAuthZ` method. This part represents the client application obtaining the token and presenting the same to the RP.

Listing 10-14. Console Application

```
class Program
{
    static void Main(string[] args)
    {
        string secretKey = KeyIssuer.GenerateSharedSymmetricKey();

        // Token issuer
        TokenIssuer issuer = new TokenIssuer();
        issuer.ShareKeyOutofBand("MyRelyingPartApp", secretKey);

        // Relying Party
        RelyingParty app = new RelyingParty();
        app.ShareKeyOutofBand(secretKey);

        // A client of the relying party app gets the token
        string token = issuer.GetToken("MyRelyingPartApp", "opensesame");

        // With the token, the client now presents the token and
        // calls the method requiring authorization
        app.Authenticate(token);
        app.TheMethodRequiringAuthZ();
    }
}
```

The KeyIssuer Class

I use a symmetric shared key to create the HMAC as the signature of the SWT. Listing 10-15 shows the `KeyIssuer` class, which I'm introducing here. It is similar to what the key generating code did in the `TokenIssuer` class we saw in the section "Simple Web Token" earlier in this chapter. The key generation has to be separated out because I will be building on these classes for implementing encryption in a JWT. When a public and a private key are involved, as in the case of asymmetric keys, it no longer makes sense for the token issuer to generate the keys.

Listing 10-15. Symmetric Key Generation

```
public class KeyIssuer
{
    public static string GenerateSharedSymmetricKey()
    {
        // 256-bit key
        using (var provider = new RNGCryptoServiceProvider())
        {
            byte[] secretKeyBytes = new Byte[32];
            provider.GetBytes(secretKeyBytes);

            return Convert.ToBase64String(secretKeyBytes);
        }
    }
}
```

The TokenIssuer Class

The TokenIssuer class used here is very similar to the one we used with the SWT. There is one minor enhancement to it, which is the method to the ShareKeyOutofBand() method that can be used to share the key with the issuer out of band. The token issuer stores the key in a dictionary against the audience (the RP) and retrieves it for subsequent use. Of course, I use a console application with classes representing the entities in a real scenario, but the process is mostly the same.

GetToken() creates a new instance of the JsonWebToken class passing in the symmetric key corresponding to the RP (audience) and an identifier that represents the token issuer. The latter is important for an RP to verify if the token is issued by someone it trusts. See Listing 10-16.

Listing 10-16. TokenIssuer GetToken() Method

```
public class TokenIssuer
{
    private Dictionary<string, string> audienceKeys = new Dictionary<string, string>();

    // This method is called to register a key with the token issuer against an audience or an RP
    public void ShareKeyOutofBand(string audience, string key)
    {
        if (!audienceKeys.ContainsKey(audience))
            audienceKeys.Add(audience, key);
        else
            audienceKeys[audience] = key;
    }

    public string GetToken(string audience, string credentials)
    {
        // Ignoring the credentials and adding a few claims for illustration
        JsonWebToken token = new JsonWebToken()
        {
                SymmetricKey = audienceKeys[audience],
                Issuer = "TokenIssuer",
                Audience = audience
        };

        token.AddClaim(ClaimTypes.Name, "jqhuman");
        token.AddClaim(ClaimTypes.Role, "Developer");
        token.AddClaim(ClaimTypes.Role, "Admin");

        return token.ToString();
    }
}
```

The RelyingParty Class

The RelyingParty class, shown in Listing 10-17, has a ShareKeyOutofBand() method just like the TokenIssuer class. The RP is assumed to rely on one token issuing authority and hence the key is simply stored at the class level for subsequent use.

The Authenticate() method is the means by which a client presents a JWT for authentication. The RP uses JsonWebToken.Parse() to deserialize the token into an object and get the claims from this object. Based on this claims set, a claims identity is established and a ClaimsPrincipal created and set to Thread.CurrentPrincipal for the downstream code to do access control.

One such place is the method TheMethodRequiringAuthZ(), which is access protected to be used only by the users in the role 'Developer.' For the sake of simplicity, role based-access control (RBAC) is used here. In real production strength code, using claims based access control is recommended.

Listing 10-17. Relying Party

```
public class RelyingParty
{
    private string secretKey = String.Empty;

    public void ShareKeyOutofBand(string key)
    {
        this.secretKey = key;
    }

    public void Authenticate(string token)
    {
        JsonWebToken jwt = null;

        try
        {
            jwt = JsonWebToken.Parse(token, this.secretKey);

            // Now, swt.Claims will have the list of claims
            jwt.Claims.ToList().ForEach(c => Console.WriteLine("{0} ==> {1}", c.Type, c.Value));

            Thread.CurrentPrincipal = new ClaimsPrincipal(new ClaimsIdentity(jwt.Claims, "JWT"));
        }
        catch (Exception ex)
        {
            Console.WriteLine(ex.Message);
        }
    }

    [PrincipalPermission(SecurityAction.Demand, Role = "Developer")]
    public void TheMethodRequiringAuthZ()
    {
        Console.WriteLine("With great power comes great responsibility - Uncle Ben");
    }
}
```

■ **Caution** When creating the ClaimsIdentity, the second parameter of "JWT" that appears to be innocuous and rather unimportant is indeed very important in the .NET Framework 4.5. Without this, the IsAuthenticated property of the identity remains false and your authorization will fail for no obvious reason.

The JsonWebToken Class

We now look at the class representing the signed JWT. A signed JWT uses a digital signature or simply uses an HMAC, in accordance with the JWS. I keep the signed JWT exactly like the SWT we have seen before. I use HMAC-SHA256 as the signature and use the three reserved claims of audience, issuer, and expiration that we used with a SWT. There are other reserved claims such as 'Not Before' (nbf), 'Issued At' (iat), 'Principal' (prn), and 'JWT ID' (jti), which I do not use here. You can refer to the JWT specification to see if it makes sense to include them in your token, if you happen to issue your own tokens.

I use a dictionary to store both reserved and private claims. Although there are properties corresponding to the reserved claims, the underlying data provider is the dictionary. If there are multiple private claims with the same type, I use comma-separated values so that we can use the claim type as the key for the dictionary. As per the JWT specification, JWTs with duplicate claim names must be rejected. A dictionary is a good mechanism to ensure this.

JSON Serialization and Deserialization

I use the JSON.NET library to serialize the `JsonWebToken` object into its JSON token representation and deserialize or parse the token back into its CLR object representation. The following steps show how to add JSON.NET to your project.

1. In Visual Studio, right-click the References node in Solution Explorer and select the Manage NuGet Packages... option in the shortcut menu, as shown in Figure 10-1.

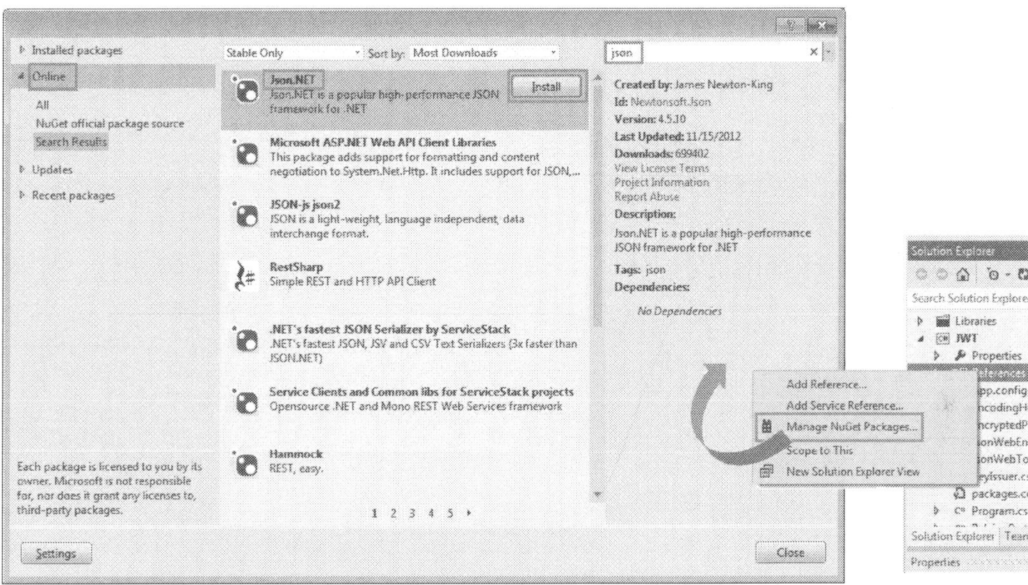

Figure 10-1. *Getting JSON.NET through NuGet*

2. Click Online and search for Json to get JSON.NET in the search result.

3. Click Install. This will make the Newtonsoft.Json.dll a part of your project and add a reference to this assembly.

In `JsonWebToken`, I have a bunch of properties defined for the header fields as well as reserved claims. I want only the header fields to be serialized into the string representation of the JWT. Hence, for those properties corresponding to the header fields I use the `JsonProperty` attribute with a name as defined in the JWT specification so that the serialized token will have the right field names in the JSON. Because compactness is the goal, the field names as defined by the JWT specification are concise. Using this approach of naming the property allows us to name the properties long enough to be descriptive and in line with any coding standards a team might have.

I do not want the properties representing the reserved claims to get serialized. Hence I use a `JsonIgnore` attribute and make sure they don't get serialized off into the string token. Similar to a SWT, we use UNIX time to track the expiration time.

Partial Implementation with the Properties

The `JsonWebToken` class with all the properties is shown in Listing 10-18. It is incomplete and without the two important methods. I will include those two soon, in the next few pages, and make this class complete and reusable when we get to Chapter 12, where we will see how to request these tokens using OAuth 2.0 and use them with ASP. NET Web API.

Listing 10-18. JsonWebToken (Partial Implementation with Properties)

```
public class JsonWebToken
{
        private const string TYPE_HEADER = "typ";
        private const string JSON_WEB_TOKEN = "JWT";
        private const string SIGNING_ALGORITHM_HEADER = "alg";
        private const string HMAC_SHA256 = "HS256";
        private const string EXPIRATION_TIME_CLAIM = "exp";
        private const string ISSUER_CLAIM = "iss";
        private const string AUDIENCE_CLAIM = "aud";

        private static readonly TimeSpan lifeTime = new TimeSpan(0, 2, 0);
        private static readonly DateTime epochStart = new DateTime(1970,01,01,0,0,0,0, DateTimeKind.Utc);

        private byte[] keyBytes = null;
        private Dictionary<string, string> claims = new Dictionary<string, string>();

        public JsonWebToken()
        {
            TimeSpan ts = DateTime.UtcNow - epochStart + lifeTime;
            this.ExpiresOn = Convert.ToUInt64(ts.TotalSeconds);
        }

        [JsonProperty(PropertyName = TYPE_HEADER)]
        public string Type
        {
            get { return JSON_WEB_TOKEN; }
        }

        [JsonProperty(PropertyName = SIGNING_ALGORITHM_HEADER)]
        public string SignatureAlgorithm
        {
            get { return HMAC_SHA256; }
        }
```

```
[JsonIgnore]
public string SymmetricKey
{
    get
    {
        return Convert.ToBase64String(keyBytes);
    }
    set
    {
        keyBytes = Convert.FromBase64String(value);
    }
}

[JsonIgnore]
public IList<Claim> Claims
{
    get
    {
        return this.claims.Keys.SelectMany(key =>
                                   this.claims[key].Split(',')
                                       .Select(value => new Claim(key, value))).ToList();
    }
}

[JsonIgnore]
public ulong ExpiresOn
{
    get
    {
        return UInt64.Parse(this.claims[EXPIRATION_TIME_CLAIM]);
    }
    private set
    {
        this.claims.Add(EXPIRATION_TIME_CLAIM, value.ToString());
    }
}

[JsonIgnore]
public string Issuer
{
    get
    {
        return this.claims.ContainsKey(ISSUER_CLAIM) ? this.claims[ISSUER_CLAIM] : String.Empty;
    }
    set
    {
        this.claims.Add(ISSUER_CLAIM, value);
    }
}

[JsonIgnore]
public string Audience
```

```
        {
            get
            {
                return this.claims.ContainsKey(AUDIENCE_CLAIM) ?
                                   this.claims[AUDIENCE_CLAIM] :
                                             String.Empty;
            }
            set
            {
                this.claims.Add(AUDIENCE_CLAIM, value);
            }
        }

        public void AddClaim(string claimType, string value)
        {
            if (this.claims.ContainsKey(claimType))
                this.claims[claimType] = this.claims[claimType] + "," + value;
            else
                this.claims.Add(claimType, value);
        }

        // Class code not complete
    }
```

Serialization (ToString Method)

Listing 10-19 shows the ToString() method that will be called by the token issuer to create the token in string form. To create the HMAC, use the base64 URL encoded first segment, which is the header, append a dot to the end, and append the base64 URL encoded first segment, which is the claim set. This is the data for which an HMAC has to be created using the SHA256 algorithm. Base64 URL encode the HMAC bytes and append to the previous segments with another dot separator. That completes the assembly of the signed JWT.

Listing 10-19. JsonWebToken: ToString()Method

```
public override string ToString()
{
    string header = JsonConvert.SerializeObject(this).ToBase64String();
    string claims = JsonConvert.SerializeObject(this.claims).ToBase64String();
    string signature = String.Empty;

    using (HMACSHA256 hmac = new HMACSHA256(keyBytes))
    {
        string data = String.Format("{0}.{1}", header, claims);
        byte[] signatureBytes = hmac.ComputeHash(Encoding.UTF8.GetBytes(data));
        signature = signatureBytes.ToBase64String();
    }

    return String.Format("{0}.{1}.{2}", header, claims, signature);
}
```

Compared to a SWT, the code to create the string representation of the JWT is concise, thanks to JSON.NET and JSON itself.

Deserialization (Parse Method)

Listing 10-20 shows the `Parse()` method of `JsonWebToken`. It does the reverse of `ToString()`; that is, it deserializes the string representation to a CLR object. Following are the steps involved in this process.

1. Ensure there are three segments.
2. Separate the three segments out and decode them.
3. Get the `JsonWebToken` object by deserializing the header JSON. The object at this point is not fully formed and has only the header data. The most important part, which is the claim set, is not added in yet.
4. Deserialize the claim set JSON back into a dictionary, which is set into the `JsonWebToken` object, to make it a full-blown object with all the data it used to contain prior to serialization.
5. Compute the signature using the header and claims segment and compare the computed signature against the incoming signature, which is the third part of the token when split by a dot. If the signature matches, validate the expiration.
6. I don't do any validation based on the issuer or the RP for brevity reasons, but any production implementation must do those checks.

Listing 10-20. JsonWebToken: Parse() Method

```
public static JsonWebToken Parse(string token, string secretKey)
{
    var parts = token.Split('.');
    if (parts.Length != 3)
        throw new SecurityException("Bad token");

    string header = Encoding.UTF8.GetString(parts[0].ToByteArray());
    string claims = Encoding.UTF8.GetString(parts[1].ToByteArray());
    byte[] incomingSignature = parts[2].ToByteArray();
    string computedSignature = String.Empty;

    var jwt = JsonConvert.DeserializeObject<JsonWebToken>(header);
    jwt.SymmetricKey = secretKey;
    jwt.claims = JsonConvert.DeserializeObject<Dictionary<string, string>>(claims);

    using (HMACSHA256 hmac = new HMACSHA256(Convert.FromBase64String(secretKey)))
    {
        string data = String.Format("{0}.{1}", parts[0], parts[1]);
        byte[] signatureBytes = hmac.ComputeHash(Encoding.UTF8.GetBytes(data));
        computedSignature = signatureBytes.ToBase64String();
    }

    if (!computedSignature.Equals(incomingSignature.ToBase64String(), StringComparison.Ordinal))
        throw new SecurityException("Signature is invalid");

    TimeSpan ts = DateTime.UtcNow - epochStart;

    if (jwt.ExpiresOn < Convert.ToUInt64(ts.TotalSeconds))
        throw new SecurityException("Token has expired");

    return jwt;
}
```

This completes the implementation of a signed JWT using a console application. In Chapter 5, the section "Implementing Claims-Based ASP.NET Web API" illustrates how to use claims using WIF classes in ASP.NET Web API. The same can be enhanced with the JWT code from this section to use the claims from JWT in ASP.NET Web API. In Chapter 12, I implement ASP.NET Web API accepting a JWT from a client application that gets the token using the OAuth 2.0 protocol from an authorization server (OAuth 2.0 terminology).

Anatomy of an Encrypted JSON Web Token

In contrast to the SWT specification, the JWT specification (JSON Web Encryption or JWE, to be exact) specifies how to go about encrypting a JWT. The cryptographic algorithms to be used while encrypting a JWT are described in the separate JSON Web Algorithms (JWA) specification.

An encrypted JWT token no longer follows the same format as the signed JWT we saw earlier. Instead of the three segments we saw with JWS, we now have five segments with JWE. As with the signed token, all these fields are base64 URL encoded and separated by a dot. Following are the five segments.

1. Header
2. Encrypted master key, produced by the key encryption process
3. Initialization vector
4. Encrypted data or the ciphertext, produced by the data encryption process
5. Tag, produced by the data encryption process

All the segments except for the header are fundamentally byte arrays. Hence, there is little merit in looking at a sample for those segments. Listing 10-21 shows a sample header.

Listing 10-21. Sample JWE Header

```
{"alg":"RSA-OAEP", "enc":"A256GCM"}
```

There are two fields in the header. These fields convey the following information about the encrypted JWT.

- "alg", or algorithm, identifies the cryptographic algorithm used to encrypt the master key. In this example, it is RSA Encryption Scheme - Optimal Asymmetric Encryption Padding (RSAES OAEP).
- "enc", or encryption method, identifies the block encryption algorithm used to encrypt the plain text to produce the ciphertext. From the perspective of an encrypted JWT, the plain text is the claim set carried by the token. As per JWE, an authenticated encryption algorithm must be used for this purpose. I explain authenticated encryption in the next section. In the preceding example, the encryption method is Advanced Encryption Standard (AES) with a key size of 256 bits used with the Galois/Counter Mode (GCM) mode of operation. GCM is a mode of operation for symmetric key cryptographic block ciphers widely adopted for efficiency and speed.

To understand how the algorithm and encryption methods are used to produce the other four segments of the encrypted JWT, you will need to understand the process of authenticated encryption as well as why the JWE specification requires authenticated encryption to be used.

Authenticated Encryption

A JWT is either signed or encrypted. If the claims payload does not contain any confidential information, encryption will not be needed and signing alone will be sufficient to ensure token integrity. When the claims payload contains confidential information, the JWT is encrypted. Although token confidentiality is ensured by authentication, it cannot ensure the token integrity. For this reason, authenticated encryption is employed.

Authenticated encryption is designed to simultaneously provide confidentiality, integrity, and authenticity assurances on the message. This type of encryption is different from the traditional encryption methods the .NET Framework supports out of the box such as Rijndael or Triple DES because it produces an authentication tag in addition to the ciphertext when encrypting plain text. The encryption methods supported by the .NET Framework are strong, no doubt. If these methods are used correctly, a malicious user will not be able to decrypt the ciphertext created by the typical encryption classes of the .NET Framework. However, a malicious user can modify the ciphertext bytes corrupting the data. Because there is no signing involved, it will not be possible to detect this tampering. The authenticated encryption algorithms solve the problem by creating the authentication tag that can be used to verify if the encrypted ciphertext was tampered with in transit.

As we saw in Chapter 6, symmetric encryption involves two inputs, apart from the plain text.

1. The symmetric key, which is a shared secret between the sender and the receiver.
2. An initialization vector, which is shared between the sender and the receiver but need not be a secret.

In the case of authenticated encryption, there is a third input.

3. Additional authenticated data (AAD), which is an input to the encryption process. The ciphertext produced by the encryption process does not contain this AAD. Hence, using the ciphertext, the AAD cannot be figured out. The sender and the receiver must agree on how the AAD will be formatted and used to encrypt and decrypt out of band. If the AAD supplied during the encryption and the decryption are different, the decryption process will fail to produce the plain text. In an encrypted JWT, the AAD is the first three segments separated by a dot.

In traditional methods, the receiver will be able to decrypt and get some plain text out of it, even if a malicious user tampers with the ciphertext. The plain text produced in this case will not match what was sent by the receiver, but the receiver will not be able to know there is a difference. However, with the authenticated encryption method, decryption itself will fail and will not produce any plain text. So, we get the benefit of both encryption and signing using authenticated encryption. Figure 10-2 illustrates the inputs and outputs of authenticated encryption and decryption.

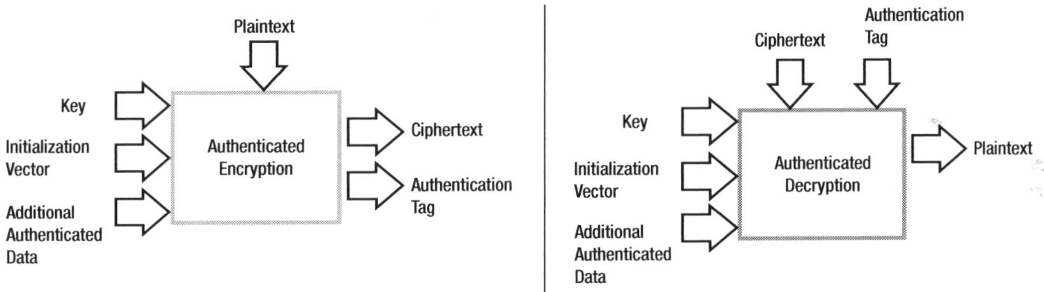

***Figure 10-2.** Authenticated encryption/decryption: inputs and outputs*

■ **Note** The .NET Framework does not support authenticated encryption out of the box. But fear not! There is a CodePlex project available by the name of CLR Security from which you can download a .NET Framework assembly with classes that will help us achieve authenticated encryption. `Security.Cryptography.dll` is the assembly and the URL for the CodePlex project is `http://codeplex.com/clrsecurity`. In Windows 8 and Windows Server 2012, the `CryptographicEngine` class of the `Windows.Security.Cryptography.Core` namespace supports the methods `EncryptAndAuthenticate` and `DecryptAndAuthenticate` respectively for authenticated encryption and authenticated decryption.

The Recipe for Creating an Encrypted JWT

The following steps show how to assemble an encrypted JWT with all five segments we saw in the previous section.

1. The first segment, the header segment, is straightforward. I use RSAES OAEP as the algorithm to encrypt the master key and AES256 GCM as the encryption method for encrypting the claim set. The base64 URL encoded header shown in Listing 10-21 forms the header segment.
2. Generate a 256-bit random master key.
3. Encrypt the master key generated in the preceding step with the public key of the RP using RSAES OAEP, the algorithm defined in the header. Base64 URL encode the ciphertext. That forms the second segment of the encrypted JWT.
4. Generate a 96-bit initialization vector (IV). Base64 URL encode the IV. That forms the third segment of the token.
5. Format the AAD by concatenating the three segments formed so far separated by a period character '.'. The AAD will be the header segment separated by a dot, followed by the base64 URL encoded encrypted master key separated by a dot, followed by the base64 URL encoded IV.
6. Perform authenticated encryption with the following as inputs (refer to Figure 10-2).
    a. Key is the 256-bit master key in plain text generated in step 2.
    b. Initialization vector is the 96-bit random value generated in step 4.
    c. AAD is the byte array corresponding to the string formatted in step 5.
    d. Plain text is the JSON representation of the set of claims that the token is supposed to carry.
7. The output of authenticated encryption produces the ciphertext and authentication tag, which are both byte arrays.
8. Base64 URL encode the cipher text. That forms the fourth segment.
9. Base64 URL encode the authentication tag. That forms the fifth and the final segment.
10. Put all five segments one after the other separated by a period character '.'. That completes the process of assembling the encrypted JWT.

To create an encrypted JWT, a token issuer needs only the public key of the RP. Everything else is generated and computed through the preceding ten steps. To validate and extract claims out of an encrypted JWT, an RP application needs only its own private key and, of course, the token itself.

Using an Encrypted JSON Web Token in a Console Application

Similar to the case of a signed JWT, I use an encrypted JWT in a console application. To keep the focus on JWT, the token issuer and the RP are all modeled as simple C# classes. In practice, these entities will be applications and not classes, just to state the obvious.

Supporting Classes

In this section, I do not show the code for the TokenIssuer and RelyingParty classes. These classes are very similar to the ones we saw with the signed JWT. The only difference is that the JsonWebEncryptedToken class is used instead of the JsonWebToken class. I'll start by showing the code in the Main method (see Listing 10-22). The token issuer has the public key corresponding to the private key of the RP. There is no X.509 certificate involved here, and the KeyIssuer class generates the key pair.

Listing 10-22. Main Method

```
static void Main(string[] args)
{
    Tuple<string, string> key = KeyIssuer.GenerateAsymmetricKey();

    TokenIssuer issuer = new TokenIssuer();
    issuer.ShareKeyOutofBand("AnotherRelyingPartApp", key.Item1); // Public Key

    RelyingParty anotherApp = new RelyingParty();
    anotherApp.ShareKeyOutofBand(key.Item2); // Private Key

    string token = issuer.GetEncryptedToken("AnotherRelyingPartApp", "opensesame");
    // With the token, the client now presents the token and calls
    // the method requiring authorization
    anotherApp.AuthenticateWithEncryptedToken(token);
    anotherApp.TheMethodRequiringAuthZ();
}
```

The GenerateAsymmetricKey method of the KeyIssuer class is shown in Listing 10-23. The RSACryptoServiceProvider class is used to generate the public-private key pair, as shown in Chapter 6. The public-private keys in the form of XML are returned to the caller as a Tuple.

Listing 10-23. GenerateAsymmetricKey Method

```
public static Tuple<string, string> GenerateAsymmetricKey()
{
    string publicKey = String.Empty;
    string privateKey = String.Empty;

    using (RSACryptoServiceProvider rsa = new RSACryptoServiceProvider())
    {
        publicKey = rsa.ToXmlString(false);
        privateKey = rsa.ToXmlString(true);
    }

    return new Tuple<string, string>(publicKey, privateKey);
}
```

There are five segments in the encrypted JWT, and it will be helpful to have a class representing the payload. Listing 10-24 shows a new class added, the EncryptedPayload class. There are five properties in this class, representing the JWT segments in the same order as how they will appear in the token. The Parse method creates an instance of the EncryptedPayload class from an encrypted token. The ToString method is simply the reverse of the Parse method. It creates the string representation of the token from the Plain Old CLR Object (POCO). There is another method, ToAdditionalAuthencticatedData(), which supplies the additional data for data encryption. It uses the first three segments from the payload.

Listing 10-24. EncryptedPayload Class

```
public class EncryptedPayload
{
    public string Header { get; set; }
    public byte[] EncryptedMasterKey { get; set; }
    public byte[] InitializationVector { get; set; }
    public byte[] CipherText { get; set; }
    public byte[] Tag { get; set; }

    public override string ToString()
    {
        return String.Format("{0}.{1}.{2}.{3}.{4}", Header.ToBase64String(),
                                                    EncryptedMasterKey.ToBase64String(),
                                                    InitializationVector.ToBase64String(),
                                                    CipherText.ToBase64String(),
                                                    Tag.ToBase64String());
    }

    public byte[] ToAdditionalAuthenticatedData()
    {
        string data =  String.Format("{0}.{1}.{2}", Header.ToBase64String(),
                                                    EncryptedMasterKey.ToBase64String(),
                                                    InitializationVector.ToBase64String());
        return Encoding.UTF8.GetBytes(data);
    }

    public static EncryptedPayload Parse(string token)
    {
        var parts = token.Split('.');
        if (parts.Length != 5)
            throw new SecurityException("Bad token");

        return new EncryptedPayload()
        {
            Header = Encoding.UTF8.GetString(parts[0].ToByteArray()),
            EncryptedMasterKey = parts[1].ToByteArray(),
            InitializationVector = parts[2].ToByteArray(),
            CipherText = parts[3].ToByteArray(),
            Tag = parts[4].ToByteArray()
        };
    }
}
```

The JsonWebEncryptedToken Class

The JsonWebEncryptedToken class, shown in Listing 10-25, does all the grunt work related to encryption and decryption. The JsonWebEncryptedToken class is very similar to JsonWebToken.

For the sake of brevity, I've removed two important methods from the listing that serialize and deserialize. We will look at those later.

Listing 10-25. JsonWebEncryptedToken

```
public class JsonWebEncryptedToken
{
    private const string TYPE_HEADER = "typ";
    private const string JSON_WEB_TOKEN = "JWT";
    private const string ENCRYPTION_ALGORITHM_HEADER = "alg";
    private const string ENCRYPTION_METHOD_HEADER = "enc";
    private const string RSA_OAEP = "RSA-OAEP";
    private const string AES_256_GCM = "A256GCM";
    private const string EXPIRATION_TIME_CLAIM = "exp";
    private const string ISSUER_CLAIM = "iss";
    private const string AUDIENCE_CLAIM = "aud";

    private static readonly TimeSpan lifeTime = new TimeSpan(0, 2, 0);
    private static readonly DateTime epochStart = new DateTime(1970, 01, 01, 0, 0, 0, 0,
                                                                              DateTimeKind.Utc);

    private Dictionary<string, string> claims = new Dictionary<string, string>();

    public JsonWebEncryptedToken()
    {
        TimeSpan ts = DateTime.UtcNow - epochStart + lifeTime;
        this.ExpiresOn = Convert.ToUInt64(ts.TotalSeconds);
    }

    [JsonProperty(PropertyName = TYPE_HEADER)]
    public string Type
    {
        get { return JSON_WEB_TOKEN; }
    }

    [JsonProperty(PropertyName = ENCRYPTION_ALGORITHM_HEADER)]
    public string EncryptionAlgorithm
    {
        get { return RSA_OAEP; }
    }

    [JsonProperty(PropertyName = ENCRYPTION_METHOD_HEADER)]
    public string EncryptionMethod
    {
        get { return AES_256_GCM; }
    }

    [JsonIgnore]
    public string AsymmetricKey { get; set; }

    [JsonIgnore]
    public IList<Claim> Claims
```

```
{
    get
    {
        return this.claims.Keys.SelectMany(key =>
                                    this.claims[key].Split(',')
                                        .Select(value => new Claim(key, value))).ToList();
    }
}

[JsonIgnore]
public ulong ExpiresOn
{
    get
    {
        return UInt64.Parse(this.claims[EXPIRATION_TIME_CLAIM]);
    }
    private set
    {
        this.claims.Add(EXPIRATION_TIME_CLAIM, value.ToString());
    }
}

[JsonIgnore]
public string Issuer
{
    get
    {
        return this.claims.ContainsKey(ISSUER_CLAIM) ? this.claims[ISSUER_CLAIM] : String.Empty;
    }
    set
    {
        this.claims.Add(ISSUER_CLAIM, value);
    }
}

[JsonIgnore]
public string Audience
{
    get
    {
        return this.claims.ContainsKey(AUDIENCE_CLAIM) ?
                    this.claims[AUDIENCE_CLAIM] :
                        String.Empty;
    }
    set
    {
        this.claims.Add(AUDIENCE_CLAIM, value);
    }
}
```

```
    public void AddClaim(string claimType, string value)
    {
        if (this.claims.ContainsKey(claimType))
            this.claims[claimType] = this.claims[claimType] + "," + value;
        else
            this.claims.Add(claimType, value);
    }

    // Incomplete class - Two methods removed for brevity
}
```

Serialization (ToString Method)

We now look at the `ToString` method that creates the string representation of the encrypted token. This is where most of the action happens! The recipe we saw earlier for creating the encrypted JWT is implemented in the `ToString` method, as shown in the following steps.

1. Using JSON.NET, serialize the object instance and the claims dictionary that contains the claims set into header and claims variables. At this point, these are just JSON representations that are not base64 URL encoded. See Listing 10-26.

   Listing 10-26. ToString Method

   ```
   public override string ToString()
   {
           string header = JsonConvert.SerializeObject(this);
           string claims = JsonConvert.SerializeObject(this.claims);
           // Rest of the logic goes here
   }
   ```

2. Generate a 256-bit random key called master key and a 96-bit IV using the `RNGCryptoServiceProvider` class, as shown in Listing 10-27. This step is the same as the one in which symmetric keys are generated in Chapter 6. There is nothing special here.

   Listing 10-27. Master Key and IV Generation

   ```
   byte[] masterKey = new byte[32];
   byte[] initVector = new byte[12];
   using (var provider = new RNGCryptoServiceProvider())
   {
       provider.GetBytes(masterKey);
       provider.GetBytes(initVector);
   }
   ```

3. Encrypt the master key generated in the previous step, using the public key of the RP, as shown in Listing 10-28. No X.509 certificate is used here. This is the same as how we implemented asymmetric encryption without a X.509 certificate in Chapter 6 using `RSACryptoServiceProvider`. I explicitly set the second parameter of the `Encrypt` method to true to use OAEP padding, because the algorithm I decided to use is RSA-OAEP.

Listing 10-28. Encryption of the Master Key

```
byte[] encryptedMasterKey = null;
using (RSACryptoServiceProvider rsa = new RSACryptoServiceProvider())
{
    rsa.FromXmlString(this.AsymmetricKey);
    encryptedMasterKey = rsa.Encrypt(masterKey, true); // OAEP Padding
}
```

4. So far, we have the header, the encrypted master key, and the IV. Load them up in an `EncryptedPayload` instance and call `ToAdditionalAuthenticatedData()` to get the AAD. This method simply base64 URL encodes the three elements (header, key, and IV), puts a dot in between, and returns the string to us. See Listing 10-29.

Listing 10-29. Additional Authenticated Data

```
var authData = new EncryptedPayload()
{
    Header = header,
    EncryptedMasterKey = encryptedMasterKey,
    InitializationVector = initVector
};

byte[] additionalAuthenticatedData = authData.ToAdditionalAuthenticatedData();
```

5. We are now all set to do the authenticated encryption. Use the `AuthenticatedAesCng` class from the Security.Cryptography.dll assembly downloaded from the CodePlex CLR Security project, as shown in Listing 10-30.
    a. Set the chaining mode to Galois/Counter Mode (GCM).
    b. The inputs to the encryption process are (1) the master key, which is a 256-bit random key we generated as is and not the encrypted one; (2) the IV, which is 96 bits we generated as is; (3) the AAD, which we got by calling the `ToAdditionalAuthenticatedData` method of the `EncryptedPayload` object; and (4) the plain text, which is the claims set in JSON format converted to an array of bytes. Two things come out: the ciphertext, or the encrypted bytes corresponding to the claims, and a tag.

Listing 10-30. Authenticated Encryption

```
byte[] tag = null;
byte[] cipherText = null;

using (var aes = new AuthenticatedAesCng())
{
    aes.CngMode = CngChainingMode.Gcm; // Galois/Counter Mode
    aes.Key = masterKey;
    aes.IV = initVector;
    aes.AuthenticatedData = additionalAuthenticatedData;

    using (MemoryStream ms = new MemoryStream())
    {
        using (IAuthenticatedCryptoTransform encryptor = aes.CreateAuthenticatedEncryptor())
```

```
        {
            using (CryptoStream cs = new CryptoStream(ms, encryptor, CryptoStreamMode.Write))
            {
                // Encrypt the claims set
                byte[] claimsSet = Encoding.UTF8.GetBytes(claims);
                cs.Write(claimsSet, 0, claimsSet.Length);
                cs.FlushFinalBlock();
                tag = encryptor.GetTag();
                cipherText = ms.ToArray();
            }
        }
    }
}
```

6. Create the final payload or the encrypted SWT by using the header, encrypted master key, IV, cipher text, and tag, all base64 URL encoded and separated by a dot, as shown in Listing 10-31.

   Listing 10-31. Assembling the Segments

   ```
   var payload = new EncryptedPayload()
   {
       Header = header,
       EncryptedMasterKey = encryptedMasterKey,
       InitializationVector = initVector,
       CipherText = cipherText,
       Tag = tag
   };

   string token = payload.ToString();

   return token;
   ```

Deserialization (Parse Method)

The receiving end—in other words, the RP—has to extract the claims out of the encrypted SWT. The method that does all the heavy lifting related to that is the `Parse()` method of `JsonWebEncryptedToken`, shown in Listing 10-32. The process here is the exact reverse of `ToString()`. Following are the steps.

1. Use the static method of `Parse` of the `EncryptedPayload` class and extract the data in the five segments. Through the properties available in the `EncryptedPayload` class, you can access the encrypted master key, IV, authentication tag, and the ciphertext.

2. The RP has the private key of the asymmetric key pair. Hence, decrypt the master key using the same.

3. Frame the additional authenticated data from the segments that have come in the token using the first three segments: header, encrypted master key, and IV. This can be accomplished by simply calling the `ToAdditionalAuthenticatedData` method on the `EncryptedPayload` object created in the first step.

4. Use the decrypted master key, IV, the AAD from the previous step, and tag to decrypt the ciphertext. If there is no tampering and all the inputs used are correct, this process will produce the plain text. The plain text is just the JSON representation of the claim set.

Deserialize it back into the claims dictionary. Also, deserialize the header and create the `JsonWebEncryptedToken` object. Then, check the expiry of the token.

5. Any other validation, such as the checks related to the issuer and the RP, are omitted for brevity.

Listing 10-32. JsonWebEncryptedToken Parse Method

```
public static JsonWebEncryptedToken Parse(string token, string privateKey)
{
    byte[] claimSet = null;
    EncryptedPayload payload = null;

    try
    {
        payload = EncryptedPayload.Parse(token);

        byte[] masterKey = null;
        using (RSACryptoServiceProvider rsa = new RSACryptoServiceProvider())
        {
            rsa.FromXmlString(privateKey);
            masterKey = rsa.Decrypt(payload.EncryptedMasterKey, true);
        }

        byte[] additionalAuthenticatedData = payload.ToAdditionalAuthenticatedData();
        using (AuthenticatedAesCng aes = new AuthenticatedAesCng())
        {
            aes.CngMode = CngChainingMode.Gcm;
            aes.Key = masterKey;
            aes.IV = payload.InitializationVector;
            aes.AuthenticatedData = additionalAuthenticatedData;
            aes.Tag = payload.Tag;

            using (MemoryStream ms = new MemoryStream())
            {
                using (CryptoStream cs = new CryptoStream(ms, aes.CreateDecryptor(),
                                                                   CryptoStreamMode.Write))
                {
                    byte[] cipherText = payload.CipherText;
                    cs.Write(cipherText, 0, cipherText.Length);
                    cs.FlushFinalBlock();

                    claimSet = ms.ToArray();
                }
            }
        }
    }
    catch (Exception ex)
    {
        throw new SecurityException("Invalid Token", ex);
    }
```

```
    var jwt = JsonConvert.DeserializeObject<JsonWebEncryptedToken>(payload.Header);
    jwt.AsymmetricKey = privateKey;
    jwt.claims = JsonConvert.DeserializeObject<Dictionary<string, string>>
                                            (Encoding.UTF8.GetString(claimSet));

    TimeSpan ts = DateTime.UtcNow - epochStart;

    if (jwt.ExpiresOn < Convert.ToUInt64(ts.TotalSeconds))
        throw new SecurityException("Token has expired");

    return jwt;
}
```

JWT Handler

In this chapter, I used console applications to demonstrate signed and encrypted JSON web tokens. I used the custom classes of `JsonWebToken` and `JsonWebEncryptedToken` for this purpose. Because I used these implementations to help you understand JWT, I did not implement all the necessary validations that a production-strength implementation will implement, such as the checks related to the issuer and the relying party.

Microsoft has released the developer preview of the JWT Security Token Handler, in the form of a NuGet package. It contains the classes to validate, parse and generate JWT tokens either on top of WIF or without any dependency on WIF's configuration. To install the JSON Web Token Handler, run the following command in the Package Manager Console: `Install-Package Microsoft.IdentityModel.Tokens.JWT`. That should bring the `Microsoft.IdentityModel.Tokens.JWT` assembly. Listing 10-33 shows the code using `JWTSecurityTokenHandler` to validate the JWT issued by `TokenIssuer`.

Listing 10-33. JWT Handler

```
public void AuthenticateUsingMsftJwt(string token)
{
    try
    {
        // Use JWTSecurityTokenHandler to validate the JWT token
        JWTSecurityTokenHandler tokenHandler = new JWTSecurityTokenHandler();

        TokenValidationParameters parms = new TokenValidationParameters()
        {
            AllowedAudience = "MyRelyingPartApp",
            ValidIssuers = new List<string>() { "TokenIssuer" },
            SigningToken = new BinarySecretSecurityToken(
                                            Convert.FromBase64String(this.secretKey))
        };

        var config = new IdentityConfiguration();
        Thread.CurrentPrincipal = config
                                .ClaimsAuthenticationManager
                                    .Authenticate("TheMethodRequiringAuthZ",
                                                tokenHandler.ValidateToken
                                                                (token, parms));
    }
```

```
    catch (Exception ex)
    {
        Console.WriteLine(ex.Message);
    }
}
```

One point to note is that the JWT specification does not allow duplicate claim types, but we have two role claims. To handle this case, I use a `ClaimsAuthenticationManager` subclass that we saw in Chapter 5 to split the comma-separated roles into individual claims, as shown in Listing 10-34.

Listing 10-34. ClaimsAuthenticationManager Subclass

```
public class AuthenticationManager : ClaimsAuthenticationManager
 {
    public override ClaimsPrincipal Authenticate(string resourceName,
                                                    ClaimsPrincipal incomingPrincipal)
    {
        if (incomingPrincipal == null)
                throw new SecurityException("Name claim missing");

        ClaimsIdentity identity = (ClaimsIdentity)incomingPrincipal.Identity;

        var newClaims = identity.Claims
                            .SelectMany(c => c.Value.Split(',')
                                .Select(value => new Claim(c.Type, value))).ToList();

        ClaimsPrincipal newPrincipal = new ClaimsPrincipal(
                                new ClaimsIdentity(newClaims, identity.AuthenticationType));

        return newPrincipal;
    }
}
```

To plug the `ClaimsAuthenticationManager` into the claims processing pipeline, modify the config file as shown in Listing 10-35.

Listing 10-35. Configuration Changes

```
<?xml version="1.0" encoding="utf-8" ?>
<configuration>
        <configSections>
                <section name="system.identityModel"
                               type="System.IdentityModel.Configuration.SystemIdentityModelSection,
                                     System.IdentityModel, Version=4.0.0.0,
                                            Culture=neutral,PublicKeyToken=B77A5C561934E089"/>
        </configSections>
        <startup>
                <supportedRuntime version="v4.0" sku=".NETFramework,Version=v4.5" />
        </startup>
```

```
    <system.identityModel>
        <identityConfiguration>
            <claimsAuthenticationManager
                        type="JWT.AuthenticationManager,JWT"/>
        </identityConfiguration>
    </system.identityModel>
</configuration>
```

Summary

A security token is a container for secure transport of the claim set over the network. Based on the format, there are three major types of tokens: SAML tokens, SWT, and JWT. A SAML token is XML based and closely related to SOAP and WS-* protocols. A client that needs a token from an STS requests and obtains one through the request-response pair of RST and RSTR, in accordance with the WS-Trust specification.

A SWT and a JWT are both web tokens because they are designed to be compact and better suited to travel in HTTP headers. The rough equivalent for WS-Trust in the REST world is OAuth 2.0, the protocol that is typically used to request and obtain web tokens. OAuth 2.0 does not require a SWT or a JWT to be used as token formats. However, in practice, when the OAuth 2.0 specification is used the tokens used are invariably web tokens.

A SWT is just HTML form encoded key name-value pairs. The token issuer and the RP decide on the exact names and the values or the claim set. The only mandatory name-value pair required by the SWT specification is HMACSHA256, the value of which is the HMAC of all the other name-value pairs in the token. The purpose of the HMACSHA256 name-value pair is to ensure token integrity and authenticity.

A JWT is based on JSON, which the JavaScript-based applications find easier to use. An important difference to note is that a SWT does not support encryption. There is nothing that prevents us from encrypting a SWT, but it is not defined as part of the SWT specification. In contrast, a JWT comes in three flavors: (1) a plain text JWT, which is neither integrity-protected nor encrypted, (2) a signed JWT with the claim set protected from tampering by an HMAC or a digital signature using PKI in accordance with JWS, and (3) an encrypted JWT with the claim set encrypted for confidentiality as well as integrity, as specified by JWE.

The JWT specification requires a special variant of base64 encoding called base64 URL encoding to be used. Base64 URL encoding is a variation on top of the standard base64 encoding, where '+' and '/' characters are respectively replaced with '-' and '_' and the padding '=' characters removed so that the payload remains just the same regardless of URL encoding or form encoding. Also, JWT employs a special type of encryption called authenticated encryption designed to provide data authenticity, integrity, and confidentiality at the same time.

CHAPTER 11

OAuth 2.0 Using Live Connect API

WS-* (pronounced WS-STAR) is the name used to refer collectively to the specifications built for SOAP-based web services. One such specification is WS-Trust, which provides a framework for requesting, issuing, and validating security tokens. I covered WS-Trust in Chapter 7. Another member of the WS-* family is WS-Security, a specification that describes how to include security tokens in SOAP messages to be presented by the client application to the web service as credentials for authentication and authorization. WS-Trust and WS-Security in combination provide a standard way for a client application to request and obtain a security token and then present it to the relying party SOAP-based web service as a credential for authentication.

In the world of REST to which ASP.NET Web API belongs, OAuth is the specification comparable to WS-Trust and WS-Security. Basically, OAuth stands for open authorization. The OAuth framework enables a client application to access a web API in one of two ways: on behalf of the end user by orchestrating an approval interaction between the user and the underlying web application, which is generally referred to as three-legged OAuth, and by allowing the client application to access the web API on its own behalf, which is generally referred to as two-legged OAuth.

The heart of the OAuth specification is the access token. OAuth specifies how a client application can request an access token from the authorization server and present the token to a resource server (read web API) to access the protected resource.

OAuth 1.0 was the initial version created in late 2006. It evolved into the current OAuth 2.0, with no backward compatibility to OAuth 1.0. In this book, I limit coverage to OAuth 2.0. We start our exploration mainly from the point of view of the client consuming a web API. Microsoft Live Connect implements the OAuth 2.0 protocol to authenticate users, and I use Live Connect API in this chapter to demonstrate OAuth 2.0 in action.

Use Case for OAuth: App-to-App Data Sharing

OAuth solves the problem of one web application trying to access another web application on behalf of a user without having to share the credentials. Suppose I own a small, specialized retail store. I have an e-mail web application where I maintain all my customer contact information, not for just the customers with whom I communicate through e-mails, but for everyone. Before I can do anything useful, the application requires me to login with my user ID and password, which is very typical for any public-facing web application.

I use another public-facing web application, Promotion Manager, to manage my promotions, offers, and deals. When I have a promotion ready to roll, I need Promotion Manager to retrieve the list of contacts and short list the contacts, based on some given criteria, and start sending e-mails. To do this, Promotion Manager needs the contact information from my e-mail application.

I could hand out my e-mail application credentials to the Promotion Manager web application, but I'm uncomfortable with that option. The Promotion Manager web application is a public web application. If I share credentials with it, it is likely that it will store the credentials or log them somewhere, intentionally or otherwise. Thus, someone in that organization could send my credentials to a competitor of mine, who could then get the details of my entire customer base. It would be devastating to my business. Maybe the developers of Promotion Manager followed sound security practices, but I can't count on that. Too much is at stake to even consider sharing the credentials.

Fortunately, there is another option. Let's say Promotion Manager needs to access my contact information. Instead of requiring my credentials, it redirects me to the e-mail web application where I can confidently enter my credentials and consent to share a subset of my contact information. The e-mail web application issues a temporary token to Promotion Manager and puts me back on the Promotion Manager web page. Promotion Manager uses the token, pulls the contact information, and displays the information to me. I review the list and, once satisfied, click a button and start the process that sends e-mails to those on the list. In this case, I never need to share the e-mail application credentials with the Promotion Manager application. I'm happy!

This is how OAuth helps me get around the rather uncomfortable situation of having to provide my credentials for my contacts application to another application. In the preceding scenario, the Promotion Manager web application in all probability will not issue a request for some web page from the e-mail application and start extracting the data from the HTML through web-scraping techniques. It is very likely that the communication here is through some sort of web API, the hallmark of the programmable web and a key piece of Web 2.0. There you are! After taking a little bit of a detour, we are back on track with web APIs.

The best real-world analogy for an OAuth scenario is the valet parking analogy provided by Eran Hammer, the former lead author and editor of the OAuth specifications. You give the attendant the valet key, but not the "real" key, to park the car on your behalf. The valet key works in the ignition, but it does not open the glove compartment or the trunk. So the temporary token issued by the e-mail web application in the preceding example is the valet key. It is not a substitute for the real key. The valet key can perform only a subset of what the real key can do. Similarly, by using the token the Promotion Manager web application can retrieve only a subset of contact information but cannot freely access every bit of information from the e-mail web application.

OPENID VS. OAUTH

OpenID and OAuth are two different things, although they are related. They are both open standards and that should explain why they both start with the letter 'O.' OAuth is related to authorization, whereas OpenID is related to authentication. But they both belong to the world of security.

Many web users try to reuse their credentials, mainly the password, which is a poor practice from a security perspective. If you are diligent, you need to maintain at least 10 or 20 credentials, depending on the extent to which you have embraced the web in your daily life. OpenID tries to solve this problem by describing a standard for consolidated digital identities.

For example, let's say you create an identity with an OpenID provider like Google, and you use the same identity to login to another web application. Even though you use the same identity, you do not need to enter your Google credentials in the other web application. When the web application requires you to authenticate, it doesn't show you a login page where credentials are entered; instead, it redirects you to a page hosted by Google, the OpenID provider. Because you are on a page within the Google domain, you can confidently enter your Google credentials. When Google successfully authenticates you, you are considered logged in to the relying party web application under the identity specified by the given OpenID.

OAuth 2.0 Roles

OAuth 2.0 defines four roles. This terminology is very important to understanding OAuth. You can find additional information in the OAuth 2.0 specification Request for Comments (RFC) 6749, "The OAuth 2.0 Authorization Framework" via the URL `http://tools.ietf.org/html/rfc6749`.

1. Resource Owner—Typically the end user who grants access to the protected resource. In the preceding example where I discussed the interaction between the e-mail application and the Promotion Manager web application, the resource owner is me and the resource is the list of contacts.

2. Resource Server—The server that hosts the protected resource and is capable of accepting access tokens and servicing the request. In the preceding example, the server running the e-mail web application is the resource server.

3. Client—An application that needs access to the protected resource. In the preceding example, the client is the Promotion Manager web application.

4. Authorization Server—The server that issues the access token to the client application after authenticating the resource owner and getting authorization from the resource owner. In the preceding scenario, the resource server and authorization server are the same. They can be separate as well.

There are two components of the e-mail application in play: the web application and the web API. The resource server hosts the web API, say `www.my-email.com/api/contacts`. The authorization server hosts the web page, `www.my-email.com/oauth`, where I enter my credentials and consent to give access. In this case, `www.my-email.com` is both the authorization and resource server, but the web application represents the authorization server and the web API represents the resource server.

■ **Note** From the standpoint of securing ASP.NET Web API, the resource server as defined by OAuth 2.0 corresponds to your ASP.NET Web API that needs to be secured. The client as defined by the OAuth 2.0 specification is the client application that consumes your ASP.NET Web API. The client application obtains an access token from the authorization server and presents it to ASP.NET Web API as the credential to access the protected resources hosted by the resource server.

OAuth 2.0 Client Types

OAuth 2.0 defines two client types:

1. **Confidential clients**—Clients that are capable of maintaining the confidentiality of their credentials. This can be a web application running in a server, such as an ASP.NET MVC web application, where the server-side code such as your controller acting as the client is a confidential client. In this case, the end user, even if he is the resource owner, does not have access to any keys, secrets, or tokens issued by the authorization server.

2. **Public clients**—Clients that are incapable of maintaining the confidentiality of their credentials. Examples of public clients are a Windows Presentation Foundation (WPF) application running on a client machine, a web page running JQuery in a browser, or a plug-in such as Silverlight running within a browser.

OAuth 2.0 Client Profiles

In the preceding scenario of an e-mail application and the Promotion Manager application, the client is a web application. The OAuth 2.0 specification refers to this type of client application as a client profile and defines three such profiles.

1. **Web application**—A web application is a confidential client running on a web server. In the context of OAuth 2.0, this refers to the server-side code that executes in the web server such as the controller action methods in the case of ASP.NET MVC or even the C# code in the views but not the JavaScript code, even if it is part of an ASP.NET MVC Web application.

2. **User agent-based application**—A public client that runs under the context of a web browser, such as JQuery or a Silverlight plug-in.

3. **Native application**—A public client that is installed and executed on the client side on a device used by a resource owner. This includes WPF or a WinForms application that runs on a laptop or desktop, a Microsoft Windows 8 application running on Surface, or native applications running on an iPhone or possibly an iPad. Unlike the user agent-based application profile, native applications do not have full browser capabilities.

OAuth 2.0 Authorization Grant Types

An authorization grant is the credential representing the resource owner's consent to allow or grant access to the protected resources. A client application uses the authorization grant to obtain an access token, which is a string representing an authorization granted to the client by the resource owner. The OAuth 2.0 specification defines four out-of-the-box grant types, with an extension mechanism for adding additional grant types.

1. Authorization code
2. Implicit
3. Resource owner password
4. Client credentials

Authorization Code Grant

An authorization code grant is applicable to a web application profile, the code that executes in a server. As the name indicates, there is an authorization code that is associated with the grant type. There are two major steps that happen as part of this grant type.

1. Once the resource owner grants access to the protected resource, the authorization server returns an authorization code to the client by redirecting the browser to the callback URI specified in the request, along with the authorization code in the query string.
2. The web application, which is the client, exchanges this authorization code for an access token with the authorization server. The authorization server can optionally return a refresh token to the client.

This two-step process is designed to ensure both the access and refresh tokens remain confined to the client web application (the server side) and never get passed to the browser. Even the resource owner will not be able to see the tokens. Only the authorization code is visible to the browser and resource owner. The secret sauce that the OAuth 2.0 specification uses to restrict the tokens from leaking into the browser, and hence into the hands of a resource owner or malicious user, is the client secret.

For anyone to exchange an authorization code for an access token, two things are required: the client ID and the client secret. Only the client application knows the client secret. The resource owners will not know the secret and therefore cannot obtain an access token themselves, even with the authorization code available to the browser. For this reason, the tokens obtained through this grant type never get leaked to browsers, and hence an authorization server can optionally return a refresh token. A refresh token is a long-lived token that can be used by a client application to obtain new access tokens without going through the steps of getting user consent again. I cover refresh tokens later in this chapter.

■ **Note** It might sound obvious, but there is a point to be clarified here. An end user is the resource owner or the actual user of your application in production. If you mistake yourself, the developer, as the end user, you might think you know the client secret and that you can get tokens. In an IT organization that follows the right security procedures, the client secret for the application running in production will not be known even to the development team that created the application. Only system administrators will copy those values into a configuration file that gets encrypted, from which your code reads the values.

Implicit Grant

An implicit grant is applicable to user agent-based applications such as JavaScript running under the context of a web browser. It is a simplified version of an authorization code grant. The access token is immediately returned to the client application in a hash fragment of the callback URI as soon as the resource owner grants access to the protected resource. There is no exchange of any code involved. Because the access token is available to the browser and hence the end user, refresh tokens are not applicable to this grant type. If an access token expires, there is no refresh token for the client application to automatically obtain a new access token. The client application must again go through the original steps of asking for user consent and subsequently getting a new access token.

Resource Owner Password Grant

A resource owner password grant might sound like an oxymoron, for the client exchanges the resource owner password for an access token after receiving the password from the resource owner (end user). This grant type might give you the impression that it is against the basic premise of OAuth, which is to not share credentials of one application with another. However, this grant type does have use cases. It is used with clients that a user can trust as well as the authorization server. For example, if I'm trying to use a web API provided by Google, I'll be comfortable entering my Google credentials on a web page hosted in Google. I should be equally comfortable to enter it in a client application if the client application itself is created by Google, such as an application Google has created to run on my mobile phone.

It is important to note that the client application that is designed to work with this type of grant does not keep the credentials anywhere. It is obtained from the end user and immediately exchanged for an access token. The client application must not log the credentials or store it somewhere for later use.

There is a performance benefit to be gained by using this grant type. In the absence of this grant type, the only available option is to directly send the end user credentials—the user ID and password—to the resource server while invoking the web API. The resource server (or web API) needs to authenticate the credentials as part of every single request. This generally means hitting a data store. By using a resource owner password grant, credentials are exchanged for a token, and the token can contain enough information to establish identity without authentication.

As a simple example, imagine a token containing just the user ID and some additional data, all encrypted and possibly signed using an HMAC. As long as the web API is able to decrypt and validate the HMAC, it can get the data from the token and establish identity without hitting the data store. This is easily possible if the resource server and the authorization server (typically from the same organization) share the same key for encryption and signing. As long as the web API is able to decrypt and validate the HMAC, it is proof that the token can be trusted. Identity can be established based on that.

Client Credentials Grant

With a client credentials grant, a client application exchanges its own credentials for an access token. This type of grant applies to scenarios where the protected resource is not owned by a specific user. In the scenario I provided earlier in this chapter, the resource is the list of "my" contacts. I am a specific user who owns the list. In contrast, if a resource is not specific to a user and is common to all, a client credentials grant can be used. A good example is application preferences or things of that nature that can be modified through the API exposed by the resource server. These preferences are not specific to any individual end user, but applicable only to the client application.

This type of grant is also applicable when a user consents to provide access to the protected resource outside the OAuth flow, perhaps through an out-of-band process, and expects the client to access the protected resource seamlessly without bothering her for authorization every time. The flow associated with this grant type is referred to as two-legged because the client interacts with the resource server with no user involvement.

The obvious disadvantage is that this grant type is not suitable for protected resources owned by individual users. Also, this grant type depends only on the client ID and client secret. If these two are compromised, anyone can get access tokens and use the web API.

The surface area for the attack can be minimized by keeping the number of APIs that accept tokens obtained through the client credentials grant as small as possible. Also, you can build additional security on top of this flow by employing a preshared key.

Access Token

We saw in the preceding scenario involving an e-mail application and the Promotion Manager application that the client, which is the Promotion Manager application, gets a token. To be more precise, the token is an access token issued by the authorization server and is based on the authorization granted by the resource owner or by me. The client accesses the protected resource, which is the list of contacts, by presenting the access token to the resource server. The resource server validates the access token for freshness and scope.

An access token is just a string representing an authorization granted to the client. Because an access token is issued by an authorization server and consumed by a resource server, the contents of the token are usually opaque to the client. The OAuth 2.0 specification neither defines how the access token must be structured or formatted nor defines how the token must be validated. It is up to the resource server (consumer) and the authorization server (producer). An access token can be built according to some other specification; for example, an access token can be a Simple Web Token (SWT) or JSON Web Token (JWT). The OAuth 2.0 specification does refer to a companion specification RFC 6750, "The OAuth 2.0 Authorization Framework: Bearer Token Usage," that describes how to use bearer tokens in HTTP requests to access OAuth 2.0 protected resources.

We briefly looked at the concept of bearer tokens vs. holder-of-key tokens in Chapter 9, with SAML tokens issued by AD FS. In short, a bearer token is like cash: finders keepers and no questions asked about the ownership. Holder-of-key tokens require supporting cryptographic material such as a key, symmetric or otherwise, to prove token ownership.

OAuth 1.0 supports cryptographic signatures, which is a must without HTTPS or SSL/TLS (transport security). OAuth Web Resource Authorization Profiles (WRAP), the predecessor to OAuth 2.0, drops the signature requirements in favor of transport security and introduces the bearer tokens, making TLS mandatory for such tokens.

Access Token as a Bearer Token

OAuth 2.0 basically specifies ways for different types of clients to obtain an access token from an authorization server and present the token to a resource server to gain access to a protected resource, which in our case is a web API. Presenting the access token to a web API can be done in the following three ways.

1. HTTP header, using the Authorization HTTP request header, as defined by RFC 2617, "HTTP Authentication: Basic and Digest Access Authentication," which we saw in Chapter 4, to send the access token.

2. Message body, using the HTTP request entity-body. RFC 6750 states several conditions that must be met to use an access token in the request body. One notable condition is that the entire request body can contain only ASCII characters. Also, there is no request body in the case of HTTP GET.

3. Query string, using the HTTP request URI. RFC 6750 specifies this approach only as the last resort if the previous two approaches are not feasible, given the security weakness associated with passing a token in the query string, such as a token getting logged and so on.

Given these three options, the preferred way is to use the HTTP authorization header because it can be consistently used for all HTTP methods and the request content types of XML, JSON, and headers do not get cached or logged. In fact, web tokens such as SWT and JWT strive to keep the tokens compact for transportation in the HTTP authorization request header. SAML tokens, being XML, are not designed for a smaller size; this is one of the reasons web tokens are favored in the world of RESTful web APIs, as we saw in Chapter 10.

When the access token rides in the HTTP authorization request header, the corresponding scheme used is the bearer scheme. Listing 11-1 shows an example of a request header using a bearer scheme.

Listing 11-1. HTTP Authorization Header Bearer Scheme

```
GET /api/employees/12345 HTTP/1.1
Host: my-server.com
Authorization: Bearer DFJQNC694GisUrPVZap5pdyWLohFK==
```

Refresh Token

Refresh tokens are issued to the client by the authorization server along with an access token. The purpose of a refresh token is for the client application to present the refresh token to the authorization server and obtain a new access token when the current access token becomes invalid. Like an access token, a refresh token is just a string representing an authorization granted to the client, and the content of the refresh token is opaque to the client. However, unlike an access token, a refresh token is never presented to a resource server and is meant to be used only with the authorization server.

A refresh token is the distinguishing attribute of an authorization code grant, which is applicable to a web application (a confidential client). Compared to an implicit grant, an authorization code grant is a bit complex. There is an extra step of exchanging the code for tokens. The specifications like OAuth were created by a bunch of smart people, after a lot of thinking and deliberation! They didn't include an extra step for no reason. This extra step, or the abstraction, is to make sure tokens stay only within the server side of the web application. As mentioned in the previous section, all the user agent or the end user gets to see is the authorization code, which has no value on its own unless it is sent along with the client secret to exchange it for a token. For this reason, even the resource owner who grants the access to the resource will not have access to the token.

Why should you be careful to ensure the tokens do not get passed to the browser or the end user? The reason is the refresh token. A refresh token is a long-lived token, whereas an access token has a short life span. However, using the refresh token, a valid access token can be obtained from an authorization server without getting the user's consent to share the protected resource. Hence, a refresh token is a prized possession. Because of its long life, a refresh token can be saved by client web applications for later use. Because of the security implications related to refresh tokens, they are not issued with an implicit grant, which does not have that abstracting step of an authorization code exchange.

Why have an additional refresh token? Why not just make the access token long lived? As Eran Hammer stated in response to these types of questions in a forum, the reasons are for security and performance.

1. **From a security standpoint:** With bearer tokens, TLS (HTTPS) is a must. But even with that, it is not as good as a holder-of-key token that has cryptographic backup. For the sake of argument, imagine a token landing in the hands of a malicious user. If the token has message security implemented through encryption and signing using keys shared out of band, a man-in-the-middle or unintended recipients can do little with it because message security ensures end-to-end security. Transport security is a great option, and it is not possible to get the token out of the transport channel, but it cannot guarantee end-to-end security. So with the bearer token being comparatively weaker, giving it a short life span reduces the window of opportunity for misuse by a malicious user.

2. **From a performance standpoint:** For revoking the access granted, authorization providers typically provide a web site. To be revoked, the token has to be invalidated. This means authorization providers have to store the access tokens in some persistent store and hit it for every web API request to see if the grant has been revoked or if it is still valid. No one wants to do this for performance reasons. Instead, they just keep the lifetime of the access token relatively small and let it die its natural death at the hands of time, when the previously granted access is revoked.

However, the authorization providers must store the refresh token because a subsequent request can come through to get a new access token based on it. But those requests are not as frequent as the actual API calls, and they can remove the refresh token from their data store when access is revoked.

Using Live Connect APIs

We have had quite a bit of theory on OAuth 2.0 so far. We now look at **using** OAuth 2.0 to consume Live Connect APIs from an ASP.NET MVC application. Live Connect is a collection of REST-based APIs that Microsoft provides so that we can integrate any application with services like SkyDrive, Hotmail, and Messenger.

I can write pages after pages of theory, but unless you see OAuth in action through a couple of examples it will be difficult to appreciate the theory. At this point, we are on the other side of the table. That is, we are the client trying to use Live Connect APIs. We are not yet at the point where we can implement authorization in our ASP.NET Web API. We will move to the other side of the table as soon as we are comfortable on this side of the table!

Registering Your Application in the Live Connect Portal

Before you can do anything with Live Connect, you must create an entry for your application in the Microsoft Live Application Management portal. The URL is `https://manage.dev.live.com`. Of course, you do need a Live ID to even log into the management portal. The following steps show how to register your application.

1. After logging into the portal, you will land on a page, as shown in Figure 11-1. Give a name to the application and click I accept.

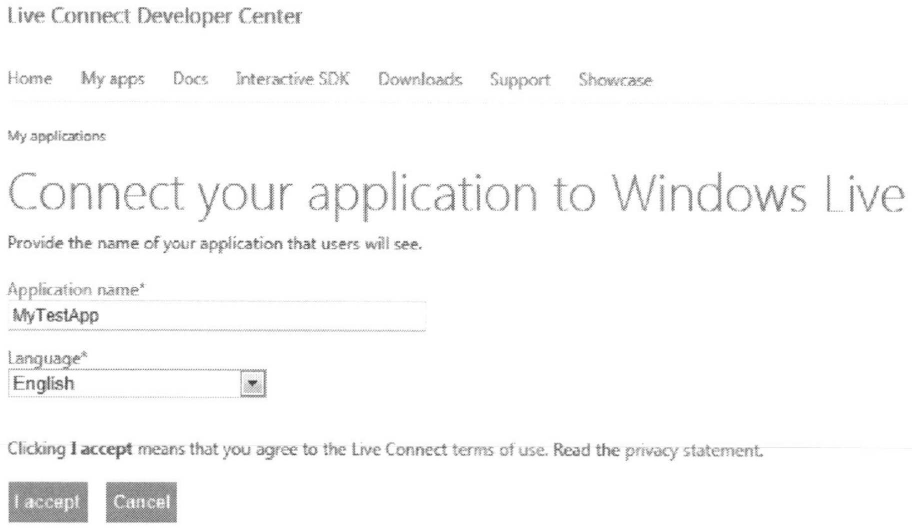

Figure 11-1. *Registration in the Application Management portal*

2. That creates the application and puts you on the next screen, shown in Figure 11-2. On this page, we are interested in the client ID and client secret. We will use them in our code. In the Redirect domain text box, you must enter a valid domain. You cannot use `http://localhost`, for example. The portal is unforgiving and needs a valid domain name. If you own one, you can go ahead and use your domain name, such as `http://www.my-server.com`. If you don't have a valid domain, you can trick the browser on your computer into thinking that it is going to `www.my-server.com` by making an entry in the hosts file. You can find the file in `C:\Windows\System32\drivers\etc`. The file name is hosts, without any extension. Just add an entry, `127.0.0.1 www.my-server.com`, to the file. If you now ping `www.my-server.com`, it will ping 127.0.0.1. In other words, Live Connect is happy that you have provided a proper domain name, and your browser will be happy because it will be able to resolve the server address to an IP, which happens to be your loopback IP. Leave the No radio button selected for Mobile client app.

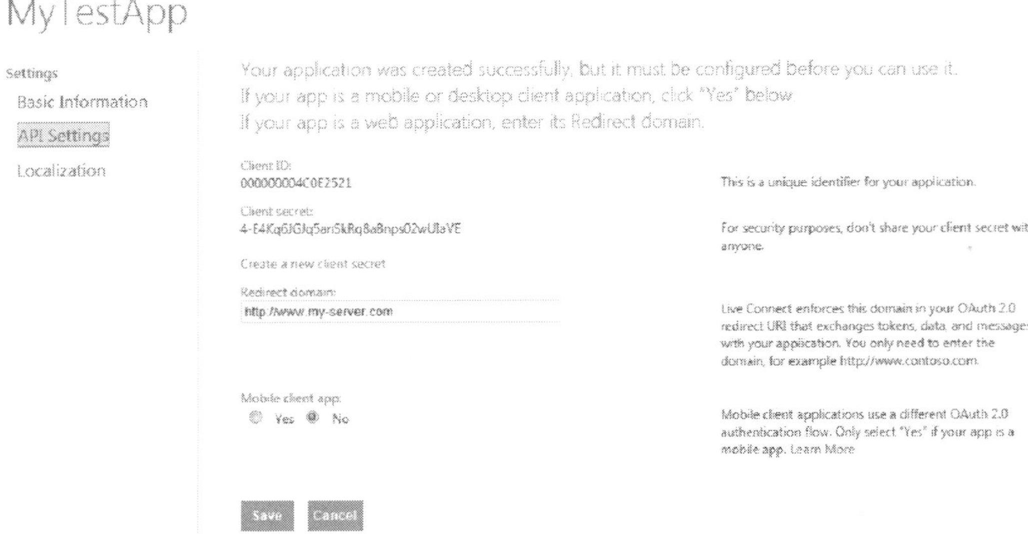

Figure 11-2. *API settings*

Using an Implicit Grant to Access Live Connect

Now we are all set to see OAuth 2.0 in action. We start by looking at an implicit grant, as that is the simplest flow. You might recall from an earlier section that the implicit grant type is applicable to user agent-based applications such as JavaScript running under the context of a web browser, and that there is no authorization code to exchange, which will keep things simple for starters.

I use a basic ASP.NET MVC application for illustration. I use two action methods within `HomeController`: `Index` and `Parse`. As part of the view corresponding to the `Index` action method, I have JavaScript code to make a token request to the Live Connect authorization endpoint `https://login.live.com/oauth20_authorize.srf`, specifying the other action method /Home/Parse as the callback URI. Live Connect redirects the browser to the callback URI, passing the token in the hash fragment. The JavaScript rendered by `/Home/Parse` picks up this token, makes a call to Live Connect, and displays the data returned by the API, which in this case is the name of the user. The following steps summarize the process that happens as part of the implicit grant flow.

1. The client application, which in this case is the ASP.NET MVC application, starts the flow by directing the user's browser to the Live Connect authorization endpoint, passing in the client ID, the scopes, a redirection URL, and a value of the token for response_type in the query string.

2. The user is prompted to enter her Live Connect credentials, and after authentication the user grants or denies the client's access request.

3. Live Connect redirects the browser to the URI specified in the initial request. As part of the URI, an access token is passed in the URI fragment like this: `http://www.my-server.com/OAuthLiveAPI/Home/Parse#access_token=<token>`.

4. The browser follows the redirect by making the request to the server. In our case, the GET request is made to/Home/Parse, the `Parse` action method runs, and the corresponding view is sent back to the browser. URI fragments are not sent to the server.

5. The HTML returned to the browser as a result of the rendering of the /Home/Parse view contains the necessary JavaScript to read the fragment and extract the token. In our example, `location.hash.slice(1)` is the code that does it, although it is too simple to handle any other elements returned or the error.

Once the token is extracted, a call to the API can be made using the token. Figure 11-3 illustrates the preceding steps of the implicit grant flow to obtain the access token.

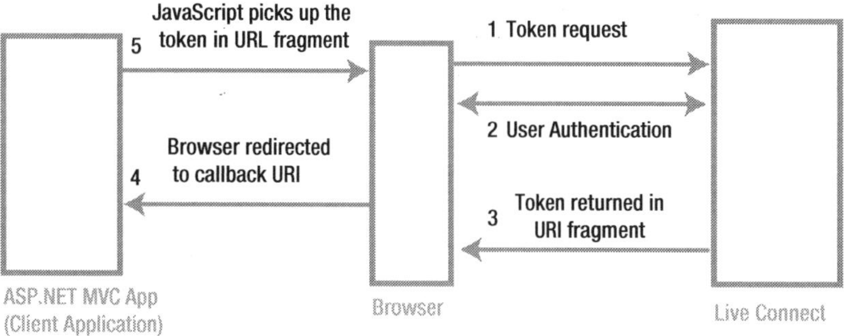

***Figure 11-3.** Implicit grant*

The following detailed steps show the use of an implicit grant flow to obtain an access token from Live Connect and subsequently call the Live Connect API, presenting the token as the credential.

1. Launch Microsoft Visual Studio as an administrator and create a basic ASP.NET MVC project with the name OAuthLiveAPI. We will limit our changes to only the views. There is no real need for an MVC project here, but it will make life a bit easier because Visual Studio can create a virtual directory for us in local IIS. You can create static HTML pages and put them in a virtual folder if you would like.

RUNNING ON IIS

I'm using a local IIS server to run this application so that I don't need to deal with ports. To open the code sample that accompanies this book, you must run Visual Studio as an administrator and open the solution file for the project to load correctly. As a reminder, you can find the code samples in the Source Code/Download area of the Apress web site at `www.apress.com`.

If you run IIS 7.0 or IIS 7.5, your IIS could have difficulty handling extension-less URLs that are common with ASP.NET MVC and web API. You can install a hot fix (`http://support.microsoft.com/kb/980368`) to resolve this issue or you can set `runAllManagedModulesForAllRequests="true"` in the web.config file, as shown here.

```
<system.webServer>
        ...
<modules runAllManagedModulesForAllRequests="true"/>
</system.webServer>
```

For more information on routing, refer to Thomas Marquardt's MSDN blog entry," How ASP.NET MVC Routing Works and its Impact on the Performance of Static Requests."

2. Add a `HomeController` and create the view for /Home/Index. Right-click the Index action method in Visual Studio and select Add View... to create the view. Delete the entire content of the view and copy and paste the code from Listing 11-2. It just runs JavaScript to format a URL with a bunch of query strings and redirects you to that URL. It is important to note that the query string field names are coming out of the specification. You need to use exactly the same names with correct values, as defined in the specification, for the protocol to work.

   a. The client identifier is copied and pasted from the application management portal.

   b. The redirect URI is where Live Connect will put us back after obtaining user consent. It is given as /Home/Parse. For this to work, we do need to provide a /Home/Parse controller action method.

   c. The scope defines the things the user would like to authorize you to access. Here the list is hard-coded, but it is generally based on what the user has consented to authorize.

   d. The response type is hard-coded to "token."

Listing 11-2. Index View

```
@section scripts{
<script type="text/javascript">
        $(document).ready(function () {
            var clientId = 'copy paste your client id here';
            var redirectUri = 'http://www.my-server.com/OAuthLiveAPI/Home/Parse';
            var scope = 'wl.signin%20wl.basic';

            var url = 'https://login.live.com/oauth20_authorize.srf';
            url += '?response_type=token&redirect_uri=' + redirectUri;
```

```
                url += '&client_id=' + clientId + '&scope=' + scope;

                document.location.href = url;

        });
</script>
}
```

3. Create a new action method `Parse` that does nothing but returns the view - `public ActionResult Parse() { return View(); }`. In the view, shown in Listing 11-3, extract the access token from the hash and simply stick the access token in the query string of the URL of the API. The code is ultra-simple. It neither handles the case of a user denying access nor other extra fields coming as part of the location hash. After you put the token into the URL, use JQuery to make a GET to the API and show the name of the user in a div. Use `getJSON()`for this because Live Connect returns a JSON response.

Listing 11-3. Parse View

```
@section scripts{
<script type="text/javascript">
        $(document).ready(function () {
            var url = 'https://apis.live.net/v5.0/me?' + location.hash.slice(1);

            $.getJSON(url, function (data) {
                $('#data').html(data.name);
            });
        });
</script>
}

<div id="data"></div>
```

▒ **Note** The Parse.cshtml razor view uses the JQuery `getJSON` method to get the API response from Live Connect. We are trying to access `https://apis.live.net` from JavaScript running under the context of my-server.com, which is against the same origin policy that we saw in Chapter 5. Because the `XDomainRequest` object must be used with Internet Explorer for cross-site scripting, we must use an alternative browser like Mozilla Firefox to run this code. If you must use Internet Explorer 9.0 or lower, then it gets a bit tricky. You have to use XDR for sure, but it needs the requestor URI and requested URI to use the same scheme. Because apis.live.net is in HTTPS, you must run this MVC application from IIS with HTTPS enabled for XDR to work. Or you can include `$.support.cors = true;` and simply enable cross-domain requests.

Testing the ASP.NET MVC Application

If you run the MVC application, you will start with /Home/Index. There is no code in the controller to execute other than returning the corresponding view. In the view, however, you get redirected to the Live Connect authorization endpoint of `/oauth20_authorize.srf`, using JavaScript.

If you are not logged in, Live Connect will prompt you for your user ID and password. The important point to note here is that you are providing the credentials only with Live Connect and not anywhere in the JavaScript.

Next, it will ask you to grant the authorization rights, as shown in Figure 11-4. Because we have used wl.signin and wl. Basic, Live Connect asks for permission for these two things. Click the Yes button to grant access.

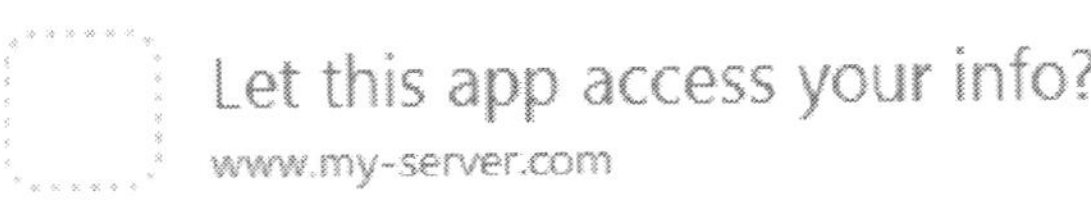

MyTestApp needs your permission to:

Sign in automatically
Signing in with your Microsoft account will automatically sign you in to this app.

View your profile info and contact list
MyTestApp will be able to see your profile info, including your name, gender, display picture, contacts, and friends.

You can change these application permissions at any time in your account settings.

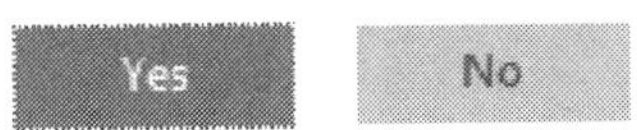

Figure 11-4. *Live Connect asking the user to grant access*

After you grant the rights, Live Connect sends back an access token corresponding to the scope. It puts you in the redirect URI, which is /Home/Parse, and sends the token in the location hash, which looks something like this: http://www.my-server.com/OAuthLiveAPI/Home/Parse#access_token=<token>. Corresponding to this GET, the Parse method of the Home controller runs and renders the JavaScript to pick up the token from the URI fragment. It then invokes the Live Connect API to get the user name as JSON and shows that in the page.

Using an Authorization Code Grant to Access Live Connect

Similar to an implicit grant, I use an ASP.NET MVC application as the client application that uses the authorization code grant to obtain an access token from Live Connect. Unlike an implicit grant, the client application must be a web application, which is a confidential client. I use two action methods within HomeController:Login and Exchange. The Login method redirects the browser to the Live Connect authorization endpoint through a server-side redirect, making a request for an authorization code. Live Connect returns the authorization code in the query string by redirecting to the callback URI specified in the request. The callback URI corresponds to the second action method, which is the Exchange method. It retrieves the token and makes the call to Live Connect API. In sharp contrast to the code we wrote for an implicit grant, where everything is done at the client side, here we write all the code on the server side (the controller). The following process happens as part of the authorization code grant flow.

The client, which is the ASP.NET MVC application, starts the flow by directing the browser of the end user to the Live Connect authorization endpoint, passing in the client ID, the scopes, the redirect URI, and a value of "code" for the response_type field in the query string.

1. Live Connect shows the login screen to the user, authenticates the credentials entered, and asks the user for consent to share the protected resource.
2. When the user grants access, Live Connect redirects the browser to the redirection URI specified in the initial request, which is /Home/Exchange. Live Connect specifies a query string with the authorization code.
3. The browser makes a GET to the URI /Home/Exchange?code=authzcode.
4. The `Exchange` action method has a parameter named code, to which the authorization code is bound by the MVC framework. Using the code, client ID, client secret, the redirect URI used before, and the grant_type of the authorization_code, the client MVC application makes a POST to the Live Connect authorization endpoint.
5. Live Connect validates the input—the authorization code, client ID, client secret, and so on—and returns a JSON response containing access and refresh tokens. The refresh tokens are stored for future use.

Using the access token, the MVC web application makes a request to the Live Connect web API passing in the access token. Figure 11-5 illustrates the preceding steps of the authorization code grant flow to obtain an access token.

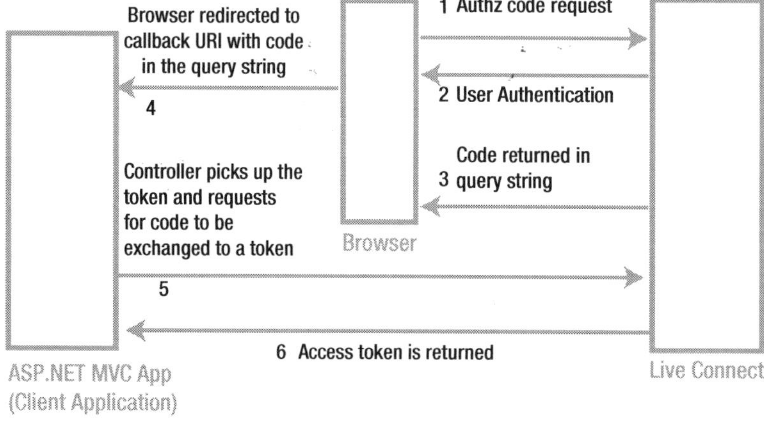

Figure 11-5. *Authorization code grant flow*

Following are the detailed steps that show you the use of the authorization code grant flow to obtain an access token from Live Connect and subsequently call the Live Connect API, presenting the token as the credential.

1. Launch Microsoft Visual Studio as an administrator.
2. Use the same ASP.NET MVC application we created in the preceding section about implicit grants.
3. Add an action method `Login` to `HomeController`, as shown in Listing 11-4. The logic is very simple, as shown in the following steps.
   a. Build a URI based on the same authorization endpoint that we have been working on: `https://login.live.com/oauth20_authorize.srf`.
   b. The query string parameters are exactly the same as those we used with the implicit grant, except for one difference: The value for the field response_type is "code," standing in for the authorization code.

c. Specify another action method, Exchange, as the redirect URI.

d. Pass in a new scope wl.offline_access for the authorization endpoint to return a refresh token. The details on using a refresh token are covered in a later section.

e. Finally, redirect to the URI of the Live Connect authorization endpoint.

Listing 11-4. Login Action Method

```
public ActionResult Login()
{
    string clientId = "your client Id";
    string redirectUri = "http://www.my-server.com/OAuthLiveAPI/Home/Exchange";
    string scope = "wl.signin%20wl.basic%20wl.offline_access";

    string url = "https://login.live.com/oauth20_authorize.srf";
    url += "?response_type=code&redirect_uri={0}&client_id={1}&scope={2}";

    url = String.Format(url, redirectUri, clientId, scope);

    return Redirect(url);
}
```

■ **Note** Because the /Home/Index action method is already used for the implicit grant flow, you need to make a change to `RouteConfig.cs` in the `App_Start` folder to make the `Login` method the default action. You need to do this so that when you run the application it starts with /Home/Login and hence starts the authorization code flow. Edit `routes.MapRoute()` to set the defaults like this: `defaults: new { controller = "Home", action =` **"Login"**, `id = UrlParameter.Optional }`.

---

4. Add the action method Exchange, as shown in Listing 11-5. The authorization code that is sent by Live Connect is available to you through the parameter named code. If you are not experienced in ASP.NET MVC, here is a brief primer on binding: MVC binds the action method parameters to the incoming data, the form fields, or the query string; by binding, it pulls the value out of those elements and puts them here in the parameters. How convenient!

Listing 11-5. Exchange Action Method

```
public ActionResult Exchange(string code)
{
    string result = String.Empty;

    // Remainder of the code goes here - look at the following steps
}
```

5. Use the authorization code and make an HTTP POST to the authorization endpoint using an instance of the `HttpClient` class, as shown in Listing 11-6. One important point to note in the HTTP POST is that the client secret is passed. As mentioned in the preceding section, this is the secret sauce that is known only to the client application, which ensures

no other entity except the client application can obtain an access token. Along with the client secret, other parameters like client ID, the redirect URI, the authorization code this action method receives as a parameter, and a grant type of "authorization_code" are sent in the request body.

Listing 11-6. Exchange Code for a Token

```
using (HttpClient client = new HttpClient())
{
        var postData = new List<KeyValuePair<string, string>>();
        postData.Add(new KeyValuePair<string, string>("client_id", "your client id"));
        postData.Add(new KeyValuePair<string, string>("redirect_uri",
                                        "http://www.my-server.com/OAuthLiveAPI/Home/Exchange"));
        postData.Add(new KeyValuePair<string, string>("client_secret", "your client secret"));
        postData.Add(new KeyValuePair<string, string>("code", code)); // retrieved from query string
        postData.Add(new KeyValuePair<string, string>("grant_type", "authorization_code"));

        HttpContent content = new FormUrlEncodedContent(postData);

        var tokenResponse = client.PostAsync("https://login.live.com/oauth20_token.srf", content)
                                                                                        .Result;

        if (tokenResponse.IsSuccessStatusCode)
        {
             // Use the token - look atthe following steps
        }
}
```

■ **Note** In Listing 11-6, the client ID and the client secret are sent in the message body. OAuth 2.0 does allow these two getting sent, respectively, as the user ID and password in the HTTP authorization request header using the basic scheme.

---

6. Live Connect sends back a JSON response, as shown in Listing 11-7. The tokens are trimmed for brevity.

   Listing 11-7. JSON Response from Live Connect

```
{
        "token_type":"bearer",
        "expires_in":3600,
        "scope":"wl.signin wl.basic wl.offline_access",
        "access_token":"EwAw...YAAA=",
        "refresh_token":"CicFtyZ...pl7UCp",
        "authentication_token":"eyJh...3Rhg1C80E"
}
```

7. Parse the JSON response and extract the access token using `System.Json`. You need to get it through NuGet. Right-click References of the project in Solution Explorer of Visual Studio and click Manage NuGet Packages. Click Online ➤ All, search for 'System.Json,' and install it (see Figure 11-6).

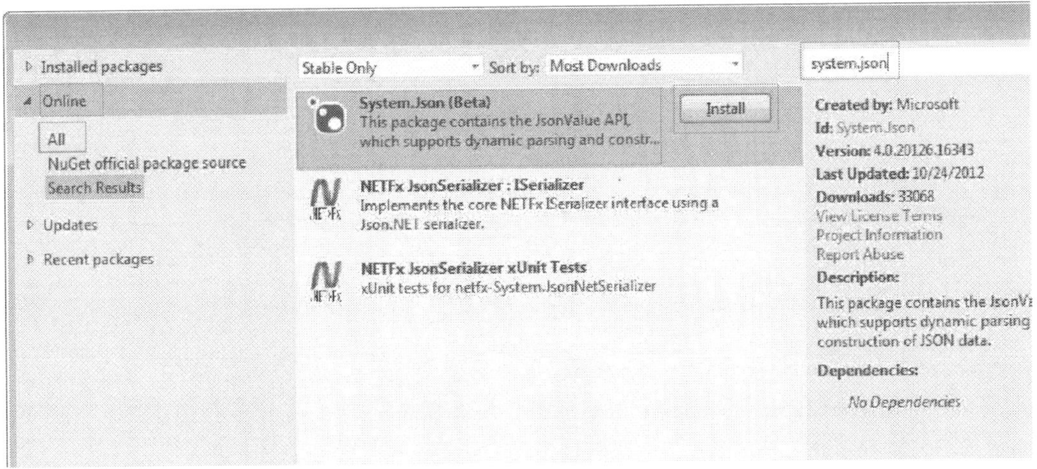

Figure 11-6. *System.Json NuGet*

8. After extracting the token, invoke the Live Connect API passing on the token and get back the result, which is once again JSON. See Listing 11-8.

Listing 11-8. Extracting a Token and Calling Live Connect API

```
var token = tokenResponse.Content.ReadAsStringAsync().Result;

JsonValue value = JsonValue.Parse(token);
string accessToken = (string)value["access_token"];

var apiResponse = client
                    .GetAsync("https://apis.live.net/v5.0/me?access_token=" + accessToken)
                        .Result;

if (apiResponse.IsSuccessStatusCode)
{
    result = apiResponse.Content.ReadAsStringAsync().Result;
}
```

9. Parse the response JSON from Live Connect API, retrieve the name, and return that as the text output. There is no view associated with the action method. The text value returned is just rendered by the browser. See Listing 11-9.

Listing 11-9. Returning the API Response to View

```
if (String.IsNullOrEmpty(result))
    return new EmptyResult();
else
    return Content((string)JsonValue.Parse(result)["name"]);
```

Testing the ASP.NET MVC Application

If you run the MVC application, you will start off with /Home/Login, because Login is configured as the default action now. At this point, the user (in other words, the resource owner) is redirected to the Live Connect login screen to enter the credentials. Once Live Connect authenticates the user, a screen is displayed to the user asking for consent, as shown in Figure 11-7.

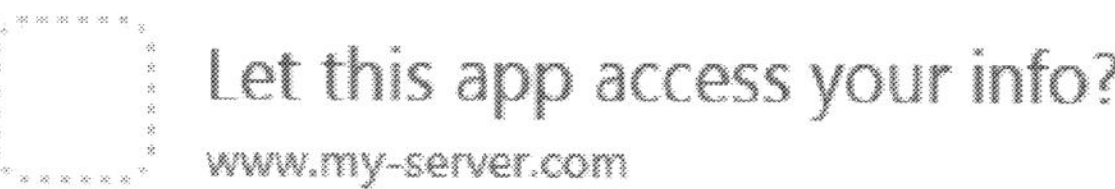

MyTestApp needs your permission to:

Sign in automatically
Signing in with your Microsoft account will automatically sign you in to this app.

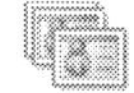

View your profile info and contact list
MyTestApp will be able to see your profile info, including your name, gender, display picture, contacts, and friends.

Access your info anytime
MyTestApp will be able to see and update your info, even when you're not using this app.

You can change these application permissions at any time in your account settings.

Figure 11-7. *Live Connect asking a user to grant access*

In the preceding section of the implicit grant, the scopes sent in are wl.signin and wl.basic. For an authorization code grant, an additional scope of wl.offline_access is also passed. The screenshot in Figure 11-7 shows three entries corresponding to the scopes in the request, when Live Connect asks the user for consent to share. The importance of this additional scope is that Live Connect returns the refresh token for this scope. I cover the use of a refresh token to get an access token in a later section.

When the user clicks the Yes button, the browser is redirected to `http://www.my-server.com/OAuthLiveAPI/Home/Exchange?code=<authz code>`. The authorization code is sent in the query string. The `Exchange` action method receives the code, exchanges it for an access token, and subsequently invokes Live Connect API passing the token.

■ **Note** Unlike an implicit grant, an authorization code grant never exposes the access and refresh tokens to the browser. Even the resource owner will not be able to see the tokens. Only the authorization code is visible to the browser and resource owner.

Using a Refresh Token to Obtain an Access Token

A refresh token is sent along with the access token in the authorization code grant when the client makes a request to the authorization server to exchange the authorization code for an access token. A refresh token can be used to obtain a new access token without asking the user once again for consent, which I show here.

I showed you in the preceding section how to use System.Json to parse the JSON response from the authorization server and extract the access token. Listing 11-10 shows the same code that we saw in Listing 11-8, but modified to get the refresh token. The additional lines of code are shown in bold type. The refresh token is added into a dictionary using a hard-coded key of "userId". That is done basically to illustrate how refresh tokens can be used. In practice, refresh tokens are stored in a persistent store because they are long-lived.

Listing 11-10. Extracting a Refresh Token

```
var token = tokenResponse.Content.ReadAsStringAsync().Result;

JsonValue value = JsonValue.Parse(token);
string accessToken = (string)value["access_token"];
string refreshToken = (string)value["refresh_token"];

tokens["userId"] = refreshToken;

var apiResponse = client
                    .GetAsync("https://apis.live.net/v5.0/me?access_token=" + accessToken)
                        .Result;

if (apiResponse.IsSuccessStatusCode)
{
    result = apiResponse.Content.ReadAsStringAsync().Result;
}
```

Of course, the client ID and client secret are needed, but the user does not have to give his consent for this refresh process because it is done automatically. Having said that, Live Connect does ask the user at the point when it asks for the user's consent for the first time (see the third item in Figure 11-7).

Now let's see how to get an access token from a refresh token. See Listing 11-11. The logic is similar to the logic of getting an access token. Note the use of "refresh_token" as the grant type as against "authorization_code" while exchanging the authorization code for an access token. The refresh token must be sent in for obvious reasons. Also, note the client secret is needed for this, just like the code-to-token exchange. The response from Live Connect contains the access token, which is extracted out, similar to the earlier code for the code-to-token exchange.

Listing 11-11. Access Token from a Refresh Token

```
public ActionResult Refresh()
{
    string result = String.Empty;

    using (HttpClient client = new HttpClient())
    {
        var postData = new List<KeyValuePair<string, string>>();
        postData.Add(new KeyValuePair<string, string>("client_id", "your client id"));
        postData.Add(new KeyValuePair<string, string>("redirect_uri",
                                            "http://www.my-server.com/OAuthLiveAPI/Home/Exchange"));
```

```
        postData.Add(new KeyValuePair<string, string>("client_secret", "your client secret"));
        postData.Add(new KeyValuePair<string, string>("refresh_token", tokens["userId"]));
        postData.Add(new KeyValuePair<string, string>("grant_type", "refresh_token"));

        HttpContent content = new FormUrlEncodedContent(postData);

        var tokenResponse = client.PostAsync("https://login.live.com/oauth20_token.srf", content)
                                                                                       .Result;

        if (tokenResponse.IsSuccessStatusCode)
        {
            var token = tokenResponse.Content.ReadAsStringAsync().Result;

            JsonValue value = JsonValue.Parse(token);
            string accessToken = (string)value["access_token"];

            var apiResponse = client.GetAsync("https://apis.live.net/v5.0/me?access_token=" +
                                                                          accessToken).Result;
            if (apiResponse.IsSuccessStatusCode)
            {
                result = apiResponse.Content.ReadAsStringAsync().Result;
            }
        }
    }

    if (String.IsNullOrEmpty(result))
        return new EmptyResult();
    else
        return Content("Refreshed " + (string)JsonValue.Parse(result)["name"]);
}
```

■ **Note** The authorization code grant ensures that access and refresh tokens are confined only to the server-side component of the client web application. I used an ASP.NET MVC application, and all the code is implemented on the server side. Now, what if you implement the authorization code grant in JQuery on the client side? No one can check how you are making requests to the endpoint from a server-side program or a client-side program. But the OAuth 2.0 specification specifies things for a reason. You can go right ahead and break the standard, but your implementation in that case is not only noncompliant to OAuth 2.0 but also leaves your implementation vulnerable to attacks.

Revoking the Grant

Once a resource owner or a user grants access, it is not cast in stone. There are scenarios where a user would like to revoke the grant. For this purpose, Microsoft provides a portal where grants provided by a resource owner can be revoked. The URL is `https://consent.live.com`. See Figure 11-8.

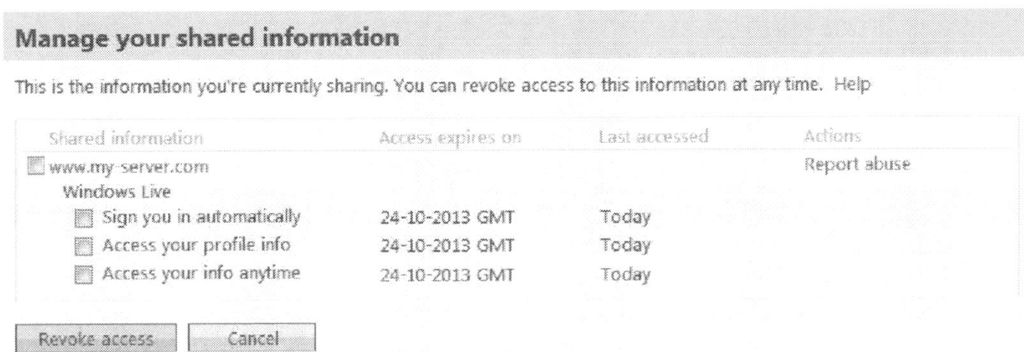

Figure 11-8. *Revoking the grant*

To revoke the access granted, select all the check boxes and click Revoke access. This invalidates the refresh token, and anymore requests for a new access token based on the refresh token will fail.

Using a Resource Owner Password Grant

Live Connect does not support a resource owner password grant type. If it did, the flow would be the same as the following list of steps.

1. The client application, which is generally a native application created by the same organization that owns the resource server, shows a screen to the user where credentials can be entered.

2. The user enters the credentials directly in the client application, knowing full well that she is entering the credentials in a client application. The user is confident the client application is also from the same entity that hosts the resource and hence is trustworthy.

3. The client makes a POST to the authorization endpoint, sending the credentials along with the grant_type of password.

4. The authorization server validates the request and returns the access token.

Figure 11-9 illustrates this process.

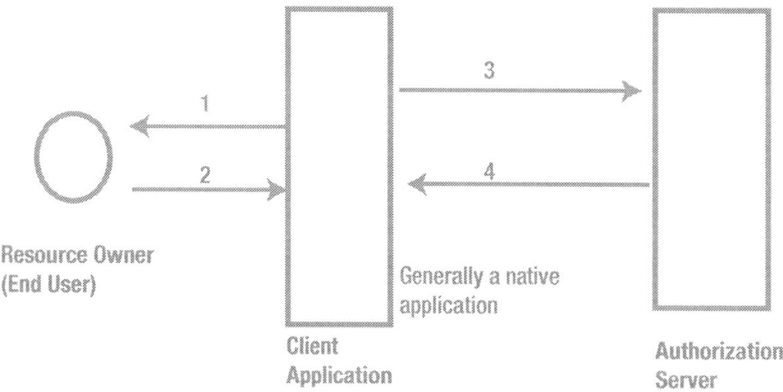

Figure 11-9. *Resource owner password grant*

If you write code to use a resource owner password grant to obtain an access token from Live Connect, it will be similar to the one shown in Listing 11-12. The grant type (grant_type) of the password is passed in the request along with the other usual elements, like client ID and client secret. The credentials of the resource owner are sent in the message body, and the client ID and client secret are sent in the HTTP authorization header. Depending on the implementation, everything can get sent in the message body. Regardless of the implementation, one thing for sure with these calls is that they must make use of transport security.

Listing 11-12. Resource Owner Password Grant

```
using (HttpClient client = new HttpClient())
{
    string creds = String.Format("{0}:{1}", "your client id", "your client secret");
    byte[] bytes = Encoding.UTF8.GetBytes(creds);
    var header = new AuthenticationHeaderValue("Basic", Convert.ToBase64String(bytes));
    client.DefaultRequestHeaders.Authorization = header;

    var postData = new List<KeyValuePair<string, string>>();
    postData.Add(new KeyValuePair<string, string>("username", "jqhuman"));
    postData.Add(new KeyValuePair<string, string>("password", "p@ssw0rd"));
    postData.Add(new KeyValuePair<string, string>("grant_type", "password"));
    postData.Add(new KeyValuePair<string, string>("scope", "wl.signin wl.basic"));

    HttpContent content = new FormUrlEncodedContent(postData);

    var httpMessage = client.PostAsync("https://authorizationserver.com/endpoint", content).Result;

    if(httpMessage.IsSuccessStatusCode)
        Console.WriteLine(httpMessage.Content.ReadAsStringAsync().Result);
}
```

Using a Client Credentials Grant

Live Connect does not support the client credentials grant. However, the flow is very simple, as shown in the following steps.

1. The client application makes a POST to the authorization server endpoint, sending the client ID, the client secret, and the grant_type of client credentials.
2. The authorization server returns the access token, after validating the client ID and client secret.

Listing 11-13 shows code that illustrates the use of a client credentials grant to obtain an access token.

Listing 11-13. Client Credentials Grant

```
using (HttpClient client = new HttpClient())
{
    string creds = String.Format("{0}:{1}", "your client id", "your client secret");
    byte[] bytes = Encoding.UTF8.GetBytes(creds);
    var header = new AuthenticationHeaderValue("Basic", Convert.ToBase64String(bytes));
    client.DefaultRequestHeaders.Authorization = header;

    var postData = new List<KeyValuePair<string, string>>();
    postData.Add(new KeyValuePair<string, string>("grant_type", "client_credentials"));

    HttpContent content = new FormUrlEncodedContent(postData);

    var httpMessage = client.PostAsync("https://authorizationserver.com/endpoint", content).Result;

    if(httpMessage.IsSuccessStatusCode)
        Console.WriteLine(httpMessage.Content.ReadAsStringAsync().Result);
}
```

As shown in the preceding example, the client ID and client secret, respectively client_id and client_secret, can get passed in the message body in some implementations, unlike being passed in the HTTP authorization header.

Summary

For SOAP-based web services, WS-Trust and WS-Security provide a standard way for a client application to request and obtain a security token and then present it to the relying party SOAP-based web service as a credential for authentication. In the world of REST to which ASP.NET Web API belongs, OAuth is the specification comparable to WS-Trust and WS-Security. OAuth 1.0 was the initial version created in 2006, and it evolved into the OAuth 2.0 of today, with no backward compatibility to OAuth 1.0. The coverage of OAuthin this book is limited to OAuth 2.0 (RFC 6749, “The OAuth 2.0 Authorization Framework”).

OAuth stands for open authorization. The heart of the OAuth specification is the access token. OAuth specifies how a client application can request an access token from the authorization server by itself or by orchestrating an approval interaction between the resource owner or the end user and the underlying web application. An authorization grant is the credential representing the resource owner’s consent to allow or grant access to the protected resources. A client application uses the authorization grant to obtain an access token. The OAuth 2.0 specification defines four out-of-the-box grant types.

1. Authorization code grant, which is applicable to the web application profile, the code that executes in a server.
2. Implicit grant, which is applicable to user agent-based applications such as JavaScript running under the context of a web browser.
3. Resource owner password grant, which can be used only with the clients that a user can trust as well as the authorization server.
4. Client credentials grant, which is applicable to scenarios where the protected resource is not owned by a specific user but by the client application itself.

The OAuth 2.0 specification refers to the companion specification RFC 6750, "The OAuth 2.0 Authorization Framework: Bearer Token Usage," which describes how to use an access token as a bearer token in the authorization HTTP request header to access OAuth 2.0 protected resources.

Microsoft Live Connect implements the OAuth 2.0 protocol to authenticate users. I used Live Connect API in this chapter to demonstrate OAuth 2.0 in action.

CHAPTER 12

OAuth 2.0 from the Ground Up

In this chapter, I show you how to implement OAuth 2.0–based authorization in ASP.NET Web API from scratch, using two ASP.NET MVC web applications, so that you understand the nuts and bolts of OAuth 2.0. The objective of this chapter is to help you gain in-depth knowledge of how the authorization code grant type of OAuth 2.0 works by building a working example from the ground up. I focus my coverage on the authorization code grant type for this exercise because it involves a more complex flow than the other grant types.

Although I show you how to build from scratch in this chapter, I do not suggest that you build OAuth 2.0 this way for your applications. There is a great open source .NET Framework library, DotNetOpenAuth (DNOA), that you can use to implement OAuth 2.0–based authorization in ASP.NET Web API. I cover DNOA in depth in Chapter 13. However, building from scratch—although it is hard work—helps you appreciate how a library such as DNOA can help you in your implementation. Also, when things do not work the way they are supposed to, it gives you the confidence to pop the hood and take a look at what is going on inside.

Keep in mind that some enterprises might restrict the use of open source in production. For that or any other reason, if you wish to write your own implementation this chapter lays the groundwork for you to build on.

Scenario: Sharing Contact Information

Our scenario in this chapter is similar to the scenario in Chapter 11: An end user, John Q. Human, wants to share the contact information contained in his contacts application with the Promotion Manager application. However, he doesn't want to divulge to the Promotion Manager application the login credentials he uses to access the contacts application. Table 12-1 shows the OAuth 2.0 roles, along with the players, for this scenario.

Table 12-1. *OAuth 2.0 Roles*

OAuth 2.0 Role	Player
Resource owner	The resource owner (in this case, the user) is John Q. Human, a small-time retail store owner who maintains all his customer contact information. He is not willing to share his `my-contacts.com` login credentials with the third party `my-promo.com` for fear of business-critical data leaking to his competition.
Resource server	The resource server, `www.my-contacts.com/contacts/api/contacts`, exposes the contact information in the form of a web API implemented using ASP.NET Web API. The protected resource is the contact information.
Authorization server	The authorization server, `www.my-contacts.com/contacts/OAuth20`, works with the resource owner to get consent and ultimately creates and sends a token, which the client can present to the resource server and access the contact information.
Client	The client is the Promotion Manager application, `www.my-promo.com/promo`, which is an ASP.NET MVC 4.0 web application. John uses this application to send promotional e-mails.

■ **Note** I do not own the domains `my-contacts.com` and `my-promo.com` mentioned in Table 12-1. I use them so you clearly know where you are in terms of the application (as indicated by the browser in the URL bar) when you test the flow. A name is better for recognizing an application than the port numbers. I use the same hosts file trick that I showed you in Chapter 11 to add two entries with these names both pointing to 127.0.0.1. If you are a user of the real sites with these addresses, you will need to remove the entries from the hosts file once you are done testing. Also, if you are lucky enough to be able to spend time at work running these applications from a work computer that is behind a proxy, you might need to bypass the proxy for these addresses for the hosts file trick to work.

There are two major flows associated with our scenario.

1. **Contacts Manager flow**—The user logs in directly into Contacts Manager using the credentials and manages the contacts, such as viewing, adding, editing, and removing contacts.
2. **Promotion Manager flow**—This involves sharing contact information. This is the more important flow to us because this is where ASP.NET Web API figures in. The user goes to the Promotion Manager application and performs an action that requires the contact information from the Contacts Manager application. In our example scenario, this action will be a user clicking a button to get contact information. Promotion Manager redirects the user to the Contacts Manager, where the user is asked to provide credentials and authenticate before Contacts Manager consents to share the contacts information with Promotion Manager. On consent, Promotion Manager pulls the contact information using the web API provided by Contacts Manager and displays the list to the user.

Figure 12-1 illustrates the Promotion Manager flow. We have not gotten into the implementation details yet, but the screenshots will help you get an overall picture of the steps involved.

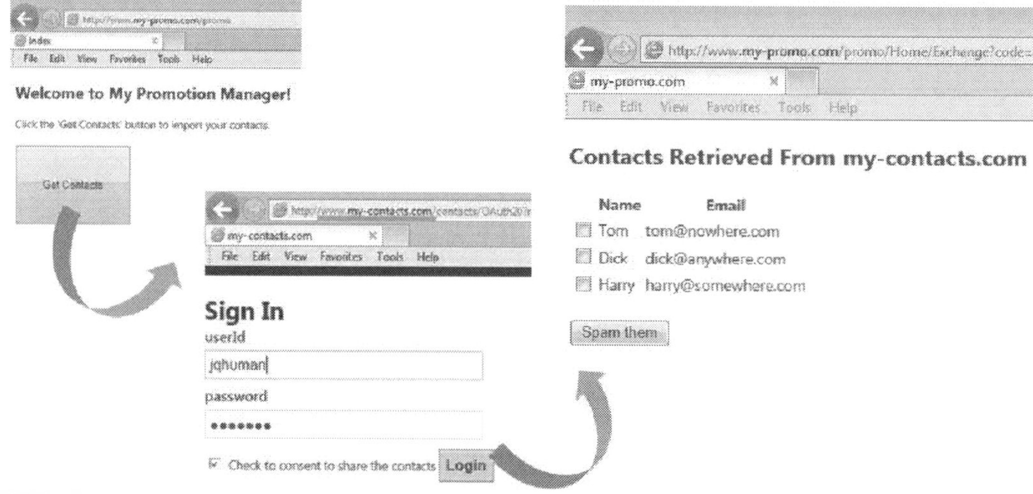

Figure 12-1. *Promotion Manager flow*

Design

We will create two ASP.NET MVC 4.0 projects in Visual Studio as part of our solution.

1. **MyContacts**: This will be an ASP.NET MVC 4.0 project created using the Web API template. We can have both MVC controllers and WebAPI controllers in the same project. This project represents both the resource server and the authorization server. Although both servers can be owned by the same organization and hence can be part of the same domain, a logical separation is generally needed. I'm combining them both into a single project here so I can store the data that has to be shared between them in memory. This approach will help me keep the code in the listings brief and stay focused on OAuth 2.0 without getting into the extraneous persistence details.
2. **MyPromo**: This will be an ASP.NET MVC 4.0 project created with the Basic template. I use the Basic template because I don't plan to have any web API or authentication mechanism for this application, but you could use any template. MyPromo represents the client web application that requires the protected resource to function.

Both projects use local IIS (not IIS Express). The project URLs are `http://localhost/Contacts` for the MyContacts project and `http://localhost/Promo` for the MyPromo project. Instead of using local host, I use the names defined in the hosts file, respectively: `http://www.my-contacts.com/contacts` and `http://www.my-promo.com/promo`.

■ **Note** To open the Visual Studio solution corresponding to this chapter from the source code accompanying this book, you must run Visual Studio as an administrator for the projects to load correctly.

Before we dive into these projects in depth, I want to explain the format of the access token. We'll implement the authorization code grant type to issue an access token, which will be a signed JSON Web Token (JWT). For signing and validation, we'll use a symmetric key that is exchanged between the resource server and the authorization server out of band. We'll use the same JWT implementation we used in Chapter 10.

MyContacts Project

Table 12-2 shows the classes in the MyContacts project, with a brief description of each class. I show all the classes in the table to give you an overview, but later we will look into the code of the individual classes in a logical grouping. We will get to know the classes up close and personal, but not necessarily in the same order shown here.

Table 12-2. *Classes in the MyContacts Project*

Class Name	Namespace	Description
`HomeController`	`MyContacts.Controllers`	Contains the action methods for login and listing the contacts. This MVC controller is all about contact management.
`OAuth20Controller`	`MyContacts.Controllers`	Accepts the requests for authorization codes as well as requests for exchanging codes to access tokens. This MVC controller is the authorization endpoint.
`ContactsController`	`MyContacts.Controllers`	Returns the list of contacts. The only API controller.

(continued)

Table 12-2. *(continued)*

Class Name	Namespace	Description
`LoginRequired`	`MyContacts.Filters`	Establishes identity based on the value stored in a cookie. If no cookie exists, it redirects to a login page, similar to implementing Forms authentication in the contacts app.
`EncodingHelper` `EncryptionHelper`	`MyContacts.Helpers`	Provides extension methods for base64 URL encoding (straight out of Chapter 10) and symmetric key TripleDES encryption. I chose TripleDES for no particular reason. You can use any strong algorithm you like for this purpose, such as Rijndael.
`AuthorizationManager`	`MyContacts.Infrastructure`	Implements claims-based access control for a web API. This class is a subclass of `ClaimsAuthorizationManager`. The scope granted by the user directly equates to the claim for this purpose.
`JsonWebToken`	`MyContacts.Infrastructure`	CLR representation of the JSON web token. Straight out of Chapter 10.
`OAuthTokenHandler`	`MyContacts.Infrastructure`	Establishes identity based on the claims in the incoming JWT bearer token. This is a message handler.
`AuthzCodeRequest`	`MyContacts.Models`	Represents the request for an authorization code. This is a model class.
`TokenRequest`	`MyContacts.Models`	Represents the request for an access token. This is a model class.
`Contact`	`MyContacts.Models`	Represents the contact entity. This is a model class.

MyPromo Project

Table 12-3 shows the classes in the MyPromo project, with a brief description of each class.

Table 12-3. *Classes in the MyPromo Project*

Class Name	Namespace	Description
`HomeController`	`MyPromo.Controllers`	Requests an authorization code, exchanges it for a token, makes the web API call, and shows the contacts retrieved to the user.
`Contact`	`MyPromo.Models`	Represents a subset of the contact business entity with only the name and e-mail.

HTTP Transactions

I covered the authorization code grant flow in Chapter 11, where I showed how to consume the web API of Live Connect. In this section I show the details; namely, the HTTP request and the HTTP response for each of the steps involved.

The flow that we are interested in here is the one that originates from the Promotion Manager web application (see preceding Figure 12-1 for an illustration of the flow through screenshots). I don't cover the flow corresponding to the user logging in directly into Contacts Manager and performing create, read, update, and delete (CRUD) operations on the contacts. I mentioned that flow briefly earlier in this chapter simply for the sake of completeness.

The following HTTP transactions happen in the Promotion Manager flow.

1. John Q. Human goes to the Promotion Manager web application home page. This is the page with the big Get Contacts button.

Request	GET `http://www.my-promo.com/promo` HTTP/1.1 Host: `www.my-promo.com`
Response	HTTP/1.1 200 OK Content-Length: 647 <!DOCTYPE html><html>...</html>

2. John clicks the Get Contacts button, triggering an HTTP POST. An HTML form containing the only control of the Get Contacts button in the /Home/Index view gets posted to itself. The action method in the controller redirects to the authorization endpoint `http://www.my-contacts.com/contacts/OAuth20`, making the request for an authorization code. Because this is an authorization code grant, which is applicable for the server-side components of the web application, I'm making the request from the MVC controller itself, although it can be done using JQuery as well from the client side. The redirect URI specified in the request must be a controller action so that the important step of exchanging the authorization code to a token runs in the server side.

Request	POST `http://www.my-promo.com/promo` HTTP/1.1 Referer: `http://www.my-promo.com/promo` Content-Type: application/x-www-form-urlencoded Host: `www.my-promo.com` go=Get+Contacts
Response	HTTP/1.1 302 Found Location: `http://www.my-contacts.com/contacts/OAuth20?response_type=code&redirect_uri=http://www.my-promo.com/promo/Home/Exchange&client_id=0123456789&scope=Read.Contacts` <html><!-- HTML response body omitted for brevity --></html>

3. The redirect results in the GET to the `OAuth20Controller`'s `Index` action method. It returns a view that corresponds to the sign-in page, where John enters his credentials and expresses his consent to share the contact information by selecting the checkbox. It is important to note that John currently is in the `my-contacts.com` domain and no longer in `my-promo.com`.

Request

```
GET http://www.my-contacts.com/contacts/OAuth20?response_
type=code&redirect_uri=http://www.my-promo.com/promo/Home/
Exchange&client_id=0123456789&scope=Read.Contacts HTTP/1.1
Referer: http://www.my-promo.com/promo
Host: www.my-contacts.com
```

Response

```
HTTP/1.1 200 OK

<!DOCTYPE html>
<html><!-- Response body omitted for brevity. It is basically the sign-in
page --></html>
```

4. As John clicks the login button, the form gets posted with his credentials along with a ciphertext. I'll cover the details of the ciphertext later in this chapter when we get to the implementation details. `OAuth20Controller` handles this POST and redirects to the URI specified in the request, along with the authorization code in the query string. I use a GUID as the authorization code. At this point, John is getting redirected back to the Promotion Manager application.

Request

```
POST http://www.my-contacts.com/Contacts/OAuth20/Authenticate
HTTP/1.1
Referer: http://www.my-contacts.com/contacts/OAuth20?response_
type=code&redirect_uri=http://www.my-promo.com/promo/Home/
Exchange&client_id=0123456789&scope=Read.Contacts
Content-Type: application/x-www-form-urlencoded
Host: www.my-contacts.com

userId=jqhuman&password=jqhuman&isOkayToShare=true&
CipherText=IpByUN0bx9aX...oQ%3D%3D
```

Response

```
HTTP/1.1 302 Found
Location: http://www.my-promo.com/promo/Home/
Exchange?code=45a92420-92a2-4825-9a06-35b439ef8b01

<html><head><title>Object moved</title></head><body> ...</html>
<!-- Response body omitted for brevity-->
```

5. The redirect results in a GET to the `Exchange` action method of `HomeController` of the Promotion Manager web application. For this request, see the following substeps a, b, and c. The response to the request is generated only as part of substep c. This entire step, including the substeps, must run only on the server side (a confidential client), as specified by OAuth 2.0. As covered in the previous chapter, exchanging the authorization code for a token requires a client secret, which must remain a secret that only the client application has access to. The user agent (browser) or the end user must not know the secret and hence must not be able to exchange the code and obtain a token themselves.

Request

```
GET http://www.my-promo.com/promo/Home/Exchange?code=45a92420-92a2-
4825-9a06-35b439ef8b01 HTTP/1.1
Referer: http://www.my-contacts.com/contacts/OAuth20?response_type=...
Host: www.my-promo.com
```

a. The Exchange action method exchanges the code it received for an access token by making a POST request using HttpClient from within the action method.

Request

```
POST http://www.my-contacts.com/contacts/OAuth20 HTTP/1.1
Content-Type: application/x-www-form-urlencoded
Host: www.my-contacts.com

client_id=0123456789&
redirect_uri=http%3A%2F%2Fwww.my-promo.com%2Fpromo%2FHome%2FExchange&
client_secret=TXVtJ3MgdGhlIHdvcmQhISE%3D&
code=39ebbe3a-e68d-4728-bdff-f239c8504b63&
grant_type=authorization_code
```

Response

```
HTTP/1.1 200 OK
Content-Type: application/json; charset=utf-8

{"access_token":"eyJ0eXI1NiJ9.eyJcyJ9.pG6rXQXXledLg9alZQ"}
```

---

b. The Exchange action method finally invokes the web API by passing the token in an HTTP request authorization header and gets the list of contacts in the form of JSON.

Request

```
GET http://www.my-contacts.com/contacts/api/contacts HTTP/1.1
Authorization: Bearer eyJ0eXI1NiJ9.eyJcyJ9.pG6rXQXXledLg9alZQ
Host: www.my-contacts.com
```

Response

```
HTTP/1.1 200 OK
Content-Type: application/json; charset=utf-8
Content-Length: 133

[{"Name":"Tom","Email":"tom@nowhere.com"},
{"Name":"Dick","Email":"dick@anywhere.com"},
{"Name":"Harry","Email":"harry@somewhere.com"}]
```

---

c. The JSON response is parsed into a list, which is sent to the view as a model. The view corresponding to the Exchange action method shows the list of contacts retrieved from the Contacts Manager application.

Response

```
HTTP/1.1 200 OK

<!DOCTYPE html>
<html>...</html><!-- Response body omitted for brevity. List of contacts retrieved -->
```

■ **Note** The refresh token can also be sent to the client in the HTTP response for Step 5a, if the scope requested is related to offline access. For this exercise, I'm not including a refresh token to keep the code small enough to be covered in this chapter.

Building the Contacts Manager Application

The Contacts Manager application is the underlying web application associated with the web API. I'm including the code for this application in this chapter only for the sake of completeness. The Contacts Manager application is the part of the resource server with which a user interacts directly. After logging in using the credentials, the user can add, modify, delete, and view the contacts. For the sake of brevity, the following code supports only a listing of contacts.

1. Launch Visual Studio 2012 as an administrator.
2. Create a new ASP.NET MVC 4.0 project using the Web API template and name it MyContacts.
3. Configure Visual Studio to use local IIS so that the project URL becomes `http://localhost/Contacts`. Select Use Local IIS Web server and clear the Use IIS Express checkbox. Click Create Virtual Directory to create the virtual directory in IIS (see Figure 12-2).

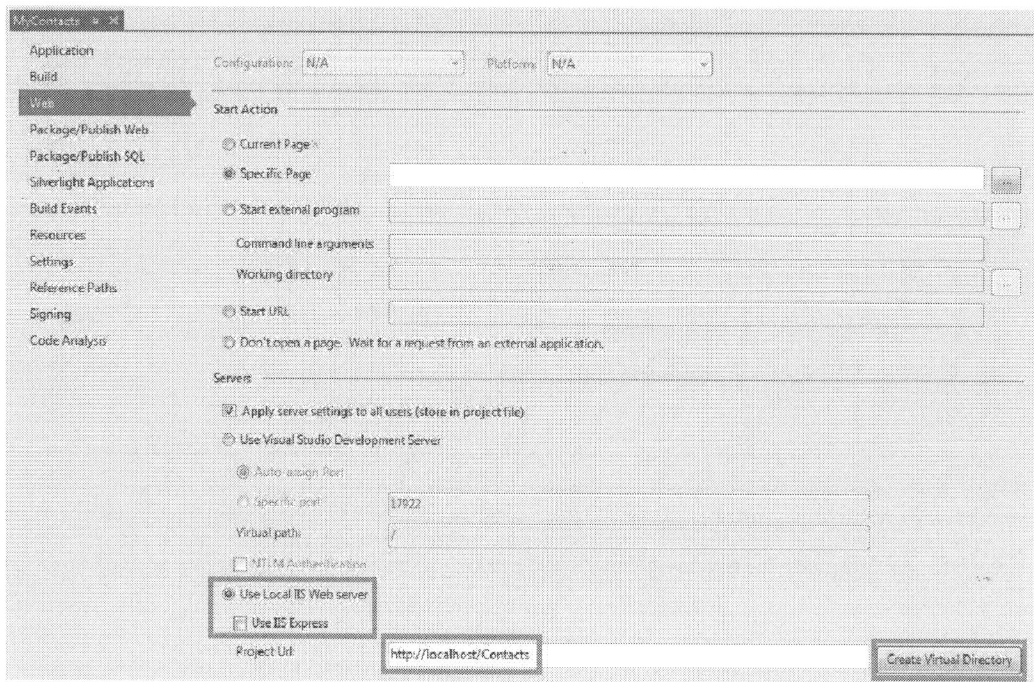

Figure 12-2. *Configuring Visual Studio to use IIS*

4. Visual Studio creates an MVC controller `HomeController` as part of the project. This will be the major component of the Contacts Manager application. Listing 12-1 shows the `HomeController` class with the `Index` action method, which corresponds to the home page of the Contacts Manager application. It calls the static `GenerateContacts` method in the `Contact` class that returns a hard-coded list of contacts and filters the contacts using the name of the identity. In other words, it displays only the contacts that belong to the logged-in user (I show the full coverage of the `Contact` class in the last step of this sequence). Forms authentication is not used and a simple mechanism based on an action filter is used. Note the application of the `LoginRequired` filter on the action method (shown in bold type).

Listing 12-1. HomeController Class in the MyContacts Project

```
public class HomeController : Controller
{
    [LoginRequired]
    public ActionResult Index()
    {
        string owner = Thread.CurrentPrincipal.Identity.Name;

        return View(Contact.GenerateContacts()
                       .Where((c => c.Owner == owner));
    }

    // Login methods go here
}
```

5. The `LoginRequired` filter shown in Listing 12-2 ensures a user is logged in before starting to use the application. The `OnActionExecuting` base method is overridden to check for the presence of a cookie named ".contacts". If the cookie is present, an identity is established with the name that is the same as the value read from the cookie. If the cookie is not present, it redirects to Login action, which is the login screen.

Listing 12-2. LoginRequired Filter

```
public class LoginRequired : ActionFilterAttribute
{
    public override void OnActionExecuting(ActionExecutingContext context)
    {
        HttpCookie cookie = context.HttpContext.Request.Cookies[".contacts"];
        if (cookie != null)
        {
            Thread.CurrentPrincipal = new GenericPrincipal(new GenericIdentity(cookie.Value), null);
        }
        else
        {
            context.Result = new RedirectToRouteResult(
                                        new RouteValueDictionary(
                                            new { Action = "Login", Controller = "Home" }));
        }
    }
}
```

6. Add the `Login` action method to `HomeController`, as shown in Listing 12-3. Decorate this action method with the `HttpGet` attribute so that it handles only HTTP GET.

Listing 12-3. Login Action Method for GET

```
[HttpGet]
public ActionResult Login()
{
        return View();
}
```

7. Right-click the Login action method and select Add View... in the resulting pop-up menu to create a new view. Leave the default selection of "Razor (CSHTML)" as the view engine. Copy and paste the code from Listing 12-4 into the newly generated view file (Login.cshtml in the Views\Home folder).

Listing 12-4. Login View (Login.cshtml)

```
@using (Html.BeginForm())
{
<div class="editor-label"> @Html.Label("userId") </div>
<div class="editor-field"> @Html.TextBox("userId")</div>

<div class="editor-label">@Html.Label("password")</div>
<div class="editor-field">@Html.Password("password")</div>

<input type="submit" value="Login" />
}
```

8. Add the Login action method to HomeController, as shown in Listing 12-5. This time, decorate the action method with the HttpPost attribute so that it handles only HTTP POST. If you are not familiar with ASP.NET MVC, model binding is what ensures the values entered by the user get passed into our action method as arguments. We follow the naming convention and make sure the text boxes in the HTML form are named userId and password, matching the parameter names of the Login action method for POST. As shown in the listing, the action method performs the authentication as just a check of the password matching the user ID for the purpose of illustration. If successful, the ".contacts" cookie is set and the browser is redirected to /Home/Index, which is the home page. The LoginRequired filter I covered earlier looks for this cookie to establish identity before the Index action method runs.

Listing 12-5. Login Action Method for POST

```
[HttpPost]
public ActionResult Login(string userId, string password)
{
        if (!String.IsNullOrWhiteSpace(userId))
        {
            if (userId.Equals(password)) // consider this an authentic user
            {
                Thread.CurrentPrincipal = new GenericPrincipal(new
                                                            GenericIdentity(userId), null);

                // create cookie with userId
                // Encrypt this - never use clear text cookies
                Response.Cookies.Add(new HttpCookie(".contacts", userId));

                return RedirectToAction("Index");
            }
        }

        return View();
}
```

■ Caution Never write plain text cookies as shown in Listing 12-5 unless you are writing that code to illustrate a concept in a book you are writing! Production code must always encrypt sensitive data before stuffing the data into a cookie.

9. As a result of the redirect in the previous step, the Index action method discussed in Step 4 will be run. Because the `LoginRequired` filter has been applied to it, the filter runs first and creates the principal object based on the cookie from the previous step. When the actual method runs, it filters the contacts based on the principal and uses the same as the model to render the view. The view for /Home/Index is shown in Listing 12-6. It just enumerates the model (the list of contacts) and displays each contact in a table row.

Listing 12-6. View for /Home/Index - Index.cshtml

```
@model IEnumerable<MyContacts.Models.Contact>

@{
    ViewBag.Title = "My Contacts";
}

<h2>My Contacts</h2>

<p>
    @Html.ActionLink("Create New", "Create")
</p>
<table>
<tr>
<th>@Html.DisplayNameFor(model => model.Name) </th>
<th>@Html.DisplayNameFor(model => model.Email) </th>
<th>@Html.DisplayNameFor(model => model.Address) </th>
<th>@Html.DisplayNameFor(model => model.DollarsSpentInStore) </th>
<th>@Html.DisplayNameFor(model => model.LoyaltyPoints) </th>
<th></th>
</tr>

@foreach (var item in Model) {
<tr>
<td>@Html.DisplayFor(modelItem => item.Name) </td>
<td>@Html.DisplayFor(modelItem => item.Email) </td>
<td>@Html.DisplayFor(modelItem => item.Address) </td>
<td>@Html.DisplayFor(modelItem => item.DollarsSpentInStore) </td>
<td>@Html.DisplayFor(modelItem => item.LoyaltyPoints) </td>
<td>
            @Html.ActionLink("Edit", "Edit", new { /* id=item.PrimaryKey */ }) |
            @Html.ActionLink("Details", "Details", new { /* id=item.PrimaryKey */ }) |
            @Html.ActionLink("Delete", "Delete", new { /* id=item.PrimaryKey */ })
</td>
</tr>
}
</table>
```

10. The final piece is the `Contact` class, the entity for which this application provides the user interface to accomplish CRUD operations. Listing 12-7 shows this class. It has several properties and a static method `GenerateContacts`, which we already used in Listing 12-1. Create this class in the `Models` folder.

Listing 12-7. Contact Class

```
public class Contact
{
    public string Name { get; set; }
    public string Email { get; set; }
    public string Address { get; set; }
    public decimal DollarsSpentInStore { get; set; }
    public int LoyaltyPoints { get; set; }
    public string Owner { get; set; }

    public static IEnumerable<Contact> GenerateContacts()
    {
        yield return new Contact()
        {
            Name = "Tom",
            Email = "tom@nowhere.com",
            Address = "123 Oak Circle, GermanTown, AB 12345",
            DollarsSpentInStore = 1234.56M,
            LoyaltyPoints = 1000,
            Owner = "jqhuman"
        };

        yield return new Contact()
        {
            Name = "Dick",
            Email = "dick@anywhere.com",
            Address = "987 Cedar Circle, DutchTown, YZ 98765",
            DollarsSpentInStore = 1784.96M,
            LoyaltyPoints = 1500,
            Owner = "jqhuman"
        };

        yield return new Contact()
        {
            Name = "Harry",
            Email = "harry@somewhere.com",
            Address = "567 Birch Circle, FrenchTown, UA 34589",
            DollarsSpentInStore = 14567.43M,
            LoyaltyPoints = 12000,
            Owner = "jqhuman"
        };

        yield return new Contact()
        {
            Name = "Tom",
            Email = "tom@missing.com",
```

```
                Address = "493 Hemlock Circle, SpanishTown, MB 53293",
                DollarsSpentInStore = 145.47M,
                LoyaltyPoints = 100,
                Owner = "jqlaw"
            };
        }
    }
```

That completes the Contacts Manager web application, a small and trivial application I have covered here mainly for completeness. The Contacts Manager web application exposes the contact information through a web API for other applications to consume. One such application is the Promotion Manager application, which I cover in the next section.

In this section I highlighted some of the fundamental concepts of MVC, such as binding and naming conventions, for those of you who are yet to use the great ASP.NET MVC framework for building web applications.

Building the Promotion Manager Application

The Promotion Manager web application is the client application. It is an ASP.NET MVC 4.0 Web application. The Promotion Manager application needs the contact information from the Contacts Manager application. The contact information is the resource protected by OAuth 2.0. There are two screens in this application: (1) the home page /Home/Index and (2) the contacts listing page /Home/Exchange, as shown on the left and right sides, respectively, of Figure 12-3.

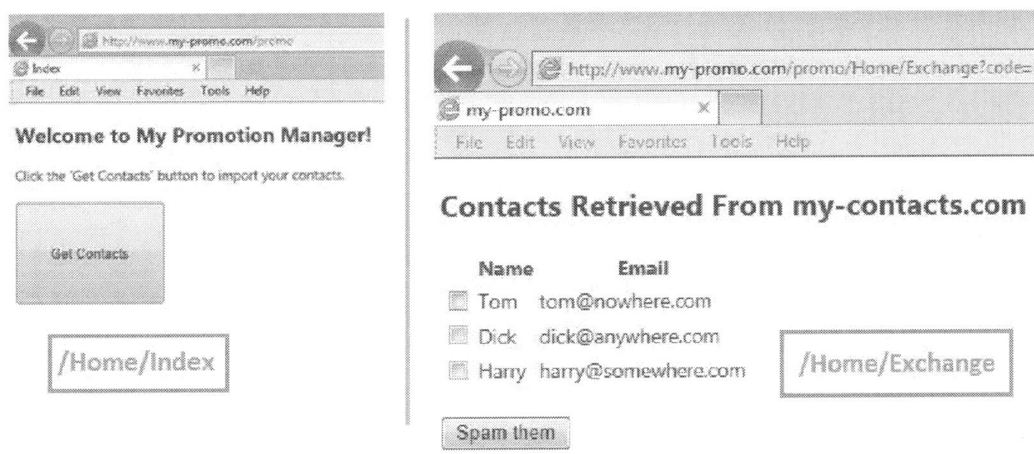

Figure 12-3. *Promotion Manager application*

The following steps show how to build our client application.

1. Launch Visual Studio 2012 as an administrator.
2. Create a new ASP.NET MVC 4.0 project using the Basic template and name it MyPromo.
3. Configure Visual Studio to use local IIS so that the project URL becomes `http://localhost/Promo`. Select Use Local IIS Web server and clear the Use IIS Express checkbox. Click Create Virtual Directory to create the virtual directory in IIS.

4. Add a new MVC controller and name it HomeController. This controller is the major component of the application. It has two action methods: Index and Exchange, which correspond to the two screens. Because this is an authorization code grant that is applicable to web applications, it should not surprise you to find all OAuth 2.0–related logic in the HomeController action methods with views having no knowledge of OAuth 2.0.

5. Add a view Index.cshtml in the Views\Home folder. Use the code in Listing 12-8.

Listing 12-8. Index.cshtml

```
@{
    ViewBag.Title = "Welcome to My Promotion Manager!";
}

<h2>Welcome to My Promotion Manager!</h2>

Click the 'Get Contacts' button to import your contacts.<br /><br />

@using (Html.BeginForm())
{
<input type="submit" name="go" value="Get Contacts" style="width: 150px; height: 100px;"/>
}
```

6. Add the action method Index to HomeController, as shown in Listing 12-9. The same action method of Index handles both GET and POST. If the incoming parameter go is empty, it is a GET. Otherwise, it is a POST. The parameter go corresponds to the button inside the form and the value of the button gets passed to the action method if the user submits the HTML form by clicking the Get Contacts button. The first time the user navigates to the home page of /Home/Index, the view displays the big Get Contacts button. When the user clicks the button, the OAuth 2.0 authorization code grant type flow starts. The browser is redirected to the authorization server http://www.my-contacts.com/contacts/OAuth20, passing the following data in the query string.

    a. The client ID, which is a hard-coded value of 0123456789. This is the same as the client ID that we used with Live Connect in Chapter 11, although there will be no screens here to register Promotion Manager with the authorization server. The values are simply hard-coded into the respective classes.

    b. The scope of "Read.Contacts". This is the only scope supported by the authorization server in our example scenario.

    c. A redirect or the callback URI of /Home/Exchange that points to the Exchange action method of HomeController. It is important to note that the code that runs to handle the callback must be on the server side. In our case, when the authorization server redirects to the callback URI, the browser will make a GET to /Home/Exchange and the code that runs to handle it will be in the MVC controller (HomeController), which is the server-side code.

    d. The response type specified as "code", indicating this is a request for an authorization code.

Listing 12-9. HomeController: Index Action Method

```
public class HomeController : Controller
{
    string clientId = "0123456789";
    string clientSecret = "TXVtJ3MgdGhlIHdvcmQhISE=";

    public ActionResult Index(string go)
    {
        if (!String.IsNullOrWhiteSpace(go)) // Form Post
        {
            string redirectUri = "http://www.my-promo.com/promo/Home/Exchange";
            string scope = "Read.Contacts";

            string url = "http://www.my-contacts.com/contacts/OAuth20";
            url += "?response_type=code&redirect_uri={0}&client_id={1}&scope={2}";

            url = String.Format(url, redirectUri, clientId, scope);

            return Redirect(url);
        }

        return View();
    }

    // Exchange action method goes here
}
```

7. At this point, the authorization server prompts for the user ID and credentials. After authentication, it asks for consent to share the contact information. After getting consent, it generates the authorization code and redirects the browser to the callback URI passing the authorization code in the query string. This will be covered in the following section, but I mention this point here for continuity.

8. The redirect or the callback URI is specified as /Home/Exchange, which corresponds to the Exchange action method shown in Listing 12-10.

    a. The GET request resulting out of the redirect is handled by the Exchange action method. The MVC binding magic makes sure the authorization code sent by the authorization server is passed into the Exchange action method as an argument. You need to ensure the parameter is named code to match the query string field.

    b. Use `HttpClient` to exchange the authorization code for an access token through a POST to the authorization server passing in the client ID, the client secret, a hard-coded value of "code" for the code field, and "authorization_code" as the grant type. As we saw in Chapter 11 with Live Connect, the client secret is the secret sauce that ensures only the client application, not the resource owner or the end user, can obtain the access token. This is the specialty of the authorization code grant.

    c. The response message to POST in the previous step is a JSON containing an access token. From the client application point of view, the token is just an opaque string. All that needs to be done is to send it to the web API as the credential.

d. Stuff the access token into the Authorization request header using the bearer scheme and make a GET request to ASP.NET Web API to retrieve the list of contacts.

e. The response message of the GET is again a JSON, which is deserialized back into an `IEnumerable<Contact>` using `Newtonsoft.Json.JsonConvert` and passed to the view as the model for rendering.

Listing 12-10. Exchange Action Method

```
public ActionResult Exchange(string code)
{
        using (HttpClient client = new HttpClient())
        {
            var postData = new List<KeyValuePair<string, string>>();
            postData.Add(new KeyValuePair<string, string>("client_id", clientId));
            postData.Add(new KeyValuePair<string, string>("redirect_uri",
                                                "http://www.my-promo.com/promo/Home/Exchange"));
            postData.Add(new KeyValuePair<string, string>("client_secret", clientSecret));
            postData.Add(new KeyValuePair<string, string>("code", code));
            postData.Add(new KeyValuePair<string, string>("grant_type", "authorization_code"));

            HttpContent content = new FormUrlEncodedContent(postData);

            var tokenResponse = client.PostAsync("http://www.my-contacts.com/contacts/OAuth20", content)
                                                        .Result;

            if (tokenResponse.IsSuccessStatusCode)
            {
                var token = tokenResponse.Content.ReadAsStringAsync().Result;

                string accessToken = (string)(JObject.Parse(token).SelectToken("access_token"));

                client.DefaultRequestHeaders.Authorization =
                                        new AuthenticationHeaderValue("Bearer", accessToken);

                var apiResponse = client.GetAsync("http://www.my-contacts.com/contacts/api/contacts")
                                                        .Result;

                if (apiResponse.IsSuccessStatusCode)
                {
                    string result = apiResponse.Content.ReadAsStringAsync().Result;

                    var contacts = JsonConvert.DeserializeObject<IEnumerable<Contact>>(result);

                    return View(contacts);
                }
            }
        }

        return Content("Failed to Exchange the authz code. Hope you find this message informative!");
}
```

9. The view that renders the model, which is `IEnumerable<Contact>`, is shown in Listing 12-11.

   Listing 12-11. Exchange Action Method's View: Exchange.cshtml

```
@model IEnumerable<MyPromo.Models.Contact>
<h2>Contacts Retrieved From my-contacts.com</h2>

<table>
<tr>
<th></th>
<th>@Html.DisplayNameFor(model => model.Name)</th>
<th>@Html.DisplayNameFor(model => model.Email)</th>
</tr>

@foreach (var item in Model) {
<tr>
<td>@Html.CheckBox(item.Email)</td>
<td>@Html.DisplayFor(modelItem => item.Name)</td>
<td>@Html.DisplayFor(modelItem => item.Email)</td>
</tr>
}
</table>
<br />
<input type="button" value="Spam them" />
```

10. Here is the `Contact` class corresponding to the JSON response sent by the web API. It just contains two properties: Name and `Email`, as shown in Listing 12-12. Add this class to the Models folder.

    Listing 12-12. Contact Class in Promotion Manager

```
public class Contact
{
    public string Name { get; set; }
    public string Email { get; set; }
}
```

■ **Note** The client application we just built is very similar to the application we built using the authorization code grant and Live Connect in Chapter 11. That is, after all, one of the benefits of sticking to a standard. Your client code will hardly change if you change the server implementation. A standard like OAuth 2.0 makes this possible.

Building the Authorization Server

In the scenario we have been working on so far, `www.my-contacts.com/contacts/OAuth20` is the authorization endpoint. This corresponds to the `OAuth20Controller` class that will be part of the MyContacts project. One of the design decisions I made was to keep the Contacts Manager web application, the authorization server, and the resource server (ASP.NET Web API) all part of the same project. So, our authorization server or the endpoint `OAuth20Controller` and other classes that are covered in this section will need to be added to the same MyContacts project that we created earlier, when we built the Contacts Manager application.

If you can imagine the authorization server as a black box, as shown in Figure 12-4, there are three requests coming in.

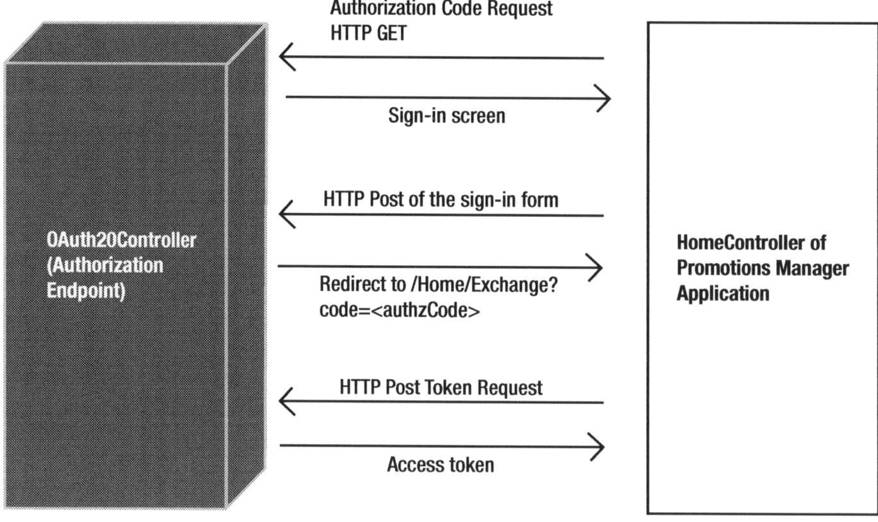

Figure 12-4. *Authorization server as a black box*

1. The authorization code request, which is an HTTP GET resulting from the redirect made from the Promotion Manager home page. There are four fields in the request here: response_type (of value "code"), redirect_uri, client_id, and scope. This request will be handled by the `Index` action method (decorated with the `HttpGet` attribute) in `OAuth20Controller`.
2. An HTTP POST of the sign-in form with credentials as well as the user consent to share the protected resource. In Live Connect, user consent happens on another screen as the next step, but here it is combined into one for brevity. This request will be handled by the `Authenticate` action method (decorated with the `HttpPost` attribute) in `OAuth20Controller`.
3. A token request, which is an HTTP POST of the authorization code. There are five fields in the request here: redirect_uri, client_id, client_secret, code, and grant_type (of value "authorization_code"). This request will be handled by the `Index` action method (decorated with the`HttpPost` attribute) in `OAuth20Controller`.

We start with the `OAuth20Controller` class without the action methods, and then add three action methods corresponding to the preceding three requests as we proceed with implementing the functionality. Listing 12-13 shows the controller without the action methods. There are two class level fields: `applicationRegistry` and `codesIssued`.

1. The `applicationRegistry` dictionary has the key as the client ID and the value is a `Tuple` that contains the client secret and the domain. This basically represents the data associated with the application registration screens in Live Connect. Currently, we are storing the values corresponding to that of our one and only one client—in other words, what is hard-coded in the `HomeController` of the Promotion Manager application.

2. The codesIssued dictionary is a concurrent dictionary with a key as the authorization code, which is System.Guid. When the authorization server issues an authorization code, it is inserted here so that when a subsequent token request comes in asking for an authorization code to be exchanged for a token, the controller can validate the code to see if it had issued one in the past. The value is a Tuple that stores the user identifier, the redirect URI, and the scope against which an authorization code is issued. These values are stored to be used in validating the subsequent token request.

The dictionary objects used in the OAuth20Controller class are just placeholders for persistent storage mechanisms such as a database. This code will not work when deployed in a load-balanced environment or even on the same machine using a web garden. A persistent store must replace these dictionary objects in such a scenario.

Add a new MVC controller namedOAuth20Controller to the MyContacts project. See Listing 12-13 for the controller class without action methods. We add the action methods into this class as we progress through the next sections.

Listing 12-13. OAuth20Controller Without Action Methods

```
public class OAuth20Controller : Controller
{
    private Dictionary<string, Tuple<string, string>> applicationRegistry = new Dictionary<string,
                                                                          Tuple<string, string>>();
    private static ConcurrentDictionary<Guid, Tuple<string, string, string>> codesIssued =
                                                     new ConcurrentDictionary<Guid, Tuple<string,
                                                                              string, string>>();

    public OAuth20Controller()
    {
        // client id, client secret and domain
        applicationRegistry.Add("0123456789", new Tuple<string, string>("TXVtJ3MgdGhlIHdvcmQhISE=",
                                                                    "http://www.my-promo.com"));
    }

    // Action methods go here

}
```

Index Action Method for HTTP GET

Now let's add the Index action method that handles the redirect from the Promotion Manager home page. An HTTP GET resulting out of this redirect is handled by the Index action method described in this section. The view corresponding to this action method shows the sign-in screen for the user to enter credentials and give consent to share the contacts information, as shown in Figure 12-5.

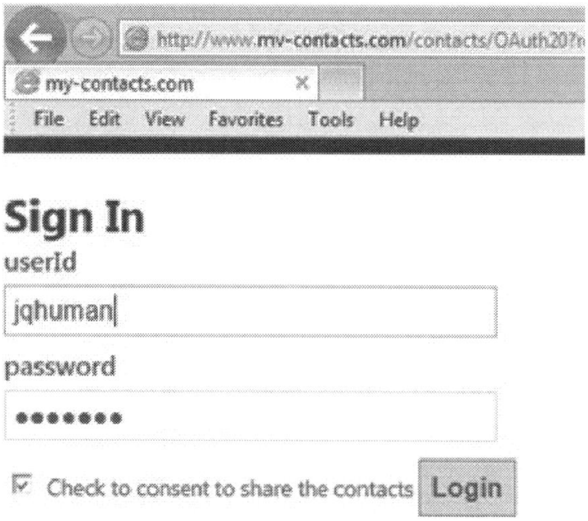

Figure 12-5. Authorization server sign-in (OAuth20/Index View)

1. When the Promotion Manager home page redirects the browser to the authorization endpoint, it passes several values in the query string. These values will be bound to the properties of the parameter of the action method, which is an `AuthzCodeRequest` object by the MVC framework. The `AuthzCodeRequest` class represents the data coming in the query string. The properties of this class match the field names in the query string, as specified by OAuth 2.0. To make matters simple, I have named the properties exactly the same as fields defined in OAuth 2.0, with the underscore and all, which is generally against the C# naming convention. It is possible to get around this using a custom binder, but that will be too much of a detour. So, I'll stick with property names containing underscores. Listing 12-14 shows the `AuthzCodeRequest` class. Because all the fields in the query string are mandatory, we can simply annotate the corresponding properties with the `Required` attribute. If any of these fields are missing in the request, the model state will be invalid. It is convenient to just check for `ModelState.IsValid` instead of checking the fields individually for presence. Create the class `AuthzCodeRequest` in the Models folder of the MyContacts project.

Listing 12-14. AuthzCodeRequest Class

```
public class AuthzCodeRequest
{
    [Required]
    public string response_type { get; set; }

    [Required]
    public string redirect_uri  { get; set; }

    [Required]
    public string client_id { get; set; }

    [Required]
    public string scope { get; set; }
}
```

2. Add the Index action method to OAuth20Controller, as shown in Listing 12-15. The following steps constitute the Index action method execution.

   a. Ensure all the properties in the input `AuthzCodeRequest` parameter are populated by looking at `ModelState.IsValid`.

   b. Check if the client ID is present in the registry. If so, retrieve the domain registered and ensure the redirect URI is part of this domain.

   c. The only scope that is supported is `Read.Contacts`. Ensure the incoming scope is the same. Reject any other scope.

   d. Finally, ensure that the response type is "code". If all these conditions are satisfied, move ahead. If not, direct to a generic error page.

   e. When all is well at this point, we are ready to show the sign-in page (see Figure 12-5) where the user enters credentials and the consent to share the contact information. One challenge ahead is when the user clicks the Login button, we get the credentials entered and the boolean value indicating the user's consent to share. To issue an authorization code at that time, we will need two values that we currently have in our input `AuthzCodeRequest` object: the scope and the redirect URI. We just validated the URI and scope, and we want the same values available to use while we issue the authorization code. But the values will not come in again from the user. We need to store it on the server side and pick it up using some kind of correlation ID that comes in later. As another option, we could just create a blob of stuff containing these two values, decipherable to no one but us, and put that in the sign-in form as a hidden field that we pick up when the sign-in form gets posted. I chose the second approach to avoid writing any persistence logic for the sake of simplicity. So, we create a string with a redirect URI and scope delimited with a pipe, encrypt this string, convert the resulting bytes into base64 encoding, and stuff that in a `ViewBag` property, which is rendered into a hidden field in the sign-in form.

Listing 12-15. Index Action Method

```
[HttpGet]
public ActionResult Index(AuthzCodeRequest request)
{
    bool isRequestValid = false;
    if (ModelState.IsValid)
    {
        if (applicationRegistry.ContainsKey(request.client_id))
        {
            var registryInfo = applicationRegistry[request.client_id];
            if (request.redirect_uri.StartsWith(registryInfo.Item2))
            {
                if (request.scope.Equals("Read.Contacts"))
                {
                    if (request.response_type.Equals("code"))
                        isRequestValid = true;
                }
            }
        }
    }
```

```
        if (!isRequestValid)
            return RedirectToAction("Error");

        ViewBag.CipherText = String.Format("{0}|{1}", request.redirect_uri, request.scope)
                                   .ToCipherText();

        return View(); // shows login screen that posts to Authenticate
    }
```

3. To implement the ToCipherText extension method used in Listing 12-15, create a folder called Helpers and create the static class EncryptionHelper inside this folder. See Listing 12-16. For more information on encryption, see Chapter 6.

Listing 12-16. ToCipherText Extension Method

```
public static class EncryptionHelper
{
    private static byte[] initVector = new byte[] { 13, 62, 115, 120, 34, 163, 226, 86 };
    private static byte[] key = new byte[] { 186, 20, 218, 62, 141, 209, 50, 89, 181, 54, 61,
                                             108, 144, 128, 224, 86, 207, 106, 6, 68, 182,
                                                                                 166, 44, 236 };

    public static string ToCipherText(this string clearText)
    {
        TripleDESCryptoServiceProvider provider = new TripleDESCryptoServiceProvider();

        byte[] clearBytes = Encoding.UTF8.GetBytes(clearText);
        byte[] foggyBytes = Transform(clearBytes, provider.CreateEncryptor(key, initVector));

        return Convert.ToBase64String(foggyBytes);
    }

    private static byte[] Transform(byte[] textBytes, ICryptoTransform transform)
    {
        using (MemoryStream buf = new MemoryStream())
        {
            using (CryptoStream stream = new CryptoStream(buf, transform, CryptoStreamMode.Write))
            {
                stream.Write(textBytes, 0, textBytes.Length);
                stream.FlushFinalBlock();
                return buf.ToArray();
            }
        }
    }
}
```

4. Now create the view for the preceding Index action method and copy and paste the code from Listing 12-17.

Listing 12-17. Index.cshtml

```
<h1>Sign In</h1>
@using (Html.BeginForm("Authenticate", "OAuth20"))
{
<div class="editor-label">@Html.Label("userId")</div>
<div class="editor-field">@Html.TextBox("userId")</div>
<div class="editor-label">@Html.Label("password")</div>
<div class="editor-field">@Html.Password("password")</div>

@Html.CheckBox("isOkayToShare")<text> Check to consent to share the contacts</text>

@Html.Hidden("CipherText", (string)ViewBag.CipherText)

<input type="submit" value="Login" />
}
```

Authenticate Action Method

An HTML form rendered by the Index view in Listing 12-17 specifies the `Authenticate` action method of `OAuth20Controller` as the target. There is a check box that the user can select to give consent to share contact information. There also is a hidden field rendered using the value we just passed in the `ViewBag`. Both these and the textboxes named userId and password get sent to the `Authenticate` action method, shown in Listing 12-18. Following are the steps that constitute the `Authenticate` action method execution.

1. The `Authenticate` action method has four parameters with names matching exactly the form fields we saw in Listing 12-17. Thus, after getting the userId and password, authenticate the same. Here, I just check that userId and password are the same for a user to be considered authentic. Of course, this is done purely from an illustration point of view.
2. If the user has agreed to share by selecting the checkbox, the boolean parameter `isOkayToShare` will be true. If that is the case and the credentials are authentic, perform the following steps.
    a. Decrypt the content of the hidden field that has come to the action method in the `CipherText` parameter using the `ToClearText` extension method and recover the URI and scope.
    b. Along with these two and the user ID, create a `Tuple`.
    c. Generate a GUID as the authorization code and using that as the key, store the `Tuple` in the concurrent dictionary.
    d. Finally, redirect to the redirect URI specified in the initial request passing the code as a query string.

Listing 12-18. Authenticate Action Method

```
[HttpPost]
public ActionResult Authenticate(string userId, string password,
bool isOkayToShare, string CipherText)
{
    // Authenticate
    bool isAuthentic = !String.IsNullOrWhiteSpace(userId) && userId.Equals(password);
```

```
            if (!isAuthentic)
                return RedirectToAction("Error");

            if (isOkayToShare)
            {
                var tokens = CipherText.ToClearText().Split('|');
                string uri = tokens[0];
                string scope = tokens[1];

                Guid code = Guid.NewGuid();
                codesIssued.TryAdd(code, new Tuple<string, string, string>(userId, uri, scope));

                uri += "?code=" + code.ToString();

                return Redirect(uri);
            }

            return RedirectToAction("Index", "Home");
        }
```

Add a new static method ToClearText to the static class EncryptionHelper we saw earlier, as shown in Listing 12-19. For more information on decryption, see Chapter 6.

Listing 12-19. ToClearText Extension Method

```
public static string ToClearText(this string cipherText)
{
    TripleDESCryptoServiceProvider provider = new TripleDESCryptoServiceProvider();
    byte[] foggyBytes = Convert.FromBase64String(cipherText);

    return Encoding.UTF8.GetString(Transform(foggyBytes, provider.CreateDecryptor(key, initVector)));
}
```

As a result of the redirect, the browser will go to the Promotion Manager application and the Exchange action method we saw in the previous section extracts this code and makes a POST request to exchange the code for an access token. The Index action method with the HttpPost attribute will handle that POST. I cover this process in the next section.

Index Action Method for HTTP POST

The Index action method of OAuth20Controller handles the HTTP POST from the Promotion Manager application to exchange the authorization code for an access token. The following steps complete the implementation of this action method.

1. The fields in the request entity-body of the HTTP POST can be represented by a class, similar to the Index action method that we created for GET. Create a TokenRequest class in the Models folder of the MyContacts project, as shown in Listing 12-20. Because all the fields in the request are mandatory, we can simply annotate the properties with the Required attribute. If any of these fields is missing in the request, the model state will be invalid. It is convenient to just check for ModelState.IsValid instead of checking the fields individually for presence.

Listing 12-20. TokenRequest Class

```
public class TokenRequest
{
    [Required]
    public string redirect_uri { get; set; }

    [Required]
    public string client_id { get; set; }

    [Required]
    public string code { get; set; }

    [Required]
    public string client_secret { get; set; }

    [Required]
    public string grant_type { get; set; }
}
```

2. Create the Index action method with the `HttpPost` attribute in `OAuth20Controller`, as shown in Listing 12-21. To summarize the action, it just performs a bunch of validations. If all are successful, it creates a JSON Web Token and sends that back as the `JsonResult` in the access_token field. Following are the validations performed before an access token is issued.

    a. All the required fields are present. This validation is accomplished by just checking `ModelState.IsValid`.

    b. The client ID is in the registry and the client secret passed in matches the client secret stored in the registry against the client ID.

    c. The grant type is "authorization_code".

    d. The authorization code in the request is present in the concurrent dictionary; in other words, the code is something we issued at some point in the past. The current implementation does not enforce any limit as to how old the authorization code can be.

    e. The redirect URI in the request matches the URI specified in the initial request.

If all conditions are satisfied, the authorization code is removed from the dictionary and a JSON Web Token is issued as the access token.

Listing 12-21. Index Action Method (POST)

```
[HttpPost]
public JsonResult Index(TokenRequest request)
{
    bool isRequestValid = false;
    Tuple<string, string, string> grantData = null;

    // All required inputs are present
    if (ModelState.IsValid)
    {
        // client id is in the registry
```

```
        if (applicationRegistry.ContainsKey(request.client_id))
        {
            var registryInfo = applicationRegistry[request.client_id];
            // client secret is the registy against the client id
            if (request.client_secret.Equals(registryInfo.Item1))
            {
                // grant type is correct
                if (request.grant_type.Equals("authorization_code"))
                {
                    Guid code = Guid.Parse(request.code);
                    // we have issued the code, since it is present in our list of codes issued
                    if (codesIssued.TryGetValue(code, out grantData))
                    {
                        // Token request is for the same redirect URI for which we
                        // previously issued the code
                        if (grantData != null && request.redirect_uri.Equals(grantData.Item2))
                        {
                            // all is well - remove the authz code from our list
                            isRequestValid = true;
                            codesIssued.TryRemove(code, out grantData);
                        }
                    }
                }
            }
        }
    }

    if (isRequestValid)
    {
        JsonWebToken token = new JsonWebToken()
        {
            SymmetricKey = EncryptionHelper.Key,
            Issuer = "http://www.my-contacts.com/contacts/OAuth20",
            Audience = "http://www.my-promo.com/promo/Home"
        };

        token.AddClaim(ClaimTypes.Name, grantData.Item1);
        token.AddClaim("http://www.my-contacts.com/contacts/OAuth20/claims/scope", grantData.Item3);

        return Json(new { access_token = token.ToString() });
    }

    // OAuth 2.0 spec requires the right code to be returned
    // For example, if authorization code is invalid, invalid_grant must be returned
    // I'm just returning 'invalid_request' as a catch-all thing, just for brevity
    return Json(new { error = "invalid_request" });
}
```

3. JWT is a signed token and it contains two claims: a standard name claim representing the user identifier used to sign in and a custom claim representing the scope. I take the `JsonWebToken` class, along with the helper class it depends on, `EncodingHelper`, straight from Chapter 10 and put them in the `Infrastructure` and `Helpers` folder, respectively. Create the `Infrastructure` folder before copying the files.

4. For any error, I return a blanket error. OAuth 2.0 clearly specifies the error code that must be returned for different situations. You can easily implement the logic to return the appropriate error after reading the specification. `OAuth20Controller` has the `Error` action method, which returns a static view with some wording that something has gone wrong while processing the request. Other action methods redirect to this when a validation fails. I'm not showing the code in a separate listing because it has just a `return View();` as the method body.

▒ **Note** I use the `EncryptionHelper` class to expose the key it uses for encryption, through a static read-only property, which I use for the JWT signing (see Listing 12-21). This class is part of the same project as `OAuth20Controller` that creates the JWT and `OAuthTokenHandler` that validates the JWT signature. Hence, I use the key in both places simply through a direct call to `EncryptionHelper.Key`. There is no out-of-band key sharing.

Building the Resource Server

Finally, we are back to writing code related to ASP.NET Web API. `ContactsController` is an `ApiController` that has just one method to return the contacts. The ultimate objective of a client application is to invoke this method. However, the method is protected by a door in the form of a message handler and the access token is the key that can unlock this door. Following are the steps to build the resource server.

1. Start with the message handler shown in Listing 12-22. The handler looks at the authorization request header and if the scheme is "Bearer", it pulls out the value in the header and deserializes the value into a `JsonWebToken`. The signature validation and expiry is checked by `Parse()`, as we saw in Chapter 10. Ultimately, the claims in the token are used to create a `ClaimsIdentity` object and subsequently a `ClaimsPrincipal` object that is set in `Thread.CurrentPrincipal`.

Listing 12-22. OAuthTokenHandler

```
public class OAuthTokenHandler : DelegatingHandler
{
    protected override async Task<HttpResponseMessage> SendAsync(HttpRequestMessage request,
                                                                 CancellationToken cancellationToken)
    {
        try
        {
            var headers = request.Headers;
            if (headers.Authorization != null)
            {
                if (headers.Authorization.Scheme.Equals("Bearer"))
                {
                    string accessToken = request.Headers.Authorization.Parameter;
                    JsonWebToken token = JsonWebToken.Parse(accessToken, EncryptionHelper.Key);

                    var identity = new ClaimsIdentity(token.Claims, "Bearer");
                    var principal = new ClaimsPrincipal(identity);

                    Thread.CurrentPrincipal = principal;

                    if (HttpContext.Current != null)
                        HttpContext.Current.User = principal;
                }
            }
```

```
            var response = await base.SendAsync(request, cancellationToken);

            if (response.StatusCode == HttpStatusCode.Unauthorized)
            {
                response.Headers.WwwAuthenticate.Add(
                            new AuthenticationHeaderValue("Bearer",
                                "error=\"invalid_token\""));
            }

            return response;
        }
        catch (Exception)
        {

            var response = request.CreateResponse(HttpStatusCode.Unauthorized);

            response.Headers.WwwAuthenticate.Add(
                    new AuthenticationHeaderValue("Bearer", "error=\"invalid_token\""));

            return response;
        }
    }
}
```

2. The message handler is plugged into the pipeline by adding the `config.MessageHandlers.Add(new OAuthTokenHandler());` line in the `WebApiConfig.cs` file in the `App_Start` folder.

3. Create a new `ApiController` named `ContactsController`, as shown in Listing 12-23. It uses the `GenerateContacts()` method of the `Contact` class, filters the list using the name of the identity, and creates a list of `MailingContact` objects. The message handler establishes the identity, but if the authorization header is not passed in it does not reject the request by sending back an unauthorized response. By decorating the `Get()` method in Listing 12-23 with a `ClaimsPrincipalPermission` attribute, I make sure the API works only if the identity is established and the necessary claims are there to invoke the method.

Listing 12-23. ContactsController: Web API

```
public class ContactsController : ApiController
{
    [ClaimsPrincipalPermission(SecurityAction.Demand, Operation = "Get", Resource = "Contacts")]
    public IEnumerable<MailingContact> Get()
    {
        return Contact.GenerateContacts()
                        .Where(c => c.Owner == User.Identity.Name)
                        .Select(c => new MailingContact()
                        {
                            Name = c.Name,
                            Email = c.Email
                        }).ToList();
    }
}
```

4. Create a class `MailingContact` with the `Name` and `Email` properties, as shown in Listing 12-24. I have this class inside `ContactsController.cs`, but you can create it in the Models folder if you like to organize your classes that way.

Listing 12-24. MailingContact Class

```
public class MailingContact
{
    public string Name { get; set; }
    public string Email { get; set; }
}
```

5. The claims needed to invoke the web API are not hard-coded in the `ApiController`, but I use a `ClaimsAuthorizationManager` subclass, shown in Listing 12-25. This is not a new concept for us because we looked at this class in Chapter 5.The authorization manager looks for a claim of type `http://www.my-contacts.com/contacts/OAuth20/claims/scope` and a value of "Read.Contacts", which is our one and only scope to decide if the API can be allowed to be invoked or not. It is currently trivial, but any changes to be made to the authorization logic in the future will be isolated to only this class and will not affect the API.

Listing 12-25. ClaimsAuthorizationManager Subclass

```
public class AuthorizationManager : ClaimsAuthorizationManager
{
    public override bool CheckAccess(AuthorizationContext context)
    {
        string resource = context.Resource.First().Value;
        string action = context.Action.First().Value;

        if (action == "Get" && resource == "Contacts")
        {
            ClaimsIdentity id = (context.Principal.Identity as ClaimsIdentity);

            if (!id.IsAuthenticated)
                    return false;

            return (id.Claims.Any(c =>
                     c.Type == "http://www.my-contacts.com/contacts/OAuth20/claims/scope"
                                  && c.Value.Equals("Read.Contacts")));
        }

        return false;
    }
}
```

6. To plug the `ClaimsAuthorizationManager` subclass into the claims pipeline, modify Web.config, as shown in Listing 12-26.

Listing 12-26. Web.config Changes

```
<configuration>
      <configSections>
          <section name="system.identityModel"
```

```
                type="System.IdentityModel.Configuration.SystemIdentityModelSection,
                System.IdentityModel, Version=4.0.0.0, Culture=neutral,
            PublicKeyToken=B77A5C561934E089"/>
        </configSections>
            ...
        <system.identityModel>
                <identityConfiguration>
                        <claimsAuthorizationManager
                                type="MyContacts.Infrastructure.AuthorizationManager,
                                MyContacts"/>
                </identityConfiguration>
        </system.identityModel>
</configuration>
```

After all this hard work, you are ready to enjoy the fruits of your labor. Start from the Promotion Manager application. Browse to `http://www.my-promo.com/promo`. I assume you have edited the hosts file in your computer for this to work.

Click on the big Get Contacts button and enter the credentials of **jqhuman** and **jqhuman** as the user ID and password. Do remember to select the check box and click Login. Promotion Manager will display the contacts: Tom, Dick, and Harry. You have just implemented the authorization code grant flow of OAuth 2.0!

Although it is not production strength and does not cover refresh tokens, which is the reason most of us labor with the authorization code grant, it is still a working model from which you can build your production-strength code.

Security Considerations

The authorization code grant that we just implemented from scratch is done primarily so you can understand the nuts and bolts. We have not given too much thought to the security aspects other than making sure the authorization code to the access token exchange is done in the server-side code so that only the client application will be able to obtain the access token using the client secret. This is not a security consideration but a requirement from the OAuth 2.0 specification for the authorization code grant.

In this section, I briefly cover the security aspects you need to consider while implementing OAuth 2.0. I point out the areas that need focus here so you can follow along as you design and implement. Covering every single aspect of security and providing code that you can readily reuse is not possible in a book of reasonable size, at least not one that can be held with two hands!

In addition to the following considerations, you can also review section 10 of the OAuth 2.0 specification (RFC 6749), which is dedicated to security considerations.

1. In the preceding scenario, we did not use transport security. In a production environment, HTTPS will be mandatory to ensure confidentiality of user credentials as well as the authorization code and tokens. OAuth 2.0 heavily banks on HTTPS.

2. The client secret, as the name indicates, must remain a secret. It must never be disclosed to anyone, including legitimate end users. Even the development team need not have access to the client secret used in production environments. Apart from one or two administrators, only the client application should have access to the client secret.

3. OAuth 2.0 does not specify the format for access tokens, but it goes without saying that the tokens must be protected for integrity as well as confidentiality in most of the production scenarios. Transport security in the form of HTTPS will be a great help, but message security accomplished using signing and encryption can also be considered for end-to-end protection.

4. RFC 6750 specifies the use of access tokens as bearer tokens. Bearer tokens do not have cryptographic support to prove token ownership, unlike the holder-of-key tokens. Hence, HTTPS is a must to secure the channel through which the client application presents the bearer token to the resource server.

5. A refresh token is a convenient mechanism to get a new access token without troubling the user to authenticate and consent to share. But from a security point of view, it is a headache to manage because the refresh tokens are long-lived. Refresh tokens must be protected both in motion as well as at rest. If a malicious user gets to your data store where you have stored the refresh tokens, it will be a disaster. One technique that is worth considering with refresh tokens is the technique that is mentioned in section 10 of RFC 6749, which is to employ a use-and-throw refresh token that expires with the first request to refresh the access token. The response message to such an access token refresh request can contain the new access token as well as a new refresh token.

6. The authorization code is sent in the query string that can get logged and stored in the browser history as well. Authorization codes must be use-and-throw as well as short-lived. In the implementation that we saw in this chapter, an authorization code that is issued never expires, which is something for you to take note of.

7. The security threats typical to a web application, such as XSS, XSRF, click jacking, and so on, are all applicable here as well. You must ensure you handle them effectively. ASP.NET MVC provides you with antiforgery tokens to use against XSRF. See Chapter 15 for more information related to XSS and XSRF.

8. A redirect or callback URI is passed in the request for authorization code, and the authorization code is sent in the query string while the authorization server redirects to the URI. To prevent a malicious user from manipulating this URI, you must always check that the callback URI in the request is part of the domain registered at the time of the client application registration.

9. In the case of an authorization code grant type, by ensuring that only the client application has access to the client secret you can make sure a request to your web API comes only from the client application in a non repudiation sense. With an implicit grant, the token is sent to the browser, and hence the users have access to the token. You will not know if the client application is making the API call, if a legitimate user is directly making the call, or if Mallory the malicious user is making the call! For an implicit grant, HTTPS is a must because the token is sent in the URI fragment.

10. It is worth noting that section 10 of RFC 6749 recommends minimizing the resource owner password credentials grant type given the fact that it is riskier than other types because it maintains the password antipattern that OAuth 2.0 strives to avoid.

11. The client credentials grant type is two-legged because there is no user involvement. Take the case of an authorization code grant, which is three-legged: The user must supply the credentials and the client application must supply the client secret for the token to be issued, more along the lines of the two-man rule. Hence, from a security standpoint, the client credentials grant type is not comparatively robust. Of course, there are use cases for this type, but it is better to minimize the use of this grant type. If the client credential is a symmetric key, be sure to rotate it regularly.

OPENID CONNECT

Can an OAuth-based access token be used to authenticate a user? The answer is yes. For example, the Promotion Manager application can establish the identity of the user based on the access token it receives from the Contacts Manager application. What if the token is an encrypted token readable only by an authorization server? Promotion Manager can simply make the API call passing the token, and if the API call goes through successfully it can infer that the user is an authenticated user. This type of indirect authentication is generally referred to as pseudo-authentication. However, this is not the right approach.

The right approach is to use OpenID Connect, which is built on top of OAuth 2.0. OpenID Connect allows clients to verify the identity of the user (the resource owner) based on the authentication performed by the authorization server. To make an OpenID Connect request, the client constructs a regular OAuth 2.0 request to obtain an access token, as in the case of an authorization code grant. A special mandatory scope of **openid** is included as one of the requested scopes.

After the user authorizes the request, the client receives the authorization code. The authorization code is exchanged for an access token and an additional token called ID token (id_token), which is a JWT containing a few mandatory claims, including the user ID (user_id). The OAuth 2.0 specification does not specify the attributes of the access token because it is just an opaque string as far as the client is concerned. However, OpenID Connect specifies the ID token to be JWT. It does make sense because the ID token is meant for client consumption, and the need for standardization is far greater here with the client being very distinct from the resource and authorization servers in the majority, if not all, of the cases.

To obtain additional attributes of the user or any other additional tokens, the client makes a GET or POST request to a special endpoint called **UserInfo** passing in the access token in the HTTP authorization request header using the bearer scheme.

What we have just seen is an OpenID Connect Basic Client Profile. At the time of the writing of this book, OpenID Connect is in an Implementor's Draft Review Period, and hence there will be no detailed treatment of the topic in this book apart from this sidebar.

Summary

In this chapter, I walked you through the scenario of John Q. Human using two web applications: The Contacts Manager application for managing his contact information and the Promotion Manager application for managing the promotions he runs for his retail store. The Promotion Manager application needs the contact information from the Contacts Manager application to send the promotions. However, John does not want to share his Contacts Manager password with the Promotion Manager application.

We implemented Contacts Manager and Promotion Manager as ASP.NET MVC applications, with the protected resource of the contact information shared to Promotion Manager through a web API that expects an access token obtained through an OAuth 2.0 authorization code grant. The client application, which in this case is Promotion Manager, obtains the access token from the Contacts Manager authorization server and presents the same to ASP.NET Web API in the bearer scheme to receive the contact information in the form of JSON. For the access token, I used a JWT and reused the JSON web token implementation from Chapter 10 for this purpose.

In the next chapter, we look at using DotNetOpenAuth to work with OAuth 2.0.

CHAPTER 13

OAuth 2.0 Using DotNetOpenAuth

In this chapter, we implement OAuth 2.0-based authorization in ASP.NET Web API using DotNetOpenAuth (DNOA). DotNetOpenAuth (`http://www.dotnetopenauth.net/`) is a well-established **open source** .NET Framework library that can help you implement production-grade OAuth 2.0-based authorization for your web API.

DNOA provides a nice API for you to work with as you implement OAuth 2.0. There are classes available to represent the OAuth 2.0 roles of resource server, authorization server, and client: `ResourceServer`, `AuthorizationServer`, and `WebServerClient`, respectively. These classes provide you with methods that abstract away the complexity and the procedural steps that are needed to request, create, obtain, and validate the access token.

For example, to start the OAuth 2.0 flow from the client side you simply need to call the `RequestUserAuthorization` method of `WebServerClient` passing the scope and the callback URI. In the action method corresponding to the callback URI, after calling the `ProcessUserAuthorization` method to get the authorization you can just extract the access token through the `AccessToken` property. In fact, you do not even need to know that there are HTTP redirects and posts happening, which we saw in the previous chapter, to get the access token. That is the kind of abstraction DNOA provides to make your life easier.

As you work through this chapter, you will appreciate how fewer lines of code give you a richer functionality than what we implemented in the previous chapter. In this chapter, you will see more lines of code in the infrastructure side to store the data related to the clients, client authorizations, and so on rather than lines of code related to the core OAuth 2.0. Of course, that is understandable because hard-coding a client ID, client secrets, and authorization codes at the class level, as we did in the previous chapter, cannot get you very far in your objective to write production-strength code. Although DNOA helps us move away from hard-coded data to nicely modeled classes, I stick to my principle of database avoidance for the sake of brevity. In your implementation, you can easily replace the in-memory storage with durable storage such as a database.

We use the same scenario that we used in Chapter 11: An end user, John Q. Human, wants to share the contact information contained in his contacts application with a Promotion Manager application without divulging his contacts application login credentials to the Promotion Manager application. We implement authorization code grant for this scenario. Instead of building from the ground up, as we did in Chapter 12, we will use DNOA. We end with a quick look at implementing implicit grant flow.

Note DotNetOpenAuth helps you implement production-grade OAuth 2.0–based authorization. However, if you need a prebuilt implementation that issues tokens through OAuth 2.0, Thinktecture.IdentityServer v2 is a good open-source option for you to evaluate. Go to `https://github.com/thinktecture/Thinktecture.IdentityServer.v2`.

Design

As with Chapter 12, we have two ASP.NET MVC 4.0 projects as part of our Visual Studio solution.

1. **MyContacts**: This is an ASP.NET MVC 4.0 project created using the Web API template. We can have both MVC controllers and WebAPI controllers in the same project. This project represents both the resource server and the authorization server.
2. **MyPromo**: This is an ASP.NET MVC 4.0 project created using the Basic template. MyPromo represents the client web application that requires the protected resource to function.

As in Chapter 12, both projects use local IIS (not Express IIS). The project URLs are `http://localhost/Contacts` for the MyContacts project and `http://localhost/Promo` for the MyPromo project. Instead of using localhost, use the names defined in the hosts file of `http://www.my-contacts.com/contacts` and `http://www.my-promo.com/promo`. This will make testing easier and less susceptible to confusion.

■ **Note** We will not use a JSON Web Token or any other standard token format in this chapter. DNOA, at the time of writing this book, does not support any of those formats. It is not a concern, though, because DNOA is used at both ends: DNOA mints the token at the authorization server end and DNOA reads and validates the token at the resource server end.

MyContacts Project

Table 13-1 shows the classes in the MyContacts project, with a brief description of each class. Class names with a star (*) are new classes for the MyContacts project that we didn't work with in Chapter 12. The controller classes remain the same as the controller classes for the MyContacts project in Chapter 12. There are no fundamental changes to the design. I leverage forms authentication here, and for this purpose `AuthenticationController` is included.

***Table 13-1.** Classes in the MyContacts Project*

Class Name	Namespace	Description
`HomeController`	`MyContacts.Controllers`	Acts as just a placeholder for the Contacts Manager web application. This is an MVC controller.
`OAuth20Controller`	`MyContacts.Controllers`	Accepts a request for authorization codes as well as requests for exchanging codes to access tokens. This MVC controller is the authorization endpoint.
`ContactsController`	`MyContacts.Controllers`	Returns the list of contacts. The only API controller in our project.
`AuthenticationController*`	`MyContacts.Controllers`	Provides authentication or the login functionality. Forms authentication redirects to this controller for authentication.
`CertificateHelper*`	`MyContacts.Helpers`	Helps convert the subject name of a certificate to a certificate object. This is an extension method to string.

(*continued*)

Table 13-1. *(continued)*

Class Name	Namespace	Description
AuthorizationManager	MyContacts.Infrastructure	Controls access to the web API based on the claims. This is a subclass of ClaimsAuthorizationManager.
OAuthTokenHandler	MyContacts.Infrastructure	Establishes identity based on the OAuth access token. It uses the ResourceServer DNOA object. This is a message handler.
ServerHost*	MyContacts.Infrastructure	Implements IAuthorizationServerHost needed to instantiate the AuthorizationServer class of DNOA.
DataStore*	MyContacts.Infrastructure.Store	Acts as the façade of all the classes related to storage. This is a singleton.
Client* ClientAuthorization* CryptoKeyStore* Nonce* NonceStore* SymmetricCryptoKey*	MyContacts.Infrastructure.Store	Provide functionalities related to storing client details such as a client ID, client secret, client authorization, nonce, and symmetric keys.
Contact	MyContacts.Models	Represents the contact entity. This is a model class.
AuthorizationRequest*	MyContacts.Models	Helps in rendering the view or the screen that asks the user for consent to share data. This is a view model class.

One major change for the better is the inclusion of several classes under `Infrastructure.Store` representing the entities for persistence. As I mentioned in the introduction to this chapter, I do not use a database. I store the objects in the application domain itself, but it is not difficult to store them in a database if you prefer.

■ **Note** If you plan to use a database, you will need to make minor changes in the `Store` classes. Because I'm not dealing with a relational database, I don't have to deal with the impedance mismatch between relational and object worlds. I store the object graph directly in the AppDomain, but you would need to employ an object-relational mapper (ORM) like the Entity Framework and design your tables with PK-FK relationships. These classes would need to reflect that.

MyPromo Project

Table 13-2 shows the two classes in the MyPromo project, with a brief description of each class. The classes are similar to the two classes in the MyPromo project in Chapter 12. The reason the project structure does not change is because this is the client using OAuth 2.0. The impact is only on the server side because we are using DNOA to build the server. However, implementation details do change in this chapter because of the DNOA `WebServerClient` class used here.

Table 13-2. *Classes in MyPromo Project*

Class Name	Namespace	Description
`HomeController`	`MyPromo.Controllers`	Requests authorization code, exchanges it for a token, makes the web API call, and shows the contacts retrieved to the user. It uses the `WebServerClient` DNOA class to initiate the OAuth 2.0 flow as well as to extract the token from the response.
`Contact`	`MyPromo.Models`	Represents a subset of the contact business entity with only the name and e-mail.

HTTP Transactions

Before we look at HTTP transactions, you need to be aware of a slight change to the screen flow in this chapter compared to Chapter 12. In Chapter 12, we saw that the user provides consent in the same screen he uses to sign in to the authorization server. In this chapter, there is a separate authorization screen for the user to give consent to share. Figure 13-1 shows the screen flow.

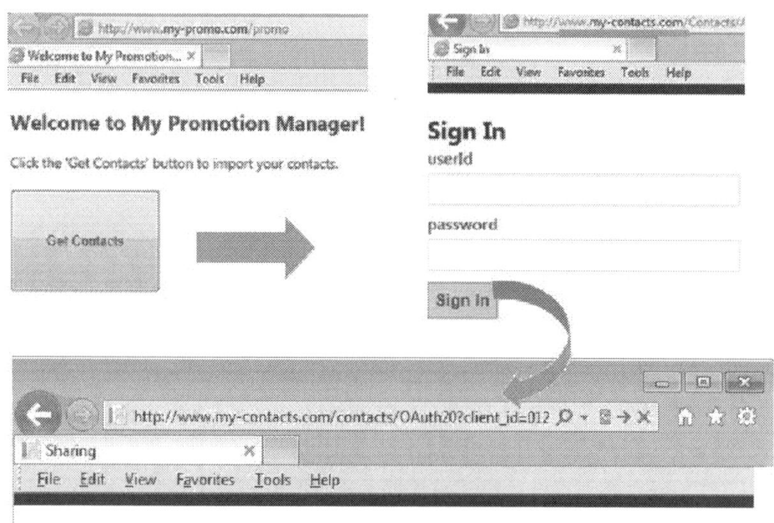

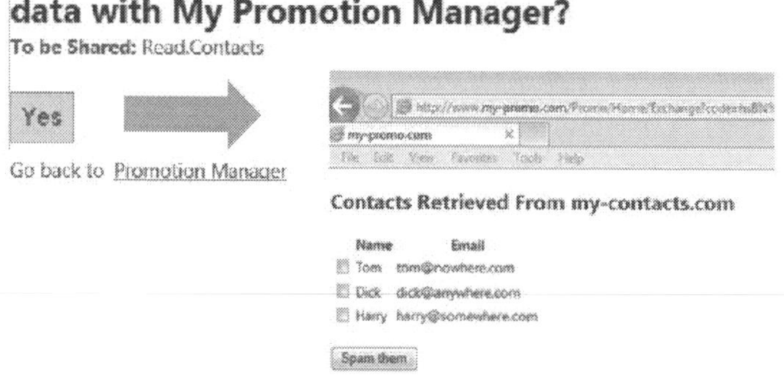

Figure 13-1. *Promotion Manager flow*

The HTTP transactions generated by DNOA are similar, but not exactly identical, to the transactions we saw in Chapter 12. In addition to the new authorization screen, there is an additional redirect in the scenario in this chapter because we use forms authentication.

Except for these changes, the fundamental structure of the flow related to the authorization code grant that we saw in Chapter 11 remains unchanged. After all, the flow is defined in the OAuth 2.0 specification and must remain essentially the same regardless of implementation details. The following HTTP transactions happen in the Promotion Manager flow.

1. John goes to the Promotion Manager web application home page. This is the page with the big Get Contacts button.

Request	GET `http://www.my-promo.com/promo` HTTP/1.1 Host: `www.my-promo.com`
Response	HTTP/1.1 200 OK Content-Type: text/html; charset=utf-8 <!DOCTYPE html> <html>... Promotion Manager home page with big button

2. John clicks the Get Contacts button, triggering an HTTP POST. The /Home/Index form with only that button gets posted to itself. DNOA tries to redirect the browser to the authorization endpoint `http://www.my-contacts.com/contacts/OAuth20`, making the request for an authorization code.

Request	POST `http://www.my-promo.com/promo` HTTP/1.1 Referer: `http://www.my-promo.com/promo` Host: `www.my-promo.com` go=Get+Contacts
Response	HTTP/1.1 302 Found Content-Type: text/html; charset=utf-8 Location: `http://www.my-contacts.com/contacts/OAuth20?client_id=0123456789&redirect_uri=http%3A%2F%2Fwww.my-promo.com%2FPromo%2FHome%2FExchange&state=apqv345snyz5ghqimdt2awkd&scope=Read.Contacts&response_type=code` `Set-Cookie: ASP.NET_SessionId=apqv345snyz5ghqimdt2awkd; path=/;` HttpOnly

3. The redirect results in another redirect. Because the authorization endpoint is protected with an `Authorize` attribute, it results in forms authentication making another redirect to the `Authentication` controller.

Request	GET `http://www.my-contacts.com/contacts/OAuth20?client_id=0123456789&redirect_uri=http%3A%2F%2Fwww.my-promo.com%2FPromo%2FHome%2FExchange&state=apqv345snyz5ghqimdt2awkd&scope=Read.Contacts&response_type=code` HTTP/1.1 Referer: `http://www.my-promo.com/promo` Host: `www.my-contacts.com`
Response	HTTP/1.1 302 Found Location: /Contacts/Authentication?ReturnUrl=%2fcontacts%2fOAuth20%3f client_id%3d0123456789%26 redirect_uri%3dhttp%253A%252F%252F`www.my-promo.com%252FPromo%252FHome` `%252FExchange%26` state%3dapqv345snyz5ghqimdt2awkd%26scope%3dRead.Contacts%26response_type...

4. The redirect results in a GET to Authorization/Index, which renders the login page for the user to enter credentials.

Request

GET http://www.my-contacts.com/Contacts/Authentication?
ReturnUrl=%2fcontacts%2fOAuth20%3f... HTTP/1.1
Referer: http://www.my-promo.com/promo
Host: www.my-contacts.com

Response

HTTP/1.1 200 OK
Content-Type: text/html; charset=utf-8

<html>. . . . Login page generated by AuthenticationController

---

5. John enters the credentials and submits the form, resulting in a POST.

Request

POST http://www.my-contacts.com/Contacts/Authentication?
ReturnUrl=%2fcontacts%2fOAuth20%3fclient_id%3d0123456789%26
redirect_uri%3dhttp%253A%252F%252Fwww.my-promo.com%252FPromo%252F
Home%252FExchange%26
state%3dapqv345snyz5ghqimdt2awkd%26scope%3dRead.Contacts%26
response_type%3dcode&client_id=0123456789&
redirect_uri=http%3A%2F%2Fwww.my-promo.com%2FPromo%2FHome%2FExchange
&state=apqv345snyz5ghqimdt2awkd&scope=Read.Contacts
&response_type=code HTTP/1.1
Referer: http://www.my-contacts.com/Contacts/Authentication?ReturnUrl...
Host: www.my-contacts.com

userId=jqhuman&password=jqhuman

Response

HTTP/1.1 302 Found
Location: /contacts/OAuth20?client_id=0123456789&redirect_
uri=http%3A%2F%2Fwww.my-promo.com%2FPromo%2FHome%2FExchange
&state=apqv345snyz5ghqimdt2awkd&scope=Read.Contacts&response_type=code
Set-Cookie: .MyContacts=67AF4EA87E. . . 0694AA; path=/; HttpOnly

---

6. After authentication, the browser is redirected to the authorization endpoint. This is the same as Step 3 except that it will go through this time, in contrast to the last time when it failed with a 401 and got redirected for want of a forms authentication ticket. Now, the request contains the cookie .MyContacts, which is the ticket. Because of this, John gets to see the authorization screen, where he can give his consent to share the data.

Request

GET http://www.my-contacts.com/contacts/OAuth20?client_id=0123456789&
redirect_uri=http%3A%2F%2Fwww.my-promo.com%2FPromo%2FHome%2FExchange&
state=apqv345snyz5ghqimdt2awkd&scope=Read.Contacts&response_type=code HTTP/1.1
Referer: http://www.my-contacts.com/Contacts/Authentication?ReturnUrl=%2f
contacts%2fOAuth20%3f...
Cookie: <Other cookies> .MyContacts=67AF4EA87E3...694AA
Host: www.my-contacts.com

Response	HTTP/1.1 200 OK Content-Type: text/html; charset=utf-8 <!DOCTYPE html> <html>. . . . Authorization screen where user clicks 'Yes' to give consent to share

7. DNOA does an HTTP POST to the authorization endpoint, specifying the redirect URI as `http://www.my-promo.com/promo/Home/Exchange` and the response_type as code. The authorization endpoint redirects to this URI passing along the authorization code in the query string.

Request	POST `http://www.my-contacts.com/contacts/OAuth20?client_id=0123456789&`
	`redirect_uri=http%3A%2F%2Fwww.my-promo.com%2FPromo%2FHome%2FExchange&`
	`state=apqv345snyz5ghqimdt2awkd&scope=Read.Contacts&response_type=code` HTTP/1.1
	Referer: `http://www.my-contacts.com/contacts/OAuth20?client_id=0123456789&`
	`redirect_uri=http%3A%2F%2Fwww.my-promo.com%2FPromo%2FHome%2FExchange&`
	`state=apqv345snyz5ghqimdt2awkd&scope=Read.Contacts&response_type=code`
	Host: `www.my-contacts.com`
	Cookie: .MyContacts=67AF4EA8 . . . . 41FD0694AA
	
	client_id=0123456789&redirect_uri=http%3A%2F%2F`www.my-promo.com%`
	2FPromo%2FHome%2FExchange&
	state=apqv345snyz5ghqimdt2awkd&scope=Read.Contacts&
	response_type=code&userApproval=Yes

Response	HTTP/1.1 302 Found Location: `http://www.my-promo.com/Promo/Home/Exchange?` **code=eMSd% . . . 2Fnw**&state=apqv345snyz5ghqimdt2awkd

8. DNOA exchanges the authorization code for a token by making an HTTP request. Next, the `/Home/Exchange` action method makes a GET to the `ContactsController` web API with the OAuth 2.0 access token in the HTTP authorization header (bearer scheme) to get the JSON response, which is passed to the view as the model for rendering.

Request	GET `http://www.my-promo.com/Promo/Home/Exchange?code=eMSd%` . . . 2Fnw&state=apqv345 snyz5ghqimdt2awkd HTTP/1.1 Referer: `http://www.my-contacts.com/contacts/OAuth20?`client_id=0123456789& redirect_uri=http%3A%2F%2F`www.my-promo.com%2FPromo%2FHome%2FExchange&` state=apqv345snyz5ghqimdt2awkd&scope=Read.Contacts&response_type=code Cookie: ASP.NET_SessionId=apqv345snyz5ghqimdt2awkd Host: `www.my-promo.com`
Response	HTTP/1.1 200 OK Content-Type: text/html; charset=utf-8 <!DOCTYPE html> <html> . . . Contacts shown . . . .

Step 8 has substeps, the most notable one being DNOA making a POST request with the client ID and client secret as the username and password in the authorization header using a basic scheme to obtain an access token.

Request	POST `http://www.my-contacts.com/contacts/OAuth20/Token HTTP/1.1` Content-Type: application/x-www-form-urlencoded; charset=utf-8 User-Agent: DotNetOpenAuth/<version> **Authorization: Basic MDEyMzQ1Njc4OTpUOSjNNZ2RHaGxJSGR2Y21RaElTRT0=** Host: `www.my-contacts.com` code=eMSd%21IAA . . . &redirect_uri=http%3A%2F%2F`www.my-promo.com`%2FPromo%2FHome%2FExchange&grant_type=authorization_code
Response	HTTP/1.1 200 OK Content-Type: application/json; charset=utf-8 { **"access_token":"gAAAAGih . . . AzoE"**, "token_type":"bearer", "expires_in":"120", "refresh_token":"T2C9!IAAAAO...Q0UQ", "scope":"Read.Contacts" }

Once the access token is retrieved, the Promotion Manager `/Home/Exchange` uses the access token as a bearer token and makes the call to the Contacts Manager web API. The HTTP request and the resulting JSON response are exactly identical to the transaction we saw in Chapter 12; for this reason, I don't repeat the information here.

■ **Note** The previous step is important from the perspective of implementation. The older versions of DNOA send two requests: the first one without the credentials that results in a 401 – Unauthorized, followed by one with the credentials. Refer to the issue `https://github.com/DotNetOpenAuth/DotNetOpenAuth/issues/195` for more details.

Implementation Ground Work

First, we add the DotNetOpenAuth library into our projects and make a few configuration changes to get it working. The following are the steps.

1. Right-click the References node under the project MyPromo in the Visual Studio Solution Explorer and select Manage NuGet Packages.
2. Go to Online ➤ All and search for DotNetOpenAuth.
3. In the search results, locate the file with the name of DotNetOpenAuth (unified). It is a single .dll with everything in it. I'm using version 4.2.1.13026. Figure 13-2 shows the Manage NuGet Packages Visual Studio window so you can verify you are using the right DNOA assembly, the same assembly as the one I use.

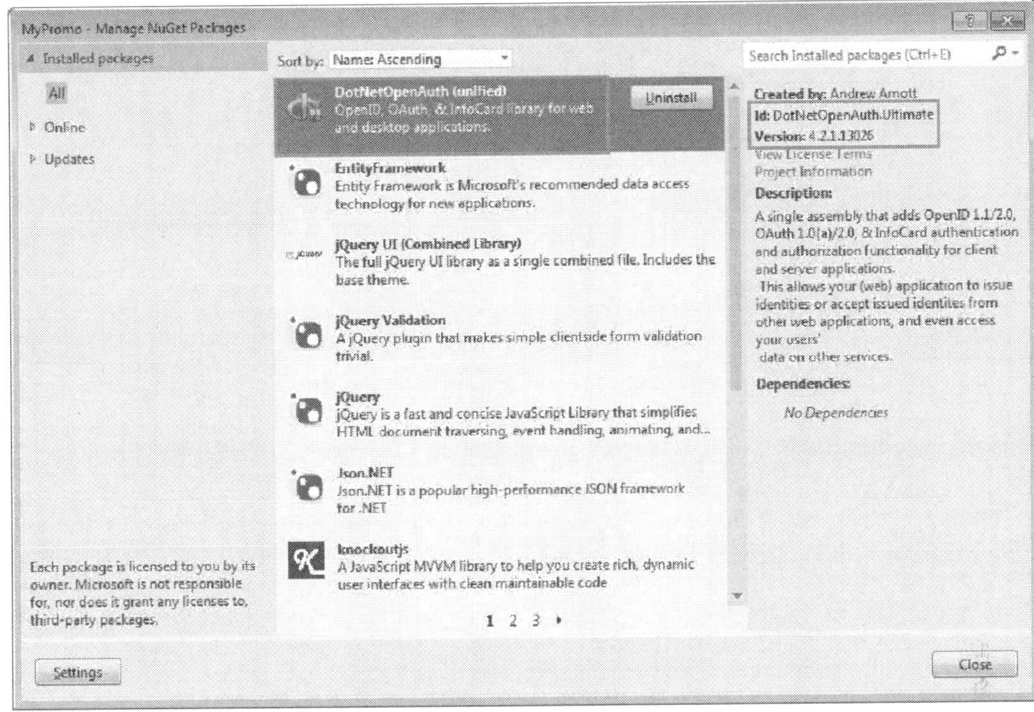

Figure 13-2. *Manage NuGet Packages*

4. Install the DNOA assembly in the MyContacts project as well, similar to the previous steps.
5. I use Visual Studio 2012 in Windows 7 targeting the .NET Framework 4.5. Depending on the version, you might get a slightly different behavior. If you get a configuration error that "There is a duplicate 'uri' section defined," you might need to comment out the line `<section name="uri" type="System.Configuration.UriSection...` under `<configSections>` in both projects.
6. Because we do not use HTTPS for the sake of simplicity, edit the messaging node under dotNetOpenAuth to add an attribute such as `<messaging relaxSslRequirements="true">` in both projects.

■ **Caution** Never go to production without HTTPS. OAuth 2.0 heavily banks on transport security.

Building the Client Application

The Promotion Manager web application is the client application. This is an ASP.NET MVC 4.0 Web application. `HomeController` is the major component of this application and there are two action methods: `Index` and `Exchange`. There is not much change to this application compared to the implementation in Chapter 12. `HomeController` has the exact same methods, an `Index` and an `Exchange` method. The following steps show how to build our client application.

1. Because we used the Basic template to create the MyPromo project in Visual Studio, you must manually add the HomeController class. Create a new MVC controller for this purpose. Listing 13-1 shows the bare-bones HomeController with a few fields, to which we add the action methods, as we progress through the steps. The following is an overview of the fields and the variables.

    a. The token issuance and authorization endpoints of the authorization server are stored in two constants. This is a slightly different behavior compared to the previous chapter where there is only one endpoint.

    b. The client ID and client secret are hard-coded here for the sake of simplicity. At least the client secret must be read from the encrypted configuration in a production environment.

    c. A static object of type AuthorizationServerDescription is created using the authorization server endpoints. The same is used to create an instance of the WebServerClient object, which is central to the working of HomeController.

Listing 13-1. HomeController

```
public class HomeController : Controller
{
        const string TOKEN_ENDPOINT = "http://www.my-contacts.com/contacts/OAuth20/Token";
        const string AUTHZ_ENDPOINT = "http://www.my-contacts.com/contacts/OAuth20";

        private readonly string clientId = "0123456789";
        private readonly string clientSecret = "TXVtJ3MgdGhlIHdvcmQhISE=";
        private readonly WebServerClient client;

        private static AuthorizationServerDescription authServer = new
                                                              AuthorizationServerDescription()
        {
            TokenEndpoint = new Uri(TOKEN_ENDPOINT),
            AuthorizationEndpoint = new Uri(AUTHZ_ENDPOINT),
        };

        public HomeController()
        {
            client = new WebServerClient(authServer, clientId, clientSecret);
        }

        // Action methods go here
}
```

2. Add the Index action method, as shown in Listing 13-2. As with the previous chapter, this action method handles both GET and POST. When the user clicks the Get Contacts button, the RequestUserAuthorization() method of the WebServerClient object is called passing in the scope and the redirect URI. This call sets the wheels in motion and the OAuth flow is triggered. A browser redirection happens a few times when the user enters the credentials for authentication and gives consent to share data. Finally the browser is redirected to the redirect URI, which corresponds to the Exchange action method.

Listing 13-2. Index Method

```
public ActionResult Index(string go)
{
            if (!String.IsNullOrWhiteSpace(go))
            {
                client.RequestUserAuthorization(new[] { "Read.Contacts" },
                                    new Uri(Url.Action("Exchange", "Home", null,
                                                                    Request.Url.Scheme)));
            }

            return View();
}
```

3. Add the Exchange action method, as shown in Listing 13-3. Note the following points.

   a. In the Exchange action method, the `ProcessUserAuthorization` method of the `WebServerClient` object is called to get the access token as well as the refresh token.

   b. Refreshing the access token that is about to expire or has already expired is just a single line of code. The `RefreshAuthorization` method of the `WebServerClient` object refreshes the tokens. The second parameter of this method takes in a `TimeSpan`, which is the cutoff based on which token is refreshed. If the remaining lifetime of the access token exceeds this `TimeSpan`, the token will not be refreshed.

   c. Once the access token is obtained, the call to the web API is the same as how it was done in the previous chapter; that is, pass the token in the authorization header in the bearer scheme.

Listing 13-3. Exchange Action Method

```
public ActionResult Exchange()
{
            var authorization = client.ProcessUserAuthorization();
            if (authorization != null)
            {
                if (authorization.AccessTokenExpirationUtc.HasValue)
                    client.RefreshAuthorization(authorization, TimeSpan.FromSeconds(30));

                string token = authorization.AccessToken;

                string result = String.Empty;
                using (HttpClient httpClient = new HttpClient())
                {
                    httpClient.DefaultRequestHeaders.Authorization = new
                                            AuthenticationHeaderValue("Bearer", token);
                    var apiResponse = httpClient.GetAsync(
                    "http://www.my-contacts.com/contacts/api/contacts").Result;
```

```
                        if (apiResponse.IsSuccessStatusCode)
                        {
                            result = apiResponse.Content.ReadAsStringAsync().Result;

                            var contacts = JsonConvert.DeserializeObject<IEnumerable<Contact>>
                                                                                    (result);

                            return View(contacts);
                        }
                    }
                }

                return View();
        }
```

4. Because we replaced the custom code in the controller with equivalent DNOA calls, the views remain the same as the ones in Chapter 12, so I don't repeat the views here. Copy the `Contact` class and two views—Home/Index view (`Index.cshtml`) and Home/Exchange view (`Exchange.cshtml`)—from the previous chapter into the `Models` folder and `Views\Home` folder, respectively, to complete the MyPromo project.

In contrast to the ground-up implementation in Chapter 12, where we dealt with the nuts and bolts of OAuth 2.0 using HTTP, DNOA provides a great class here: `WebServerClient`. If you think about the overall authorization code grant flow, a client needs to request user authorization and process the authorization to obtain a token. That is what happens with the call to `RequestUserAuthorization()` and then `ProcessUserAuthorization()`.

Building the Authorization Server

The authorization server includes two logical components: (1) the façade provided by `OAuth20Controller` in terms of the endpoints for requesting an authorization code and the access token, and (2) the DNOA-specific classes powering our authorization server from behind the scenes. The process of building the preceding two components can be broken down into the following steps.

1. Creating the infrastructure classes needed by DNOA to manage the client, client authorizations, and so on.
2. Creating the `IAuthorizationServerHost` implementation.
3. Creating the `OAuth20Controller` class. DNOA requires two endpoints specified in the authorization server, one for authorization and one for getting the token. We used the URI `www.my-contacts.com/contacts/OAuth20` in the previous chapter. We retain that as the authorization endpoint and use `www.my-contacts.com/contacts/OAuth20/Token` as the endpoint for token issuance. The two action methods, `Index` and `Token`, of `OAuth20Controller` represent the two endpoints.
4. Securing the endpoints exposed by `OAuth20Controller` by implementing forms authentication using another MVC controller, `AuthenticationController`.

Creating the Infrastructure

The first step in building the authorization server with DNOA is creating the infrastructure for the DNOA classes to store and retrieve the client details, authorizations by the client, the associated authorization codes, and the cryptographic keys to encrypt and sign authorization codes and refresh tokens.

Design

I have a singleton class, `DataStore`, acting as the façade of the other infrastructure classes. Figure 13-3 shows the class diagram generated by Visual Studio for `DataStore` and the two infrastructure classes related to the client details and the authorizations granted by the resource owners, namely `Client` and `ClientAuthorization`.

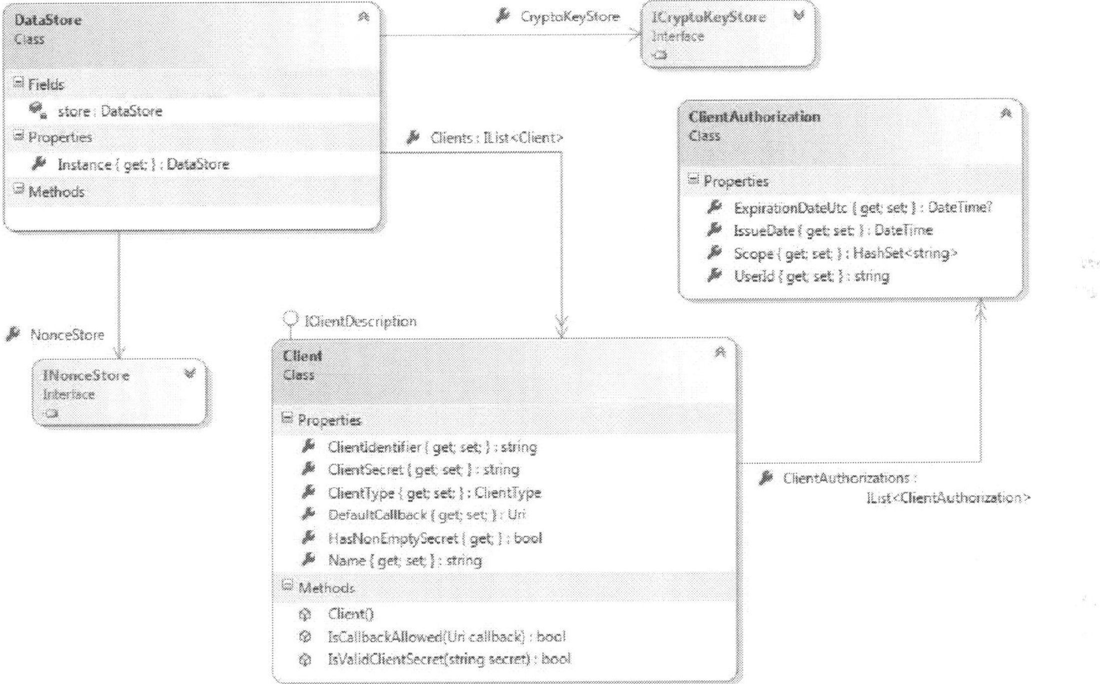

***Figure 13-3.** Infrastructure classes*

`DataStore` has a list of `Client` with each of these objects representing a client application. In our case, Promotions Manager is the only client application. The `Client` class implements the `IClientDescription` interface provided by DNOA. `Client` has a list of `ClientAuthorization`, with each instance of this class representing a user authorization against which a token is issued.

`DataStore` has two properties of type `ICryptoStore` and `INonceStore`, respectively. The implementations for these interfaces that are provided by DNOA are `CryptoKeyStore` and `NonceStore` classes, respectively. `NonceStore` stores `Nonce` objects and `CryptoKeyStore` stores `SymmetricCryptoKey` objects, as shown in Figure 13-4. These classes are used by DNOA classes internally in the OAuth 2.0 flow. `CryptoKeyStore` represents the store for storing crypto keys used to symmetrically encrypt and sign authorization codes and refresh tokens. `NonceStore` represents the store for storing authorization codes. The purpose of this store is to ensure authorization codes are used only once. A nonce is a number used once.

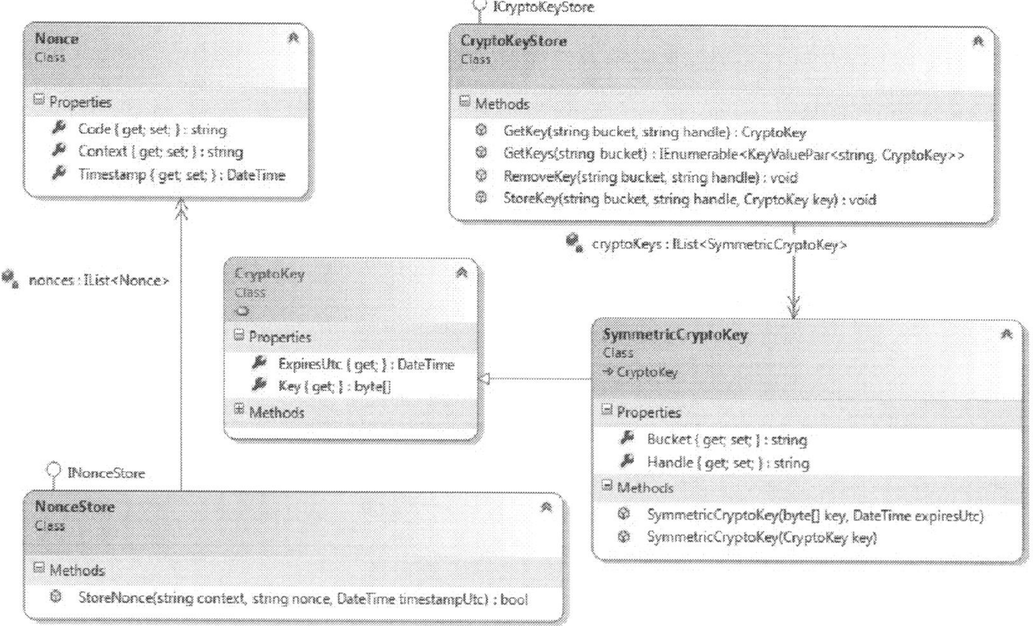

Figure 13-4. *Nonce and Crypto Stores*

Implementing the Infrastructure Classes

The following steps show how to implement the classes covered in the previous section. All classes in this section will be created in the `Store` folder under the `Infrastructure` folder.

1. Create the folder `Infrastructure` and the child folder `Store`.

2. Create the `DataStore` class, as shown in Listing 13-4. It has a static reference to an object of type `DataStore` and all access is through the `Instance` property, making this a singleton. It has a list of `Client` objects. Currently, the list has one `Client` object representing Promotions Manager.

Listing 13-4. DataStore

```
public class DataStore
{
    private static DataStore store = null;

    static DataStore()
    {
        store = new DataStore();
    }

    private DataStore()
    {
        this.Clients = new List<Client>();
        this.CryptoKeyStore = new CryptoKeyStore();
        this.NonceStore = new NonceStore();
```

```
        this.Clients.Add(
                    new Client()
                    {
                        Name = "My Promotion Manager",
                        ClientIdentifier = "0123456789",
                        ClientSecret = "TXVtJ3MgdGhlIHdvcmQhISE=",
                        DefaultCallback = new Uri("http://www.my-promo.com/promo"),
                        ClientType = ClientType.Confidential
                    });
    }

    public static DataStore Instance
    {
        get
        {
            return store;
        }
    }


    public IList<Client> Clients { get; set; }

    public ICryptoKeyStore CryptoKeyStore { get; set; }
    public INonceStore NonceStore { get; set; }
}
```

3. Create the `ClientAuthorization` class, as shown in Listing 13-5. An authorization is given by the user for a scope. Hence, `ClientAuthorization` has these two properties: `UserId` and Scope. In our example, we deal with one scope only but there can be multiple scopes. For this reason, scope is defined as `HashSet<string>`. No duplicates are allowed.

Listing 13-5. ClientAuthorization Class

```
public class ClientAuthorization
{
    public DateTime IssueDate { get; set; }

    public string UserId { get; set; }

    public HashSet<string> Scope { get; set; }

    public Nullable<DateTime> ExpirationDateUtc { get; set; }
}
```

4. `ClientAuthorization` cannot exist without a `Client`. There will be multiple authorizations against a `Client`. Create the `Client` class, as shown in Listing 13-6. `Client` implements `IClientDescription`, an interface provided by DNOA. Following are the points to note about this class.

a. A redirect URI provided by the client application (Promotion Manager, in our case) while making the requests is passed to the IsCallbackAllowed method for you to verify if the URI is valid and acceptable. The host, port, and scheme (HTTP/HTTPS) of the incoming URI is compared against the default callback registered against the client in the DataStore class. It is up to you to implement the logic here based on how lenient or how rigid you want to be with respect to checking the redirect URI coming in the requests.

b. The property HasNonEmptySecret and the method IsValidClientSecret are plain vanilla implementations. The code itself is self-explanatory. DNOA calls these methods at various times to make sure the request is valid.

Listing 13-6. Client Class

```
public class Client : IClientDescription
{
    public string ClientIdentifier { get; set; }

    public string ClientSecret { get; set; }

    public Uri DefaultCallback { get; set; }

    public string Name { get; set; }

    public ClientType ClientType { get; set; }

    public IList<ClientAuthorization> ClientAuthorizations { get; set; }

    public Client()
    {
        this.ClientAuthorizations = new List<ClientAuthorization>();
    }

    public bool HasNonEmptySecret
    {
        get { return !string.IsNullOrEmpty(this.ClientSecret); }
    }

    public bool IsCallbackAllowed(Uri callback)
    {
        return callback.Scheme == this.DefaultCallback.Scheme &&
                    callback.Host == this.DefaultCallback.Host &&
                        callback.Port == this.DefaultCallback.Port;
    }

    public bool IsValidClientSecret(string secret)
    {
        return MessagingUtilities.EqualsConstantTime(secret, this.ClientSecret);
    }
}
```

5. Create the Nonce class, as shown in Listing 13-7. Nonce represents the authorization code generated by the authorization server. For subsequent validation, Nonce is stored in a NonceStore.

Listing 13-7. Nonce Class

```
public class Nonce
{
    public string Context { get; set; }

    public string Code { get; set; }

    public DateTime Timestamp { get; set; }
}
```

6. Create the NonceStore class, as shown in Listing 13-8. By virtue of implementing the INonceStore interface, NonceStore implements the StoreNonce method. When DNOA calls this method with a nonce, context, and timestamp that is not already present, we insert and return true. When this combination is already present, we return false and DNOA rejects the request because it could be a replay attack.

Listing 13-8. NonceStore and Nonce Classes

```
public class NonceStore : INonceStore
{
    private IList<Nonce> nonces = new List<Nonce>();

    public bool StoreNonce(string context, string nonce, DateTime timestampUtc)
    {
        if (nonces.Any(n => n.Context == context &&
                                            n.Code == nonce &&
                                                 n.Timestamp == timestampUtc))
            return false; // Possibly a replay attack, return false
        else
        {
            Nonce newNonce = new Nonce { Context = context, Code = nonce, Timestamp = timestampUtc };

            nonces.Add(newNonce);
            return true;
        }
    }
}
```

Caution While exchanging the authorization code for a token, the older versions of DNOA send two requests: one without the credential resulting in 401 – Unauthorized, followed by the request with credentials. For this reason, the *StoreNonce* method in the class implementing *INonceStore* (Listing 13-8) gets called twice in the implementations using the older versions of DNOA. Our current logic would fail the second request, assuming it is a replay. Ensure you use the latest version of DNOA.

---

7. Create the SymmetricCryptoKey class, as shown in Listing 13-9. The SymmetricCryptoKey class inherits the CryptoKey class provided by DNOA and, by virtue of inheritance, gets the Key and ExpiresUtc properties. Because symmetric keys are shared between two parties, DNOA changes them periodically. ExpiresUtc is important from that perspective. ExpiresUtc defines the lifetime of a key, after which a key is discarded and a new one is generated by DNOA.

   Listing 13-9. SymmetricCryptoKey Class

```
public class SymmetricCryptoKey : CryptoKey
{
    public SymmetricCryptoKey(byte[] key, DateTime expiresUtc) : base(key, expiresUtc) {
}

    public SymmetricCryptoKey(CryptoKey key) : base(key.Key, key.ExpiresUtc) { }

    public string Bucket { get; set; }

    public string Handle { get; set; }
}
```

8. Create the CryptoKeyStore class, as shown in Listing 13-10. DNOA uses symmetric keys to encrypt and sign authorization codes and refresh tokens. These keys are stored in the crypto key store, an object implementing ICryptoKeyStore. DNOA calls the methods defined in this interface to store and retrieve keys.

Listing 13-10. CryptoKeyStore Class

```
public class CryptoKeyStore : ICryptoKeyStore
{
    private IList<SymmetricCryptoKey> cryptoKeys = new List<SymmetricCryptoKey>();

    public CryptoKey GetKey(string bucket, string handle)
    {
        return cryptoKeys.Where(k => k.Bucket == bucket && k.Handle == handle).FirstOrDefault();
    }

    public IEnumerable<KeyValuePair<string, CryptoKey>> GetKeys(string bucket)
    {
        return cryptoKeys.Where(k => k.Bucket == bucket)
                    .OrderByDescending(o => o.ExpiresUtc)
```

```
                  .Select(kvp => new KeyValuePair<string, CryptoKey>(kvp.Handle, kvp));
    }

    public void RemoveKey(string bucket, string handle)
    {
        var key = cryptoKeys.FirstOrDefault(k => k.Bucket == bucket && k.Handle == handle);
        if (key != null)
            cryptoKeys.Remove(key);
    }

    public void StoreKey(string bucket, string handle, CryptoKey key)
    {
        cryptoKeys.Add(new SymmetricCryptoKey(key) { Bucket = bucket, Handle = handle });
    }
}
```

With this, we have completed the implementation of classes that are needed by DNOA to issue authorization codes and tokens. DNOA classes call our classes as part of the OAuth 2.0 flow.

Creating the IAuthorizationServerHost Implementation

All the infrastructure classes that we have seen so far—`Client`, `ClientAuthorization`, `CryptoKeyStore`, and `NonceStore`—are all brought together by one class, the `ServerHost` class that implements the `IAuthorizationServerHost` interface. `ServerHost` does all the heavy lifting related to dealing with the infrastructure classes.

The `AuthorizationServer` class provided by DNOA is the underpinning of the server side OAuth. We have seen `WebServerClient` in action in the client side. The server-side equivalent of the `WebServerClient` is `AuthorizationServer`. To instantiate `AuthorizationServer`, an instance of `ServerHost` is needed. The `CryptoKeyStore` and `NonceStore` infrastructure classes are available to DNOA through the properties exposed by the `IAuthorizationServerHost` interface. The following steps show how to build the `ServerHost` class.

1. Create a class `ServerHost` in the `Infrastructure` folder, as shown in Listing 13-11.
    a. Implement `CryptoKeyStore` and `NonceStore` properties returning the corresponding properties of our infrastructure façade `DataStore`.
    b. I chose not to implement the `TryAuthorizeClientCredentialsGrant`, `TryAuthorizeResourceOwnerCredentialGrant`, `CheckAuthorizeClientCredentialsGrant`, and `CheckAuthorizeResourceOwnerCredentialGrant` methods of the `IAuthorizationServerHost` interface because these methods are not relevant for the authorization code grant.
    c. Implement the `GetClient` method to return the `Client` object corresponding to the incoming client ID from the list of clients maintained in the `DataStore`.

Listing 13-11. ServerHost Class (Partially Implemented)

```
public class ServerHost : IAuthorizationServerHost
{
    public ICryptoKeyStore CryptoKeyStore
    {
```

```
        get { return DataStore.Instance.CryptoKeyStore; }
    }

    public INonceStore NonceStore
    {
        get { return DataStore.Instance.NonceStore; }
    }

    public IClientDescription GetClient(string clientIdentifier)
    {
        return DataStore.Instance.Clients.First(c => c.ClientIdentifier == clientIdentifier);
    }

    public bool TryAuthorizeClientCredentialsGrant(IAccessTokenRequest accessRequest)
    {
        throw new NotImplementedException();
    }

    public bool TryAuthorizeResourceOwnerCredentialGrant(string userName, string password,
                                                         IAccessTokenRequest accessRequest,
                                                             out string canonicalUserName)
    {
        throw new NotImplementedException();
    }

    public AutomatedAuthorizationCheckResponse CheckAuthorizeClientCredentialsGrant(
                                                         IAccessTokenRequest accessRequest)
    {
        throw new NotImplementedException();
    }

    public AutomatedUserAuthorizationCheckResponse
                                                  CheckAuthorizeResourceOwnerCredentialGrant(
                                                      string userName, string password,
                                                      IAccessTokenRequest accessRequest)
    {
        throw new NotImplementedException();
    }
}
```

2. Implement the `IsAuthorizationValid` method, as shown in Listing 13-12. Look for a client authorization that has not expired yet, with the user ID matching the incoming user ID. Ensure the scope list requested is a subset of the scopes granted by the user for this matching authorization. In our example scenario it is just one scope, yet the code is future-proof to handle multiple scopes.

Listing 13-12. IsAuthorizationValid Method

```
public bool IsAuthorizationValid(IAuthorizationDescription authorization)
{
    var client = DataStore.Instance.Clients
                                .First(c => c.ClientIdentifier ==
                                                    authorization.ClientIdentifier);

    var authorizations = client.ClientAuthorizations
                                .Where(a => a.UserId == authorization.User &&
                                        a.IssueDate <=
                                              authorization.UtcIssued.AddSeconds(1) &&
                                        (!a.ExpirationDateUtc.HasValue ||
                                              a.ExpirationDateUtc.Value >=
                                                        DateTime.UtcNow));
    if (!authorizations.Any()) // No authorizations
        return false;

    var grantedScopes = new HashSet<string>();
    authorizations.ToList().ForEach(a => grantedScopes.UnionWith(a.Scope));

    return authorization.Scope.IsSubsetOf(grantedScopes);
}
```

3. Implement the CreateAccessToken method that creates the token, which will be signed and encrypted, as shown in Listing 13-13. We will use X.509 certificates to provide us with the public-private key pairs for this purpose. The token will be signed with the private key of the authorization server and encrypted with the public key of the resource server. The X.509 certificate corresponding to the authorization server will contain both public and private keys in the server running the authorization server. In the server running the resource server, the same authorization server certificate will contain only the public key. This is just the opposite for the resource server certificate. Figure 13-5 shows the keys distribution in a typical production environment. However, I use the same machine for running both servers and hence both certificates with both keys are present on my computer.

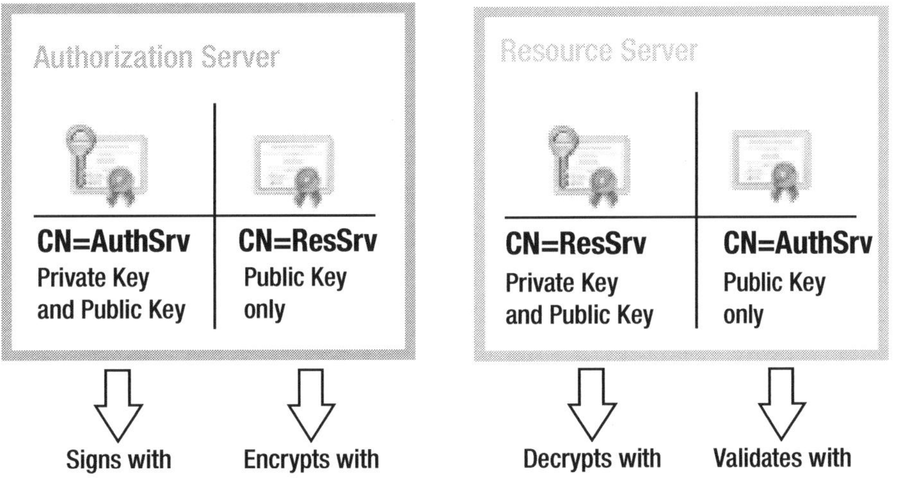

Figure 13-5. *Signing and encryption keys distribution*

Listing 13-13. CreateAccessToken Method

```
public AccessTokenResult CreateAccessToken(IAccessTokenRequest request)
{
        var accessToken = new AuthorizationServerAccessToken();
        accessToken.Lifetime = TimeSpan.FromMinutes(2);

        // Using the certificate of our one and only resource server blindly
        accessToken.ResourceServerEncryptionKey = (RSACryptoServiceProvider)WebApiApplication
                                                        .EncryptionCertificate.PublicKey.Key;

        accessToken.AccessTokenSigningKey = (RSACryptoServiceProvider)WebApiApplication
                                                             .SigningCertificate.PrivateKey;

        var result = new AccessTokenResult(accessToken);
        return result;
    }
```

One more point to note about the `CreateAccessToken()` method is that, because we have only one resource server in the form of the contacts manager, I blindly return the key corresponding to it. If one authorization server serves multiple resource servers, the certificate corresponding to the resource server for which the token is being requested must be used. For this purpose, DNOA passes in an object of type `IAccessTokenRequest` for us to inspect.

4. Define the keys needed by the `CreateAccessToken` method at the application level as static properties in `Global.asax.cs`, as shown in Listing 13-14.

Listing 13-14. Global.asax.cs: WebApiApplication

```
public class WebApiApplication : System.Web.HttpApplication
{
    private static X509Certificate2 signingCertificate = "CN=AuthSrv".ToCertificate();
    private static X509Certificate2 encryptionCertificate = "CN=ResSrv".ToCertificate();

    public static X509Certificate2 SigningCertificate
    {
        get
        {
            return signingCertificate;
        }
    }

    public static X509Certificate2 EncryptionCertificate
    {
        get
        {
            return encryptionCertificate;
        }
    }
```

```
    protected void Application_Start()
    {
        ...
    }
}
```

X.509 certificates corresponding to the subject names CN=AuthSrv and CN=ResSrv are generated using the Makecert tool, as we saw in Chapter 6. The extension method that returns the `X509Certificate2` object from the subject name string is also from Chapter 6. Copy this class into the `Helpers` folder.

RUNNING THE APPLICATION IN IIS

If you are deploying the applications in IIS, our application will have difficulty accessing the private keys of the certificates. You will need to give the IIS application pool account access to the private keys of both certificates.

On my machine, I use the default application pool. I have given access to the private keys to IIS_IUSRS group, which is the built-in group used by IIS.

To give access to private keys, use the following steps.

1. Use Microsoft Management Console (MMC). You can launch MMC by typing mmc in the Run box.
2. Select File ➤ Add/Remove snap-in.
3. On the left side of Available snap-ins, select the Certificates snap-in and click Add.
4. Select Computer account, local computer to see the certificates on your computer.
5. Locate the certificate under Personal ➤ Certificates. Right-click the certificate and select Manage Private Keys . . . in the shortcut menu and add the user account, as shown in Figure 13-6.

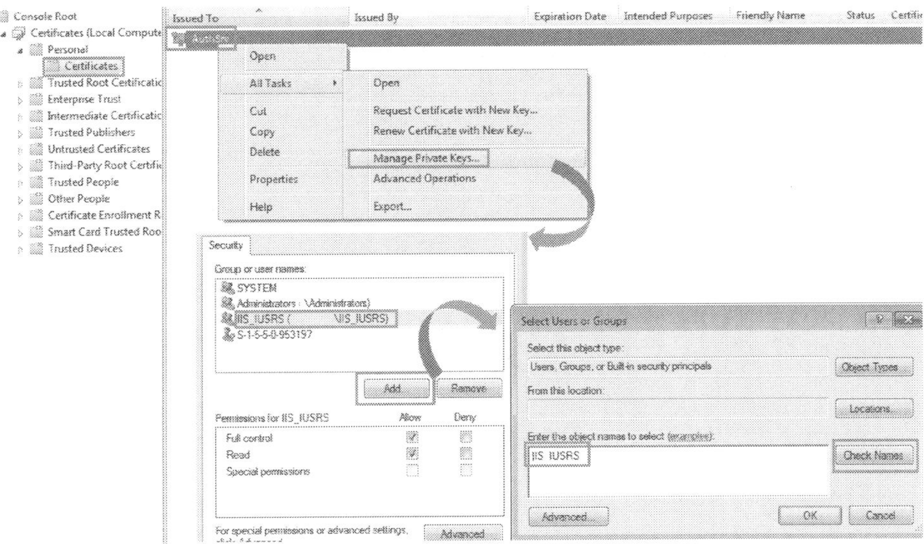

Figure 13-6. Providing access to private keys through MMC

Creating OAuth20Controller

`OAuth20Controller` has `Index` and `Token` action methods representing the authorization and token issuance endpoints, respectively. There are three action methods in the controller.

1. **Index action method that handles HTTP GET**: This action method handles the redirect request, which is the first step of the authorization code grant flow. The view that this action method returns is the authorization page where a user consents to share the protected resource, which in our scenario is the contact information.
2. **Index action method that handles HTTP POST**: This action method handles the form post triggered by the user clicking the Yes or No button on the authorization page. If the user consents to share, this action method returns an authorization code in the query string of the redirect URI.
3. **Token action method**: This action method returns the access token.

The following steps show how to create the `OAuth20Controller` class.

1. Unlike the `OAuth20Controller` that we saw in Chapter 12 that dealt with the nuts and bolts, this controller will be simple because it uses the `AuthorizationServer` class provided by DNOA. An instance of `AuthorizationServer` is created by passing in an instance of the `ServerHost` class that we saw in the preceding subsection. Create a new MVC controller, as shown in Listing 13-15.

   Listing 13-15. OAuth20Controller

```
public class OAuth20Controller : Controller
{
    private readonly AuthorizationServer server = new AuthorizationServer
    (new ServerHost());

    // Action methods go here
}
```

2. Add the `Index` action method that handles HTTP GET. Read the authorization request by calling the `ReadAuthorizationRequest()` method on the `AuthorizationServer` instance. Create an instance of the view model `AuthorizationRequest` and send that to the view for rendering. See Listing 13-16. Pay attention to the `Authorize` filter applied to this action method. I cover the details related to this in the next section.

   Listing 13-16. Index Action Method (HTTP GET)

```
[Authorize]
public ActionResult Index()
{
    var request = this.server.ReadAuthorizationRequest();
    if (request == null)
        throw new HttpException((int)HttpStatusCode.BadRequest, "Bad request");

    var model = new AuthorizationRequest
    {
        ClientApp = DataStore.Instance.Clients
                        .First(c => c.ClientIdentifier == request.ClientIdentifier).Name,
        Scope = request.Scope,
```

```
            Request = request,
        };

        return View(model);
    }
```

3. Create the `AuthorizationRequest` view model class in the `Models` folder. See Listing 13-17.

Listing 13-17. AuthorizationRequest View Model

```
public class AuthorizationRequest
{
    public string ClientApp { get; set; }

    public HashSet<string> Scope { get; set; }

    public EndUserAuthorizationRequest Request { get; set; }
}
```

4. Create the view corresponding to the Index action method, as shown in Listing 13-18.

Listing 13-18. Index View Index.cshtml: View of /OAuth20/Index

```
@model MyContacts.Models.AuthorizationRequest

@{
    ViewBag.Title = "Sharing";
}

<h2>Would you like to share the MyContacts application data with @Model.ClientApp?</h2>
<div>
    <b>To be Shared: </b>
    @String.Join(" ", Model.Scope.ToArray())
</div>

@using (Html.BeginForm())
{
    @Html.Hidden("client_id", Model.Request.ClientIdentifier)
    @Html.Hidden("redirect_uri", Model.Request.Callback)
    @Html.Hidden("state", Model.Request.ClientState)
    @Html.Hidden("scope", DotNetOpenAuth.OAuth2.OAuthUtilities.JoinScopes(Model.Request.Scope))
    @Html.Hidden("response_type", "code")
    <br />
        <input type="submit" name="userApproval" value="Yes"/>
}

Go back to <a href="http://www.my-promo.com/promo">Promotion Manager</a>
```

5. The AuthorizationRequest view model is rendered by the view in Step 4. The resulting screen, which is the authorization screen, asks the user for consent to share the data listing the scopes in the request. When the user clicks the Yes or No button, the HTML form is posted to /OAuth20/Index with the response_type of code. Create the Index action method to handle this POST, as shown in Listing 13-19. The following steps constitute the processing that happens in this method.

    a. Read the request using the ReadAuthorizationRequest method of the AuthorizationServer instance.

    b. If the user agrees to share data by clicking Yes, the userApproval parameter of the action method will be nonempty. Based on this parameter, store the authorization against the user and the client, respectively John Q. Human (jqhuman) and the Promotion Manager web application.

    c. If the user agrees to share the protected resource of the contact information, call the PrepareApproveAuthorizationRequest method on the AuthorizationServer instance.

    d. The message thus prepared is passed into the PrepareResponse method and ultimately the ActionResult object is sent back. The response thus sent contains the authorization code.

    e. WebServerClient, which we used in the client side from the Promotion Manager HomeController, retrieves this code and makes a request to /OAuth20/Token to exchange the code for an access token.

Listing 13-19. Index Action Method (HTTP POST)

```
[Authorize, HttpPost]
public ActionResult Index(string userApproval)
{
    var request = this.server.ReadAuthorizationRequest();
    if (request == null)
        throw new HttpException((int)HttpStatusCode.BadRequest, "Bad request");

    if (!String.IsNullOrWhiteSpace(userApproval))
    {
        // Record the authorization against the client and user
        DataStore.Instance.Clients
            .First(c => c.ClientIdentifier == request.ClientIdentifier)
                .ClientAuthorizations.Add(
                    new ClientAuthorization
                    {
                        Scope = request.Scope,
                        UserId = User.Identity.Name,
                        IssueDate = DateTime.UtcNow
                    });

        var response = this.server.PrepareApproveAuthorizationRequest(request,
                                                                      User.Identity.Name);
```

```
            return this.server.Channel.PrepareResponse(response).AsActionResult();
        }

        return View();
    }
```

6. Create the Token action method, as shown in Listing 13-20. From the Token action method, just call the HandleTokenRequest method on the AuthorizationServer instance. DNOA takes care of minting the token and sending it back to the client.

Listing 13-20. Token Action Method

```
public ActionResult Token()
{
    return this.server.HandleTokenRequest(this.Request).AsActionResult();
}
```

Thus, we have added the endpoints of our authorization server, realized through the action methods of OAuth20Controller. Currently, they are secured through the Authorize attribute but they are not fully functional because there is one more piece that is missing, which we will see in the next section.

Securing the OAuth20Controller Endpoints

We secure the MyContacts project, including the OAuth20Controller, through forms authentication. Make an entry in the Web.config file, as shown in Listing 13-21.

Listing 13-21. Web.config with Forms Authentication Enabled

```
<system.web>
    <!--<authentication mode="None" />-->
    <authentication mode="Forms">
        <forms name=".MyContacts" protection="All" cookieless="UseCookies" loginUrl="Authentication" />
    </authentication>
    ...
</sytem.web>
```

When an action method is decorated with the Authorize attribute, a 401 – Unauthorized response gets generated. But FormsAuthenticationModule captures this and redirects the browser to the login URL specified in the configuration file. In this case, the login URL is specified as Authentication, which is /Authentication/Index. Listing 13-22 shows the corresponding controller class, AuthenticationController.

Listing 13-22. AuthenticationController

```
public class AuthenticationController : Controller
{
    [HttpGet]
    public ActionResult Index()
    {
        return View();
    }

    [HttpPost]
```

```
    public ActionResult Index(string userId, string password, string returnUrl)
    {
        bool isAuthentic = !String.IsNullOrWhiteSpace(userId) && userId.Equals(password);

        if(isAuthentic)
            FormsAuthentication.SetAuthCookie(userId, false);

        return Redirect(returnUrl ?? Url.Action("Index", "Home"));
    }
}
```

The Index action for GET just renders the view, the screen where a user can enter login credentials and click the Sign In button. The post back is handled by the Index action with the HttpPost attribute. As with the other places, authentication is just a check to make sure the user ID and password are the same, for the purpose of illustration. If that condition is satisfied, a forms authentication ticket is created and written into a cookie. Listing 13-23 shows the view corresponding to the Index action. The names of the text boxes match the parameter names of the Index action method.

Listing 13-23. Index View

```
@{
    ViewBag.Title = "Sign In";
}

<h2>Sign In</h2>

@using (Html.BeginForm())
{
    <div class="editor-label">
        @Html.Label("userId")
    </div>
    <div class="editor-field">
        @Html.TextBox("userId")
    </div>

    <div class="editor-label">
        @Html.Label("password")
    </div>
    <div class="editor-field">
        @Html.Password("password")
    </div>
    <input type="submit" value="Sign In" />
}
```

Forms authentication thus implemented ensures that the user is authenticated as the Promotion Manager application redirects the browser to the resource server; that is, the action methods of OAuth20Controller. The Token action method is not explicitly protected by forms authentication. Since the exchange for the authorization code to the token will be made by the server side of the client application, which will not share the cookie containing the ticket, this action method cannot be protected explicitly. However, it is implicitly protected because a valid authorization code is needed to get a token and a valid code can be obtained only by going to the forms authentication secured endpoints.

Building the Resource Server

The resource server remains the same as what we saw in Chapter 12. The access token is passed in the HTTP authorization request header using the bearer scheme. The `ClaimsPrincipal` object is created based on the token and set to `Thread.CurrentPrincipal` by a message handler.

The `ApiController` action method is decorated with the `ClaimsPrincipalPermission` attribute, and authorization is based on the true or false returned by the `ClaimsAuthorizationManager` subclass. You can plug this class into the claims processing pipeline by making an entry in Web.config.

To summarize, the resource server in action is exactly the same as the resource server we saw in Chapter 12, so I do not repeat those steps here. However, in Chapter 12 the token issued was a JSON Web Token and here the access token is created by DNOA. We need to use the `ResourceServer` class provided by DNOA to read the token.

The `OAuthTokenHandler` class that does this activity is shown in Listing 13-24. In contrast to how we used the keys in the authorization server side (the private key of the signing certificate and the public key of the encryption certificate), we use the public key of the signing certificate and the private key of the encryption certificate to read the token in the resource server.

■ **Note** Copy the classes `ContactsController`, `Contact`, and `AuthorizationManager` from Chapter 12 and modify Web.config to plug `AuthorizationManager` into the pipeline. Also, add `OAuthTokenHandler` to the handlers collection in `WebApiConfig.cs` in the `App_Start` folder to complete the MyContacts project.

Listing 13-24. OAuthTokenHandler

```
public class OAuthTokenHandler : DelegatingHandler
{
        protected override async Task<HttpResponseMessage> SendAsync(HttpRequestMessage request,
                                                            CancellationToken cancellationToken)

        {
            try
            {
                var headers = request.Headers;
                if (headers.Authorization != null)
                {
                    if (headers.Authorization.Scheme.Equals("Bearer"))
                    {
                        string accessToken = request.Headers.Authorization.Parameter;

                        ResourceServer server = new ResourceServer(
                                        new StandardAccessTokenAnalyzer(
                                               (RSACryptoServiceProvider)
                                                      WebApiApplication.SigningCertificate
                                                            .PublicKey.Key,
                                               (RSACryptoServiceProvider)
                                                      WebApiApplication.EncryptionCertificate
                                                            .PrivateKey
                                        )
                                    );

                        OAuthPrincipal principal = server.GetPrincipal() as OAuthPrincipal;
```

```
                    if (principal != null && principal.Identity != null &&
                                                     principal.Identity.IsAuthenticated)
                    {
                        var claims = new List<Claim>();

                        foreach (string scope in principal.Roles)
                            claims.Add(new Claim(
                            "http://www.my-contacts.com/contacts/OAuth20/claims/scope", scope));

                        claims.Add(new Claim(ClaimTypes.Name, principal.Identity.Name));

                        var identity = new ClaimsIdentity(claims, "Bearer");

                        var newPrincipal = new ClaimsPrincipal(identity);

                        Thread.CurrentPrincipal = newPrincipal;

                        if (HttpContext.Current != null)
                            HttpContext.Current.User = newPrincipal;
                    }
                }
            }

            var response = await base.SendAsync(request, cancellationToken);

            if (response.StatusCode == HttpStatusCode.Unauthorized)
            {
                response.Headers.WwwAuthenticate.Add(
                            new AuthenticationHeaderValue("Bearer",
                                "error=\"invalid_token\""));
            }

            return response;
        }
        catch (Exception)
        {
            var response = request.CreateResponse(HttpStatusCode.Unauthorized);

            response.Headers.WwwAuthenticate.Add(
                    new AuthenticationHeaderValue("Bearer", "error=\"invalid_token\""));

            return response;
        }
    }
}
```

To test the application, you can run the MyPromo project directly from Visual Studio, but change the URL in the Internet Explorer address bar from `http://localhost/Promo/` to `http://www.my-promo.com/promo` because this is the callback URL we have registered with `DataStore`.

■ **Note** In the code we saw in this chapter, some of the security-related aspects such as clickjacking mitigation and use of antiforgery tokens that are used in the DNOA samples have been removed to keep the focus on OAuth. If you plan to build production code based on the examples from this chapter, you will need to include those protections. Please do review the DNOA samples from `https://github.com/DotNetOpenAuth/DotNetOpenAuth`.

Implicit Grant

With the authorization code grant implemented using DNOA, it is quite easy now to implement an implicit grant. The authorization and resource server pieces will remain the same. Only the client will be different. An implicit grant is for client-side applications such as JavaScript executing within the context of a web browser. The following steps show how to implement an implicit grant flow.

1. Although it is possible to use just static HTML to illustrate an implicit grant, I'll use ASP.NET MVC. We just need to add an additional action method to `HomeController` in the MyPromo project, as shown in Listing 13-25.

   Listing 13-25. Action Method in HomeController for an Implicit Grant

   ```
   public ActionResult Implicit()
   {
       return View();
   }
   ```

2. The `Implicit()` action method does nothing much, as expected. Because this is an implicit grant, we will have all the code in JavaScript. The view corresponding to the `Implicit()` action method is shown in Listing 13-26. Add the view by right-clicking the action method in Visual Studio and selecting Add View on the shortcut menu.

   Listing 13-26. View Corresponding to the Implicit Action Method

   ```
   @{
       ViewBag.Title = "Implicit Grant";
   }

   <h2>Welcome to My Promotion Manager! (Implicit Grant)</h2>

   Click the 'Get Contacts' button to import your contacts.<br />
   <br />

   @using (Html.BeginForm())
   {
       <input type="button" id="btnGo" name="go" value="Get Contacts" style="width: 150px;
                                                                          height: 100px;" />
   }
   <br />
   <div id="result" style="display:none">
       <table id="contacts">
           <tr>
               <th></th>
   ```

```
                <th>Name</th>
                <th>Email</th>
            </tr>
        </table>
        <br />
        <input type="button" value="Spam them" />
    </div>

    @section scripts{
        <script src="@Url.Content("~/Scripts/implicitgrant.js")" type="text/javascript"></script>
    }
```

3. The view generates the HTML to show a big Go button, like the home page of the My Promo application we saw earlier. All the action happens in implicitgrant.js, shown in Listing 13-27. Add this file to the `Scripts` folder. When the Go button is clicked, the `getContacts()` function is called. This method formats a URL corresponding to the authorization endpoint we have been using in this chapter. It passes the client ID, a hard-coded scope of 'Read.Contacts,' and the redirect URI and response_type of `token` in the query string. For the authorization code grant, we used response_type of `code`. Finally, it sets the `document.location` to the URL it has just formatted.

Listing 13-27. Implictgrant.js

```
$(document).ready(function () {
    $('#btnGo').click(getContacts);

    var hashIndex = document.location.href.indexOf('#');
    if (hashIndex > 0) {
        // rest of the code goes here
    }
});

function getContacts(evt) {
    var url = 'http://www.my-contacts.com/contacts/OAuth20';
    url = url + '?client_id=0123456789';
    url = url + '&scope=Read.Contacts'; // hard-coded scope for illustration only
    url = url + '&redirect_uri=' + encodeURIComponent('http://www.my-promo.com/promo');
    url = url + ='&response_type=token';

    document.location = url;
};
```

4. At this point, the user is taken to the sign-in page and subsequently the page where the user consents to share the contacts. From an end-user perspective, the screen flow will be exactly the same as the authorization code grant flow. However, after the user consents to share the data, the authorization endpoint does not send the authorization code; instead, it sends the token itself in the redirect URI fragment.

5. The redirect URI is `http://www.my-promo.com/promo`, which is `/Home/Index`. However, our action method is `Implicit`. Just to keep things simple, we can tweak the `RouteConfig.cs` file in the `App_Start` folder to make the action method `Implicit` the default action method so that `http://www.my-promo.com/promo` corresponds to the `/Home/Implicit` action method. The correct way to do this is to change the server code to accommodate the new redirect URI, but that will be a bigger change that will take the focus away from the implicit grant flow. Hence, I'm opting to tweak `RouteConfig.cs`, as shown in Listing 13-28.

Listing 13-28. RouteConfig.cs

```
public class RouteConfig
{
    public static void RegisterRoutes(RouteCollection routes)
    {
        routes.IgnoreRoute("{resource}.axd/{*pathInfo}");

        // Change default action of "Index" to "Implicit" to test implicit grant flow
        routes.MapRoute(
            name: "Default",
            url: "{controller}/{action}/{id}",
            defaults: new { controller = "Home", action = "Implicit",
            id = UrlParameter.Optional }
        );
    }
}
```

6. As a result of this change, after the user clicks the button to consent to share the contacts, the `/Home/Implicit` action method is invoked and the corresponding view is rendered. As the browser renders the HTML, script from the file (`implicitgrant.js`) starts to execute (see Listing 13-29). First, we look for a hash in the URI and extract out the fragment, which happens to contain key value pairs. The key we are interested in is 'access_token', and the corresponding value is the access token.

Listing 13-29. Retrieving an Access Token

```
var fragment = document.location.href.substring(hashIndex + 1);
var accessToken = null;

var keyValuePairs = fragment.split('&');
for (var i = 0; i < keyValuePairs.length; i++) {
    var keyValue = keyValuePairs[i].split('=');
    var key = decodeURIComponent(keyValue[0]);
    if (key == 'access_token') {
        var value keyValue[1];
        accessToken = decodeURIComponent(value);
        break;
    }
};
```

7. At this point, the access token is visible in the address bar of the browser, which means the end user as well as the script code have access to the token. Contrasting this to the authorization code grant flow, only the authorization code is visible in the address bar and the server-side code ultimately exchanges it for a token without the user's knowledge. Once the token is extracted out of the URL fragment, we can just stuff the token in the authorization header using the bearer scheme and make the web API call from JavaScript. When the Web API JSON response is received, we use JQuery to build the HTML table, displaying the contacts. We use JQuery to call the My Contacts web API from the My Promo application. Clearly, this is a violation of the same origin policy and browsers will not tolerate it. To get around this, we have to use CORS. I'm using `$.support.cors = true;` to bypass the same origin check altogether for Internet Explorer, which is not good from a security standpoint. When you test this flow by running the application, Internet Explorer will warn you and ask for a confirmation to continue. I'm taking this shortcut for the purpose of brevity. The shortcut, however, will not work with other browsers such as Firefox. Production-strength code will use CORS and send the Access-Control-Allow-Origin response header that we saw in Chapter 4. See Listing 13-30.

Listing 13-30. Making the API Call

```
if (accessToken) {
    $.support.cors = true; // Allows cross-domain requests in case of Internet Explorer

    $.ajax({
        type: 'GET',
        url: 'http://www.my-contacts.com/contacts/api/contacts',
        dataType: 'json',
        contentType: 'application/json; charset=utf-8',
        headers: { 'Authorization=': ='Bearer ' + accessToken },
        success: function (data) {
            $('#result').show();
            $.each(data, function (i, contact) {
                $('#contacts').append($('<tr>')
                    .append($('<td>')
                        .append($('<input>')
                            .attr('type', 'checkbox')
                        )
                    )
                    .append($('<td>')
                        .text(contact.Name)
                    )
                    .append($('<td>')
                        .text(contact.Email)
                    )
                );
            });
        }
    });
}
```

8. One last thing remains. We have to make a minor modification to the Index view of OAuth20Controller to get this thing working. When we were building the authorization code grant, we hard-coded the value of code as the response_type in Listing 13-18. To make the same authorization endpoint work, we need to make a change, as shown in bold type in Listing 13-31, to choose the right response_type at runtime.

Listing 13-31. Change to the OAuth20/Index View

```
@model MyContacts.Models.AuthorizationRequest

@{
    ViewBag.Title = "Sharing";
}

<h2>Would you like to share the MyContacts application data with @Model.ClientApp?</h2>
<div>
       <b>To be Shared: </b>
       @String.Join(" ", Model.Scope.ToArray())
</div>

@{
    bool isImplictGrant = Model.Request.ResponseType ==
                               DotNetOpenAuth.OAuth2.Messages
                                      .EndUserAuthorizationResponseType
                                              .AccessToken;

    string responseType = isImplictGrant ? "token" : "code";
}

@using (Html.BeginForm())
{
    @Html.Hidden("client_id", Model.Request.ClientIdentifier)
    @Html.Hidden("redirect_uri", Model.Request.Callback)
    @Html.Hidden("state", Model.Request.ClientState)
    @Html.Hidden("scope", DotNetOpenAuth.OAuth2.OAuthUtilities.JoinScopes
                                                                     (Model.Request.Scope))
    @Html.Hidden("response_type", responseType)
    <br />
        <input type="submit" name="userApproval" value="Yes"/>
}

Go back to <a href="http://www.my-promo.com/promo">Promotion Manager</a>
```

To test this flow, navigate to `http://www.my-promo.com/promo`. Because we have the `Implicit` action method as the default method of `HomeController`, you will be shown the screen corresponding to the `Implicit` action. It is very similar to the `/Home/Index` screen. When you click the big Go button it triggers the implicit grant flow. Figure 13-7 shows the new screen displaying the contact information after the button click.

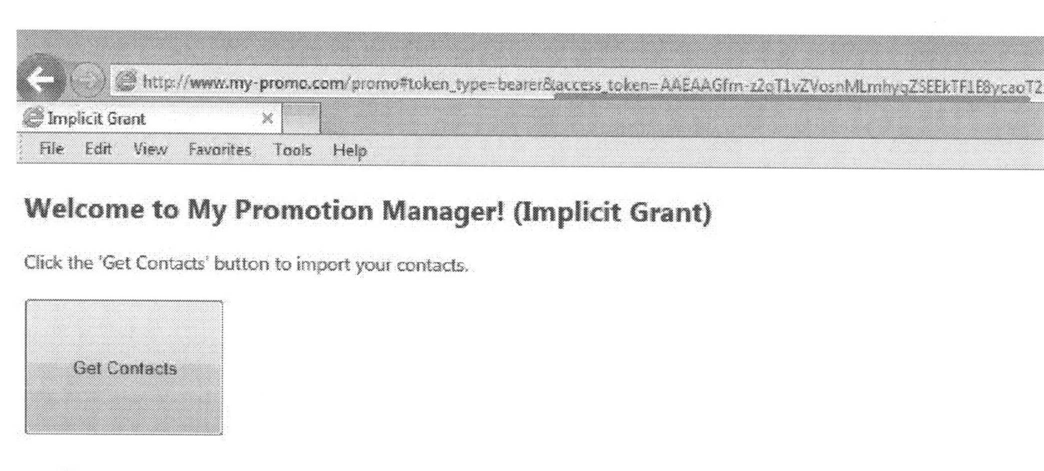

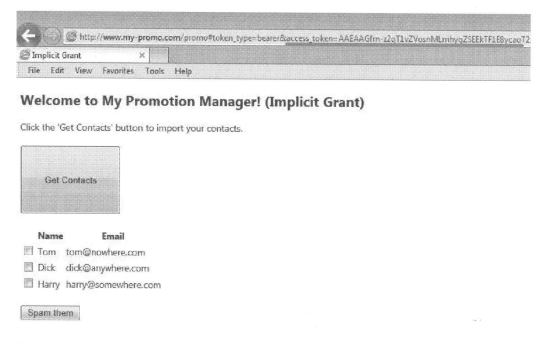

Figure 13-7. *Screen for the implicit grant flow*

Summary

In this chapter, we implemented the same authorization code grant flow that we implemented in Chapter 12, but in this chapter we used DotNetOpenAuth, an open source .NET Framework library. Instead of having to work at the lower level by making HTTP calls, DNOA provides a nice API for us to work with and achieve the same flow in a more robust way. We used the following major classes provided by DNOA:

1. The `AuthorizationServer` class in our authorization server endpoint `OAuth20Controller` to manage and respond to authorization code and token requests.
2. The `ResourceServer` class in the message handler `OAuthTokenHandler` to read the access token.
3. The `WebServerClient` class from the `HomeController` of the client application to issue requests and get the token using the OAuth 2.0 authorization code grant flow.

CHAPTER 14

Two-Factor Authentication

A system identifies a user through a user identifier, commonly abbreviated to user ID. The process by which a system confirms that a user really is who the user claims to be is called authentication. We saw in Chapter 5 that there are three types of credentials through which a user can be authenticated: knowledge factor (what a user knows), ownership factor (what a user owns), and inherence factor (what a user is).

When you have an authentication mechanism that leverages a combination of two of these factors, it is called two-factor authentication (TFA, T-FA, or 2FA). A real-life example for TFA is an automated teller machine (ATM). Before you can transact with an ATM, you need to authenticate by providing your debit card as well as your PIN. The debit card is something you own (ownership factor) and the PIN is something you know (knowledge factor). You are required to use a valid debit card and the corresponding PIN to transact. Because this authentication process is based on two factors, it is a TFA. Another example of TFA is a corporate network that requires the use of a hardware token or USB dongle along with a user ID and password combination.

It goes without saying that from a security standpoint TFA is more robust than single-factor authentication. In this chapter, I show you how to secure ASP.NET Web API by implementing TFA.

Two Ways to Implement TFA

In Chapter 2, we looked at the stateless constraint, which is one of the constraints a service must satisfy to be called a RESTful service. The concept of a server-side session does not exist in the stateless world that ASP.NET Web API belongs to. Unlike a typical UI-based application where authentication happens only once at the time a user starts using the application, authentication typically happens in every service call for RESTful services. This is a key consideration for designing the authentication for RESTful services in general.

Using the authentication code generated by a token such as RSA SecurID® is very common in TFA implementations. An RSA token (not to be confused with a security token that is a container of claims that we saw in Chapter 5) generates a code that changes after a fixed duration, usually a minute. Every minute a new code is generated, and the user must enter the code that the token shows when the application prompts for the code. If the user enters the correct code, it proves to the application that the user owns the token. The knowledge factor in these implementations is typically the password that needs to be entered in addition to the RSA code.

In the case of ASP.NET Web API-powered RESTful services, it is not practical to implement TFA with a credential that changes constantly over time, such as that of codes generated by a token. It is feasible for a user to refer to the token and enter the generated code at the time of login in the case of a UI-based application, but it is not practical for the same user to enter the token-generated code with every single call to the web API. Hence, you will not be able to employ time-sensitive credentials to implement TFA with ASP.NET Web API for all API calls. You can use only credentials that do not change with time to implement TFA for all calls.

However, it is possible to leverage the token-generated authentication code to implement two-factor security for a few selective, occasional but important calls. Normally, the application works with one factor, say a knowledge factor such as password, for authenticating the service calls. When a user makes a request to perform a sensitive action, the web API elevates the security need to two-factor security and demands the authentication code generated by the token as the ownership factor in addition to the base knowledge factor of the user ID and password.

Let's take the example of a banking application. When you try to do something important such as adding a new payee for the funds transfer, the corresponding API call can demand an additional ownership factor while accepting a single factor for the other typical requests. Adding a payee is always important because a malicious user with your credentials can add himself as a payee and drain your account. Hence TFA always make sense for this type of request.

In some other cases, TFA will be required on a need basis even for selective actions, depending on the input or some other parameter. An example for such a case is a funds transfer. If you transfer $50, you will not want to reach out to the token to get the authentication code to complete the transfer. Two-factor security for that use case becomes an irritant. However, if you transfer $50,000, you no doubt will want the extra protection TFA offers.

Considering the preceding points related to implementing TFA with ASP.NET Web API, I classify the TFA techniques I cover in this chapter into the following two categories.

1. **Blanket TFA:** All the ASP.NET Web API calls need TFA. Because it is not feasible for an end user to supply the credentials for every call, the client application must get the credentials once and reuse the same for all subsequent calls. The credentials that do not change with time are critical for the implementation of this type of TFA. By combining the authentication factors I covered in the earlier chapters on knowledge-based and ownership-based security, I illustrate the implementation of this type of TFA. For the example implementation, I take the knowledge factor of the password presented to ASP.NET Web API in the HTTP basic authentication scheme and the ownership factor of the X.509 client certificate.

2. **Per-request TFA:** ASP.NET Web API normally operates with authentication based on one factor, the knowledge factor of a password. For a few important API calls, ASP.NET Web API elevates the security to two-factor security and demands an additional ownership factor to successfully authenticate and service the request. I use an application called Google Authenticator to implement this type of TFA. Google Authenticator is a mobile-based application designed to work as a software token, generating authentication codes for TFA. The client application must be programmed to interpret the response from the web API and demand the additional credential for certain operations. In this type of TFA, the symmetric key entered into Google Authenticator at the time an application is registered in it is the ownership factor (not the mobile phone). The per-request TFA can further be classified into two types:

    a. Constant TFA, where a specific action method of the `ApiController` always needs TFA.

    b. On-demand TFA, where a specific action method of the `ApiController` needs TFA on a need basis, based on the request or some other parameter.

Implementing Blanket TFA with ASP.NET Web API

To implement TFA for all API calls to ASP.NET Web API, I use the knowledge factor of a password in an HTTP basic authentication scheme and the ownership factor of an X.509 client certificate. Both these credentials do not change with time, and a client application can get the credentials from an end user once and use the same credentials to make the subsequent API calls for a reasonable duration of time. There is one more reason for my choice of combining basic authentication and a client certificate. They both need HTTPS and hence are good candidates to be selected as the individual factors for TFA.

In Chapter 9, I covered the steps you will need to perform to set up HTTPS and generate and use a client X.509 certificate as a credential. I don't repeat those steps here. I show only the message handler that can be used to implement the TFA logic. The logic is basically a combination of what we saw with X.509 client certificates in Chapter 9 and basic authentication in Chapter 8.

Create a new class for the message handler and remember to plug in the handler into the handlers list by making an entry in `WebApiConfig.cs` under the `App_Start` folder. Listing 14-1 shows `TwoFactorAuthenticationHandler`, which is a message handler that can be plugged into the ASP.NET Web API pipeline to perform TFA of every request coming in. The message handler first pulls the client certificate off the request using the `GetClientCertificate` extension method defined in the `System.Net.Http` namespace for `HttpRequestMessage`. The `X509Chain` class is used to validate the certificate by building the chain. I ignore the revocation list but in production, that line must be commented out. I also make sure the issuer of the client certificate is CN=WebApiCA.

Listing 14-1. TwoFactorAuthenticationHandler

```
public class TwoFactorAuthenticationHandler : DelegatingHandler
{
    private const string SCHEME = "Basic";

    protected override async Task<HttpResponseMessage> SendAsync(HttpRequestMessage request,
                                                                CancellationToken cancellationToken)

    {
        X509Certificate2 cert = request.GetClientCertificate();

        if (cert != null)
        {
            X509Chain chain = new X509Chain();
            chain.ChainPolicy.RevocationMode =
                        X509RevocationMode.NoCheck; // Not production strength

            if (chain.Build(cert) && cert.Issuer.Equals("CN=WebApiCA"))
            {
                var headers = request.Headers;

                if (headers.Authorization != null && SCHEME.Equals(headers.Authorization.Scheme))
                {
                    Encoding encoding = Encoding.GetEncoding("iso-8859-1");

                    string credentials = encoding.GetString(
                                            Convert.FromBase64String(
                                                    headers.Authorization.Parameter));
                    string[] parts = credentials.Split(':');
                    string userId = parts[0].Trim();
                    string password = parts[1].Trim();

                    string subjectName = cert.Subject.Substring(3); // ignoring CN=

                    // Perform the validation of user ID and password here
                    // For illustration purposes, the factor is considered valid,
                    // if user ID and password are the same


                    bool areTwoFactorsValid = !String.IsNullOrWhiteSpace(userId) &&
                                                userId.Equals(password) &&
                                                    userId.Equals(subjectName);
```

```
                    if (areTwoFactorsValid)
                    {
                        var claims = new List<Claim>
                        {
                                new Claim(ClaimTypes.Name, userId)
                        };

                        var principal = new ClaimsPrincipal(new[] { new ClaimsIdentity(claims, "2FA") });

                        Thread.CurrentPrincipal = principal;

                        if (HttpContext.Current != null)
                            HttpContext.Current.User = principal;
                    }
                }
            }
        }

        var response = await base.SendAsync(request, cancellationToken);

        if (response.StatusCode == HttpStatusCode.Unauthorized)
        {
            response.Headers.WwwAuthenticate.Add(
                        new AuthenticationHeaderValue(SCHEME));
        }

        return response;
    }
}
```

For the knowledge factor, the validation is simple. Just pull the user ID and password off the authorization request header and validate them. In the preceding example, I check for the user ID and password to be equal for the knowledge factor to be considered authentic. In real production systems, this means validating the credentials against a membership store such as a database.

If both factors are valid and the certificate subject name is the same as the user ID coming in the authorization header, an authenticated identity is established.

To test the preceding TFA, we don't need a special test harness because we are working within the boundaries of the mechanisms defined in the HTTP specification. We can use a browser like Internet Explorer to issue requests directly to the web API and exercise the 2FA-related code. Internet Explorer knows how to send the client certificate as long as the client certificate is installed and ready for use, as shown in Chapter 9.

When sending back the 401 – Unauthorized response, we send the WWW-Authenticate header with the basic scheme. Because of this, Internet Explorer knows that it has to pop up a window to gather the user ID and password from the user and package the same in the HTTP Authorization header in the basic scheme before making the subsequent request.

Google Authenticator

To implement per-request TFA, you can use the preceding combination of HTTP basic authentication and an X.509 client certificate. However, I chose to implement per-request TFA using Google Authenticator. Google Authenticator is a mobile-based application developed by Google that is meant to work as a soft token to generate authentication codes for the implementation of TFA for Google services. It generates a six-digit number that users must provide in addition to their username and password to log in to Google services. The validity of the six-digit number lasts only 30 seconds.

After that, a new number is generated and displayed. It is not feasible to use such a time-sensitive credential as a second factor for implementing TFA with ASP.NET Web API for all the calls on a blanket basis. Tokens are great candidates for per-request TFA. For this reason I choose to use a token-based mechanism for implementing the per-request TFA.

I chose Google Authenticator as the token for two main reasons:

1. Google Authenticator is a soft token. It can be installed on a mobile phone, which most of us own and carry around nowadays. There is no dongle to carry around with a mobile phone acting as the token. Google Authenticator generates the authentication code on the mobile device without depending on anything external such as an Internet connection.

2. Google Authenticator uses an HMAC-based One-Time Password (HOTP) algorithm specified in RFC 4226 and a Time-based One-Time Password (TOTP) algorithm specified in RFC 6238. The algorithms Google Authenticator implements are not proprietary. If you prefer implementing them yourself without a dependency on Google Authenticator, it is quite easy to do so.

Google offers Authenticator implementations for iOS, BlackBerry, and Android. Google Authenticator can be used by any application to implement two-factor security, on top of the traditional user ID and password authentication, which is a knowledge-factor authentication.

Google Authenticator runs in a mobile phone and a mobile phone is something you own. By running Google Authenticator on your mobile phone and entering the code it generates, you are proving ownership. As we will see in the following sections, the ownership you are proving is not that of your mobile phone, but a preshared secret between you and the application. The secret sauce is the preshared key (PSK) that we examined in Chapter 9. Google Authenticator is available on Google Code at the following URL: `https://code.google.com/p/google-authenticator`.

How Does Google Authenticator Work from a User Perspective?

I'll show you how Google Authenticator fits into the TFA scheme of things from the perspective of an end user named Alice. Alice uses the client application hosted at `www.company.com` (a fictitious name I use here and not to be confused with the real site with this name) that uses our ASP.NET Web API. The following are the steps that Alice performs.

1. Alice registers with the client application `www.company.com`. The user profile gets created with the user ID of `alice.work@company.com` and a password for Alice to use the client application.

2. As part of the registration process, the client application generates a key, say WXBJY3DPEZPK3ESH, and displays it to the user on the screen either as the key itself or as a QR code in the form of an image that Alice can scan instead of manually entering the key.

3. The client application shares the generated key with ASP.NET Web API through an out-of-band process, informing the web API that this key is for the user Alice. If the client application is the underlying application, the functionality of which is exposed through the web API, the web API itself can have direct access to the key in Alice's user profile, obviating the need for any key-sharing process.

4. Alice adds the account created to Google Authenticator running on her mobile phone. See Figure 14-1 for the screenshots. She provides the account name of `alice.work@company.com` and manually enters the key generated in the preceding step, choosing Time based for the type of key. She clicks the Save button to save the account entry.

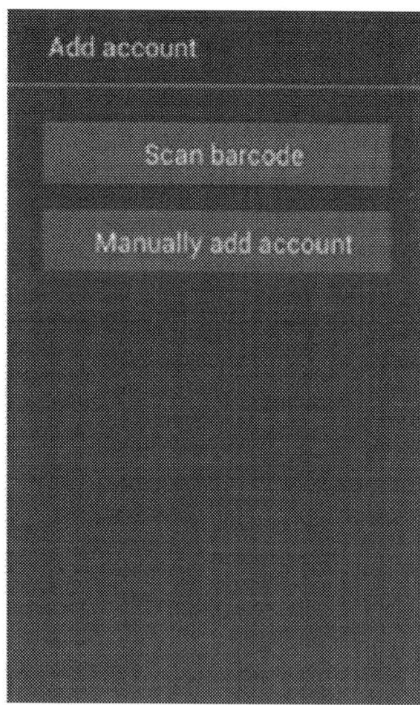

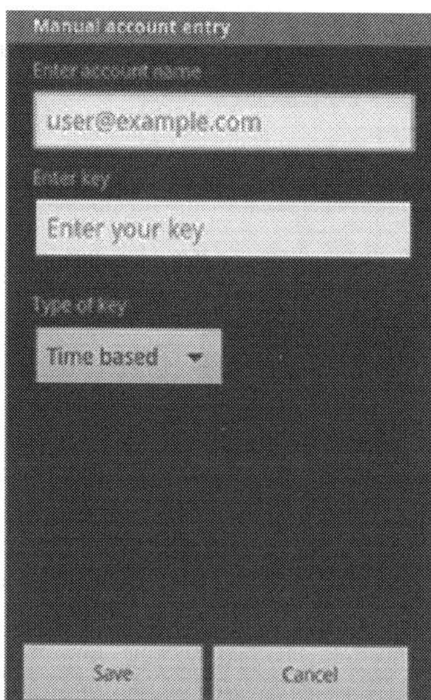

Figure 14-1. *Adding an account with Google Authenticator*

5. Although the key is the most important aspect with Google Authenticator, an account name is also there because it is easier to remember and human friendly. For example, Alice registers the cryptic code generated by the client application against her user account of `alice.work@company.com` in Google Authenticator. From that point onward, she doesn't need to worry about the key.

6. Alice starts using the client application using the credentials she got from the registration process (first step). The client application keeps calling ASP.NET Web API, passing a knowledge-based credential of a password with every call. This password can be the same as the one Alice uses with the client application or it can be different. For our purposes, that detail is not important.

7. Alice comes to a screen in the client application where she needs to perform a sensitive operation. The corresponding web API call that the client application invokes requires an additional ownership credential to authenticate before moving ahead. ASP.NET Web API returns an error code to the client application indicating the same.

8. The client application asks Alice to enter the code generated by Google Authenticator.

9. Alice opens Google Authenticator and enters the six-digit code it shows at that instant against `alice.work@company.com`. Although the underlying ownership factor is the PSK, Alice does need to have her mobile phone with her to see the code and enter it in the application. However, the user-friendly aspect of this TFA mechanism is that Alice no longer needs to retrieve the cryptic key from somewhere and enter it, but only needs to enter a comparatively smaller, simpler six-digit code of 838610, as shown in Figure 14-2.

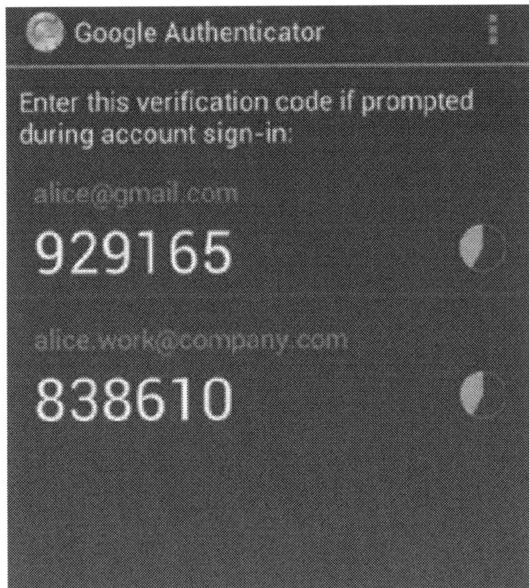

Figure 14-2. *Google Authenticator code*

10. The client application immediately sends this code to ASP.NET Web API as the additional ownership credential.
11. ASP.NET Web API authenticates this new credential and, if authentic, proceeds with servicing the request to perform the sensitive action.

The last step is the most important step from your perspective (i.e., the perspective of a developer). The current code of 838610 is valid for maybe another 10 seconds, and a new code that is completely unrelated to that code will appear in Google Authenticator. After 30 seconds, another new code will be generated, and so on. When the client application asks for this code, Alice immediately looks up the code in the Google Authenticator application on her mobile phone and enters it in the application to complete the transaction that requires additional credentials. How is it possible for ASP.NET Web API to know this rapidly changing code to validate if Alice has correctly entered the code? To get an answer to this question, you need to pop the shiny hood of Google Authenticator and take a look at what goes on inside.

■ **Note** Using Google Authenticator does not mean the data associated with it, such as your account user ID or the secret key, will go through Google servers. What gets passed between you and "your" server, not the Google server, is only that six-digit code.

Under the Hood of Google Authenticator

Google Authenticator has two modes of working: counter based and time based. It uses the HOTP algorithm specified in RFC 4226 and the TOTP algorithm specified in RFC 6238, respectively, to generate the code. In this chapter, I use only the time-based mode because it is the most convenient. The downside is that, technically, the time in your mobile phone where Google Authenticator runs and the time in the server that runs ASP.NET Web API must be in sync to a reasonable extent. Because all time calculations are based on UTC, you don't need to worry about the time zone a server is located in compared to the time zone the user is in, such as a time zone with daylight savings time.

The HOTP algorithm generates a one-time password based on HMAC (SHA-1). The output of HMAC-SHA-1 is 160 bits. It is not practical for any human being to enter this data into a screen not only because it is an onerous task, but also because it is extremely error prone to manually enter such data.

HOTP generates a number from this hash that can be entered easily, such as a six-digit number, in place of the long cryptic value. If C is a counter value (which is just a number) and K is the secret key, an HOTP algorithm can be represented as HOTP value = Truncate(HMAC-SHA-1(K,C)) mod 1000000. The magical number of a million is 10 raised to the power 6, where 6 is the number of digits we would like to have present in our HOTP code.

TOTP builds on the HOTP algorithm. The inputs to the HOTP algorithm are the counter value and the secret key. Assuming the counter remains the same, the HOTP code generated for a secret remains the same regardless of the passage of time. TOTP introduces a time-based moving factor into the mix. If we somehow derive a number from the current date and time and use it as the counter to create the HOTP code, it will start to vary continuously with time.

As you start thinking about deriving a number based on the date and time, one thing that should immediately spring to mind, based on the earlier chapters, is the mechanism we have been using all along with the tokens to denote the expiry, which is computing the seconds elapsed since midnight of January 01, 1970 UTC.

If we plug that number in, the HOTP generated will differ every second. It will not be very useful in that form because it changes very rapidly. If we instead generate the number corresponding to 00 second of the current minute and let it remain constant for the next 30 seconds, it becomes usable. Even a very slow user can look at the six-digit code and enter it in a screen within this time period.

Suppose the current time is 08:37:00 (hours:minutes:seconds). At that precise second of 00, we calculate the seconds elapsed since epoch start and plug that into the HOTP to get the code. The code thus calculated remains valid until 8:37:29. We calculate the code again at 08:37:30, which remains valid until 08:38:00, and so on. In other words, the TOTP code gets refreshed every 30 seconds.

Now that we've had a brief primer on HOTP and TOTP, let's see how Google Authenticator generates the six-digit code and how ASP.NET Web API, or any service for that matter, validates the code on receiving the same as the additional ownership credential. The following steps show how Google Authenticator generates the code.

1. As we saw in the preceding section, the most important input to Google Authenticator is the key. It is an 80-bit key. The user enters the key in base32-encoded format. The first step is to decode it. I cover the details of this base32 encoding in a later section.

2. Google Authenticator gets the current date and time from the mobile phone where it runs. It rounds down the time to the previously elapsed 00 second or 30 seconds of the current minute, and for that time it calculates the corresponding UNIX time. For example, if the current time is 08:00:07, it takes the time as 08:00:00. If the time is 08:00:31, it takes the time as 08:00:30.

3. Google Authenticator creates an HMAC of the UNIX time through the SHA-1 algorithm using the 80-bit key.

4. Google Authenticator truncates the hash thus generated and does a mod 10 power six (which is one million). It then pads 0 to the left of the number thus generated to make it six digits. That is the code shown by Google Authenticator.

When ASP.NET Web API receives this code, it basically repeats these steps. Because it knows the user ID from the first factor of user ID and password, it can fetch the corresponding shared key and precisely perform the preceding steps. If the code thus generated matches the code sent in by the client application, ASP.NET Web API considers the ownership-based credential to be authentic as well.

■ **Note** The ownership factor is the 80-bit key. Of course, you can register the same account and key combination on multiple phones. It will still work because the secret sauce is the key and not the mobile phone. Google Authenticator does two things to make the key human-friendly. First, it stores the key on the mobile phone that a user carries, and second, it uses the TOTP algorithm to reduce the big cryptic key to a six-digit code that can be easily read from the mobile phone and entered into any application when the application asks for it.

Listing 14-2 shows the pseudo-code used by Google Authenticator to generate the six-digit code.

Listing 14-2. Google Authenticator Code Generation

```
function GenerateCode(string secret) // secret coming in is base32 encoded string
     key = base32decode(secret)
     message = current Unix time ÷ 30
     hash = HMAC-SHA1(key, message)
     offset = last nibble of hash
     truncatedHash = hash[offset..offset+4]  //4 bytes starting at the offset
     Set the first bit of truncatedHash to zero  //remove the most significant bit
     code = truncatedHash mod 1000000
     pad code with 0 until length of code is 6
     return code
```

Base32 Encoding and Decoding

Before we start implementing the pseudo-code in Listing 14-2 in C#, we have to understand base32 encoding as well as how it is used by Google. Base32 encoding is one of the encoding schemes described in RFC 4648, "The Base16, Base32, and Base64 Data Encodings." Base 32 encoding uses a restricted set of symbols that can be conveniently used by humans. The alphabet for base32 was selected to avoid similar-looking symbols. For example, the numbers 1, 8, and 0 are not included because they can be confused with the letters I, B, and O. So, it basically uses the 26 English letters A through Z and the numbers 2 through 7. Table 14-1 shows the 32 alphabets of base32.

Table 14-1. *Base32 Alphabet*

Value	Symbol	Value	Symbol	Value	Symbol	Value	Symbol
0	A	9	J	18	S	27	3
1	B	10	K	19	T	28	4
2	C	11	L	20	U	29	5
3	D	12	M	21	V	30	6
4	E	13	N	22	W	31	7
5	F	14	O	23	X		
6	G	15	P	24	Y		
7	H	16	Q	25	Z		
8	I	17	R	26	2		

Google Authenticator uses base32-encoding to help assist users in the manual entry of the key during the registration process. A user can enter the individual characters of the key without any confusion, such as entering 1 when they must enter I or 0 when they must enter O, and so on.

Google uses an 80-bit key so that the resultant base32-encoded string is 16 characters long: 5 bits are grouped and mapped to an alphabet. The client application must generate the 80-bit key and base32 encode it before sharing it with the user to be added to Google Authenticator. However, there are no Convert.ToBase32 or Convert.FromBase32 functions in the .NET Framework. So we have to write it, but it is easy.

To generate a random 10 bytes (80 bits), use `RNGCryptoServiceProvider` as we have been using in other chapters in this book. See Listing 14-3.

Listing 14-3. Key Generation and Base32 Encoding

```
byte[] key = new byte[10]; // 80 bits

using (var rngProvider = new RNGCryptoServiceProvider())
{
        rngProvider.GetBytes(key);
}
```

The following steps show how to base32 encode the byte array we generated in Listing 14-3.

1. Take an individual byte from the byte array and convert it into the bit form.
2. Ensure there are 8 bits by padding with leading 0 bits.
3. Perform the previous two steps for the other bytes in the byte array. Now you have 80 bits.
4. Split them into 16 groups of 5 bits each. The biggest number in the decimal system that 5 bits can represent is 11111, which is 31. Hence, this encoding is base32.
5. Refer to Table 14-1 to get the corresponding base32 alphabet for each of these 16 groups. Now you get the 16 character string, which is the base32-encoded representation of the 10 bytes (or 80 bits) we generated.

Figure 14-3 illustrates the base32-encoding process for an example byte array: `byte[] { 72, 101, 108, 108, 111, 33, 222, 173, 190, 239 }`.

byte[10]	72	101	108	108	111	33	222	173	190	239
bits	01001000	01100101	01101100	01101100	01101111	00100001	11011110	10101101	10111110	11101111

Concatentated bits 01001000011001010110110001101100011011110010000111011110101011011011111011101111

Bits Group of 5 bits	01001	00001	10010	10110	11000	11011	00011	01111	00100	00111	01111	01010	11011	01111	10111	01111
Decimal form	9	1	18	22	24	27	3	15	4	7	15	10	27	15	23	15
Mapped Base32 Alphabet	J	B	S	W	Y	3	D	P	E	H	P	K	3	P	X	P

Figure 14-3. *Base32 encoding*

We will write an extension method on byte[] to implement the base32-encoding logic. See Listing 14-4.

Listing 14-4. ToBase32String Extension Method

```
public static class StringHelper
{
        private static string alphabet = "ABCDEFGHIJKLMNOPQRSTUVWXYZ234567";

        public static string ToBase32String(this byte[] secret)
        {
            var bits = secret.Select(b => Convert.ToString(b, 2)
                                                .PadLeft(8, '0'))
                                                        .Aggregate((a, b) => a + b);

            return Enumerable.Range(0, bits.Length / 5)
                            .Select(i => alphabet.Substring(
                                                        Convert.ToInt32(
                                                                    bits.Substring(i * 5, 5), 2), 1))
                                .Aggregate((a, b) => a + b);
        }
}
```

Now, let's move to the decoding part. As you saw in Listing 14-2, Google Authenticator first decodes the base32-encoded string registered with it and uses it for code generation. Similarly, if our ASP.NET Web API has to generate the TOTP code, we have to base32 decode the secret.

Decoding is simply the reverse of encoding. We take the first character and get the value from the map. So, if it is J we take 9 and write the bit representation of 9, which is 1001. We then make sure this is at least 5 bits wide by prefixing it with a zero. Now we have 01001. We do this for every other character and concatenate all the bits. Then, we break this huge string of concatenated bits by groups of 8 (a byte) and thus we get a byte array, which is the shared key. Because a Google-generated key is 16 characters wide, we will get 80 bits and hence ultimately a byte[10].

A picture is worth thousand words, Figure 14-4 illustrates how a base32-encoded string of JBSWY3DPEHPK3PXP is decoded back to a byte array.

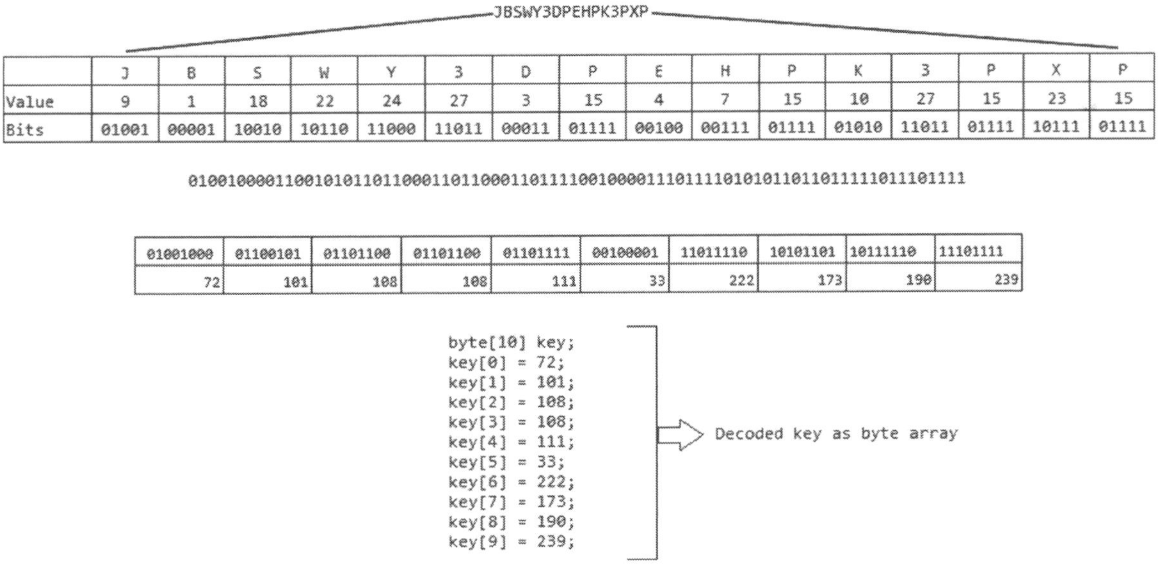

JBSWY3DPEHPK3PXP

	J	B	S	W	Y	3	D	P	E	H	P	K	3	P	X	P
Value	9	1	18	22	24	27	3	15	4	7	15	10	27	15	23	15
Bits	01001	00001	10010	10110	11000	11011	00011	01111	00100	00111	01111	01010	11011	01111	10111	01111

01001000011001010110110001101100011011110010000111011110101011011011111011101111

01001000	01100101	01101100	01101100	01101111	00100001	11011110	10101101	10111110	11101111
72	101	108	108	111	33	222	173	190	239

```
byte[10] key;
key[0] = 72;
key[1] = 101;
key[2] = 108;
key[3] = 108;
key[4] = 111;
key[5] = 33;
key[6] = 222;
key[7] = 173;
key[8] = 190;
key[9] = 239;
```

Decoded key as byte array

Figure 14-4. *Base32 decoding*

■ **Note** The encoding logic you saw in Listing 14-4 and the decoding logic you are about to see in Listing 14-5 are tailor made for Google Authenticator. Google uses 80-bit keys, which divide exactly into 16 groups of 5 bits. Our logic will not handle any other lengths.

Listing 14-5 shows the C# code to base32 decode, exactly along the lines of the steps just outlined. It might not be the most efficient implementation, but the code exactly mimics the preceding steps for your easy understanding.

Listing 14-5. Base32 Decoding

```
public static byte[] ToByteArray(this string secret)
{
        var bits = secret.ToUpper().ToCharArray().Select(c =>
                                                Convert.ToString(alphabet.IndexOf(c), 2)
                                                        .PadLeft(5, '0'))
                                                            .Aggregate((a, b) => a + b);

        return Enumerable.Range(0, bits.Length / 8)
                                .Select(i => Convert.ToByte(bits.Substring(i * 8, 8), 2))
                                    .ToArray();
}
```

`Convert.ToString(int, 2)` gives the corresponding bits in the string representation. So, `Convert.ToString(9, 2)` is 1001. `PadLeft` adds the prefix and the LINQ Aggregate operator just concatenates the padded bit strings to a single huge string. The next line of code breaks the huge string of bits into chunks of 8 bits each and `Convert.ToByte(string, 2)` converts the bits in the form of a string into a byte. So, `Convert.ToByte("01001000", 2)` returns a byte of value 72.

Implementing TOTP Algorithm in a Console App

We will now implement the HOTP and TOTP algorithm as used by Google Authenticator in a console application written in C#. The secret is 80 bits and the HOTP code generated is six digits. Listing 14-6 shows the code to generate HOTP. Although I use TOTP in this chapter, I show you HOTP here because TOTP uses HOTP internally, as you will see in this section. The following are the steps to generate an HOTP.

1. The two inputs to the HOTP generating function are the secret and a counter. The secret is a string that is base32 encoded. The counter is just a number.
2. Get the bytes corresponding to the counter using `BitConverter`. A small wrinkle here is that Windows uses the little endian convention in storing bytes, and we need to reverse the byte array by calling the `Reverse method to` get it the way we want it.
3. Decode the base32-encoded secret. For this, use the extension method, which we saw in Listing 14-5.
4. Create an HMAC SHA-1 of the byte array from Step 2 using the base32-decoded secret as the key.
5. Truncate the hash. I use the logic taken straight out of the example from RFC 4226 Section 5.4 for this purpose. The truncated hash modulus 10 raised to the power of 6, which is a million, is the HOTP.
6. As the final step, make sure the code is six digits by prefixing zeros and return it as string.

Listing 14-6. HOTP Generator

```
public static string GetHotp(string base32EncodedSecret, long counter)
{
    byte[] message = BitConverter.GetBytes(counter)
                            .Reverse().ToArray(); // Assuming Intel machine (little endian)

    byte[] secret = base32EncodedSecret.ToByteArray();

    HMACSHA1 hmac = new HMACSHA1(secret, true);

    byte[] hash = hmac.ComputeHash(message);

    int offset = hash[hash.Length - 1] & 0xf;
    int truncatedHash = ((hash[offset] & 0x7f) << 24) |
                            ((hash[offset + 1] & 0xff) << 16) |
                                ((hash[offset + 2] & 0xff) << 8) |
                                    (hash[offset + 3] & 0xff);

    int hotp = truncatedHash % 1000000; // 6-digit code and hence 10 power 6, that is a million

    return hotp.ToString().PadLeft(6, '0');
}
```

We now implement the TOTP algorithm building on top of the HOTP implementation. Listing 14-7 shows the code. The TOTP generator uses the HOTP generator to generate the code. There is no counter parameter here because it is deduced from the current date and time. The number of seconds elapsed since midnight on January 1, 1970 UTC is divided by 30 and rounded down to the nearest whole number. This number is used as the input to the HOTP logic, and the resultant code is returned as TOTP.

Listing 14-7. TOTP Generator

```
public static string GetTotp(string base32EncodedSecret)
{
    DateTime epochStart = new DateTime(1970, 01, 01, 0, 0, 0, 0, DateTimeKind.Utc);

    long counter = (long)Math.Floor((DateTime.UtcNow - epochStart).TotalSeconds / 30);

    return GetHotp(base32EncodedSecret, counter);
}
```

Finally, Listing 14-8 shows the code for the Main method of the console application that uses our TOTP generator to generate codes. I print the TOTP code every three seconds.

Listing 14-8. Test Program

```
static void Main(string[] args)
{
    string secret = "JBSWY3DPEHPK3PXP";
```

```
    while (true)
    {
        Console.WriteLine("{0} {1}", DateTime.Now, GetTotp(secret));
        Thread.Sleep(1000 * 3);
    }
}
```

The output of the console application is shown in Figure 14-5. As you can see, the generated TOTP code remains valid for 30 seconds. When it is 0 second or 30 seconds of the minute, a new code is generated.

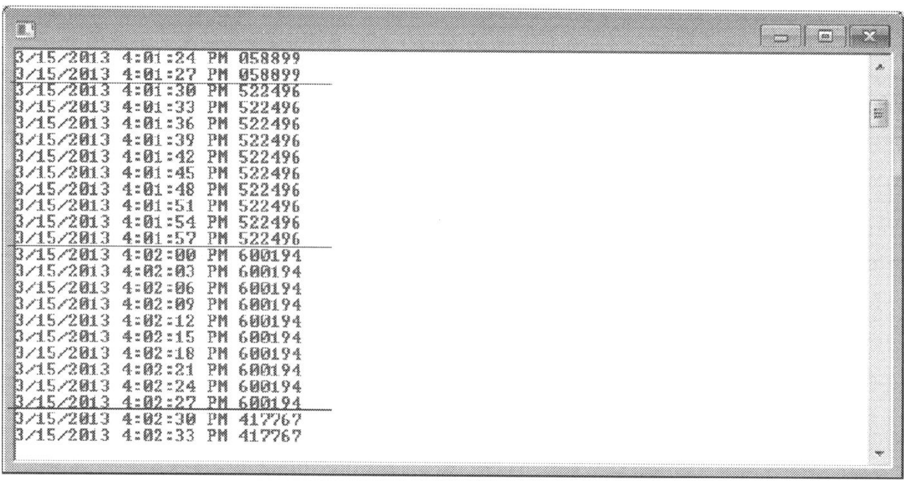

Figure 14-5. *Output*

At this point, our logic is in line with Google Authenticator. If you have a mobile phone running iOS, a BlackBerry, or Android, you can get the Google Authenticator application and add an account using some mail ID and the secret key of JBSWY3DPEHPK3PXP.

Once an account is added with this secret key, the code generated by Google Authenticator for that account and our little console application will be exactly the same at any given instant. As Google Authenticator shows a new code at the change of the second to 0 or 30, our console application also will print the same code as if it is magic!

What you are seeing is the fundamental idea behind two-factor security using Google Authenticator. At any point in time, any application implementing the TOTP algorithm and Google Authenticator application will display the same TOTP code, as long as the same secret key is used in Google Authenticator as well as the application.

If you don't have a compatible phone, there are several third-party implementations available, including the one for Windows Phone. If you don't want to use any mobile phone at all for testing, there is even an HTML 5–based implementation available in Github. If you have the Google Chrome browser, the same HTML 5 implementation is available as an add-on, GAuth Authenticator, in the Chrome Web Store.

See Figure 14-6 for a screenshot of the Chrome add-on showing the TOTP code. Because I have used the same secret used by this add-on for `alice@google.com`, the codes generated by the add-on and the console application are exactly the same at any given point in time.

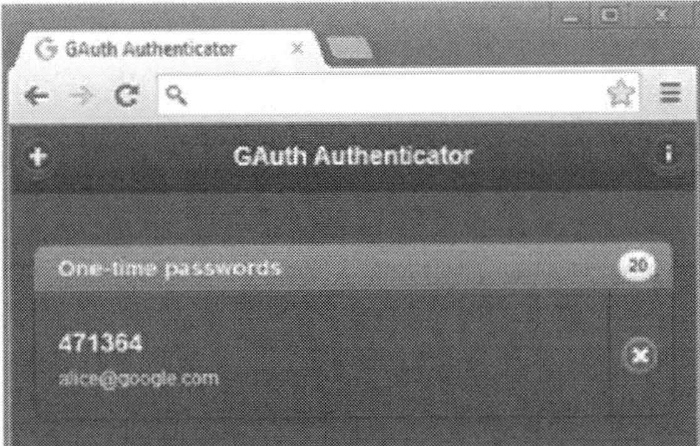

Figure 14-6. *Google Chrome GAuth Authenticator add-on*

Now that we have tested our TOTP generation logic and we are satisfied that it is generating the code exactly the same as Google Authenticator, let's move on to implementing TFA with ASP.NET Web API.

Implementing Constant Per-Request TFA

I now show you how to implement what I call constant per-request TFA, with ASP.NET Web API using TOTP codes generated by Google Authenticator. ASP.NET Web API normally operates with authentication based on one factor, the knowledge factor of a password sent in the HTTP authentication header basic scheme. For a few important API calls, ASP.NET Web API elevates the security to two-factor security and demands the TOTP code as the additional ownership factor to successfully authenticate and service the request.

The action method that handles HTTP POST in the `TransfersController` class is what we will try to secure using TFA. Because we need to secure action methods selectively, I chose to subclass the `Authorize` filter to implement TFA. This filter expects the TOTP code to be sent by the client application in a custom HTTP request header by the name of X-TOTP. The knowledge factor of the password is needed for all API calls. Hence, the corresponding authentication logic will be implemented in a message handler. The following are the steps to implement constant per-request TFA for the HTTP POST action method of the `TransfersController` class.

1. Open Visual Studio 2012 and create a new ASP.NET MVC 4 Web Application using the Web API template and name it GoogleAuthWebApi.
2. Create a folder named `Infrastructure`.
3. Create a new message handler class, as shown in Listing 14-9. This is the same as the message handler we saw in Chapter 8 when we implemented basic authentication.

Listing 14-9. Basic Authentication Delegating Handler

```
public class BasicAuthenticationHandler : DelegatingHandler
{
    private const string SCHEME = "Basic";

    protected override async Task<HttpResponseMessage> SendAsync(HttpRequestMessage request,
                                                            CancellationToken cancellationToken)
    {

        var headers = request.Headers;
        if (headers.Authorization != null && SCHEME.Equals(headers.Authorization.Scheme))
```

```
            {
                string credentials = Encoding.UTF8.GetString(
                                                    Convert.FromBase64String(
                                                        headers.Authorization.Parameter));
                string[] parts = credentials.Split(':');
                string userId = parts[0].Trim();
                string password = parts[1].Trim();

                // TODO - Do authentication of user ID and password against your credentials store here
                if (true)
                {
                    var claims = new List<Claim>
                    {
                        new Claim(ClaimTypes.Name, userId)
                    };

                    var principal = new ClaimsPrincipal(new[] {new ClaimsIdentity(claims, SCHEME) });

                    Thread.CurrentPrincipal = principal;

                    if (HttpContext.Current != null)
                        HttpContext.Current.User = principal;
                }
            }

            var response = await base.SendAsync(request, cancellationToken);

            if (response.StatusCode == HttpStatusCode.Unauthorized)
            {
                response.Headers.WwwAuthenticate.Add(
                            new AuthenticationHeaderValue(SCHEME));
            }

            return response;

        }
}
```

4. Add the message handler to the list of message handlers by making an entry in WebApiConfig.cs under the `App_Start` folder: `config.MessageHandlers.Add (new BasicAuthenticationHandler());`

5. Add an extension method to the `HttpRequestMessage` class, as shown in Listing 14-10. Create a new static class named `RequestHelper` in the `Helpers` folder. Create the folder before creating the class. The logic is simple. If the TOTP code is present in the X-TOTP header, the method retrieves it. It then calls a static method `GetPastCurrentFutureOtp` on the `Totp` class that returns three TOTP codes corresponding to the last 30-second block, the current TOTP, and the TOTP corresponding to the next 30-second block. As an example, let's say the time this code runs is 08:35:07 AM. The three TOTP codes returned in the list, respectively, will be as follows.

    a. TOTP code corresponding to the time period 08:34:30 AM–08:34:59 AM (Past).

    b. TOTP code corresponding to the time period 08:35:00 AM–08:35:29 AM (Current).

    c. TOTP code corresponding to the time period 08:35:30 AM–08:35:59 AM (Future).

Listing 14-10. TOTP Code Validation

```
public static class RequestHelper
{
    public static bool HasValidTotp(this HttpRequestMessage request, string key)
    {
        if (request.Headers.Contains("X-TOTP"))
        {
            string totp = request.Headers.GetValues("X-TOTP").First();

            // We check against the past, current, and future TOTP
            if (Totp.GetPastCurrentFutureOtp(key).Any(p => p.Equals(totp)))
                return true;
        }

        return false;

    }
}
```

6. If the incoming TOTP matches one of the three, authentication is considered successful. The reason for this slight complexity is to accommodate the clock skew between the server where this code runs and the clock of the mobile phone where the user-entered TOTP was generated by Google Authenticator. By looking at the past and the future one, we are a little easy on the user. It does take them a little bit of time to enter the code. If they enter the code a few seconds before expiry, by the time the request comes to ASP.NET Web API we are probably on the next TOTP. If we reject the user entry, the user will mostly likely not realize what happened, unless the user has knowledge of how TOTP works, network latency, and so on. To a typical end user, it will just be a bad system. So we try to be a bit accommodating.

7. In the `Infrastructure` folder, create another class named `Totp`. Listing 14-11 shows the `Totp` class. Only the new method of `GetPastCurrentFutureOtp` is shown in the listing. Copy and paste the method `GetHotp` from Listing 14-6.

Listing 14-11. Totp Class

```
public class Totp
{
    public static IList<string> GetPastCurrentFutureOtp(string base32EncodedSecret)
    {
        DateTime epochStart = new DateTime(1970, 01, 01, 0, 0, 0, 0, DateTimeKind.Utc);

        long counter = (long)Math.Floor((DateTime.UtcNow - epochStart).TotalSeconds / 30);

        var otps = new List<string>();
        otps.Add(GetHotp(base32EncodedSecret, counter - 1)); // previous OTP
        otps.Add(GetHotp(base32EncodedSecret, counter)); // current OTP
        otps.Add(GetHotp(base32EncodedSecret, counter + 1)); // next OTP

        return otps;
    }
```

```
    private static string GetHotp(string base32EncodedSecret, long counter)
    {
        // Same logic we saw in Listing 14-6
    }
}
```

8. Copy and paste the `StringHelper.cs` file containing the static class `StringHelper` with the two extension methods `ToByteArray` and `ToBase32String` that we saw in Listings 14-4 and 14-5.

9. Create the `TwoFactorAttribute` class in the `Infrastructure` folder by extending `System.Web.Http.AuthorizeAttribute`, as shown in Listing 14-12. This filter is based on the assumption that the delegating handler that runs earlier in the pipeline will have established the authenticated identity based on the knowledge factor of the password.

    a. Override the `IsAuthorized` method to pull the username from `Thread.CurrentPrincipal`, which is established by the message handler.

    b. Get the secret key for this user. This step is not implemented in listing 14-12. I just use a hard-coded key.

    c. Using the extension method `HasValidTotp`, validate the incoming TOTP and return true if the incoming TOTP is valid. Otherwise, return false.

    d. Returning false here would result in a response status code of 401 – Unauthorized. Along with 401, send a reason phrase back stating that TOTP is required by overriding the `HandleUnauthorizedRequest` method.

Listing 14-12. TwoFactorAttribute

```
public class TwoFactorAttribute : AuthorizeAttribute
{
    protected override bool IsAuthorized(HttpActionContext context)
    {
        IIdentity identity = Thread.CurrentPrincipal.Identity;
        if (identity.IsAuthenticated && !String.IsNullOrWhiteSpace(identity.Name))
        {
            // TODO - Using a hard-coded key for illustration
            // Get the key corresponding to identity. Name from the membership store
            string key = "JBSWY3DPEHPK3PXP";

            if (context.Request.HasValidTotp(key))
            {
                return true;
            }
        }

        return false;
    }

    protected override void HandleUnauthorizedRequest(HttpActionContext actionContext)
    {
        actionContext.Response = new HttpResponseMessage(HttpStatusCode.Unauthorized)
                                            {
                                                ReasonPhrase = "TOTP code required"
                                            };
    }
}
```

10. Create a new Web API Controller with a name of `TransfersController`, as shown in Listing 14-13. Apply the `TwoFactor` filter on the `Post` action method. The action filter makes sure the request contains an X-TOTP header with a valid TOTP. If not, a 401 - Unauthorized status code is sent back. The granularity we can achieve with this filter is the action method level, which is exactly what we need to implement per-request TFA.

Listing 14-13. TransfersController API Controller

```
[TwoFactor]
public HttpResponseMessage Post(AccountTransfer transfer)
{
        // Transfer logic goes here
}

public class AccountTransfer
{
        public decimal Amount { get; set; }
}
```

That completes our per-request TFA implementation. I used a funds transfer example because I will build on the same example when I cover on-demand TFA in the next section. However, a better example for this constant per-request TFA scenario is a user adding a payee that requires elevated security all the time, regardless of the input or any other parameter. If you transfer a small amount, you will not want to reach out to your phone to complete the transfer. Two-factor security for that use case becomes an irritant. If you transfer a bigger amount, it does make sense. We see how we can modify our approach to meet this on-demand TFA need in the next section.

Implementing On-Demand Per-Request TFA

The fundamental idea of using Google Authenticator–based TOTP code remains the same to implement two-factor security on demand, based on the data that is being handled. We still have the first factor as user ID and password and use basic authentication accomplished in a message handler. That portion remains unchanged. Instead of an action filter, we use another message handler. The following are the steps.

1. As we go down this path of having two handlers, you need to be aware of the fact that the handler validating TOTP must run only after the basic authentication handler. This is very simple to accomplish: The sequence of how we register with configuration determines the calling sequence. We have a `TotpHandler` in addition to the `BasicAuthenticationHandler`. These two handlers must be registered in WebApiConfig, in the `App_Start` folder, as shown in Listing 14-14.

Listing 14-14. Handler Registration

```
public static class WebApiConfig
{
    public static void Register(HttpConfiguration config)
    {
        config.Routes.MapHttpRoute(
            name: "DefaultApi",
            routeTemplate: "api/{controller}/{id}",
            defaults: new { id = RouteParameter.Optional }
        );
```

```
            config.MessageHandlers.Add(new BasicAuthenticationHandler());

            // Must be after BasicAuthenticationHandler
            config.MessageHandlers.Add(new TotpHandler());
        }
    }
```

2. Add a new message handler to the `Infrastructure` folder of the project we used in the preceding section. Give it the name `TotpHandler` and copy and paste the code shown in Listing 14-15. This handler runs for all the requests. However, it does nothing if the X-TOTP header is absent. If present, it validates the TOTP exactly how we performed the validation in the preceding section by calling the `HasValidTotp` method. If TOTP is valid, add a new custom claim of type `http://badri/claims/totp` and value of `true` to the claims-based identity established by `BasicAuthenticationHandler`.

Listing 14-15. TotpHandler

```
public class TotpHandler : DelegatingHandler
{
    protected override async Task<HttpResponseMessage> SendAsync(HttpRequestMessage request,
                                                             CancellationToken cancellationToken)
    {
        var headers = request.Headers;

        IIdentity identity = Thread.CurrentPrincipal.Identity;
        if (request.Headers.Contains("X-TOTP") &&
                        identity.IsAuthenticated &&
                                !String.IsNullOrWhiteSpace(identity.Name))
        {
            // TODO - Using a hard-coded key for illustration
            // Get the key corresponding to identity.Name from the membership store
            string key = "JBSWY3DPEHPK3PXP";

            if (request.HasValidTotp(key))
            {
                ClaimsIdentity claimsIdentity = identity as ClaimsIdentity;

                if (identity != null)
                    claimsIdentity.AddClaim(new Claim("http://badri/claims/totp", "true"));
            }
        }

        return await base.SendAsync(request, cancellationToken);
    }
}
```

3. With this mechanism in place, the whole thing at this point becomes a case of implementing claims-based authorization in ASP.NET Web API, which we did in Chapter 5. We will subclass `ClaimsAuthorizationManager` and implement our claims checking logic there. See Listing 14-16 for the subclass implementation. The `ClaimsAuthorizationManager` subclass looks for a resource claim of type `http://badri/claims/TransferValue`. Only when the value exceeds 50,000 does it check for the user claim added by `TotpHandler`, a claim of type `http://badri/claims/totp` with a value that can be parsed to a Boolean value of true. For small transfers, no checking is done.

Listing 14-16. ClaimsAuthorizationManager Subclass

```
public class AuthorizationManager : ClaimsAuthorizationManager
{
    public override bool CheckAccess(AuthorizationContext context)
    {
        var resource = context.Resource;
        var action = context.Action;

        string resourceName = resource.First(c => c.Type == ClaimTypes.Name).Value;
        string actionName = action.First(c => c.Type == ClaimTypes.Name).Value;

        if (resourceName == "Transfer" && actionName == "Post")
        {
            ClaimsIdentity identity = (context.Principal.Identity as ClaimsIdentity);
            if (!identity.IsAuthenticated)
                return false;

            var claims = identity.Claims;

            string claimValue = resource
                                .First(c =>
                                        c.Type == "http://badri/claims/TransferValue")
                                .Value;
            decimal trasferValue = Decimal.Parse(claimValue);

            if (transferValue > 50000M)
            {
                if (claims.Any(c => c.Type == "http://badri/claims/totp" &&
                                                        Boolean.Parse(c.Value)))

                    return true;
            }
            else
                return true;
        }

        return false;
    }
}
```

4. With this, the action method in ApiController must call CheckAccess() passing in the resource claim, which is the transfer amount. The AccountTransfer class is very simple and has one property of Amount for the web API to bind the incoming value. Based on the return value of the method CheckAccess, transfer processing is continued or dropped. The action method is shown in Listing 14-17.

Listing 14-17. Action Method

```
public HttpResponseMessage Post(AccountTransfer transfer)
{
    // Based on ID, retrieve employee details and create the list of resource claims
    var transferClaims = new List<Claim>()
    {
        new Claim("http://badri/claims/TransferValue", transfer.Amount.ToString())
    };

    if (User.CheckAccess("Transfer", "Post", transferClaims))
    {
        //repository.MakeTransfer(transfer);
        return new HttpResponseMessage(HttpStatusCode.OK);
    }
    else
        return new HttpResponseMessage(HttpStatusCode.Unauthorized)
        {
                ReasonPhrase = "TOTP code required" };
        }
}
```

5. Plugging our custom implementation of ClaimsAuthorizationManager into the claims processing pipeline and the extension method of CheckAccess method on IPrincipal interface are all covered in Chapter 5. I don't repeat that process here. With this implementation, the transfers can work at normal security level for the typical smaller amounts. Two-factor security kicks in only for the larger amounts, and the ownership factor is authenticated, in addition to the already authenticated knowledge factor. From the point of view of the end users, for doing large transfers they have to reach out to their mobile phones and enter the code that Google Authenticator shows at that instant into the application consuming our web API. The application will relay back the code to our API when the API is invoked. This is a great thing for end users. For large transfers, there is an additional level of protection, which kicks in only when required without annoying them.

To test the on-demand TFA, here is a simple JQuery powered UI (see Listing 14-18). Copy and paste the following code in /Home/Index view.

Listing 14-18. Index View

```
@section scripts{
    <script type="text/javascript">
        $(document).ready(function () {
            $('#transfer').click(function () {
                $('#result').empty();

                // Basic authorization hard-coded for jqhuman:jqhuman
                $.ajax({
                    type: "POST",
```

```
                headers: {
                    "X-TOTP": $("#otp").val(),
                    "Authorization": "Basic anFodW1hbjpqcWh1bWFu"
                },
                url: "http://localhost:19927/api/transfers",
                data: { "Amount": "50001" },
                success: function (data) {
                    $('#result').html("Transfer successful");
                },
                error: function (error) {
                    alert(error);
                    $('#result').val("Transfer failed " + error);
                }
            });
        });
    });
    </script>
}
<h2>Transfer amount exceeds $50,000. Enter the code from Google Authenticator</h2>
<div>
    <div>
        <input type="text" id="otp" />
        <input id="transfer" type="button" value="Transfer" />
    </div>
    <div id="result"/>
</div>
```

Two-Factor Security through Mobile Phones

In this chapter, I have covered TFA implementation realized through the use of TOTP codes generated by Google Authenticator. The ownership factor is not the mobile phone running Google Authenticator but the secret key generated by the client application and shared with the web API as well as Google Authenticator. Because it will be difficult for a user to enter the long and cryptic PSK, the TOTP algorithm generates a six-digit code corresponding to the PSK, which is easier for a user to enter. Google Authenticator is just a handy means to look at the six-digit code coming out of the TOTP algorithm, for the PSK and the 30-second interval corresponding to that point in time.

An important point to note is that Google Authenticator is not tied to a specific phone. You can install Google Authenticator on any phone that is supported and add the account with the shared key. It will start generating the correct TOTP. A mobile phone, therefore, is not the ownership factor.

However, it is possible to implement two-factor security using a mobile phone as the second ownership factor. For example, if a web API can generate a small code and send it to the mobile number in the form of an SMS message, it can expect this number to be entered to complete a transaction. This is two-factor security with the mobile phone serving as the ownership factor.

At the time of registration, the user enters her mobile phone number into the application. Typically, the application that supports the registration functionality collects the phone number from the user and immediately validates that the user is in possession of a phone with that number by sending a One-Time PIN or Password (OTP) to the mobile phone through SMS. The user has to enter the OTP to complete the registration. By entering the OTP that the system has sent, the user is proving to the system that she is indeed the owner of the mobile phone.

In the future, for any transaction that requires elevated security, the web API can simply generate a new OTP and send it to the already registered phone number. If the user retries the transaction by sending the OTP received in the mobile phone and it matches with the one the web API has stored in the system, the transaction continues.

In this method, TOTP is not used. The web API generates a code, usually a smaller one that is four to six digits long, and sends that in the SMS. Before sending, the code is stored against the user in a persistent store to compare against. The code stored will get invalidated by one or more incorrect attempts or the passage of time.

So, this SMS-based method differs from the Google Authenticator approach in two primary ways: (1) There is no time-based logic and the code generated can be any random code, and (2) the code generated must be persisted to validate subsequently when the code comes back in the request. But for these two fundamental differences, the rest of the logic can remain the same.

The additional capability required from the web API point of view is sending an SMS message. Of course, there are providers available that offer SMS capabilities to an application at a cost. From a technical point of view, SMS capabilities are available as a REST API for our ASP.NET Web API to use and send SMS.

There are advantages and disadvantages in the mobile-phone-based two-factor security, compared to the HOTP-based approach implemented through Google Authenticator. Unlike Google Authenticator, the user has to wait for the code to arrive in SMS. However, the advantage with this method is that an additional application like Google Authenticator is not needed, and the SMS can be sent to any phone, not just smart phones capable of running Google Authenticator.

Google Authenticator is not tied to a phone. A user does not have to register a phone number. It is a great thing from the perspective of privacy. An average user who values privacy will hesitate to share his mobile number. The common link in the case of a mobile phone/SMS-based approach is the mobile number itself, whereas with the Google Authenticator approach it is only an 80-bit randomly generated secret key.

Summary

The process by which a system confirms that a user is really who the user claims to be is called authentication. There are three types of credentials through which a user can be authenticated: knowledge factor (what a user knows), ownership factor (what a user owns), and inherence factor (what a user is). When you have an authentication mechanism that leverages a combination of two of these factors, it is called two-factor authentication.

RESTful services are stateless. Unlike a typical UI-based application where authentication happens only once when a user starts using the application, authentication typically happens in every service call for RESTful services. In the case of ASP.NET Web API-powered RESTful services, it is not practical to implement TFA with a credential that changes constantly over time, such as that of codes generated by a token such as RSA SecurID®. Whereas it is feasible for a user to refer to the token and enter the generated code at the time of login in the case of a UI-based application, it is not practical for the same user to enter the token-generated code with every single call to the web API. Hence, you will not be able to employ time-sensitive credentials to implement TFA with ASP.NET Web API for all API calls. You can use only credentials that do not change with time to implement TFA for all calls.

However, it is possible to leverage the token-generated authentication code to implement two-factor security for a few selective important calls. Normally, the application works with one factor, say a knowledge factor such as a password, for authenticating the service calls. When a user makes a request to perform a sensitive action, the web API elevates the security need to two-factor security and demands the authentication code generated by the token as the ownership factor in addition to the base knowledge factor of user ID and password. Considering the preceding points related to implementing TFA with ASP.NET Web API, I classified the TFA techniques that I covered in this chapter into the following two categories.

1. **Blanket TFA:** All the ASP.NET Web API calls need TFA. The credentials that do not change with time are critical for the implementation of this type of TFA. By combining the authentication factors I covered in the earlier chapters on knowledge-based and ownership-based security—a password using HTTP basic authentication and the X.509 client certificate, respectively—I illustrated the implementation of this type of TFA.

2. **Per-request TFA:** ASP.NET Web API normally operates with authentication based on one factor, the knowledge factor of a password. For a few important API calls, ASP.NET Web API elevates the security to TFA and demands an additional ownership factor to successfully authenticate and service the request. I used an application called Google Authenticator to implement this type of TFA. Google Authenticator is a mobile-based application designed to work as a software token generating authentication codes for TFA using HOTP and TOTP algorithms. In this type of TFA, the symmetric key entered into Google Authenticator at the time an application is registered is the ownership factor (not the mobile phone). A per-request TFA can be further classified into two types:

    a. Constant TFA, where a specific action method always needs TFA.

    b. On-demand TFA, where a specific action method needs TFA on a need basis, based on the request or some other parameters.

We finished the chapter with a quick overview of implementing two-factor security using mobile phones with a one-time PIN or a password transmitted through an alternative means, which is SMS.

CHAPTER 15

Security Vulnerabilities

We saw in Chapter 1 that the term *information security* means protecting information and information systems from unauthorized access, use, disclosure, disruption, modification, or destruction to ensure confidentiality, integrity, and availability. Related to this, we have seen how an application can identify and authenticate entities using the three factors based on knowledge, ownership, and inherence to control the access of protected application resources from unauthorized entities. Also, we examined how cryptography can help ensure the two important aspects of message security: confidentiality through encryption and integrity through digital signing techniques. We also looked at transport security achieved through TLS over HTTP (HTTPS).

Now that you have gained a new understanding of the security techniques I've covered in previous chapters, I show you in this final chapter how you can learn from the mistakes of other organizations by becoming familiar with the Open Web Application Security Project (OWASP) Top Ten list for 2013. At the time of the writing of this book, the list is a release candidate. The list identifies the top ten application security vulnerabilities or risks. OWASP is a worldwide, not-for-profit organization focused on improving the security of software. The OWASP Top Ten list aims to raise awareness about application security by identifying some of the most critical security risks facing organizations.

RFC 4949, "Internet Security Glossary, Version 2," defines a *vulnerability* as a flaw or weakness in a system's design, implementation, operation, or management that could be exploited to violate the system's security policy. If a vulnerability is exploited with no harmful result, the vulnerability is not considered to be a risk. Starting in 2010, the OWASP Top Ten lists risks rather than vulnerabilities. However, as a developer, application designer, or application architect, you need to be aware of all the possibilities that can leave your ASP.NET Web API vulnerable, risky or not. I cover the OWASP risks in this chapter from the perspective of vulnerability.

Attacks are the techniques that an attacker uses to exploit the vulnerabilities in your application. In previous chapters we have seen multiple types of attacks such as man-in-the-middle (MITM) and replay attacks. The action or the technique employed to counter an attack is a *countermeasure*. A good countermeasure is typically a combination of hardware, software, and processes. The term software here includes both the system software, such as the operating system, and the application software, which is the code you write or the code you reuse. To drive home this point, I cover a couple of attacks and the corresponding countermeasures in this chapter.

Finally, I briefly cover two sound practices related to securing ASP.NET Web API: logging (or auditing) and input validation.

OWASP Application Security Risks

Following are the OWASP top ten application security risks for 2013. At the time of writing, this list is a release candidate.

1. Injection
2. Broken Authentication and Session Management
3. Cross-Site Scripting (XSS)
4. Insecure Direct Object References

5. Security Misconfiguration
6. Sensitive Data Exposure
7. Missing Function Level Access Control
8. Cross-Site Request Forgery (CSRF)
9. Using Known Vulnerable Components
10. Unvalidated Redirects and Forwards

Injection

An application is vulnerable to injection attacks if it sends untrusted data to an interpreter. There are many types of injections: SQL, LDAP, XPATH, and so on. From the point of view of ASP.NET Web API, I cover two types of injections, namely SQL injection and overposting.

SQL Injection

SQL injection attacks operate by manipulating the input data that is subsequently used in a SQL query as is without sanitization in such a way that the SQL query performs a database operation not intended by the developer. Almost all applications, whether web applications or otherwise, must use some kind of store to persist data resulting from the interactions with the end user or other systems or as a result of the internal processing of the inputs. The most common type of data stores are relational databases or SQL databases. The defining characteristic of a SQL database is its support for Structured Query Language (SQL) to manage the stored data.

A SQL query consists of one or more SQL statements such as `SELECT`, `INSERT`, `UPDATE`, and `DELETE`. If a query contains multiple statements, a semicolon (;) separator is used to separate the statements. A SQL statement consists of language elements such as clauses, expressions, and so on.

A `SELECT` SQL statement is the most common, and the `WHERE` clause of the `SELECT` statement is as famous as the `SELECT` statement itself. The `WHERE` clause gives us the ability to get precisely the data we need. In an organization with 10,000 employees, a table storing the employee records will have as many records as the number of employees. If I'm interested in getting the details of an employee, a simple `SELECT` statement such as `SELECT * FROM employee WHERE employee_id = 12345` can return the details of the employee with an identifier of 12345. The `WHERE` clause is very flexible. I can query the employee table not only by the ID, but also by using any other attribute (of the field in the world of the database), such as `WHERE first_name = 'John'`.

SQL statements themselves are just strings, and in a language such as C# we can declare a variable of type string and store the SQL statement, such as `string sql = "SELECT * FROM employee WHERE employee_id = 12345"`. When the input data to the `SELECT` statement, which is the employee ID of 12345, has to change based on user input, an easy way to frame the `SELECT` statement is to concatenate the ID with the skeleton SQL. So, you will start off with `string sql = "SELECT * FROM employee WHERE employee_id ={0}";` and then plug in the value, which is from the user input using `String.Format()` or even just plain concatenation. This approach is the root cause for SQL injection attacks, specifically when the user input is plugged in as is without any validation or sanitization. The input plugged in need not be from a user input on a screen. In the case of a web API, it can be based on the value coming in the request header, URI, query string, or the message body. Let's take an example. Listing 15-1 shows a simple GET action method that returns an `Employee` object based on the ID passed in.

Listing 15-1. GET Action Method

```
public Employee Get(string id)
{
        return repository.GetEmployee(id);
}
```

The controller might be using good practices related to design such as dependency injection and repository pattern, but the incoming ID is never validated and is simply passed into the repository method. The `GetEmployee` repository method can pass the unsanitized value further down. Finally, in the data access layer (if there is one), the ID is simply concatenated to a SQL string to form a `SELECT` statement and executed against the database, as shown in Listing 15-2.

Listing 15-2. SQL Execution

```
string connectionString = "Put your connection string here";
string sql = "SELECT * FROM employee WHERE employee_id = " + id; // id is straight from the URI
using (var connection = new SqlConnection(connectionString))
{
        using (var cmd = new SqlCommand(sql, connection))
        {
                connection.Open();
                // use the reader returned by cmd.ExecuteReader(); to create Employee object
        }
}
```

This web API is vulnerable to SQL injection attacks. If a user sends a GET to `http://server/api/employees/12345`, the approach just discussed works great. If another user sends a GET to `http://server/api/employees/12345;%20update%20employees%20set%20password='abc'; --`, two statements executed will be `SELECT * FROM employees WHERE employee_id=12345;` and `UPDATE employees SET password='abc'; --`. Now, the user who issued the previous GET can log in as any other employee, assuming the employees table stores the password in clear text in the password column. It is a far too simplistic of an example, but it is good enough to demonstrate the risk potential.

If the user issues a GET to `http://server/api/employees/12345;Truncate%20table%20employees`, it can have an even more devastating effect, provided the SQL user account under which the connection is established is authorized to truncate tables. There are three methods to defend against SQL injection attacks.

1. The first line of defense in the world of ASP.NET Web API is using model binding correctly. In the preceding example, even if the developer is not aware of SQL injection, if she has followed the basics of programming in a strongly typed language such as C# and used the correct type to declare the action parameter as integer, especially given the fact that identifiers are generally numeric, a SQL injection risk is avoided. Model binding will fail to convert the string to the expected numeric value and the request will fail with 400 - Bad Request.

2. The second line of defense is validating the input for illegal characters. If the employee identifier must be a string, such as 'jqhuman' instead of 12345, model binding is of no protection and the action parameter must be `string`. In that case, the incoming parameter can be checked for illegal values such as semicolons, quotes, comment delimiters such as --, or /* */. This approach, called blacklisting, is slightly inferior to whitelisting, where you allow only a certain set of characters. For example, if you know that the employee ID in your organization is based on names—for example, John Q. Human is jqhuman—you can simply allow only characters a through z, making any other character illegal. Of course, we are assuming here the user ID will never contain any other character even if an employee name contains one, as in the case of Richard Ricochet O'Connell.

3. The third and the most important line of defense is to never concatenate values into SQL and use parameters. I rewrote Listing 15-2 to use parameters, as shown in Listing 15-3.

Listing 15-3. SQL Execution Using Parameters

```
string sql = "SELECT * FROM employee WHERE employee_id = @ID;";
using (var connection = new SqlConnection(connectionString))
{
        using (var cmd = new SqlCommand(sql, connection))
        {
                cmd.Parameters.Add("@ID", SqlDbType.Int);
                cmd.Parameters["@ID"].Value = id; // from the URI after validation

                connection.Open();
                // use the reader returned by cmd.ExecuteReader(); to create Employee object
        }
}
```

■ **Tip** By using an object-relational mapper (ORM) like Entity Framework (EF), you can indirectly use the parameterized queries. ORM, while executing the query corresponding to your filter expression, uses parameterized queries. So, ORM is not just for smoothing out the relational world to the object world impedance mismatch. There are other benefits.

Overposting

An ASP.NET Web API application is vulnerable to overposting if it takes all the properties of the model object used in the binding blindly for further processing without any validation. One of the great things about ASP.NET Web API is that it has the same model binding capabilities of ASP.NET MVC. MVC model binding will feel like magic most of the time. The controller action method's parameters are automatically populated based on what comes in the HTTP request. Binding frees developers from writing the boilerplate code to copy the values in the request to properties of an object they want to work with. The action method code remains crisp and clean, thanks to the binding magic.

Although it is one of the coolest things, it does come with a downside. The model binder will try to map and set all the data it can in the action method parameters from the request. Let's say we have an `Employee` class, as shown in Listing 15-4.

Listing 15-4. Employee

```
public class Employee
{
    public int Id { get; set; }
    public string FirstName { get; set; }
    public string LastName { get; set; }
    public string Address { get; set; }
    public string Phone { get; set; }
    public bool IsEligibleForBonus { get; set; }
}
```

`EmployeeController` with the action method handling updates (PUT) accepts an `Employee` object as a parameter, as shown in Listing 15-5. This method is intended to be used by an internal web application for the employees to update their contact details. The web application has a screen with fields corresponding to only the contact details properties: `FirstName`, `LastName`, `Address`, and `Phone`. The `IsEligibleForBonus` property of the `Employee` class denotes if that particular employee is eligible for the annual bonus based on individual performance and a few other similar parameters. There is a database field backing this property, but the screen used by the employees to update the contact address will not show a field for a user to enter any value to be bound to this property.

Listing 15-5. PUT Action Method

```
public void Put(Employee emp)
{
    // repository.Save(emp);
}
```

Now, all a tech-savvy employee has to do is to gather the JSON representation of the `Employee` object sent back in any of the HTTP GET responses to know that the property `IsEligibleForBonus` exists. With that knowledge, he can manipulate an address change HTTP POST to send the additional field of "IsEligibleForBonus":"true" to make himself eligible for the bonus payout! The major problem here is the approach of using the domain object directly as the parameter for the action method that allows a user to overpost.

It gets even worse if the `Employee` class has a property representing the user account, as shown in Listing 15-6.

Listing 15-6. Employee Class with UserAccount Property

```
public class Employee
{
    public int Id { get; set; }
    public string FirstName { get; set; }
    public string LastName { get; set; }
    public string Address { get; set; }
    public string Phone { get; set; }
    public bool IsEligibleForBonus { get; set; }

    public UserAccount Account { get; set; }
}
```

Assuming that the `UserAccount` class has the `Password` property, sending a JSON like the one in Listing 15-7 is all it takes to set the password property of the `UserAccount` object to any random password. If the database update is done manually based on the `Employee` object, there is a good chance the password will not get updated because you will be trying to update only the employees table. If the `Employee` class is an entity class of an ORM such as EF you are trying to reuse and `Account` is a navigation property, the effects can be devastating, with the password coming in the manipulated request making it all the way to your data store.

EF is an ORM that enables.NET Framework developers to work with relational data using domain-specific objects. By specifying the mapping between your class model and the table model, you can let EF manage the database operations such as selecting, inserting, updating, or deleting table rows without writing any data-access code. For more information, see `http://msdn.microsoft.com/en-us/data/ef.aspx`.

Listing 15-7. Request JSON

```
{
        "Id":12345,
        "Address":"123 Birchwood Lane",
        "Phone":"123-456-7890",
        "IsEligibleForBonus":true,
        "Account":
        {
                "Password":"some random password"
        }
}
```

The best approach to prevent overposting vulnerabilities in ASP.NET Web API is to never use entity classes directly for model binding. Using a subset of the entity class that expects nothing more and nothing less for the scenario at hand is the best approach. For example, using the class shown in Listing 15-8 for model binding will prevent any overposting. In this case, any overposted data is simply ignored by the binder.

Listing 15-8. Employee View Model

```
public class EmployeeModel
{
    public int Id { get; set; }
    public string FirstName { get; set; }
    public string LastName { get; set; }
    public string Address { get; set; }
    public string Phone { get; set; }
}
```

Of course, you need to make sure the values stored in these properties are transferred to the `Employee` object before you can store it in the database. You can accomplish the same manually or use a convention-based object to an object mapper such as AutoMapper (`http://automapper.org/`).

Broken Authentication and Session Management

From the point of view of ASP.NET Web API, I leave out session management because it does not apply to the stateless services we build using ASP.NET Web API. I have covered authentication extensively in this book, but one point worth noting here is the use of global message handlers for authentication.

As covered in Chapter 3, the global message handlers run for all the requests. Contrast this with per-route message handlers that run for the requests falling within that route and the filters that run only for that specific action method when applied to the action method. By using a global message handler or a global filter for authentication, you can ensure that all API calls are authenticated without depending on the skills and knowledge levels of individual programmers who write the various action methods. For web-hosting, you can also use an HTTP module to ensure all the requests are authenticated.

Cross-Site Scripting (XSS)

Cross-site scripting (XSS) is all about a malicious user injecting client-side script into web pages that will be viewed by other users. This form of vulnerability is not applicable to ASP.NET Web API.

XSS comes in two flavors:

1. The nonpersistent form of XSS that occurs when the input from the client in the form of a query string is used as is by a server to generate the response without cleansing. This form of XSS is totally irrelevant to ASP.NET Web API.

2. The persistent form of XSS that occurs when the input from the client is stored in a persistent store without sanitizing and subsequently retrieved and written to the response without cleansing.

Take the case of a POST request that comes to our Employee API. Let's say we create a new employee or even update an existing employee with the name exactly the same way it comes in the request. For example, if the request comes in with the name as `<script>alert('Howdy!');</script>`, we store the same as the name of the employee without any cleaning. If this web API is used by a web application that writes the name of the employee as is into an HTTP response to a browser, we have a persistent XSS problem.

However, it is not the responsibility of the web API to encode the data and store it. The web API is HTTP based, but it can be consumed by anything and the data displayed can be in any device and by any application. Escaping this input is a moot point for, say, a WPF application displaying the name in a label in a window. It is a problem only when the name with a script tag gets written as is into the HTTP response sent to a web browser. Therefore the responsibility of preventing XSS vulnerability will be that of the web application consuming the web API.

Even if the `GetAllEmployees` method returns `<script>alert('Howdy!');</script>` instead of John Q. Law, the Home/Index view can HTML encode the name before generating the HTML for browser rendering. By default, a JavaScript library such as JQuery performs HTML encoding. So does the Razor view engine in ASP.NET MVC. To summarize, in most of the typical cases XSS will not be a concern for ASP.NET Web API.

Insecure Direct Object References

RESTful URIs are hackable and in fact they are supposed to be hackable. For example, let's say `http://server/api/employees/12345` can give information about an employee John Q. Human with an employee ID of 12345. If John gets to see his own details using that URI, it is very natural for any curious person to see what this endpoint will return for his coworker with an ID of 12346. The direct object here is the identifier of an employee. If we blindly return the data based on ID, it becomes an insecure direct object reference.

This is precisely the point of authorization. Authorization need not be limited to the level of action methods. Sometimes, it needs to be more granular than that. Failure to authorize at that level for the example we looked at is an example of insecure direct object references.

However, one point to note with respect to ASP.NET Web API compared to ASP.NET MVC is that the URI of ASP.NET Web API is not visible to a typical user even when the client application consuming the web API is a web application. In other words, if the URI of the employee details page of an ASP.NET MVC application is `http://server/hrapplication/employee/getdetails/12345`, it is highly likely a user will attempt to edit the URI and try it with another employee ID. In the case of ASP.NET Web API, the URI is not exposed to the end user. Security by obscurity is not a sound security principle, though, and you must implement authorization at the right granular level regardless of whether a user can see the URI or not.

In the preceding subsection on overposting, I suggested using a model class and gave the example of the `EmployeeModel` class (Listing 15-8). There is a property with the name `Id`. If you think about it, can a user make an HTTP POST and update the contact details of some other employee? The answer is yes. The model class does solve the overposting vulnerability, but it does not prevent a user from making unintended updates. Such vulnerability is another form of insecure direct object references. So, this form of vulnerability is not limited to URIs.

Security Misconfiguration

Security is both configured and programmed. Security misconfiguration, as the name indicates, is about not configuring security the right way. The term configuration here is not just limited to the configuration file such as Web.config that a programmer will instantly relate to as she reads the subsection title. Per OWASP, failing to keep your software updated by not applying patches; not disabling and removing unnecessary services, software, and operating system accounts; not blocking unwanted ports; and assigning the same credentials for connecting to development and production databases all belong to this category.

Although the preceding activities are related to IT administration, programmers can introduce vulnerabilities as well. Here are two such examples.

1. Sending a stack trace to the end user when there is an exception in the production environment is a security risk. Specifying the `Never` option for the error details inclusion policy in `WebApiConfig.cs` in the `App_Start` folder can stop the stack trace from getting to the client, as follows: `config.IncludeErrorDetailPolicy = IncludeErrorDetailPolicy.Never;` A programmer changing this setting to `Always` and checking it in and the build process propagating the change to production is an example of a security misconfiguration vulnerability introduced by the programmer and the software configuration management process.

2. The purpose of the `HttpRuntimeSection.EnableHeaderChecking` property is to enable encoding of the carriage return and newline characters in the response headers to prevent HTTP response splitting attacks. By default, it is true so that an ASP.NET application is not vulnerable. Setting this to false is another example of security misconfiguration.

Sensitive Data Exposure

Sensitive data exposure means failure to secure data at rest and data in motion. First, let's try to understand data in motion versus data at rest. Data in motion, as the name indicates, is about data in the network, on the move. Data at rest is stored data, such as data in files and databases. When it comes to securing data, data in motion hogs the limelight because you will naturally worry more about the data that is traveling out of the perimeter you can control than the data safely stored on the servers inside your secure data centers.

Data at Rest

If Mallory tampers with messages exchanged between Alice and Bob, the impact is relatively low because it affects only Alice and Bob. If Mallory gets her hands on sensitive stored data, though, it can affect every Tom, Dick, and Harry whose data is stored in an insecure way.

Sensitive data vulnerabilities for data at rest stem from sensitive data getting stored in clear text without any encryption, using a poor encryption algorithm written in-house, improper use of a standard encryption algorithm, or lack of better processes to secure associated cryptographic materials such as keys.

Hashing Passwords for Secure Storage

In Chapter 6, I described encryption and signing from the perspective of securing data in motion, although encryption can be used to secure data at rest as well. Now, we take a look at one of the techniques closely related to securing data at rest, which is hashing. Hashing is the process by which arbitrary data or a message is converted into a fixed-length string.

The important difference between encryption and hashing is that with hashing, the output cannot be reversed back to the original state, unlike encryption. Data encrypted can be decrypted using the same keys, as in the case of symmetric encryption, or using a different key in the case of asymmetric encryption. Data that is hashed remains hashed forever. The defining characteristic of hashed data is that the original data can never be recovered out of the hashed data. What is the use for it, then?

If I hash 'world peace' into 123456 using some algorithm and store the hash in my data store, I don't need to worry about someone with malicious intentions being able to recover the secret 'world peace' from 123456. Anytime I run 'world peace' through the algorithm, it will consistently give me 123456. Thus, a great use for hashing is to store sensitive information like a password, which the user will need to enter every time to log in to our system. We can hash the password entered and compare the hashed result with what we stored previously to make the authentication decision. Hashing therefore is a great technique for securing sensitive data at rest, such as a password.

■ **Note** Hashing is not a one-size-fits-all solution for all data at rest security needs. You can't hash a credit card number and store it for later use because a credit card number can't be recovered from the hash. Encryption is more appropriate in that case.

There are multiple algorithms available for hashing. The MD5 Message Digest algorithm is a widely used algorithm that produces a 128-bit (16-byte) hash value. It has a few weaknesses, which led the cryptography world to start using Security Hash Algorithm (SHA-1). Security flaws were identified with SHA-1 as well, and SHA-2 is the currently recommended algorithm. At the time of writing this book, a new algorithm SHA-3 is already in place, complementing SHA-2. SHA-3 is not supposed to supersede SHA-2 because no weakness has been demonstrated against SHA-2 so far.

The System.Security.Cryptography namespace in the .NET Framework has the classes corresponding to different hashing algorithms: MD5, SHA1, SHA256, SHA384, SHA512, and so on. The last three classes represent the SHA-2 family of algorithms that produce a digest of size 256, 384, and 512 bits, respectively.

Let's create an SHA256 hash for an extremely long word straight from the English dictionary, "Supercalifragilisticexpialidocious," and the small word "hello." See Listing 15-9 for the code to create the hash.

Listing 15-9. SHA256 Hash

```
string data = "Supercalifragilisticexpialidocious";
SHA256 hasher = SHA256.Create();
byte[] hash = hasher.ComputeHash(Encoding.UTF8.GetBytes(data));

string hashString = BitConverter.ToString(hash).Replace("-", "").ToLower();
```

It is extremely simple to create the hash. Just a call to the ComputeHash method will do the trick. The BitConverter class is used to convert the byte array into a hex string representation. The output for the words "Supercalifragilisticexpialidocious" and "hello" is shown in Listing 15-10.

Listing 15-10. Hash Output

```
94730f57d7e41018d963d92fbf11618dce8274ca2c1bf72274e0285a6013c17b
2cf24dba5fb0a30e26e83b2ac5b9e29e1b161e5c1fa7425e73043362938b9824
```

Although the input strings are drastically different in terms of length, the digest length in both cases is 256 bits. One important point, though, is that it is easy to crack these hashes. In other words, it is possible to get the original string if you input these hash values to any of those online hash crackers. Even that big word is no exception. The fundamental premise with which we started this section is that the original string cannot be recovered from the hash. How are online tools capable of doing the extraction? These tools are not even batching or offline programs, but online web applications that can derive the original string in a few seconds.

As we saw in Chapter 8, we can brute-force attack the hash. On the fly, we can compute the hash for a and compare it with the value entered. If no match, we proceed with b. When we reach z, we start with aa and so on. As we established in Chapter 8, it is going to take quite a bit of time and CPU power to make this happen.

It is possible to compute the hash ahead of time for well-known words, such as the words in a dictionary, and when the hash is entered it becomes simply a matter of lookup. Clearly, then, the hashing in its original form is not a good choice for storing passwords because the malicious user with the hashed passwords can easily get the original string using something like online tools do.

The fundamental problem with plain hashing is that the mapping of a specific output to the corresponding input can be precomputed and stored. An easy solution to this problem is *salting*. A salt is just a random string that is added to the data before hashing so that the output cannot be mapped back to the input using precomputed mappings. Thus, salting makes all the attacks, including the dictionary-based attacks, on the hash ineffective, with the exception of brute-force attacks. It is important to keep the salt value longer, and if a unique salt value is used for each message or data it will be all the more secure.

Salting ensures that attackers can't fast forward the attack process using lookup tables, but an attacker can mount a brute-force attack. With CPUs getting more powerful and cheaper and the availability of elastic computing power available for use on an hourly basis with no up-front investment in the hardware, a brute-force attack is not a theoretical possibility. There is a technique available known as *key stretching* that can make a brute-force attack slower. It will make it so slow, in fact, that it will be practically impossible to break the hash. In a practical world, taking a few months to crack a hash is as bad as being unable to crack it, at least from an attacker's point of view.

Password-Based Key Derivation Function 2 (PBKDF2) is a key derivation function that is part of RSA Laboratories' Public-Key Cryptography Standards (PKCS) series, specifically PKCS #5 version 2.0, also published as Internet Engineering Task Force's RFC 2898. It replaces an earlier standard, PBKDF1, which could produce only derived keys up to 160 bits long.

There are standard algorithms available for key stretching, such as the PBKDF2 algorithm. It hashes the input password or data along with a salt value and repeats the process many times to produce a derived key. This repeated hashing makes brute-force attacks time consuming and frustrating for an attacker. The recommended number of iterations is 1,000. The higher the number of iterations, the more it is going to need CPU power and hence time, but the security will be better. See Listing 15-11 for the code that generates an SHA-1 hash using salt and PBKDF2. The `Rfc2898DeriveBytes` class is SHA-1 based, and hence the resulting hash is SHA-1 and not SHA256 in this example.

Listing 15-11. SHA-1 Hash with Salt and Key Stretching

```
string data = "hello";

byte[] salt = new Byte[32];
using (var provider = new RNGCryptoServiceProvider())
{
    provider.GetBytes(salt);
}

Rfc2898DeriveBytes pbkdf2 = new Rfc2898DeriveBytes(data, salt);
pbkdf2.IterationCount = 1000;

byte[] hash = pbkdf2.GetBytes(32);

string hashString = Convert.ToBase64String(hash);
```

How do we put this to use? Assuming your user table has user_id and password columns, add another column for salt and store `hashString` and `salt` from Listing 15-11 in the password and salt columns, respectively, at the time of user registration. You can store the salt as it is; that is, as a byte array itself. Or you can base64 encode it. Listing 15-12 shows how to authenticate user credentials at the time the user logs back in.

Listing 15-12. User Credentials Authentication

```
string password = String.Empty; // Placeholder for the password from database
string saltString = String.Empty; // Placeholder for the salt from database
string userEnteredPassword = String.Empty; // User input

var pbkdf2 = new Rfc2898DeriveBytes(userEnteredPassword, Convert.FromBase64String(saltString));
pbkdf2.IterationCount = 1000;
byte[] computedHash = pbkdf2.GetBytes(32);

bool isAuthenticCredential = password.Equals(

Convert.ToBase64String(computedHash),

StringComparison.Ordinal);
```

■ **Tip** For encrypting data in a database, you will need a key. Never store this key in the database itself. If the database is compromised, such as through SQL injection, the attacker will find it easy to get and decrypt the key if it is stored in the database itself. Instead, store it in a file to which the operating system account running the database engine has no access.

Encrypting Web.Config

We saw the distinction between data at rest and data in motion in the beginning of this section. The term data at rest is not limited to application data stored in a database or file. It does include configuration data stored in a configuration file such as Web.config. Although encrypting the entire Web.config file might not be necessary for typical cases, encrypting sections selectively is a good strategy to secure sensitive information in the configuration file. The best candidates for this are database connection strings, credentials that the web API might need to use to connect to some other systems, and so on. Encrypting the Web.config file is important because it needs to reside in a web server. The web servers are typically in DMZs.

Before we look at the process of encrypting Web.config, let's see what the `connectionStrings` section of Listing 15-13 looks like when encrypted, as shown in Listing 15-14.

Listing 15-13. Web.config Clear Text

```
<connectionStrings>
  <add name="DefaultConnection" connectionString="Data Source=.\SQLEXPRESS;
                AttachDbFilename=|DataDirectory|\aspnet-MyApplication-20121110193704.mdf;
                Initial Catalog=aspnet-MyApplication-20121110193704;Integrated Security=True;
                User Instance=True"
                providerName="System.Data.SqlClient" />
</connectionStrings>
```

Listing 15-14. Web.config Encrypted

```
<connectionStrings configProtectionProvider="RsaProtectedConfigurationProvider">
  <EncryptedData Type="http://www.w3.org/2001/04/xmlenc#Element"
    xmlns="http://www.w3.org/2001/04/xmlenc#">
    <EncryptionMethod Algorithm="http://www.w3.org/2001/04/xmlenc#tripledes-cbc" />
    <KeyInfo xmlns="http://www.w3.org/2000/09/xmldsig#">
      <EncryptedKey xmlns="http://www.w3.org/2001/04/xmlenc#">
        <EncryptionMethod Algorithm="http://www.w3.org/2001/04/xmlenc#rsa-1_5" />
        <KeyInfo xmlns="http://www.w3.org/2000/09/xmldsig#">
          <KeyName>Rsa Key</KeyName>
        </KeyInfo>
        <CipherData>
         <CipherValue>fg1RaefMxjQBV6hwx3q...1qnDmdDrsWcwk=</CipherValue>
        </CipherData>
      </EncryptedKey>
    </KeyInfo>
    <CipherData>
      <CipherValue>ld0t8MkPX9euWy2bjFj...nTEYzApmlQC9A80=</CipherValue>
    </CipherData>
  </EncryptedData>
</connectionStrings>
```

Although encryption of Web.config can be done through C# code as well, let's focus on using the aspnet_regiis utility. In production environments, it is likely that a system administrator will perform this task, so using a utility is a better fit for this purpose. The aspnet_regiis tool is located in the `%windows%\Microsoft.NET\Framework\versionNumber` folder. For example, it is "C:\Windows\Microsoft.NET\Framework\v4.0.30319" on my machine.

First, you need to grant the Windows account running the IIS worker process read access to the default RSA key container, for which the pa switch is used. I have deployed the ASP.NET Web API application in the default application pool. The account I use in the first line of Listing 15-15 reflects that fact.

Listing 15-15. aspnet_regiis Commands

```
aspnet_regiis -pa "NetFrameworkConfigurationKey" "IIS APPPOOL\DefaultAppPool"

aspnet_regiis -pef "connectionStrings" "C:\Users\102628\Desktop\MvcApplication5\MvcApplication5"

aspnet_regiis -pdf "connectionStrings" "C:\Users\102628\Desktop\MvcApplication5\MvcApplication5"
```

To encrypt, the pef switch is used. Arguments are the section name and path of the application. To decrypt the Web.config file back to clear text, the pdf switch is used.

Regardless of whether the Web.config file is encrypted or not, you can use `System.Web.Configuration.WebConfigurationManager.ConnectionStrings["DefaultConnection"].ConnectionString` to read the configuration data.

Data in Motion

Securing data in motion is a broad topic. Historically, cryptography was created mainly for the purpose of securing communications, or from the perspective of data in motion. We looked at encryption and signing from the perspective of securing data in motion in Chapter 6.

First and the foremost, in the world of the web, transport security through HTTP/TLS (also known as HTTPS) is the most fundamental as well as the most important aspect in securing communications. HTTPS, when correctly done, is the easiest to work with from a programmer's point of view because there is nothing additional that needs to be done. Of course, from the point of view of IT administration, operations, and budgeting, it means procuring, installing, and managing valid certificates on the server side.

I would like to quote a couple of paragraphs from one of Eran Hammer's posts to illustrate the fact that HTTPS is not the silver bullet for all vulnerabilities related to data in motion.

> *Doesn't HTTPS Solve Everything?*
>
> *HTTPS guarantees an end-to-end secure connection. The implementation and deployment details are critical to ensure that, but when done correctly (which is not always the case), is a great solution. What HTTPS provides is a secure channel. Any secret, password, or bearer token sent over HTTPS is protected and cannot be compromised by an attacker listening in on the line. HTTPS allows a client to send a secret to its desired destination securely.*
>
> *However, HTTPS can't help if the client's desired destination is a bad place. HTTPS doesn't help prevent phishing attacks because anyone can get an SSL certificate and show the secure icon in the browser. The fact you are using a secure channel doesn't mean the entity on the other side is good. It just means that no one else can listen in on it (just the bad guys). If a client sends their bearer token to the wrong place, even over HTTPS, it's game over.*

—Eran Hammer
`http://hueniverse.com/2010/09/oauth-2-0-without-signatures-is-bad-for-the-web/`

Eran Hammer was the lead author and editor of the OAuth specifications. The preceding quote is taken from his post pertaining to the subject of bearer tokens support in OAuth 2.0. OAuth 1.0 requires cryptographic signatures to be sent with the requests. OAuth 2.0 dropped signature and cryptography in favor of bearer tokens. We have seen key-of-holder tokens versus bearer tokens when we were dealing with SAML tokens, but the concept is that bearer tokens are like cash. Finders, keepers!

Although Eran Hammer's post pertains to OAuth access tokens, the given narrative holds good for any sensitive data in motion. HTTPS is great, but it takes a great deal of discipline and deep knowledge. We tend to take the path of least resistance, especially under project schedule pressure, to get things working. If we get an error because the certificate has some problems or there is some issue related to the server configuration, we don't generally fix the ultimate problem but only the proximate problem. It is far easier to disable the certificate checking than fix the ultimate problem. Although not intentional, we make the HTTPS mechanism vulnerable to MITM attacks in this process.

Signing ASP.NET Web API Response

The transport security of HTTPS ensures no one can eavesdrop or mount MITM attacks, but it does not ensure the end-to-end security that message security provides. In this section, I show one useful little technique related to signing. When HTTPS cannot be used or if you believe in defense in depth and want to build something additional on top of HTTPS, you can incorporate a signature to a web API response to make it tamper-proof.

I use an action filter for this so that only the selective action methods have their responses signed. Listing 15-16 shows the code for the action filter. I override the `OnActionExecuted` method to implement the signing logic. The `OnActionExecuted` method runs after the action method and hence is the appropriate place for the implementation of our logic. The signature is generated using the URI, HTTP method, and the entire message body. SHA256 HMAC is stuffed into the X-Signature response header for the client to validate.

Listing 15-16. Signing Filter

```
public class SignIt : ActionFilterAttribute
{
    public override void OnActionExecuted(HttpActionExecutedContext context)
    {
        // 256-bit shared key - hard-coded here only for the purpose of this example
        string key = "foGqiGOGLeY8VGdP2PZoS9aoOB7VjkNaUc549Ac2OCkh2t5rk9";
        key += "wTBOEbj98I7LGE1mpAkAHXabU/aHTiRhud9A==";

        string response = context.Response.Content.ReadAsStringAsync().Result;

        if (!String.IsNullOrWhiteSpace(response))
        {
            string data = String.Format("{0}{1}{2}", context.Request.RequestUri.ToString(),
                                                        context.Request.Method,
                                                            response);

            byte[] bytes = Encoding.UTF8.GetBytes(data);
            using (HMACSHA256 hmac = new HMACSHA256(Convert.FromBase64String(key)))
            {
                string signature = Convert.ToBase64String(hmac.ComputeHash(bytes));
                context.Response.Headers.Add("X-Signature", signature);
            }
        }
    }
}
```

The client can validate the signature similar to the way in which it was created. The client code is shown in Listing 15-17. I use the same key on the client side and hence this is a symmetric shared key. I compute the signature and compare it with the one in the X-Signature header. Matching values indicate the response is not tampered with. The code in Listing 15-17 assumes the X-Signature response header will always be present, for brevity's sake.

Listing 15-17. Client Validating the Response Integrity

```
static void Main(string[] args)
{
    string key = "foGqiGOGLeY8VGdP2PZoS9aoOB7VjkNaUc549Ac2OCkh2t5rk9";
    key += "wTBOEbj98I7LGE1mpAkAHXabU/aHTiRhud9A==";

    using (HttpClient client = new HttpClient())
    {
        Uri uri = new Uri("http://localhost:20759/api/employees/12345");

        string creds = String.Format("{0}:{1}", "badri", "badri");
        byte[] bytes = Encoding.ASCII.GetBytes(creds);
        var header = new AuthenticationHeaderValue("Basic", Convert.ToBase64String(bytes));
        client.DefaultRequestHeaders.Authorization = header;

        var result = client.GetAsync(uri).Result;
        string response = result.Content.ReadAsStringAsync().Result;

        string message = String.Format("{0}{1}{2}", uri.ToString(), "GET", response);

        byte[] signature = Encoding.UTF8.GetBytes(message);
        using (HMACSHA256 hmac = new HMACSHA256(Convert.FromBase64String(key)))
        {
            byte[] signatureBytes = hmac.ComputeHash(signature);
            bool isValid = Convert.ToBase64String(signatureBytes)
                                    .Equals(result.Headers.GetValues("X-Signature").First(),
                                                                StringComparison.Ordinal);
        }
    }
}
```

■ **Tip** The response headers can also be included for signing, but include sensitive custom headers only because headers can be added or changed by intermediaries. It is not a good idea to include all the headers.

Missing Function Level Access Control

The missing function level access control vulnerability is attributed to applications not protecting the low-level functions properly. This is related to insecure direct object references, but there is a major difference. Whereas insecure direct object references is about input data, the missing function level access control vulnerability is about failing to protect functions.

For example, let's say `http://server/api/employees/12345` can give information about an employee with an employee ID of 12345. A user who has read-only access to the employee details can get the JSON representation and attempt an HTTP POST on the same URI after manipulating the JSON of the GET response. If ASP.NET Web API allows HTTP POST, it is vulnerable to the missing function level access control vulnerability.

Implementing a sound authorization mechanism for every API call is very important. A global message handler or a filter that runs for all the calls and controls the access based on the claims using the subclass of `ClaimsAuthorizationManager`, as we saw in Chapter 5, is the best approach to prevent this vulnerability in ASP.NET Web API.

Cross-Site Request Forgery (CSRF)

The cross-site request forgery (CSRF, pronounced *sea-surf*) is simply tricking the web browser to issue a request to a web site using an authentication token you received previously as part of regular authentication. CSRF is typically associated with cookies containing an authentication ticket, so you might wonder what CSRF has to do with ASP.NET Web API. A web API is REST-based, and I don't use a cookie. Unfortunately, a cookie is not the only thing that can be exploited by CSRF attacks. A browser does cache things other than cookies, such as a user ID and password entered by a user directly into the browser during basic authentication.

Suppose I make a request from my web browser to `http://server.com/api/Employees/123` protected by basic authentication. Because the browser receives a WWW-Authenticate response header indicating a basic scheme, the browser pops up a dialog box and gets my credentials. The credentials are sent back diligently, like a cookie, in all the subsequent requests to the same path `/api/Employees`.

The basic authenticated credential is similar to an in-memory cookie, as you need to close your browser to get rid of the cached credentials. The browser caches the credentials with good intentions. It does not want to bombard you with authentication dialog boxes for every resource requested from the server. Unfortunately, all good intentions do not ensure good consequences.

Understanding CSRF through Basic Authentication

Let's look at an example involving ASP.NET Web API to understand how HTTP basic authentication can be exploited. Because it involves basic authentication, you can deploy the application in IIS and enable HTTPS if you would like. Transport security through HTTPS, or the lack of it, is not going to alter the end result.

We need Fiddler's help to capture traffic. If you enable HTTPS, you need to enable Fiddler to decrypt HTTPS traffic. The following steps show CSRF with ASP.NET Web API protected by HTTP basic authentication.

1. Create a new ASP.NET MVC 4 project in Visual Studio using the Web API template.

2. Create a new `ApiController` (`EmployeesController`) and a class (`Employee`), as shown in Listing 15-18.

Listing 15-18. EmployeesController

```
public class EmployeesController : ApiController
{
    [Authorize]
    public IEnumerable<Employee> Get()
    {
        return new Employee[]
        {
            new Employee() { Id = 12345, FirstName = "John", LastName = "Human" },
            new Employee() { Id = 67890, FirstName = "Jane", LastName = "Public" }
        };
    }

    [Authorize]
    public Employee Get(int id)
    {
        return new Employee()
            {
                Id = id,
                FirstName = "John",
                LastName = "Human"
            };
    }
```

```
    public void Post(Employee emp)
    {
        // repository.Save(emp);
    }

    public void Put(Employee emp)
    {
        // repository.Save(emp);
    }
}

public class Employee
{
    public int Id { get; set; }
    public string FirstName { get; set; }
    public string LastName { get; set; }
}
```

3. Implement basic authentication using a message handler, as we did in Chapter 8.
4. Hook this message handler into the pipeline by adding the handler to the handlers collection in the `WebApiConfig` file in the `App_Start` folder.
5. Change the view Index.cshtml corresponding to `HomeController`, as shown in Listing 15-19.

Listing 15-19. Index.csthml: Index View of HomeController

```
@section scripts{
    <script type="text/javascript">
        $(document).ready(function () {
            $('#search').click(function () {
                $('#employees').empty();
                $.getJSON("/api/employees", function (data) {
                    $.each(data, function (i, employee) {
                        var content = employee.Id + ' ' + employee.FirstName;
                        content = content + ' ' + employee.LastName;
                        $('#employees').append($('<li/>', { text: content }));
                    });
                });
            });
        });
    </script>
}
<div>
    <div>
        <h1>
            Employees Listing</h1>
        <input id="search" type="button" value="Get" />
    </div>
    <div>
        <ul id="employees" />
    </div>
</div>
```

6. The view simply makes an AJAX call to /api/employees using JQuery and shows the result as an unordered list.

7. Create a new MVC controller, `BadController` with `Index` action. The controller action method and the view are shown in Listing 15-20 and Listing 15-21, respectively.

Listing 15-20. BadController: Index Action Method

```
public class BadController : Controller
{
    public ActionResult Index()
    {
        return View();
    }
}
```

Listing 15-21. BadController: Index Action View

```
@{
    ViewBag.Title = "Index";
}

<h2>Index</h2>
<img height="0" width="0" src="/api/employees/1234" />
@section scripts{
    <script type="text/javascript">
        document.getElementById('myForm').submit();
    </script>
}

<form id="myForm" action="/api/employees" method="post">
    <input type="hidden" name="Id" value="78956" />
    <input type="hidden" name="FirstName" value="John" />
    <input type="hidden" name="LastName" value="Human" />
</form>
```

8. In this case, `BadController` runs in the same application, but it is only a placeholder for illustration. It can be anything, such as a page served up by any site or even a static HTML page in your computer.

9. Now that we are done with the coding, let's test this using the following steps.

    a. Go to `https://server/yourapplication`, which will show the Index view of `HomeController`.

    b. If you have configured HTTPS and have not used a valid server-side certificate, the browser will complain. Ignore it for the purpose of this test.

    c. Click the Get button. The browser should pop up a dialog box, get your credentials, and show the list of employees as an unordered list.

    d. Without closing the browser, browse to any sites of your liking and come back to our application after some time. It can even be the next day.

e. Go to `https://server/yourapplication/bad`. The page will show up normal and is nothing special.

f. If you see the Fiddler capture, you will notice that the bad page has made both a GET and a POST request to the API successfully, using your cached basic credentials. As you can imagine, the bad page can be something served to you by any web server in the world. The page is just plain HTML. To the eyes, it doesn't look different. By making the image width and height zero, even that broken image is not visible.

The fact of the matter is that the web page to which you have surfed to has successfully executed a GET and a POST, tricking your browser to send the authorize header with your credentials to our web API. Through the POST request, it could have inserted a random employee into our employee database. Our GET is nullipotent, so there's not much damage there.

It is better to avoid HTTP basic authentication for a web API that will need to be accessed from a web page running inside the context of a browser. Does that mean HTTP basic authentication is practically worthless? The answer is no. We have a CSRF problem only when a browser is in the picture. For nonbrowser clients, basic authentication over HTTPS is still a good, simple option.

CSRF Involving Cookies

CSRF involving cookies is typically relevant to ASP.NET Web API when it is protected by forms authentication. Forms authentication is covered in depth in Chapter 2. When you navigate to a page for the first time, you will be redirected to a login page. On successful authentication, a cookie with an authentication ticket gets written to the HTTP response. The browser gets the cookie and starts sending the cookie back to the web application in the subsequent requests, until the time the cookie expires. If the cookie is an in-memory cookie, when the user closes the browser the cookie ceases to exist.

As long as the cookie is valid, the browser diligently sends the cookie when a request is made to the web application that has sent the cookie in the first place. The key point to note is that browser sends the cookie whether you as the user initiate an HTTP GET or POST or the browser itself makes it.

When will the browser make a request without you telling it to? When an HTML page has to be rendered, the browser makes multiple requests without getting your permission to get files like CSS, script files, and images. If there is an image with the `src` attribute set to URI `http://server.com/employee/delete/12345`, the browser will make the GET request and trigger the code execution on the server side and probably delete the employee with identifier 12345.

The resource `http://server.com/employee/delete/12345`, corresponding to an action method `Delete` in `EmployeeController`, is protected by forms authentication. If a request is made to the URI directly, the browser will be redirected to the login page. Only on successful authentication can a user can do anything useful with the web application.

The browser is making a GET to this page without your knowledge. If you have previously logged into this web application and have a session open—that is, you have a live cookie with the authentication ticket—the browser diligently sends the cookie with this GET request triggered by the browser's attempt to retrieve the image.

ASP.NET is happy because it gets the ticket and runs the code on the server side. The effect can be as devastating as someone draining your bank account, but it all boils down to what the code on the server side does. Making GET requests nullipotent is a deterrent, but not sufficient to plug this security hole. It is quite easy to post an HTML form using a few lines of JavaScript.

If possible, it is better to avoid forms authentication involving cookies with ASP.NET Web API. There is no reason for you to use cookies containing an authentication ticket to be sent back and forth between your web browser-based client and a web API, like what forms authentication does. However, if you must use such a cookie for a valid reason—honestly, I can't think of even one valid reason why cookies must be used with a web API—you have to be aware of the fact that your web API is now susceptible to CSRF attacks.

We are resigned to the fact that we have to live with a cookie. How do we prevent CSRF attacks? By looking to the people who have already designed such mechanisms for web applications, such as the antiforgery token that ASP.NET MVC provides.

One of the important characteristics of CSRF is that the malicious user is generally in the dark with respect to the interactions between the user and the web site. He simply tricks the browser to make a request that the user does intend to initiate and expects to gain something out of this unintended request. ASP.NET MVC's antiforgery token is a simple mechanism that utilizes the preceding fact (see Figure 15-1).

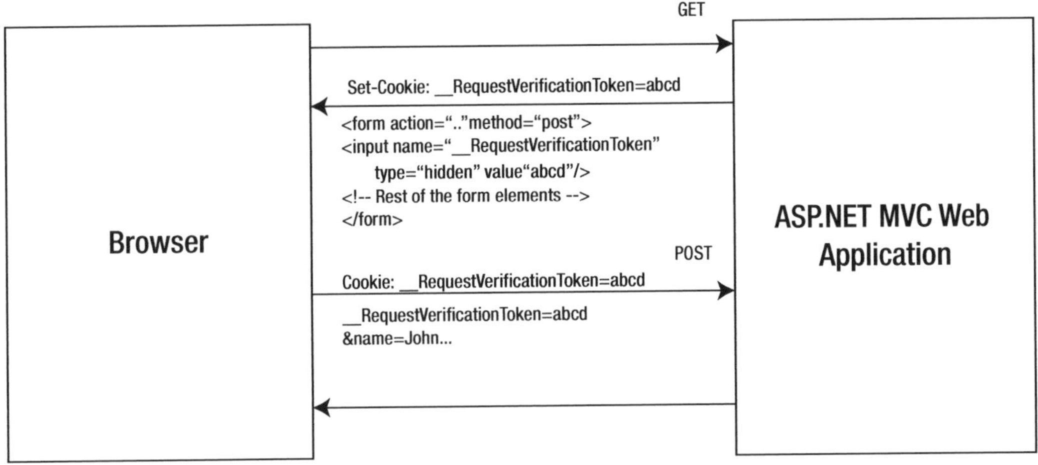

Figure 15-1. *MVC antiforgery token in action (approximated for easy understanding)*

A token is written into a hidden field that is part of the HTML form to be submitted, and the same token is written as a cookie into the response. When an authentic user makes the POST, the cookie is sent back with the token in the header and so is the hidden field with the token in the body. On the server side, a simple check that compares these two values can detect CSRF. The malicious user can trick the browser into making a request with cookies but cannot forge the request to contain the same token because he is in the dark with respect to what gets sent between the user or the victim and the web application.

In the preceding example, the attacker can trick the browser to issue a request to the web application with a `__RequestVerificationToken` cookie in the request but will not know the value abcd to put in the message body. Of course, abcd is just a placeholder and a real token will be a long, hard-to-guess cryptic string. The ASP.NET MVC web application can immediately reject the request because the message body either does not contain the `__RequestVerificationToken` field at all or, if it is present, the value will be different from the value in the cookie.

The MVC framework offers the `AntiForgeryToken()` helper method that can be used to insert the hidden field and cookie. By putting `@Html.AntiForgeryToken()` inside the form, we can accomplish the same thing. On the server side, the action method that handles the POST can be decorated with a `ValidateAntiForgeryToken` attribute that will take care of comparing the header and body token values and rejecting the forged requests.

One fundamental assumption with the implementation of an antiforgery token is that our ASP.NET MVC application does not have any XSS loophole. If there is one, a malicious user can read the antiforgery token value and use it to forge valid HTTP POSTs.

Using the ASP.NET MVC Antiforgery Token with ASP.NET Web API

It is not hard to implement a mechanism similar to the antiforgery token of ASP.NET MVC. Better yet, you can piggyback on the antiforgery mechanism itself. If you have `@Html.AntiForgeryToken()` somewhere inside your MVC view, your JavaScript should be able to read the hidden field and stuff the token in a custom header when you make the AJAX call to the web API.

Assuming that the web API and your web application are in the same domain so that the cookie containing the session ticket created by the web application can be used by the web API as well to establish identity, all three things will travel in the HTTP request headers: the cookie with the authentication ticket, the cookie with the token value, and the custom header with the token value.

On the server side, a message handler can be plugged into the web API pipeline to perform the token validation. The message handler can right away reject the request if the custom header is missing. If both the cookie and the custom header are present in the request, the handler can compare the token value in the cookie and custom header and reject the request if there is any discrepancy in the values. There is a method available, `AntiForgery.Validate(string, string)`, that the message handler code can use to perform the comparison of the token values. When your browser gets tricked to send the cookies as a result of a CSRF attack, it will send both cookies but not the custom header. Even if the header is sent, the value will not match. The following steps show how to use an antiforgery token with ASP.NET Web API.

1. We use the same project we created in the previous subsection. Create an action method `TestAft` in `HomeController` and create a view for this action, copying and pasting the code from Listing 15-22. By including the `AntiForgeryToken()` helper, we make sure a hidden field with a token gets written into the page. In the case of ASP.NET MVC, this typically will be inside a form so that this field travels in the message body when the form is submitted. In the case of an AJAX call to a web API, we simply need to take that token value and put it in a request header, which I have named X-AFT. When this view is converted into HTML and sent to the browser, in addition to the hidden field a cookie is also sent, which looks something like this: `Set-Cookie: __RequestVerificationToken_L012...I081; path=/; HttpOnly`. The browser starts sending this cookie to the server for all subsequent requests. As we make this GET request, the X-AFT request header and the cookie get sent to our web API. If the user is already forms authenticated, the ticket cookie will also get sent.

Listing 15-22. Index.csthml: Index View of HomeController

```
@section scripts{
    <script type="text/javascript">
        $(document).ready(function () {
            $('#search').click(function () {
                $('#employees').empty();

                $.ajax({
                    cache: false,
                    dataType: 'json',
                    type: 'GET',
                    headers: { "X-AFT": $('input[name="__RequestVerificationToken"]').val() },
                    contentType: 'application/json; charset=utf-8',
                    url: '/api/employees',
                    success: function (data) {
                        $.each(data, function (i, employee) {
                            var content = employee.Id + ' ' + employee.FirstName;
                            content = content + ' ' + employee.LastName;
                            $('#employees').append($('<li/>', { text: content }));
                        });
                    }
                });
            });
        });
    </script>
}
```

```
@Html.AntiForgeryToken()
<div>
    <div>
        <h1>
            Employees Listing</h1>
        <input id="search" type="button" value="Get" />
    </div>
    <div>
        <ul id="employees" />
    </div>
</div>
```

2. Create a message handler by calling `AntiForgeryTokenHandler` as shown in Listing 15-23 to validate the antiforgery token. Note the following points.

    a. The message handler extracts the cookie token and form token (in our case it becomes the header token) using `request.Headers.GetCookies(AntiForgeryConfig.CookieName)` and `request.Headers.GetValues("X-AFT")`, respectively, and passes the token values to the `AntiForgery.Validate` method.

    b. If the tokens are valid, the `Validate` method does nothing. Otherwise, it throws an exception. We swallow that, but the `isCsrf` flag will not be set to false. Based on the flag, we send a forbidden response and short-circuit the pipeline processing.

    c. The message handler is unforgiving. It assumes every request is a forged request and expects you to prove otherwise by sending the appropriate tokens. It also expects the antiforgery tokens to be sent in all kinds of requests, including GET, but how you want to handle this part is entirely up to you. You can surely show some leniency for nullipotent methods like GET.

Listing 15-23. AntiForgeryTokenHandler

```
public class AntiForgeryTokenHandler : DelegatingHandler
{
    protected override async Task<HttpResponseMessage> SendAsync(HttpRequestMessage request,
                                                        CancellationToken cancellationToken)
    {
        bool isCsrf = true;

        CookieHeaderValue cookie = request.Headers
                                        .GetCookies(AntiForgeryConfig.CookieName)
                                            .FirstOrDefault();
        if (cookie != null)
        {
            if (request.Headers.Contains("X-AFT"))
            {
                try
                {
                    AntiForgery.Validate(cookie[AntiForgeryConfig.CookieName].Value,
                                    request.Headers.GetValues("X-AFT").First());
```

```
                    isCsrf = false;
                }
                catch (Exception) { }
            }
        }

        if (isCsrf)
        {
            return request.CreateResponse(HttpStatusCode.Forbidden);
        }

        return await base.SendAsync(request, cancellationToken);
    }
}
```

3. To see this handler in action, make a GET request to `http://localhost:<port>/home/testaft` and click Get button.

■ **Note** For those with an eye for details, a 403 – Forbidden response is sent instead of 401 – Unauthorized to signify the fact that we are refusing to serve this request. 401 – Unauthorized is sent when the credentials are missing or if the credentials are incorrect. However, in our case it is a request forgery. 404 – File not found can also be sent back because we don't want to send the reason why we refuse to serve the request.

WEB API FOR JAVASCRIPT CONSUMPTION

The root cause for the CSRF evil is the web browser itself. The cookies and cached credentials are the proximate reasons, but if there is no web browser there will be no CSRF. However, browser-based applications are everywhere and nothing beats the AJAX-powered user experience in the web browsers—not just from a performance perspective, but even from an end user perception.

So if we have to develop a web API to be consumed by JavaScript, how can we secure the web API? It is a unique problem because we tend to focus on security with the assumption that endpoints are trustworthy. Alice and Bob are always good natured folks. Only Mallory and Eve are bad, aren't they?

In the case of JavaScript, any kind of security logic you write will be exposed to the users. A smart user can always figure out what is going on by reviewing the script code and debugging HTTP messages through tools like Fiddler. Thus, we cannot implement any kind of security directly in JavaScript. JavaScript must not have the knowledge of any sensitive information like credentials or the knowledge to obtain the same. Credentials should be made available to JavaScript either by the user interaction or by the server-side application on a need basis.

One option is to have the server-side code drop a token of some sort in the HTML into a hidden field for JavaScript to pick up and use as credentials to talk to a web API. This is similar to the way we used the antiforgery token. Without help from the server-side code, JavaScript cannot talk to a web API.

Another option is to use three-legged authentication involving the user. The implicit grant flow of OAuth 2.0 that we touched on in Chapter 11 and implemented using DNOA in Chapter 13 is a good candidate here. Without the user's involvement, no token can be obtained and thus no access is allowed to the web API.

Using Known Vulnerable Components

This vulnerability is not specific to ASP.NET Web API. It is always a good practice to keep all the application components, including third-party components, up to date by applying patches and fixes as soon as they are available.

Although the IT administration teams in a typical enterprise are diligent about updates to major software components such as the operating system and database engines, the task of keeping application components up to date generally falls through the cracks between IT administration and application maintenance teams. Processes must be put in place to ensure this does not happen.

Before you commit to using a third-party component, ensure the security aspects are all covered and that there is support available from the third party to address any security issue that might arise out of their code as well as the components they use.

Unvalidated Redirects and Forwards

This vulnerability is not applicable to ASP.NET Web API. However, it is worth noting the redirects that happen in OAuth 2.0 that we saw in the previous chapters. If you implement the OAuth 2.0 authorization server, ensure you have proper validations in place to make sure the redirect URI in the requests matches the URI registered with the client application.

Security = Hardware + Software + Process

Application security is a combination of hardware and software security with well-defined processes backing them. By hardware, I mean the infrastructure including the servers as well as networking components such as firewalls, routers, and so on. By software, I mean system software such as the operating system and application software, both the code you write and the code you reuse. The third one is the set of processes that need to be put in place such as rotating symmetric keys regularly, renewing the X.509 certificates that are about to expire, and so on.

However, being a programmer, all the problems will look like potential candidates for programming-based solutions; if all you have is a hammer, every problem is a nail. I use two related attacks to illustrate how to choose an effective countermeasure.

1. A denial of service (DOS) attack is about overwhelming a network resource such as ASP.NET Web API with such a high volume of requests that legitimate users do not get serviced; in other words, the users are denied service. A distributed denial of service (DDOS) is a variant of a DOS attack. Multiple systems distributed across the Internet work in unison to overwhelm a target.

2. A brute-force attack is generally about guessing a user's password and bypassing access control. It involves running through all the possible permutations of characters until the correct password is found.

A DOS attack and brute-force attack are related in the sense that both use automation through some kind of software to hit the servers, but they differ in the motive. A DOS attack is just about denial of service, whereas a brute-force attack strives to get the credentials of a user. ASP.NET Web API lends itself well to these kinds of attacks because it is extremely easy to interact with. After all, a web API is intended to be used by another application rather than an end user, as in the case of web applications. Also, programming in HTTP and parsing JSON or XML is simple and straightforward. Writing a simple C# program that runs a loop to do GETs or POSTs to a URI will be a few lines of code. In the .NET Framework, running parallel loops maximizing the usage of all the cores of the CPU in a computer is far too easy for any experience level.

If you are a programmer, the immediate thing that might come to your mind from the perspective of a countermeasure is to write an ASP.NET Web API message handler to log the requests and the timestamp and detect the DOS or brute-force patterns. However, for these kinds of attacks a message handler approach might not be efficient. Ideally, it is better to ward off these attacks much earlier in the life cycle. Even a handler running right after

`HttpServer` is too late. The request has come in through the ASP.NET pipeline, and CPU and memory resources were already spent in creating some of the ASP.NET and even web API objects.

The best solution is hardware-based defense mechanisms involving routers and firewalls. If those are not feasible, having restrictions at the web-server level, such as Dynamic IP Restrictions Extension for IIS, is better than creating our own solution (provided your ASP.NET Web API is web-hosted). Dynamic IP Restrictions for IIS can inspect the source IP of the requests, look for attack patterns, and place the offending IP on a temporary deny list. Although this is just one example, it helps to illustrate the thought process for securing an application in a holistic sense.

The following are some of the security principles that support this holistic thinking.

1. *Principle of least privilege* means giving a user only those privileges absolutely necessary to perform the task. If your ASP.NET Web API must access a database, you will need a user account to connect to your database from the web API. You can, of course, use a database system administrator account such as sa, which can do everything with your database. However, it is not according to the principle of least privilege. If you are reading and writing to tables, as any typical application does, the database user account must have the privileges to only read and update rows of the tables in your database. The obvious advantage of this approach is that if your application has a SQL injection flaw introduced by a programmer, the damage will be minimal. For example, the malicious user cannot truncate your tables.

2. *Defense in depth* is the use of multiple security countermeasures to protect your application. This is based on the military principle that it is more difficult for an enemy to defeat a multilayered defense than to overcome a single line of defense. This is another case for teamwork between different IT teams. As an example, your network administrators ensure your firewalls and routers pass only those requests coming in from a certain IP range through a certain port. Your application logic builds on top of that and ensures only authentic and authorized users access to application resources.

3. *Default denial,* also known as whitelisting, is the approach of assuming every entity is a malicious entity except those on a list of entities that the system has in its good books. The mechanism of access control that we saw in Chapter 5 is an example for this approach. If the application can identify a user and authenticate the credentials, the user can use the application subject to the rights the user has been assigned. The same principle can be applied to other layers as well, such as firewalls. By default, your enterprise firewall denies every request coming in. You make exceptions to this principle by raising requests to your network administration team to enable IP address ranges and ports.

Web Server Fingerprinting

As you know, fingerprints identify human beings. In the world of the web, fingerprinting is a process that identifies a web server based on response messages, specifically the response headers and the order of the headers produced by the web server. Fingerprinting produces details about the web server such as server type, server software, and platform details. Attackers can use this data maliciously because security vulnerabilities typically are related to platforms and versions of the software.

I cover this topic because wiping the web server fingerprints clean off the server responses can come to you as an action item to comply with the policies of your security administration team or the operations team. Sometimes, reports based on penetration tests do highlight fingerprints as a vulnerability. Removing fingerprints is accomplished more along the lines of security through obscurity, which is all about using secrecy to provide security. It is debatable if security through obscurity is a solid approach, but at times it is good to keep the head down. Without question, what really helps is keeping the Windows OS and all server-side software updates by patching them when a new fix or a service pack is available, although it generally is not something that a programmer, software designer, or a technology architect would do, especially in production servers.

Listing 15-24 shows the response headers that are produced by the IIS running on my machine. It is obvious from the response headers that the server is IIS and that we are using the ASP.NET framework.

Listing 15-24. Response Headers

```
HTTP/1.1 200 OK
Cache-Control: no-cache
Pragma: no-cache
Content-Type: application/json; charset=utf-8
Expires: -1
Server: Microsoft-IIS/7.5
X-AspNet-Version: 4.0.30319
X-Powered-By: ASP.NET
Date: Wed, 07 Nov 2012 17:15:48 GMT
Content-Length: 244
```

To remove X-AspNet-Version and X-Powered-By or just change X-Powered-By to something else, you need to edit the Web.config file of your application, as shown in Listing 15-25.

Listing 15-25. Web.config Changes

```
<system.web>
        ...
        <httpRuntime targetFramework="4.5" enableVersionHeader="false" />
        ...
</system.web>
<system.webServer>
        ...
        <httpProtocol>
                <customHeaders>
                        <remove name="X-Powered-By" />
                         <add name="X-Powered-By" value="Biofuel" />
                </customHeaders>
        </httpProtocol>
</system.webServer>
```

The Server header can be removed using the UrlScan free utility from Microsoft, in the case of IIS 6.0 and IIS 7.0 classic mode. For the IIS 7.0 integrated pipeline, where the .NET Framework–based modules are first-class citizens, you can write a native module. Even better, write just a few lines of code in your Global.asax.cs to remove the Server header, as shown in Listing 15-26.

Listing 15-26. Global.asax.cs

```
public class WebApiApplication : System.Web.HttpApplication
{
    protected void Application_Start() { ... }

    protected void Application_PreSendRequestHeaders(object sender, EventArgs e)
    {
        HttpContext.Current.Response.Headers.Remove("Server");
    }
}
```

Logging, Auditing, and Tracing

Logging, auditing, and tracing are technically the same: They are all about creating records of the events happening in an application. However, the purpose is what differentiates them. There are no hard and fast rules to demarcate logging, auditing, and tracing, but it is helpful to understand the differences at a broader level.

Logging is writing the details of events happening in an application to a persistent store. Logging can be about recording normal events as well as abnormal events such as errors or exceptions. The purpose of logging is mainly from the operations perspective to get the operational metrics as well as to help ensure a service-level agreement (SLA). It is typical to have specialized software monitoring the logs for specific events and alerting the team supporting the application. Logging is generally a nonfunctional requirement.

Auditing or audit logging, to be exact, is a specialized case of logging aimed at capturing logs of events from the perspective of security such as authentication and authorization failures or a user accessing a protected resource and making changes. Whereas logging is about recording the details of the events themselves, auditing is about recording the user identity as well—the user who was responsible for the event or who acted as the trigger. Depending on the nature of the business, some applications create audit logs for pretty much everything, some for a critical subset, and some create no audit logs at all. Audit logging can be a functional or nonfunctional requirement, again depending on the nature of the application.

Tracing is associated with the development phase of the systems development life cycle (SDLC). Tracing is a special case of logging that aims at recording information about an application's code execution. Tracing is used by programmers for debugging code. Tracing is generally not considered a functional or nonfunctional requirement because it is not about the user actions. It mainly is about the application itself and is just a tool for the development team.

The techniques relevant to any software application with respect to logging holds good for ASP.NET Web API. The logging mechanism defined in your organizational standards can be employed with a web API as well. However, ASP.NET Web API does have built-in tracing that can trace the execution of the code in the web API pipeline in addition to your own code.

Implementing Tracing in ASP.NET Web API

We now look at the tracing mechanism available out of the box in ASP.NET Web API. The most fundamental step in enabling tracing is to create a class that implements the `System.Web.Http.Tracing.ITraceWriter` interface, as shown in Listing 15-27.

Listing 15-27. Trace Writer

```
public class WebApiTracer : ITraceWriter
{
    public void Trace(HttpRequestMessage request,
                             string category,
                                  TraceLevel level,
                                      Action<TraceRecord> traceAction)
    {
        TraceRecord rec = new TraceRecord(request, category, level);
        traceAction(rec);

        using (Stream xmlFile = new FileStream(@"C:\Path\log.xml", FileMode.Append))
        {
            using (XmlTextWriter writer = new XmlTextWriter(xmlFile, Encoding.UTF8))
            {
                writer.Formatting = Formatting.Indented;
```

```
                writer.WriteStartElement("trace");
                writer.WriteElementString("timestamp", rec.Timestamp.ToString());
                writer.WriteElementString("operation", rec.Operation);
                writer.WriteElementString("user", rec.Operator);
                writer.WriteElementString("message", rec.Message);
                writer.WriteElementString("category", rec.Category);
                writer.WriteEndElement();
                writer.WriteString(Environment.NewLine);
            }
        }
    }
}
```

ITraceWriter requires the Trace method to be implemented. I'm creating a trace file with each entry in the form of an XML element named trace. To plug this in, add a line of code in WebApiConfig under App_Start like this: config.Services.Replace(typeof(ITraceWriter), new WebApiTracer());

As it is, if you run the application and issue a web API request, it will start tracing the code execution in the web API pipeline. To trace from our code you can call the Trace method, as shown in Listing 15-28.

Listing 15-28. Tracing from ApiController

```
public class EmployeesController : ApiController
{
    [Authorize]
    public IEnumerable<Employee> Get()
    {
        Configuration.Services.GetTraceWriter().Trace(Request, "MyCategory", TraceLevel.Info,
        (t) =>
                {
                        t.Operation = Request.Method.Method;
                        t.Operator = User.Identity.Name;
                        t.Message = "Get Employees";
                 });

        return new Employee[]
        {
            new Employee() { Id = 12345, FirstName = "John", LastName = "Human" },
            new Employee() { Id = 67890, FirstName = "Jane", LastName = "Public" }
        };
    }
}
```

It is possible to trace from handlers as well. Listing 15-29 shows a message handler that logs the requests and response messages. We use the ReadAsStringAsync method of HttpMessageContent to extract the request and response messages in the raw format and write to the trace.

Listing 15-29. Tracing Handler

```
public class TracingHandler : DelegatingHandler
{
    protected override async Task<HttpResponseMessage> SendAsync(HttpRequestMessage request,
                                                                CancellationToken cancellationToken)
    {
        HttpMessageContent requestContent = new HttpMessageContent(request);
        string requestMessage = requestContent.ReadAsStringAsync().Result;

        var response = await base.SendAsync(request, cancellationToken);

        HttpMessageContent responseContent = new HttpMessageContent(response);
        string responseMessage = responseContent.ReadAsStringAsync().Result;

        GlobalConfiguration.Configuration.Services.GetTraceWriter()
            .Trace(request, "MyCategory", System.Web.Http.Tracing.TraceLevel.Info,
                (t) =>
                {
                    t.Operation = request.Method.Method;
                    t.Operator = Thread.CurrentPrincipal.Identity.Name;
                    t.Message = requestMessage + Environment.NewLine + responseMessage;
                });


        return response;
    }
}
```

■ **Caution** It is better to move the security audit files created by the web application into some other network location by a periodic batch or an offline process. When the web server is compromised, the attacker will not be able to get to the security audit files. Also, the account running the worker process must never be given the privilege to delete any of these files.

Input Validation

Input validation is relevant to ASP.NET Web API as well, although the inputs here are not direct user entries. One of the basic things to do in this area is to define the data types of the variables or properties accurately so that model binding itself will fail in the case of invalid or malicious inputs.

In addition, the web API does support validation annotations, just like ASP.NET MVC. Data annotations are attributes that are a part of the `System.ComponentModel.DataAnnotations` namespace. `Required`, `StringLength` `RegularExpression`, `Range`, and `Email` are some of the out-of-the-box attributes available to help us with the input validation. It is possible to create our own custom attributes as well, in case the validation needs are not met by the out-of-the-box attributes.

After the model binding, if any of the inputs are not valid there will be errors in the model state. We can check for errors by inspecting `ModelState.IsValid`. If this is false, the request can be rejected on the grounds of a bad request.

Summary

In this chapter, I covered the OWASP top ten vulnerabilities for the year 2013 from the perspective of ASP.NET Web API. Some of them are not applicable to ASP.NET Web API, the most notable one being XSS. Some of them are applicable to ASP.NET Web API as with any other application and do not deserve special mention. The following list shows the most relevant subset of the OWASP Top Ten.

- **Injection:** A SQL injection is applicable to ASP.NET Web API, just as with any other UI-based application. In addition, there is another form of injection vulnerability possible with ASP.NET Web API: overposting. Using a view model, which is different from an entity model, helps prevent overposting.
- **Insecure Direct Object References:** RESTful URIs can be hacked, and ASP.NET Web API lends itself well for a user to manipulate a URI or the input. Fine-grained authorization is the solution to prevent this vulnerability.
- **Missing Function Level Access Control:** Implementing a sound authorization mechanism for all API calls is important to prevent this vulnerability. A global message handler or a filter that runs for all the calls and controls the access based on the claims using the subclass of `ClaimsAuthorizationManager` is the best approach to prevent this vulnerability in ASP.NET Web API.
- **Cross-Site Request Forgery (CSRF):** CSRF is applicable not just for cookies, but also for credentials cached by the browser for basic authentication and Windows authentication. If cookies must be used with ASP.NET Web API, an antiforgery token can be employed to prevent CSRF.
- **Unvalidated Redirects and Forwards:** This vulnerability is not applicable to ASP.NET Web API, but it is worth noting the redirects that happen in OAuth 2.0. If you implement the OAuth 2.0 authorization server, ensure you validate the redirect URI in the requests.

Application security is a combination of hardware and software security with well-defined processes backing them. Hardware includes all the infrastructure aspects including networking components such as servers, firewalls, routers, and so on. Software includes the system software such as the operating system as well as application software, which includes the software you develop and third-party software. Equally important are the processes around hardware and software to ensure application security remains at the required level over the lifetime of the application.

From a programmer's perspective, input validation and logging or auditing are important to ensure security. Model binding and data annotations help a developer validate the input data. ASP.NET Web API has out-of-the-box support for tracing, which can be used to trace, log, and create audit logs.

APPENDIX

ASP.NET Web API Security Distilled

This appendix is a grand summary of this book, a recap of the various security mechanisms we have seen so far. There is no good or bad mechanism in an absolute sense. The idea of this book is to present all the mechanisms and let you decide based on your needs.

There is no mandate that you must select only one mechanism. You can design your web API to support more than one and give client applications a few options. The ASP.NET Web API pipeline helps us plug in as many handlers as we need to run. Message handlers are great enablers for achieving that goal.

If you decide to choose more than one, carefully consider the possibilities. For example, if you mix basic and digest authentication and decide to use HTTPS only for basic authentication, there is a risk of a malicious man-in-the middle (MITM) removing the **WWW-Authenticate: Digest** response header and tricking the client into sending the credentials in a basic scheme in clear text.

Mechanism	When to Use?	Merits	Demerits
Forms Authentication (Chapter 2)	Use when the client consuming the web API is an ASP.NET web application and the same IIS application hosts the web application and web API so that the same authentication ticket can be reused. A great example of this scenario is Single Page Applications (SPAs) where the single page and the web API backing the scripts can be hosted in the same IIS application.	Easy to use and familiar to ASP.NET developers. Same authentication mechanism for both the web application and the web API.	Forms authentication mechanism developed mainly for web applications rather than a web API. Cannot be used for a standalone web API. Forms authentication is based on an authentication ticket stuffed into a cookie that gets shunted up and down. Cookies are generally frowned upon in the REST- style architectures that celebrate statelessness.

(continued)

Mechanism	When to Use?	Merits	Demerits
Basic Authentication (Chapter 8)	Use when a simple user ID and password-based mechanism must be used and HTTPS can be used. This is typically the case when the client is not very sophisticated to use other mechanisms but has support for HTTP from the platform in the form of a library or otherwise to manipulate the HTTP request header as well as the ability to base64-encode strings and use transport security in the form of HTTPS. The server hosting the web API must support HTTPS as well.	Simple, lightweight, and supported by the HTTP specification.	HTTPS is a must. Susceptible to CSRF, when the client is browser based such as a JavaScript library.
Digest Authentication (Chapter 8)	Use when a user ID and password-based mechanism must be used but HTTPS cannot be used. This is the case when the client does not have support from the platform to use transport security or the server side hosting ASP.NET Web API does not support HTTPS for a reason. The client must have the capability to create an MD5 hash, generate an arbitrary number (nonce), and track and increment the nonce counter.	HTTPS is not a must. HTTP specification supported. Password is never transmitted over the wire.	Too complex, especially for a client to implement. Uses MD5 hashing, which is outdated. Needs client cooperation in terms of incrementing a nonce counter.
Windows Authentication (Chapter 8)	Use when both the client and server sides run Windows OS and all the end users will have a Windows account and clients and the server are in the same network (intranet).	Simple and easy because ASP.NET and IIS establish the identity for you, without a line of code. Impersonation capabilities.	Susceptible to CSRF, when the client is browser based such as a JavaScript library. Reliance on Microsoft stack limits the reach of a web API. May not work over HTTP proxy and hence is better suited for intranet only.
Preshared Key or API Key-Based Authentication (Chapter 9)	Use when a web API wants to establish the identity of the client but does not need to authenticate the identity. This is the case when an API deals with less sensitive data. Also useful when the client application making the API call needs to identify itself to an API regardless of user identity. When a more secure mechanism is required with a need to authenticate in addition to just identifying the client, a dual PSK can be used.	HTTPS is not a must. Easier to encrypt payload, either the whole payload or selectively, using PSK. There is no cost associated with buying any certificates.	Slightly complex mechanism to implement. An out-of band exchange of keys is a consideration for application administration as well as security. Requires both parties to safeguard the PSK effectively.

(continued)

Mechanism	When to Use?	Merits	Demerits
X.509 Client Certificate-Based Authentication (Chapter 9)	Use when HTTPS is a given and the web API has extremely sensitive information needing ownership-factor-based security in addition to or instead of the typical user ID and passwords.	A certificate, being a file, can be closely guarded by IT systems and unauthorized sharing can be prevented, unlike with passwords or keys. The web API usage can be limited to only those machines on which the certificate is installed. Can combine with other mechanisms to achieve two-factor authentication for enhanced security.	CA-issued certificates cost money. Managing certificates is an administration overhead. HTTPS is a must. Can get stifling at times, because the web API can be accessed only from the machines with a client certificate.
SAML Token-Based Authentication and Authorization (Chapter 9)	Use when the token issuance infrastructure such as AD FS or some other STS is already in place and must be leveraged for securing the web API.	Windows Identity Foundation, which is now a part of .NET Framework 4.5, has great out-of-the-box support for issuing and validating SAML tokens and the related WS-* protocol WS-Trust. Makes it possible to leverage investments in existing infrastructure. AD FS can map Windows groups to claims that can be used for authorization.	SAML is XML and hence SAML tokens tend to get heavier compared to web tokens such as SWT or JWT. Forcing clients to talk to WS-Trust endpoints to get an SAML token reduces the reach of the web API. A client not having the ability to use WS-Trust protocol will pretty much be not able to use the web API.
SWT-Based Authentication and Authorization (Chapter 10)	Use when direct presentation of credentials by the client to the web API is not suitable and brokered authentication is preferred through a common trusted service. The token contains claims and hence is suitable for claims-based architectures. Azure ACS supports issuance of SWT, and hence this mechanism is great to use with Azure ACS.	Simple and lightweight token format. Authenticity ensured through HMAC signatures.	SWT cannot be encrypted and hence HTTPS is a must if token confidentiality is required. Using Azure ACS cannot be the sole motivating factor for using SWT, because the only major WS-Trust provider supported by ACS is AD FS.

(*continued*)

Mechanism	When to Use?	Merits	Demerits
JWT-Based Authentication and Authorization (Chapter 10)	Use when direct presentation of credentials by the client to the web API is not suitable and brokered authentication is preferred through a common trusted service. The token contains claims and hence is suitable for claims-based architectures. Azure ACS supports issuance of JWT and hence this mechanism is great to use with Azure ACS.	Simple and lightweight token format. JWT supports both signing (JWS) and encryption (JWE). JSON goes well with JavaScript clients.	Slightly complex to implement, especially JWE.
Google Authenticator OTP-Based Authentication (Chapter 14)	Use when additional security in the form of two-factor authentication is required on a need basis for certain business-critical requests made to the web API.	Uses a standard HOTP/ TOTP algorithm and there is nothing proprietary. There is no cost associated, unlike other tokens such as RSA.	Needs a smartphone running iOS, BlackBerry, or Android. Reliance on Google Authenticator application. Mobile phone is not the ownership factor but only a base32-encoded easy-to-type (and hence easy-to-remember) secret key.
SMS-Delivered OTP-Based Authentication (Chapter 14)	Use when additional security in the form of two-factor authentication is required on a need basis for certain business-critical requests made to the web API.	Simple and supports any mobile phone capable of receiving SMS, with the mobile phone itself used as ownership factor, unlike PSK with Google Authenticator.	User has to wait for SMS to arrive. Costs associated with sending SMS. Privacy concerns around sharing mobile number.
OAuth 2.0 Access Token-Based Authentication and Authorization (Chapters11, 12, and 13)	Use when the web API is based on a web application in that the user registers and thereby has a user ID and password to access the application that can be leveraged to authenticate to the web API. The client is also a web application (typically).	OAuth 2.0 is a standard meant for the REST world, along the lines of WS-Trust and WS-Security in the SOAP world. Getting and presenting a token as defined by a standard is always better than creating one's own standard.	Slightly complex to implement, although the open source library DotNetOpenAuth is available to help in implementation. HTTPS is a must for bearer tokens.

OAuth 2.0 Grant Type	When to Use?	Merits	Demerits
Authorization Code-Based Grant	Use when the client application is a server-side web application such as ASP.NET running in IIS.	Long-lived refresh token is available. Both access and refresh tokens are not exposed to the browser or the end user, ensuring token confidentiality.	Refresh token has advantages but it introduces an element of risk related to refresh tokens stored in the data store getting compromised. Also, the flow is slightly complex, with the additional step of exchanging an authorization code for a token.
Implicit Grant	When the client runs within the context of a web browser such as JavaScript.	Flow is simple. No refresh tokens and hence security risk or exposure is limited. Three-legged authentication supported by implicit grant flow is one of the best ways, if not the best from the security standpoint, for JavaScript clients to talk to a web API.	No token confidentiality; browser has access to the token and so does the end user. Refresh tokens are not supported, which means as and when tokens expire, flow has to be repeated to obtain a new token.
Resource Owner Password-Based Grant (To be used only when other flows are not viable)	When the client application is also from the same organization owning the resource server, or in other words, a first-party application.	Flow is very simple: Just exchange the user ID and password for a token.	Password exposed directly to the client application. There is risk associated with the client application not being diligent with handling the password. For example, a client application storing the password somewhere is a big risk. Password must be immediately exchanged for a token and never stored for future use.
Client Credentials-Based Grant (Two-legged)	For scenarios where a protected resource is not user specific or the user has consented to provide access to the protected resource outside of the OAuth flow, might be through an out of band process.	User need not be bothered to provide authorization every time the protected resource has to be accessed. For this reason, this is referred to as two-legged (the third leg being the user).	Although it can be a slight irritant, user involvement in authorizing access is always better from a security standpoint and hence this grant type is comparatively riskier.

The right approach in securing ASP.NET Web API is choosing the appropriate mechanism for your organizational and application needs, rather than being influenced by others. For example, do not use OAuth 2.0 just because others use it.

A great thing about ASP.NET Web API and the .NET Framework in general, with claims-based identity, is that you can plug in new authentication and authorization methods and yet keep the application resistant to the effects on account of these changes. New message handlers can be plugged in to handle new authentication methods and ultimately, if the web API works based on claims, it just boils down to handlers creating appropriate claims for the identity.

Index

A, B

C

D

E, F

G

H

I, J

K

L

M, N

O

T

U, V

W, X, Y, Z